Note to the reader from the UNU

The United Nations University programme on the Human and Policy Dimensions of Global Change was initiated in recognition of the level of complexity of global environmental change and the need to formulate appropriate strategies to minimize the rate and extent of such change and likely associated consequences, as well as reduce possible adverse impacts on human societies and on ecosystems. The objectives of the programme are: (1) to increase awareness of the complex dynamics governing human interaction with the Earth as a whole system; (2) to strengthen efforts to anticipate social change affecting the global environment; (3) to analyse policy options for dealing with global environmental change; and (4) to identify broad social strategies to prevent or mitigate undesirable impacts of global environmental change.

An outcome of the UNU project of the same name, this book is intended as a comprehensive treatise on the subject of industrial restructuring for sustainable development, incorporating a comprehensive coverage of the field. The emerging concepts of "industrial metabolism" and restructuring for sustainable development focus on the long-term transformation of the technical base of the economy, with a view towards reducing the demands and pressures exerted by society on its resource base and its environment. As such, it forms an essential part of the principal answer to the challenge of sustainability.

Industrial metabolism

Industrial metabolism: Restructuring for sustainable development

Edited by Robert U. Ayres and
Udo E. Simonis

**United Nations
University Press**

TOKYO • NEW YORK • PARIS

333.7

I42

United Nations University Press
The United Nations University, 53-70, Jingumae 5-chome,
Shibuya-ku, Tokyo 150, Japan
Tel: (03) 3499-2811   Fax: (03) 3499-2811
Telex: J25442   Cable: UNATUNIV TOKYO

Typeset by Asco Trade Typesetting Limited, Hong Kong
Printed by Permanent Typesetting and Printing Co., Ltd.,
Hong Kong
Cover design by Apex Production, Hong Kong

UNUP-841
ISBN 92-808-0841-9
United Nations Sales No. E.93.III.A.3
03500 P

Contents

Acknowledgements

This book is the end result of a process that began with a conference in Tokyo in September 1988, sponsored jointly by the United Nations University (UNU), UNESCO, and the International Federation of Institutes for Advanced Study (IFIAS). This conference was convened to explore ways of broadening the International Geosphere-Biosphere Programme (IGBP) to consider explicitly the human dimensions of global change.

The term "industrial metabolism" was coined during the preparatory stages of that conference, to encapsulate this interaction. Selected papers from the Tokyo conference were published in the *International Social Science Journal* (ISSJ) in 1989. A second, follow-up, workshop on "Industrial Metabolism" was held in Maastricht, the Netherlands, under the joint auspices of the UNU and IFIAS, in 1989. The present volume was conceived at that workshop.

We are extremely grateful for the financial support of the UNU for this book, and for the personal support and assistance of Dr Walter Shearer, New York Office of the UNU, and Dr Roland Fuchs, Vice-Rector of the UNU in Tokyo. We would like to thank Professor Friedrich Schmidt-Bleek, of Wuppertal Institut, and Professor Robert H. Socolow, of Princeton University, for their valuable comments on the first draft of the manuscript.

Introduction

Robert U. Ayres and Udo E. Simonis

The term "metabolism," applied to a plant or animal, is a notion so familiar and comprehensive that it resists formal definition. Webster, nevertheless, defines it as "the sum total of the build-up and destruction of cell tissue; the chemical cellular changes providing the energies for the life process and the elimination of waste materials." It is, in other words, the totality of internal processes – both physical and chemical – that supply the energy and nutrients required by an organism as the conditions of life itself. These processes can be described, in the aggregate, in terms of the transformations of inputs (sunlight, chemical energy, nutrients, water, air) into biomass – the substance of the organism itself – and waste products.

Industrial metabolism, by analogy, is the set of physico-chemical transformations that convert raw materials (biomass, fuels, minerals, metals) into manufactured products and structures (i.e. "goods") and wastes. To an economist these processes, in the aggregate, are called "production." A further transformation of economic goods into services (and wastes) is also implied by the economic term "consumption." Thus industrial metabolism comprehends all the materials/energy transformations that enable the economic system to function, i.e. to produce and consume.

Seen from this perspective, the human economic system takes its proper place within the larger natural system of the earth (and sun). The *anthroposphere* is only a part of the *biosphere*,[1] which itself can only exist in a continuing dynamic equilibrium with the sun, the air (*atmosphere*), the oceans (*hydrosphere*) and the earth's crust (*lithosphere*).

In the pre-industrial era, the anthroposphere was in a more or less uneasy balance with the biosphere and the other elements of the earth system. Humans were a part of the natural ecosystem; and animals were harvested for food, clothing and even structural materials. Wastes were recycled by natural decay processes. Mineral and metal items – from building blocks to weapons, tools or coins – were used and re-used for centuries or even millenia.

The Industrial Revolution of the eighteenth century changed this situation radically. In pre-industrial times the only truly unsustainable consequence of human economic activity was irreversible loss of forest cover and topsoil in some regions (mainly North Africa and the Middle East). Since the Industrial Revolution, and the large-scale exploitation of fossil fuels, the list of unsustainable environmental trends has grown much larger:

– The build-up of "greenhouse gases" in the atmosphere.
– The destruction of the ozone layer in the stratosphere.
– The acidification of the soil and surface waters.
– The build-up of toxic metals in sediments and soil.
– The build-up of radioactive wastes.
– The accumulation of long-lived non-biodegradable chemicals in the environment.
– The contamination and exhaustion of groundwater.
– The loss of tropical forests, wetlands, biodiversity, etc.

Continuing with the biological metaphor, the spread of industrial activity in the last two centuries can best be described as a cancer: industrialization, in its present form, is a process of uncontrolled, unsustainable "growth" that eventually destroys its host – the biosphere.

The death of the biosphere is not necessarily unavoidable. But with every year and decade that passes without a radical change in direction and quality, the death of the biosphere becomes more likely. However, the long-range prognosis of the state of planet Earth is not the main subject of this book. Our purpose here is to elucidate – and exemplify – a new kind of analysis.

Our intellectual tradition is essentially reductionist: we try to explain complex large-scale systems by subdivision into ever smaller subsystems, components, and subcomponents. We explain the forest as a collection of trees; we explain the tree in terms of roots, trunk, branches, bark, and leaves. The infinite regression continues as the power of the microscope increases. Then, at last, when we see the forest in terms of biochemical reactions, we think we have understood it. But in so doing we have missed the essence of the forest.

Yet, there are other perspectives and other modes of analysis. The earth system can be viewed as a whole. The anthroposphere can be viewed as part of the planetary system. Industry can be examined within this larger context, not as a collection of individual firms, plants, and processes. Further, some powerful analytical tools remain at our disposal. The law of conservation of mass and energy (the "first law" of thermodynamics) is one of them. In our context this law of physics gives rise to the materials balance principle. One implication of this principle is that materials extracted from the natural environment for the production of goods and services must eventually be returned to the environment in degraded form.[2] So simple a principle, and yet with such profound implications.

The present book consists of 14 chapters which are grouped into three parts. Part 1 provides an overview of the various aspects and implications of the "industrial metabolism" paradigm. In chapter 1, Robert U. Ayres elaborates the concept in theoretical terms, and discusses some of its policy implications – not all of which are immediately obvious.

Chapter 2, by Rudolf B. Husar, presents useful metaphors to bridge biosphere and ecosphere. The question of how strong the impact of industrialization has been on the environment and whether or not a de-linking of economic activity from environmentally sensitive inputs has taken place in the industrial nations is addressed by Udo E. Simonis in chapter 3. As regards the developing countries, this question is asked by Rajendra K. Pachauri, Mala Damodaran, and Himraj Dang in chapter 4. Evolution, sustainability, and industrial metabolism are looked at in a more general, theoretical manner by Peter M. Allen in chapter 5.

In part 2, from chapters 6 to 11, a number of case-studies of industrial metabolism are presented, at various levels of aggregation. Ulrik Lohm, Stefan Anderberg, and Bo Bergbäck start with a study on chromium and lead pollution at the national level, taking Sweden as an example (chapter 6). Next are William M. Stigliani and Stefan Anderberg with a study on cadmium pollution in the Rhine basin (chapter 7). Paul H. Brunner, Hans Daxbeck, and Peter Baccini studied industrial metabolism in a Swiss region (chapter 8). Case-studies on carbon monoxide and methane emissions and sulphur and nitrogen emissions in the United States are presented by Robert U. Ayres, Leslie W. Ayres, and Joel A. Tarr (chapter 9), and Rudolf B. Husar (chapter 10) respectively. Finally, the consumptive uses and losses of toxic metals in the United States are addressed by Robert U. Ayres and Leslie W. Ayres (chapter 11).

Part 3 of the book provides some future perspectives. Timothy O'Riordan, on the basis of the industrial metabolism concept, asks, in chapter 12, how far the precautionary principle could lead in environmental management. In chapter 13, Sergio C. Trindade looks at the conditions under which a more efficient industrial metabolism could be reached in developing countries by transfer of clean(er) technologies. The physical exchanges between the industrial economy and the natural environment need improved – i.e. rather different – accounting and information systems; Marina Fischer-Kowalski, Helmut Haberl, and Harald Payer present their concept in chapter 14.

Finally, a select bibliography on industrial metabolism and industrial restructuring is presented by Rüdiger Olbrich and Udo E. Simonis.

Notes

1. The integrative notion of the "biosphere" was first introduced in the 1920s by the great Russian earth scientist Vladimir Vernadsky.
2. For the first explicit application of this principle to economics, see: R. U. Ayres and A. V. Kneese, "Production, Consumption and Externalities: A Materials-Balance Perspective," in *American Economic Review*, 59 (1969), no. 3: 382–296; and A. V. Kneese, R. U. Ayres, and R. C. d'Arge, *Aspects of Environmental Economics: A Materials Balance–General Equilibrium Approach*, Baltimore, Md.: Johns Hopkins University Press, 1970.

Part 1
General implications

1

Industrial metabolism: Theory and policy

Robert U. Ayres

What is industrial metabolism?

The word metabolism, as used in its original biological context, con-
notes the internal processes of a living organism. The organism in-
gests energy-rich, low-entropy materials ("food") to provide for its
own maintenance and functions, as well as a surplus to permit growth
and/or reproduction. The process also necessarily involves the excre-
tion or exhalation of waste outputs, consisting of degraded, high-
entropy materials. There is a compelling analogy between biological
organisms and industrial activities – indeed, the whole economic system – not only because both are materials-processing systems driven
by a flow of free energy (Georgescu-Roegen, 1971), but because both
are examples of self-organizing "dissipative systems" in a stable
state, far from thermodynamic equilibrium (Ayres, 1988).

At the most abstract level of description, then, the metabolism of
industry is the whole integrated collection of physical processes that
convert raw materials and energy, plus labour, into finished products
and wastes in a (more or less) steady-state condition (fig. 1). The
production (supply) side, by itself, is not self-regulating. The stabilizing controls of the system are provided by its human component.
This human role has two aspects: (1) direct, as labour input, and (2)

3

Robert U. Ayres

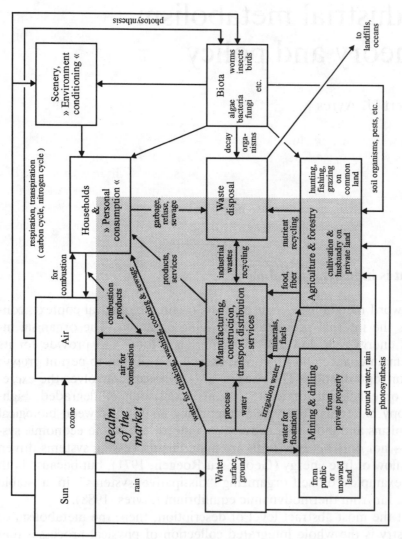

Fig. 1 The world of the market

4

indirect, as consumer of output (i.e. determinant of final demand). The system is stabilized, at least in its decentralized competitive market form, by balancing the supply of and demand for both products and labour through the price mechanism. Thus, the economic system is, in essence, the metabolic regulatory mechanism.

Industrial metabolism can be identified and described at a number of levels below the broadest and most encompassing global one. Thus, the concept is applicable to nations or regions, especially "natural" ones such as watersheds or islands. The key to regional analysis is the existence of a well-defined geographical border or boundary across which physical flows of materials and energy can be monitored.

The concept of industrial metabolism is equally applicable to another kind of self-organizing entity, a manufacturing enterprise or firm. A firm is the economic analogue of a living organism in biology.[1] Some of the differences are interesting, however. In the first place, biological organisms reproduce themselves; firms produce products or services, not other firms (except by accident). In the second place, firms need not be specialized and can change from one product or business to another. By contrast, organisms are highly specialized and cannot change their behaviour except over a long (evolutionary) time period. In fact, the firm (rather than the individual) is generally regarded as the standard unit of analysis in economics. The economic system as a whole is essentially a collection of firms, together with regulatory institutions and worker-consumers, using a common currency and governed by a common political structure. A manufacturing firm converts material inputs, including fuels or electric energy, into marketable products and waste materials. It keeps financial accounts for all its external transactions; it is also relatively easy to track physical stocks and flows across the "boundary" of the firm and even between its divisions.

The materials cycle

A third way in which the analogy between biological metabolism and industrial metabolism is useful is to focus attention on the "life cycle" of individual "nutrients."

The hydrological cycle, the carbon cycle, and the nitrogen cycle are familiar concepts to earth scientists. The major way in which the industrial metabolic system differs from the natural metabolism of the earth is that the natural cycles (of water, carbon/oxygen, nitrogen, sulphur, etc.) are *closed*, whereas the industrial cycles are *open*. In other words, the industrial system does *not* generally recycle its nutrients. Rather, the industrial system starts with high-quality materials (fossil fuels, ores) extracted from the earth, and returns them to nature in degraded form.

This point particularly deserves clarification. The materials cycle, in general, can be visualized in terms of a system of compartments containing *stocks* of one or more nutrients, linked by certain *flows*. For instance, in the case of the hydrological cycle, the glaciers, the oceans, the fresh water lakes, and the groundwater are stocks, while rainfall and rivers are flows. A system is *closed* if there are no external sources or sinks. In this sense, the earth as a whole is essentially a closed system, except for the occasional meteorite.

A closed system becomes a *closed cycle* if the system is also in steady state, i.e. the stocks in each compartment are constant and unchanging, at least on average. The materials balance condition implies that the material inputs to each compartment must be exactly balanced (on average) by the outputs. If this condition is not met for a given compartment, then the stock in one or more compartments must be increasing, while the stocks in one or more other compartments must be decreasing.[2]

It is easy to see that a closed cycle of flows, in the above sense, can only be sustained indefinitely by a continuous flow of *free* energy. This follows immediately from the second law of thermodynamics, which states that global entropy increases in every irreversible process. Thus, a closed cycle of flows can be sustained as long as its external energy supply lasts. An open system, on the contrary, is inherently unstable and unsustainable. It must either stabilize or collapse to a thermal equilibrium state in which all flows, i.e. all physical and biological processes, cease.

It is sometimes convenient to define a generalized four-box model to describe materials flows. The biological version is shown in figure 2, while the analogous industrial version is shown in figure 3. Reverting to the point made at the beginning of this section, the natural system is characterized by closed cycles, at least for the major nutrients (carbon, oxygen, nitrogen, sulphur) – in which biological processes play a major role in closing the cycle. By contrast, the industrial system is an open one in which "nutrients" are transformed into "wastes," but not significantly recycled. The industrial system, as it exists today, is therefore *ipso facto* unsustainable.

At this stage, it should be noted that nothing can be said about open cycles (on the basis of such simple thermodynamic arguments,

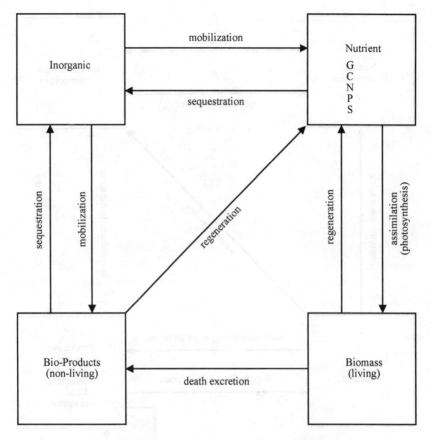

Fig. 2 Four-box scheme for bio-geo-chemical cycles

at least) with respect to any of the really critical questions. These are
as follows:
1. Will the industrial system stabilize itself without external interference?
2. If so, how soon, and in what configuration?
3. If not, does there exist any stable state (i.e. a system of closed
materials cycles) short of ultimate thermodynamic equilibrium that
could be reached with the help of a feasible technological "fix"?
4. If so, what is the nature of the fix, and how costly will it be?
5. If not, how much time do we have until the irreversible collapse of
the bio-geosphere system makes the earth uninhabitable? (If the
time scale is a billion years, we need not be too concerned. If it is
a hundred years, civilization, and even the human race, could
already be in deep trouble.)
It is fairly important to try to find answers to these questions.

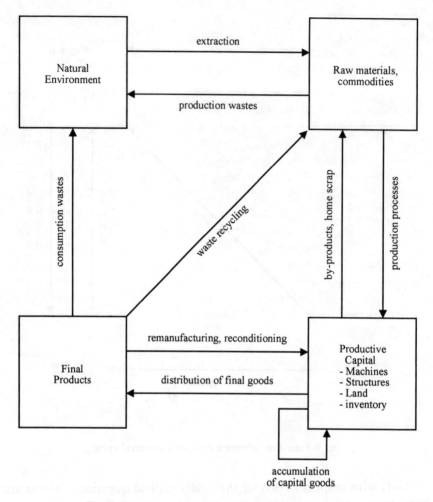

Fig. 3 Four-box scheme for industrial material cycles

Needless to say, we do not aspire to answer all these questions in the present volume.

It should also be pointed out that the bio-geosphere was not always a stable system of closed cycles. Far from it. The earliest living cells on earth obtained their nutrients, by fermentation, from non-living organic molecules whose origin is still not completely understood. At that time the atmosphere contained no free oxygen or nitrogen; it probably consisted mostly of water vapour plus some hydrogen, and hydrogen-rich gases such as methane, hydrogen sulphide, and ammonia. The fermentation process yields ethanol and carbon dioxide. The system could only have continued until the fermentation organisms used up the original stock of "food" molecules or choked on the carbon dioxide buildup. The system stabilized temporarily when a new organism (blue-green algae, or cyano-bacteria) appeared that was capable of recycling carbon dioxide into sugars and cellulose, thus again closing the carbon cycle. This new process was anaerobic photosynthesis.

However, the photosynthesis process also had a waste product: namely, oxygen. For a long time (over a billion years) the oxygen generated by anaerobic photosynthesis was captured by dissolved ferrous iron molecules, and sequestered as insoluble ferric oxide or magnetite, with the help of another primitive organism, the Stromatolites. The resulting insoluble iron oxide was precipitated on the ocean bottoms.[3] (The result is the large deposits of high-grade iron ore we exploit today.) The system was still unstable at this point. It was only the evolutionary invention of two more biological processes, aerobic respiration and aerobic photosynthesis, that closed the oxygen cycle as well. Still other biological processes – nitrification and denitrification, for instance – had to appear to close the nitrogen cycle and others.

Evidently, biological evolution responded to inherently unstable situations (open cycles) by "inventing" new processes (organisms) to stabilize the system by closing the cycles. This self-organizing capability is the essence of what has been called "Gaia." However, the instabilities in question were slow to develop, and the evolutionary responses were also slow to evolve. It took several billion years before the biosphere reached its present degree of stability.

In the case of the industrial system, the time scales have been drastically shortened. Human activity already dominates and excels natural processes in many respects. While cumulative anthropogenic changes to most natural nutrient stocks still remain fairly small in most cases,[4] the *rate* of nutrient mobilization by human industrial activity is already comparable to the natural rate in many cases. Table 1 shows the natural and anthropogenic mobilization (flow) rates for the four major biological nutrients, carbon, nitrogen, phosphorus and sulphur. In all cases, with the possible exception of nitrogen, the anthropogenic contributions exceed the natural flows by a considerable margin. The same is true for most of the toxic heavy metals, as shown in table 2.

On the basis of relatively crude materials cycle analyses, at least, it would appear that industrialization has already drastically disturbed, and *ipso facto* destabilized, the natural system.

9

Table 1 Anthropogenic nutrient fluxes (teragrams/year)

	Carbon		Nitrogen		Sulphur		Phosphorus	
	T/yr	%	T/yr	%	T/yr	%	T/yr	%
To atmosphere, total	7,900	4	55.0	12.5	93	65.5	1.5	12.5
Fossil fuel combustion and smelting	6,400		45.0		92			
Land clearing, deforestation	1,500		2.6		1			
Fertilizer volatilization[a]			7.5				1.5	
To soil, total			112.5	21	73.3	23.4	15	7.4
Fertilization			67.5		4.0		15	
Waste disposal[b]			5.0		21.0			
Anthropogenic acid deposition			30.0		48.3			
Anthropogenic (NH_3, NH_4) deposition			10.0					
To rivers and oceans, total			72.5	25	52.5	21	5	10.3
Anthropogenic acid deposition			55.0		22.5		5	
Waste disposal			17.5		30.0		5	

a. Assuming 10 per cent loss of synthetic ammonia-based fertilizers applied to land surface (75 tg/yr).
b. Total production (= use) less fertilizer use, allocated to landfill. The remainder is assumed to be disposed of via waterways.

Table 2 Worldwide atmospheric emissions of trace metals (1,000 tonnes per year)

Element	Energy production	Smelting, refining, and manufacturing	Manufacturing processes	Commercial uses, waste incineration, and transportation	Total anthropogenic contributions	Total contribution by natural activities
Antimony	1.3	1.5	—	0.7	3.5	2.6
Arsenic	2.2	12.4	2.0	2.3	19.0	12.0
Cadmium	0.8	5.4	0.6	0.8	7.6	1.4
Chromium	12.7	—	17.0	0.8	31.0	43.0
Copper	8.0	23.6	2.0	1.6	35.0	6.1
Lead	12.7	49.1	15.7	254.9	332.0	28.0
Manganese	12.1	3.2	14.7	8.3	38.0	12.0
Mercury	2.3	0.1	—	1.2	3.6	317.0
Nickel	42.0	4.8	4.5	0.4	52.0	2.5
Selenium	3.9	2.3	—	0.1	6.3	3.0
Thalium	1.1	—	4.0	—	5.1	29.0
Tin	3.3	1.1	—	0.8	5.1	10.0
Vanadium	84.0	0.1	0.7	1.2	86.0	28.0
Zinc	16.8	72.5	33.4	9.2	132.0	45.0

Source: Nriagu, 1990.

Measures of industrial metabolism

There are only two possible long-run fates for waste materials: re-cycling and re-use *or* dissipative loss.[5] (This is a straightforward im-plication of the law of conservation of mass.) The more materials are recycled, the less they will be dissipated into the environment, and vice versa. Dissipative losses must be made up by replacement from virgin sources.

A strong implication of the analysis sketched above is that a long-term (sustainable) steady-state industrial economy would necessarily be characterized by near-total recycling of intrinsically toxic or hazardous materials, as well as a significant degree of recycling of plastics, paper, and other materials whose disposal constitutes an environmental problem. Admittedly it is not possible to identify, in advance, all potentially hazardous materials, and it is quite likely that there will be (unpleasant) surprises from time to time. However, it is safe to say that heavy metals are among the materials that would have to be almost totally recycled to satisfy the sustainability criterion. The fraction of current metal supply needed to replace dissipative losses (i.e. production from virgin ores needed to maintain a stable level of consumption) is thus a useful, if partial, surrogate measure of "distance" from a steady-state condition, i.e. a condition of long-run sustainability.

Most economic analysis in regard to materials, in the past, has focused on *availability*. Data on several categories of reserves (economically recoverable, potential, etc.) are routinely gathered and published by the US Bureau of Mines, for example. However, as is well known, such figures are a very poor proxy for actual reserves. In most cases the actual reserves are greater than the amounts actually documented. The reason, simply, is that most such data are extrapolated from test borings by mining or drilling firms. There is a well-documented tendency for firms to stop searching for new ore bodies when their existing reserves exceed 20 to 25 years' supply. Even in the case of petroleum (which has been the subject of worldwide searches for many decades), it is not possible to place much reliance on published data of this kind.[6]

However, a sustainable steady state is less a question of resource availability than of recycling/re-use efficiency. As commented earlier, a good measure of unsustainability is dissipative usage. This raises the distinction between *inherently* dissipative uses and uses where the material could be recycled or re-used in principle, but is not. The latter could be termed potentially recyclable. Thus, there are really three important cases:

1. Uses that are economically and technologically compatible with recycling under present prices and regulations.
2. Uses that are not economically compatible with recycling but where recycling is technically feasible, e.g. if the collection problem were solved.
3. Uses where recycling is inherently not feasible.

Generally speaking, it is arguable that most structural metals and industrial catalysts are in the first category; other structural and packaging materials, as well as most refrigerants and solvents, fall into the second category. This leaves coatings, pigments, pesticides, herbicides, germicides, preservatives, flocculants, anti-freezes, explosives, propellants, fire retardants, reagents, detergents, fertilizers, fuels, and lubricants in the third category. In fact, it is easy to verify that most chemical products belong in the third category, except those physically embodied in plastics, synthetic rubber, or synthetic fibres.

From the standpoint of elements, if one traces the uses of materials from source to final sink, it can be seen that virtually all sulphur mined (or recovered from oil, gas, or metallurgical refineries) is ultimately dissipated in use – for example, as fertilizers or pigments – or discarded as waste acid or as ferric or calcium sulphites or sulphates. (Some of these sulphate wastes are classed as hazardous.) Sulphur is mostly (75–80 per cent) used to produce sulphuric acid, which in turn is used for many purposes. But in every chemical reaction the sulphur must be accounted for – it must go somewhere. The laws of chemistry guarantee that reactions will tend to continue either until the most stable possible compound is formed or until an insoluble solid is formed. If the sulphur is not embodied in a "useful" product, it must end up in a waste stream.

There is only one long-lived structural material embodying sulphur: plaster of Paris (hydrated calcium sulphate), which is normally made directly from the natural mineral gypsum. In recent years, sulphur recovered from coal-burning power plants in Germany has been converted into synthetic gypsum and used for construction. However, this potential recycling loop is currently inhibited by the very low price of natural gypsum. Apart from synthetic gypsum, there are no other durable materials in which sulphur is physically embodied. It follows from materials balance considerations that sulphur is entirely dissipated into the environment. Globally, about 61.5 million tonnes of sulfur *qua* sulphur – not including gypsum – were

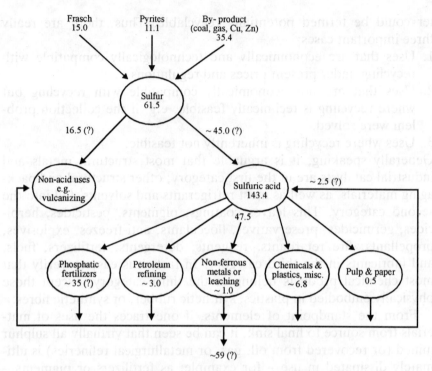

Fig. 4 Dissipative uses of sulphur, 1988 (millions of tonnes)

produced in 1988. Of this, less than 2 million were recycled (mainly as waste sulphuric acid), as indicated schematically in figure 4. Very little is currently used for structural materials. Thus, most sulphur chemicals belong in class 3.

Following similar logic, it is easy to see that the same is true of most chemicals derived from ammonia (fertilizers, explosives, acrylic fibres), and phosphorus (fertilizers, pesticides, detergents, fire retardants). In the case of chlorine, there is a division between class 2 (solvents, plastics, etc.) and class 3 (hydrochloric acid, chlorine used in water treatment, etc.).

Chlorofluorocarbon refrigerants and solvents are long-lived and non-reactive. In fact, this is the reason they pose an environmental hazard. Given an appropriate system for recovering and reconditioning old refrigerators and air-conditioners, the bulk of the refrigerants now in use could be recovered, either for re-use or destruction. Hence, they belong in class 2. However, CFCs used for foam-blowing are not recoverable.

14

Table 3 Examples of dissipative use (global)

Substance	10^6 T	Dissipative uses
Other chemicals		
Chlorine	25.9	Acid, bleach, water treatment, (PVC) solvents, pesticides, refrigerants
Sulphur	61.5	Acid (H_2SO_4), bleach, chemicals, fertilizers, rubber
Ammonia	93.6	Fertilizers, detergents, chemicals
Phosphoric acid	24.0	Fertilizers, nitric acid, chemicals (nylon, acrylics)
NaOH	35.8	Bleach, soap, chemicals
Na_2CO_3	29.9	Chemicals (glass)
Heavy metals		
Copper sulphate ($CuSO_4 \cdot 5H_2O$)	0.10	Fungicide, algicide, wood preservative, catalyst
Sodium bichromate	0.26	Chromic acid (for plating), tanning, algicide
Lead oxides	0.24	Pigment (glass)
Lithopone (ZuS)	0.46	Pigment
Zinc oxides	0.42	Pigment (tyres)
Titanium oxide (TiO_2)	1.90	Pigment
TEL	?	Gasoline additive
Arsenic	?	Wood preservative, herbicide
Mercury	?	Fungicide, catalyst

Table 3 shows the world output of a number of materials – mostly chemicals – whose uses are, for the most part, inherently dissipative (class 3). (It would be possible, with some research, to devise measures of the inherently dissipative uses of each element, along the lines sketched above.) Sustainability, in the long run, would imply that such measures decline. Currently, they are almost certainly increasing.

With regard to materials that are potentially recyclable (classes 1 and 2), the fraction actually recycled is a useful measure of the approach toward (or away from) sustainability. A reasonable proxy for this, in the case of metals, is the ratio of secondary supply to total supply of final materials: see, for example, table 4. This table shows, incidentally, that the recycling ratio in the United States has been rising consistently in recent years only for lead and iron/steel. In the case of lead, the ban on using tetraethyl lead as a gasoline additive (an inherently dissipative use) is entirely responsible.

15

Table 4 Scrap use in the United States

Material	Total consumption (million short tons)			% of total consumption in recycled scrap		
	1977	1982	1987	1977	1982	1987
Aluminium	6.49	5.94	6.90	24.1	33.3	29.6
Copper	2.95	2.64	3.15	39.2	48.0	39.9
Lead	1.58	1.22	1.27	44.4	47.0	54.6
Nickel	0.75	0.89	1.42	55.9	45.4	45.4
Iron/steel	142.40	84.00	99.50	29.4	33.4	46.5
Zinc	1.10	0.78	1.05	20.9	24.1	17.7
Paper	60.00	61.00	76.20	24.3	24.5	25.8

Source: Institute of Scrap Recycling Industries, 1988.

Another useful measure of industrial metabolic efficiency is the economic output per unit of material input. This measure can be called materials productivity. It can be determined, in principle, not only for the economy as a whole, but for each sector. It can also be measured for each major "nutrient" element: carbon, oxygen, hydrogen, sulphur, chlorine, iron, phosphorus, etc. Measures of this kind for the economy as a whole are, however, not reliable indicators of increasing technological efficiency or progress toward long-term sustainability. The reason is that increasing efficiency – especially in rapidly developing countries – can be masked by structural changes,[7] such as investment in heavy industry, which tend to increase the materials (and energy) intensiveness of economic activity. On the other hand, within a given sector, one would expect the efficiency of materials utilization – or materials productivity – to increase in general.[8]

Useful aggregate measures of the state of the environment *vis-à-vis* sustainability can be constructed from physical data that are already collected and compiled in many countries. To derive these aggregates and publish them regularly would provide policy makers with a valuable set of indicators at little cost.[9]

It is clear that other interesting and useful measures based on physical data are also possible. Moreover, if similar data were collected and published at the sectoral level, it would be possible to undertake more ambitious engineering-economic systems analyses and forecasts – of the kind currently possible only for energy – in the entire domain of industrial metabolism.

Policy implications of the industrial metabolism perspective

It may seem odd to suggest that a mere viewpoint – in contradistinction to empirical analysis – may have policy implications. But it is perfectly possible. In fact, there are two implications that come to mind. Both will recur more than once in the papers that follow. First, the industrial metabolism perspective is essentially "holistic" in that the whole range of interactions between energy, materials, and the environment are considered together, at least in principle. The second major implication, which follows from the first, is that from this holistic perspective it is much easier to see that narrowly conceived or short-run (myopic) "quick-fix" policies are very far from the global optimum. In fact, from the larger perspective, many such policies can be positively harmful.

The best way to explain the virtues of a holistic view is by contrasting it with narrower perspectives. Consider the problem of waste disposal. It is a consequence of the law of conservation of mass that the total quantity of materials extracted from the environment will ultimately return thence as some sort of waste residuals or "garbo-junk" (Ayres and Kneese, 1969, 1989). Yet environmental protection policy has systematically ignored this fundamental reality by imposing regulations on emissions by *medium*. Typically, one legislative act mandates a bureaucracy that formulates and enforces a set of regulations dealing with emissions by "point sources" only to the air. Another legislative act creates a bureaucracy that deals only with waterborne emissions, again by "point sources." And so forth.

Not surprisingly, one of the things that happened as a result was that some air pollution (e.g. fly ash and SO_x from fossil fuel combustion) was eliminated by converting it to another form of waste, such as a sludge to be disposed of on land. Similarly, some forms of waterborne wastes are captured and converted to sludges for land disposal (or, even, for incineration). Air and water pollution were reduced, but largely by resorting to land disposal. But landfills also cause water pollution (leachate), and air pollution, owing to anaerobic decay processes.

In short, narrowly conceived environmental policies over the past 20 years and more have largely shifted waste emissions from one form (and medium) to another, without significantly reducing the totals. In some cases, policy has encouraged changes that merely dilute the waste stream without touching its volume at all. The use of

17

high stacks for coal-burning power plants, and the building of longer
sewage pipes to carry wastes further offshore, exemplify this approach.

To be sure, these shifts may have been beneficial in the aggregate.
But the costs have been quite high, and it is only too obvious that the
state of the environment "in the large" is still deteriorating rapidly.
One is tempted to think that a more holistic approach, from the beginning, might have achieved considerably more at considerably less
cost.

In fact, there is a tendency for sub-optimal choices to get "locked
in" by widespread adoption. Large investments in so-called "clean
coal" technology would surely extend the use of coal as a fuel – an
eventuality highly desired by the energy establishment – but would
also guarantee that larger cumulative quantities of sulphur, fly ash
(with associated toxic heavy metals), and carbon dioxide would be
produced. The adoption of catalytic convertors for automotive engine
exhaust is another case in point. This technology is surely not the
final answer, particularly since it is not effective in older vehicles. Yet
it has deferred the day when internal combustion engines will eventually be replaced by some inherently cleaner automotive propulsion
technology. By the time that day comes, the world's automotive fleet
will be two or three times bigger than it might have been otherwise,
and the cost of substitution will be many times greater.

The implication of all these points for policy makers, of course, is
that the traditional governmental division of responsibility into a
great number of independent bureaucratic fiefdoms is dangerously
faulty.[10] But the way out of this organizational impasse is far from
clear. Top-down central planning has failed miserably, and is unlikely
to be tried again. On the other hand, pure "market" solutions to
environmental problems are limited in cases where there is no convenient mechanism for valuation of environmental resource assets
(such as beautiful scenery) or functions (such as the UV protection
afforded by the stratospheric ozone layer). This is primarily a problem of *indivisibility*. Indivisibility means that there is no possibility of
subdividing the attribute into "parcels" suitable for physical exchange. In some cases this problem can be finessed by creating ex-
changeable "rights" or "permits," but the creation of a market for
such instruments depends on other factors, including the existence of
an effective mechanism for allocating such rights, limiting their number, and preventing poaching or illicit use of the resource.

Needless to say, the policy problems have economic and socio-
political ramifications well beyond the scope of this book. However,

as the Chinese proverb has it, the longest journey begins with a single step.

Notes

1. This analogy between firms and organisms can be carried further, resulting in the notion of "industrial ecology." Just as an ecosystem is a balanced, interdependent, quasi-stable community of organisms living together, so its industrial analogy may be described as a balanced, quasi-stable collection of interdependent firms belonging to the same economy. The interactions between organisms in an ecosystem range from predation and/or parasitism to various forms of cooperation and synergy. Much the same can be said of firms in an economy.

2. A moment's thought should convince the reader that if the stock in any compartment changes, the stock in at least one other compartment must also change.

3. Another kind of primitive marine organism apparently utilized hydrogen sulphide as an energy source. The sulphur, released as a waste, combined with the dissolved iron and precipitated out as iron sulphide (pyrites).

4. However, this statement is not true for greenhouse gases in the atmosphere. Already, the concentration of carbon dioxide has increased by 20 per cent since pre-industrial times, while the concentration of methane is up 50 per cent. The most potent greenhouse gases, CFCs, do not exist in nature at all.

5. The special case of indefinite storage in deep underground mines, wells, or caverns, currently being considered for nuclear wastes, is not really applicable to industrial or consumer wastes, except in very special and rare circumstances. Surface landfills, no matter how well designed, are hardly permanent repositories, although little consideration has been given to the long-run disposal of leachates.

6. The reserve-to-production ratio has remained close to 20 years. For example, this figure was widely published in the 1920s (Graf, 1924), cited by Rogner (1987).

7. See chapter 3 of this volume.

8. This need not be true for each individual element, however. A major materials substitution *within* a sector can result in the use of one material increasing, at the expense of others, of course. The substitution of plastics for many structural materials, or of synthetic rubber for natural rubber, would exemplify this sort of substitution. For instance, currently glass fibres are in the process of substituting for copper wire as the major carrier of telephonic communications.

9. See also chapter 14 of this volume.

10. The analogous problem is beginning to be recognized in the private sector, as the legacy of Frederick Taylor is finally being challenged by new managerial/organizational forms. Taylorism has been criticized extensively, but its major problem arises from two (explicit) assumptions: (1) that the firm's activities can be subdivided into individual tasks, each of which can be performed independently of all others; (2) that maximizing output at the task level will maximize output (or projects) for the firm as a whole. The large US firms, which adopted Taylorism first and most enthusiastically at the beginning of the twentieth century, have been themselves to the new situation of intense international competition and faster technological change.

References

Ayres, Robert U. 1988. "Self Organization in Biology and Economics." *International Journal on the Unity of the Sciences* 1, no. 3.

Robert U. Ayres

Ayres, Robert U., and Allan V. Kneese. 1969. "Production, Consumption and Externalities." *American Economic Review* 59, no. 3: 282–296.
———. 1989. "Externalities: Economics and Thermodynamics." In: F. Archibugi and P. Nijkamp, eds., *Economy and Ecology: Towards Sustainable Development*. Dordrecht: Kluwer Academic Publishers.
Georgescu-Roegen, Nicholas. 1971. *The Entropy Law and the Economic Process*. Cambridge, Mass.: Harvard University Press.
Nriagu, J. O. 1990. "Global Metal Pollution." *Environment* 32, no. 7: 7–32.
Rogner, Hans-Holger. 1987. "Energy in the World: The Present Situation and Future Options." In: *Proceedings of the 17th International Congress of Refrigeration, August 24–28, 1987*.

2

Ecosystem and the biosphere: Metaphors for human-induced material flows

Rudolf B. Husar

Introduction

Long-term sustainable human development requires an understanding of the interaction between human activities and natural processes (Clark and Munn, 1986).[1] Displacement of materials by industrial and agricultural activities causes the most severe human stress on the natural system. Hence, the understanding of human-induced material flows and comparison of those to natural flows is a major step toward the design of sustainable development schemes.

A major component in the understanding of human-induced material flow is the identification of the key players and driving forces involved, i.e. the building of a conceptual model. Initially, such a model does not need to be predictive; it is sufficient for it to have explanatory power for the existing human–nature interactions. In formulating and explaining such conceptual models, it is helpful to use known existing systems as a guide, and by applying metaphors and analogies to transfer existing knowledge and concepts to the new system under consideration. Natural systems have demonstrated their capacity for sustained development and provide a rich choice of desirable metaphors for the description of human activities.

Industrial metabolism is a powerful metaphor for the illumination of the processes that mobilize and control the flow of materials and energy through industrial activities. As in nature, industrial "organisms" consume "food" for the maintenance of their functions and cause the exhalation of waste products (see chapter 1 of this volume). The industrial metabolism metaphor has the organism as its main biological entity, and industrial organizations as its human analogues. These are proper entities for the study of the internal workings of metabolism within these organisms. However, both the causes and the consequences of metabolism lie beyond the confines of an organism. These depend on the external world, which includes other organisms as well as the physico-chemical environment.

This chapter builds on the strength of the industrial metabolism metaphor and discusses the possible applicability of the ecosystem and the biosphere as extended biological analogues for human activities. The goal here is to offer multiple, complementary points of view to describe, by means of analogues, the same topic: the human-induced mobilization of materials. Hopefully, this will contribute to the illumination of this fascinating, multifaceted, and important process.

The ecosystem analogue

An ecosystem is biotic assemblage of plants, animals, and microbes, taken *together* with their physico-chemical environment (e.g. Kormondy, 1969). In an ecosystem the biological cycling of materials is

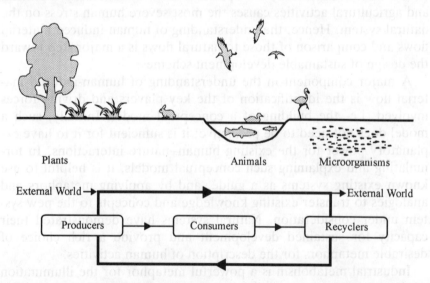

Fig. 1a The movement of chemicals and materials through the natural ecosystem

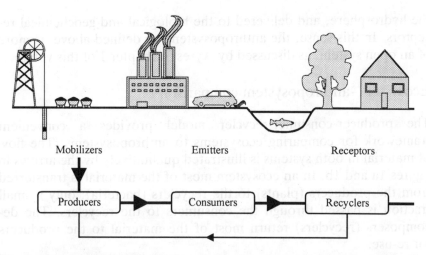

Fig. 1b The movement of chemicals and materials through a system resulting from human activity (anthroposystem)

maintained by three groups: producers, consumers, and decomposers (fig. 1a). The producers are plants and some bacteria capable of producing their own food photosynthetically or by chemical synthesis. The consumers are animals that obtain their energy and protein directly by grazing, feeding on other animals, or both. The decomposers are fungi and bacteria that decompose the organic matter of producers and consumers into inorganic substances that can be re-used as food by the producers; they are the recyclers of the biosphere. Nature is capable of sustaining the producer-consumer-decomposer cycle indefinitely, with the sun as the energy source. The smallest such entity that is self-sufficient is an ecosystem.

Functionally, human activities that perturb the natural environment can also be divided into three similar components (fig. 1b). Producing activities include energy production (fossil fuels), manufacturing (non-fuel minerals), and growing food. The consumers are humans and their domestic animals. Decomposing or recycling activities include treatment of waste water and recycling of metals. However, whereas an ecosystem relies on its decomposers for a complete recycling of its elements, the system created by human activity lacks such efficient decomposers and recyclers. As such, manufactured materials that are no longer needed and the waste by-products of industrial activity are disposed of into the physical environment. The process of adding unwanted material to the environment is called pollution. The waste products are taken up by the atmosphere and

23

the hydrosphere, and delivered to the biological and geochemical receptors. In this sense, the anthroposystem, as defined above, is more of an open system, as discussed by Ayres in chapter 1 of this volume.

Ecosystem–anthroposystem comparison

The producer-consumer-recycler model provides a convenient framework for comparing ecosystems to anthroposystems. The flow of material in both systems is illustrated qualitatively by the arrows in figures 1a and 1b. In an ecosystem most of the material is transferred from the producers (plants) to the recyclers (bacteria); only a small fraction is passed through the consumers to the recyclers. The decomposers (recyclers) return most of the material to the producers for re-use.

In the anthroposystem the flow from the producers to the recyclers is small (or even non-existent), since it would be pointless to produce (mobilize) material and immediately recycle it without a consumer in the loop. In the anthroposystem much of the mobilized material is transferred to the rest of the external environment by the producer or by the consumer. Hence, it mostly an open system, with recycling accounting for only a small fraction of the mobilized matter.

In an ecosystem, recycling and sustained development (evolution) is facilitated by a close physical proximity and functional matching between the producers and consumers. The physical proximity of producers, consumers, and recyclers in an ecosystem (e.g. plants, animals, and bacteria in a forest) assures that very little energy is required for the physical transport of matter between the plant and its symbiotic bacterial population. Also, the physical proximity allows a reasonably fast mutual adjustment if there is a perturbation in the system.

In the anthroposystem, with consumers playing a more significant role, there is usually a significant physical displacement between the producer and the consumer. The global flow of oil products is the most dramatic example. Accordingly, a significant amount of energy is required to transfer the matter back to the producer or to a recycler. This physical separation of consumers, producers, and recyclers appears to be a major difference between the ecosystem and anthroposystem.

The producer-consumer-receptor-based model is a suitable framework for economic models which study the driving forces of the material flows. It is self-evident that the economics – i.e. the allocation of material resources – will depend on production (availability), consumption (demand), and on the cost at the receptor.

The above ecosystem, i.e. the producer-consumer-receptor-based material flow model, can also be used to formulate physico-chemical models based on mass conservation principles. The next section presents such a formulation.

Ecosystem-based material flow system

The flow of matter from producers to consumers and subsequently to receptors is depicted schematically in figure 2. Most of the production of potential pollutants begins with mining, that is, the removal of a substance from its long-term geochemical reservoir. The amount of pollutant mass, fzM_i, mobilized by mining (tons/yr) is the production rate P_i (tons/yr) of the raw material (coal, oil, smelting ore, etc.)

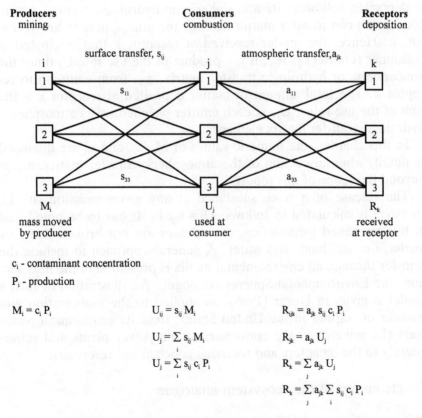

| Producers | Consumers | Receptors |
| mining | combustion | deposition |

surface transfer, s_{ij} atmospheric transfer, a_{jk}

M_i U_j R_k

mass moved   used at   received
by producer   consumer   at receptor

c_i - contaminant concentration

P_i - production

$$M_i = c_i P_i \qquad U_{ij} = s_{ij} M_i \qquad R_{ijk} = a_{jk} s_{ij} c_i P_i$$

$$U_j = \sum_i s_{ij} M_i \qquad R_{jk} = a_{jk} U_j$$

$$U_j = \sum_i s_{ij} c_i P_i \qquad R_k = \sum_j a_{jk} U_j$$

$$R_k = \sum_j a_{jk} \sum_i s_{ij} c_i P_i$$

Fig. 2 Key matrices in the flow of materials from producer to consumer to receptor

25

multiplied by the concentration c_i (gram/ton) of the impurity (sulphur, mercury, lead, etc.): $M_i c_i P_i$.

Matter is transferred from the producer to the consumer by transportation, including railroads, trucks, and ships. Functionally, transportation redistributes the mobilized substances over a large geographical area and to a multiplicity of consumers. Any producer, i, may deliver its product to any consumer, j. Mathematically, this producer-consumer transfer is characterized by a surface transfer matrix, s_{ij}.

The amount of matter, U_{ij}, originating from producer i and used at consumer j is $s_{ij}M_i$. The total amount of matter reaching consumer j is the sum of the matter produced by all producers multiplied by their respective surface transfer matrix elements.

The next transfer occurs between the consumer, or emitter, and the environmental receptors. The consumer is located where the combustion or smelting occurs, and the receptor where the pollutant is deposited following its atmospheric or hydrologic transit. Again, consumer j can transfer matter through the atmosphere to any receptor, k. Hence, the matter received at receptor k that originated at consumer (emitter) j, R_{jk}, is the product of the use rate U_j times the atmospheric or hydrologic transfer matrix, a_{jk}, from emitter j to receptor k. The total amount of matter deposited at receptor k is the sum of the use rates, U_j, at each emitter weighed by its atmospheric/ hydrologic transfer matrix element.

In this chapter, the numeric values of M_i, c_i, and s_{ij} are discussed in detail, while discussion of the atmospheric transfer matrix, a_{jk}, is beyond the scope of this report.

The release of a trace substance at any given emission site U_j (tons/yr) is calculated as follows: $U_j = s_{ij}c_iP_i$. It has to be noted that in this simplified formulation, the releases are not broken down by media, i.e. air, land, and water. A general approach to include the transfer through all environmental media is presented in the next section, the Environmental Spheres Analogue. An illustration of such a model is given in Husar (1986), as applied to the mobilization and transfer of sulphur in the United States, from its geochemical reservoirs (by mining) to the consumers at the power plants and subsequently to the receptors and receiving geochemical reservoirs.

Shortcomings of the ecosystem analogue

The ecosystem model of nature and of human activities has a major shortcoming in that it pays little heed to the physical transfer of mobilized matter. It does not answer the question of where the redistribution has occurred. Also, in that model, much of the anthroposystem had to be left open since many of the flows were out of the system as waste products. The next section is an attempt to extend the ecosystem analogue by "closing the system." In such a scheme, material is accounted for regardless of where it goes after leaving a given open system.

The environmental spheres analogue: Atmosphere, hydrosphere, lithosphere, and biosphere

Chemicals on earth are distributed among four major environmental compartments or conceptual spheres: atmosphere, hydrosphere, lithosphere, and biosphere. While such a compartmentalization of nature is rather arbitrary, it helps in organizing our existing knowledge on the distribution and flow of chemicals. A schematic representation of the four environmental compartments and their interrelationships is shown in figure 3.

The circles represent the spheres and the curved arrows the flow pathways of matter. These are used instead of boxes and straight-line connections to emphasize the close, dynamic, inseparable, organic coupling among the environmental compartments; if one compartment or linkage changes, all other compartments respond.

In this conceptual frame, every sphere has a two-way linkage to every other sphere, including itself. The two-way linkage signifies that matter may flow from one compartment to another in both directions; the two-way transfer within a given compartment indicates movement of the substance from one physical location to another without changing the sphere. Since matter cannot be created or destroyed, the question one seeks to answer is the location and chemical form of the substance at a given time.

The four spheres

The atmosphere is best envisioned as a transport-conveyer compartment that moves substances from the atmospheric sources to the receptors. Its storage capacity for matter is small compared to the other spheres, but it has an immense capability for spatially redistributing matter.

The hydrosphere may be envisioned as two compartments: a conveyor (river system) collects the substances within the watershed and delivers them to the second hydrologic compartment, oceans.

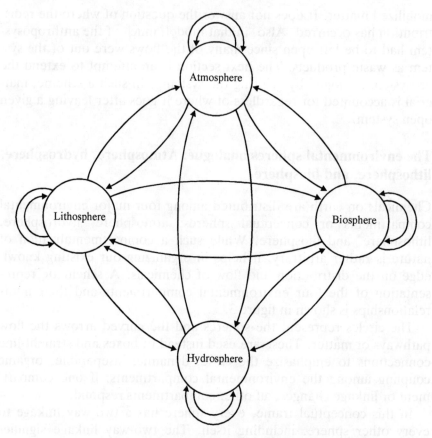

Fig. 3 The four environmental spheres

The lithosphere is the solid shell of inorganic material at the surface of the earth. It is composed of soil particles and of the underlying rocks down to a depth of 50 kilometres. The soil layer is also referred to as the pedosphere, and is a mixture of inorganic and organic solid matter, air, water, and microorganisms. Within the soil, biochemical reactions by microorganisms are responsible for most of the chemical changes of matter. However, soil and rock are mainly storage compartments for deposited matter.

The biosphere is the thin shell of organic matter on the earth's surface. It occupies the least volume of all of the spheres but it is the heart, or the chemical pump, of much of the flow of matter through nature. Weathering through the hydrological cycle, wind, and volcanic releases are the other mobilizing agents. The biosphere is responsible for the grand-scale recycling of energy and matter on

Earth. The mobilization of matter by biota is by no means restricted to small geographic regions. The periodic burning of forests and savannas, for example, not only changes the chemical form of matter, but also results in long-range atmospheric transport and deposition. Some of the biologically released chemicals, including carbon, nitrogen, and sulphur, have long atmospheric residence times, resulting in redistribution on a continental and a global scale.

Man and the biosphere

Human activities most closely resemble the function of the biosphere. In more than one way, humans are part of the biosphere. Humans and biota are responsible for grand-scale redistribution of chemicals on earth – once again with major similarities and differences. Fires and other forms of combustion result in an oxidation of both biogenic and anthropogenic elements. In nature, living plants tend to reduce their metabolized chemicals, thus ensuring a cycling of the chemicals that make up living matter.

Once again, the anthroposystem has no built-in mechanisms for reducing oxidized compounds. Man-induced oxidation products have instead to rely on biota for reduction, i.e recycling. Given the limited reduction capacity of the biosphere, many of the combustion products remain in stable oxidized form and are ultimately deposited in another long-term geochemical reservoir.

The atmosphere and the hydrosphere (rivers) are effective conveyors of matter. Consequently, many of the anthropogenic chemicals are transferred to the land oceans where they are subsequently incorporated in these long-term geochemical reservoirs. Much of the environmental damage is done in the atmosphere, hydrosphere, lithosphere, and the biosphere during the transit from one long-term geochemical reservoir to another.

Summary and conclusions

In the "industrial metabolism" metaphor, industrial organizations are likened to biological organisms that consume food and discard waste products. This chapter builds on and extends this metaphor beyond the biological organisms to an entire ecosystem. The human analogue of the ecosystem is the anthroposystem, consisting of producers, consumers, and recyclers.

Using these components, both ecosystem and anthroposystem are described by a conceptual material flow model that is also a suitable framework for an economic model. It is noted that the current anthroposystems differ from ecosystems mainly in that they lack efficient material recyclers that allow sustainable development. In this sense, the anthroposystem is an open system and the analogy with the ecosystem is incomplete.

The environmental spheres analogy extends the ecosystem analogy further by considering the flow of matter in all environmental compartments or conceptual "spheres" – air, land, water, and biota. This extension allows a closing of the system by following the flow and fate of matter regardless of the location and medium of transfer. It is concluded that human activities most closely resemble the role of the biosphere in the mobilization of matter.

The current work could be extended in several ways, in particular by combining the ecosystem and the environmental metaphors into a single "model." In principle, the multimedia "spheres" approach to material flows lends itself to rigorous mathematical formulation using basic conservation laws. In fact, it could incorporate all the features of the ecosystem approach. The resulting model could encompass the complete, end-to-end flow analysis, from the point of "production" – i.e. removal of the matter from one geochemical reservoir – to its fate in the receiving reservoir. Such a multimedia physical model would also be a suitable framework for environmental economic analysis.

Note

1. The author acknowledges the contributions of Janja D. Husar in the review and preparation of this manuscript.

References

Clark, W. C., and R. E. Munn, eds. 1986. *Sustainable Development of the Biosphere*. Cambridge, Mass.: Cambridge University Press.

Husar, R. B. 1986. "Emissions of Sulfur Dioxide and Nitrogen Oxides and Trends for Eastern North America." In: National Research Council, *Acid Deposition Long-term Trends*. Washington, D.C.: National Academy Press.

Husar, R. B., and J. D. Husar. 1990. "Sulfur." In: B. L. Turner et al., eds. *The Earth as Transformed by Human Action*. Cambridge, Mass.: Cambridge University Press.

Kormondy, E. J. 1969. *Concepts of Ecology*. Englewood Cliffs, N.J.: Prentice-Hall, Inc.

3

Industrial restructuring in industrial countries

Udo E. Simonis

Introduction

Until recently, the role of economic or industrial change as a driving force for environmental change has not been widely explored.[1] This may be due in part to the difficulty of collecting suitable data and indicators with which to describe the impacts of an economic structure on the environment. In part it may be due to the fact that the level of economic development or the growth rate of the economy was thought to be more important for explaining the changes occurring in the natural environment.[2]

The present chapter approaches the links between the various sectors (or industries) of the economy and the overall economic performance and addresses the possible delinking of polluting sectors (or industries) from the gross domestic product (GDP); it thus views restructuring as one way towards a more efficient industrial metabolism.

Such an examination could take place on the level of the individual sector (or industry) or the aggregate level of all sectors (or industries), but also at the regional level. It should at least be undertaken for those sectors (or industries) whose environmental effects are rather certain (structural environmental impacts). This would imply a mesoeconomic, not a micro-economic, approach to understanding environmental change. Such an examination may make it possible to assess current structural changes in economies and, on the basis of their environmental implications, may suggest future directions for environmentally benign structural policies.

The expression "structural change" or "restructuring" is generally used to characterize the decline or increase over time in certain sectors, groups of industries, or regions (and, sometimes, technologies) as regards gross national/domestic product.[3] One may also think of structural change in terms of a transformation in the mix of goods and services produced; or one may refer to a broader set of changes in the economy, not only in its products and employment, but also in the social relations of production (e.g. unionization, part-time *v.* full-time jobs), the means of production (handicrafts, robotics), and the forces of production (market demand, profits).

Clearly, not all possible classifications and groupings are helpful or of interest for purposes of structural research. One either has to make an explicit choice, or one has implicitly made one in using or referring to a well-known, long-established concept of structural change. In this chapter, we will use one of several concepts of structure in economics, namely the sectoral production structure – i.e. the share of sectors in the economy and their relation to gross domestic/net material product.

Economic restructuring thus subsumes *industrial* restructuring, though the terms are often used interchangeably. Any restructuring of the sectors (or industries) in an economy is, of course, linked to more profound changes in other realms. For our purposes, and within this concept, we will deliberately select sectors whose environmentally destructive potential is beyond question. Thus we will not consider the regional structure, the employment structure, and the investment structure, even though all of these might be quite relevant in explaining the given environmental situation of a country, or its change over time.

Regarding the temporal dimension of structural change, there is, as we will see, a differentiation to be made between *discontinuity* and *gradualism*. There is economic restructuring as a discontinuity, or a break in development, and there is gradualism as an evolutionary or slow transition. Discontinuity may be the outcome of subterranean historical processes, but gradualism is the everyday reality of change. Clearly, the two are not mutually exclusive, but rather two sides of the same coin.

As regards impacts, we use the term "structural environmental impact," which means the environmental stress (or burden) that results from a given sectoral production structure, irrespective of pollution-control measures in the form of *end-of-pipe* treatment.

Identifying indicators of environmentally relevant structural change

It is not so long ago that sheer quantity of output was considered to be an indicator of a nation's economic success; in some circles this still seems to be the case. In Eastern Europe the importance attached to this criterion led to "tonnage ideology." In Western societies steel production and railways tonnage were once considered to be central indicators of economic success; currently housing starts, energy consumption, and the number of cars produced play this role. This accounts for the importance of the motor industry in the political arena. For a number of reasons, however, indicators of energy and materials consumption must be understood as indicators of economic failure.

Particularly in times of high or increasing costs for energy and materials, a high consumption of such inputs may turn out to be uneconomic. And countries that have drastically reduced their specific energy and materials use are today at the top of the international list of economic performance; resource use efficiency (or "materials productivity") has a major contribution to make in evolving new strategies towards sustainable development.[4]

No wonder, then, that economists, planners, and engineers are seeking solutions to the problem of how to modify or restructure the existing patterns of energy and materials use, to switch from "high-volume production" to "high-value production."[5] At the same time, this reorientation reflects new and potentially strong environmental priorities. The hope of a "reconciliation between economy and ecology" and the envisaged "industrial metabolism" relies on the premise that a reduction in the energy and material input of production will lead to a reduction in the amount of emissions and waste, and will help to facilitate the potential for recycling and promote the option of intentionally closing cycles in industrial society.[6]

The industrial system as it exists today is *ipso facto* unsustainable (R.U. Ayres). While the natural cycles (of water, carbon, nitrogen, etc.) are closed, the industrial cycles (of energy, steel, chemicals, etc.) are basically still open.[7] In particular, the industrial system starts with high-quality materials (like fossil fuels and metal ores) and returns them to nature in a degraded form.

On the basis of materials cycle analysis, it would appear that industrial society has drastically disturbed, and still is disturbing, the natural system. Ayres proposes two main criteria or measures of an approach towards (or further away from) sustainability, the recycling ratio and materials productivity. In the form of policy suggestions, this means (1) reducing the dissipative losses by near-total recycling of intrinsically toxic or hazardous materials, and/or (2) increasing economic output per unit of material input.

In this chapter, we will use a somewhat different, but comparable, approach in focusing on structural change in the economy and its environmental impact.[8] To assess the empirical dimensions of the harmful or potentially benign environmental effects of structural change, we need suitable information concerning the material side of production. This by itself is not an easy task, especially if we look for cross-national comparisons. Resource conservation, materials productivity, and environmentally significant structural change are not appropriately described by the monetary values used in national accounts, although national accounts and, particularly, input-output tables offer some information.[9] An alternative is to select indicators that act as synonyms for certain characteristics of the production process.

Certain indicators have been in the forefront of the environmental debate since it began, and the availability of data on the emission of various (representative) pollutants has grown considerably.[10] Our present interest, however, is on environmentally relevant input factors.

Given the state of research and data availability, only a few such indicators can be tested in a cross-national comparison of Eastern and Western economies. The results of this test thus cannot give a precise picture of the real world, but can at least offer some patterns of environmentally relevant structural change from which hypotheses could be derived for further research. We use four such factors whose direct and indirect environmental relevance is indisputable: energy, steel, cement, and the weight of freight transport.[11]

Energy consumption in general is accompanied by more or less serious environmental effects, and energy-intensive industries in particular pose environmental threats. Energy consumption thus is probably *the* central ecological dimension of the production pattern of a country. For similar reasons steel consumption is also a general indicator of structural environmental stress, in that it reflects an important part of the material side of industrial society. Cement consumption is in itself a highly polluting process, and cement represents to some extent the physical reality of the construction industry. (For reasons of data availability, in the following we use the production statistics of cement only.) The weight of freight transport can be understood as a general indicator of the volume aspect of production, as nearly all kinds of transport are accompanied not only by high materials input but also by a high volume of hazardous emissions. (In the following, we use data for road and rail transport only.)

The empirical investigation covers the period from 1970 to 1987 and includes 32 countries from the East and West, i.e., nearly the whole industrialized world. As is well known, certain methodological

Table 1 Data sources

Energy consumption	International Energy Agency (IEA), *Energy Balances of OECD Countries 1970–1985 and Main Series from 1960*; Department of International Economic and Social Affairs of the United Nations, *Energy Statistics Yearbook*, *Yearbook of World Energy Statistics*, and *World Energy Supplies*
Steel consumption	Statistical Office of the United Nations, *Statistical Yearbook*; Statistical Bureau of the United States, *Statistical Abstracts of the United States*
Cement production	Statistical Office of the United Nations, *Statistical Yearbook* and *Monthly Bulletin of Statistics*
Freight transport	Economic Commission for Europe of the United Nations, *Annual Bulletin of Transport Statistics for Europe*; International Road Federation (IRF), *World Road Statistics*; International Railway Federation (UIC), *International Railway Statistics*
Population	Organisation for Economic Cooperation and Development (OECD), *Labour Force Statistics 1965–1985*; Statistical Office of the United Nations, *Demographic Yearbook*
Domestic product[a]	United States Statistical Yearbook, *Comparative International Statistics*; Statistical Bureau of the United States, *Statistical Abstracts of the United States*; Organisation for Economic Cooperation and Development (OECD), *Main Economic Indicators* and *National Accounts of OECD Countries*

a. The economic performance of the Eastern European countries is expressed in GNP or GDP terms as published in the *Comparative International Statistics* of the United States Statistical Yearbook. For calculating the GNP in US dollars, the constant GNP values were determined and then adjusted according to the East–West differences in calculation method. The conversion into US dollars is based on the exchange rates published by the World Bank. For the countries of Eastern Europe this method of calculating the GNP or GDP results in a somewhat lower growth rate than that given in their respective national statistics; nevertheless, the method of calculation employed here seems to be fairly realistic.

problems arise when comparing data on the national (domestic) product of Eastern and Western economies.[12] For the purposes of this study, we relied on the data given in the *National Accounts of OECD Countries*, on data from the Statistical Office of the United Nations, and on other well-established data series, as specified in table 1.

Structural change as environmental relief

The harmful as well as the benign environmental effects of structural (or industrial) change and the significance of a structurally oriented environmental policy have been cited in recent literature.[13] According to this insight, environmentally benign effects of structural change are to be expected by actively delinking economic growth from the consumption of ecologically significant resources, like energy and materials. Such delinking, achievable in particular by decreasing the input coefficients of these resources (dematerialization, re-use, recycling) or by increasing their effectiveness (energy and materials productivity) through better use,

- would result in a decrease in resource consumption and probably also in production costs, at least in the long term;
- would mean *ex ante* environmental protection, which is cheaper and more efficient than *ex post* installation of pollution-abatement equipment (end-of-pipe technology);
- would be environmentally more effective, since end-of-pipe technologies normally treat only single, "outstanding" pollutants, whereas integrated technologies touch upon several environmental effects simultaneously; and
- would open up a broad range of options for technological innovation or would itself be the result of such innovation.

For certain types of pollution, the effectiveness of structural change has been verified empirically. For example, structural change with respect to energy consumption had more benign environmental effects than end-of-pipe protection measures, especially as regards such emissions as SO_2 and NO_x. Several OECD reports on the state of the environment reflect this fact for a number of countries.[14] Changes in the energy structure, for instance, led to greater environmental protection effects than the installation of desulphurization plants. In Japan, energy conservation (and also water conservation) has been particularly successful;[15] conventional environmental protection has been superseded by technological and structural change.

Examples like these may support the rapid introduction of market instruments, like resource taxes and effluent charges – a policy that would accelerate structural change and lead to economic advantages as well as to environmental relief.

Environmentally relevant structural change: Empirical analysis

Environmental benefits of structural change

Before dealing with the option of accelerating environmentally benign structural change in the economy, it is necessary to consider ways to describe such processes, especially with respect to international and intertemporal comparisons.[16]

Structural change as a continuous shift of labour, capital, and skills to more intelligent uses can also be conceived of as a process of successive delinking: the contribution of traditional factors to the national product decreases whilst the contribution of other factors increases – i.e. they tend to change or lose their function over time. This chapter is concerned with the environmentally relevant factors (sectors) in this process.

Focusing on the four factors described above, figure 1 illustrates such delinking from the growth of the gross domestic product (GDP), taking the Federal Republic of Germany as a first example. The delinking of energy and weight of freight transport from the GDP became apparent by the end of the 1970s, while for cement this process began in the early 1970s; for steel consumption, delinking had already begun in the 1960s.

In the Federal Republic of Germany, structural change generated environmentally benign effects in various ways:
– The growth of the service sector of the economy was environmentally beneficial (if transport activities are excluded from consideration), at least to the extent that it added economic value at relatively little cost in terms of energy and materials.
– The stagnating consumption of primary energy made a reduction in emissions possible, in spite of a comparatively sluggish clean-air policy in this period; the desulphurization and denitrification of the power plants came into full swing only in the second half of the 1980s. The effect of energy saving could have been even more impressive if there had not been a further increase in the consumption of electricity.
– The decrease in steel consumption accounts for a considerable reduction in emissions as far as production and processing are con-

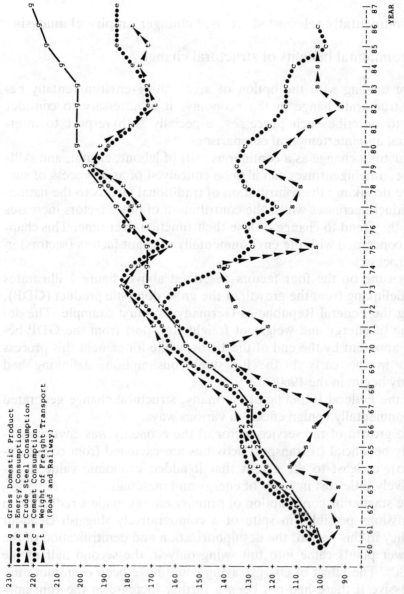

Fig. 1 Structural economic change in the Federal Republic of Germany, 1960–1987 (1960 = 100) (Source: Jänicke et al., note 8)

g = Gross Domestic Product
e = Energy Consumption
s = Crude Steel Consumption
c = Cement Consumption
t = Weight of Freight Transport
    (Road and Railway)

YEAR

cerned. The drop is especially noticeable, and is partly due to an increased recycling ratio. However, such benign environmental effects may have to be compared with the harmful effects of an increased use of steel substitutes such as plastics and other materials and their inherent environmental risks.

- The fall in cement production represents a direct environmental gratis effect as far as the emissions from cement factories are concerned. With regard to the environmentally disputed construction industry, this decrease reflects a trend away from new construction towards modernization of the housing stock. (Again this trend may be reversed owing to the large construction programmes launched since the unification of Germany.)
- From the development of the weight of freight transport it can be concluded that in the period under investigation the volume of materials employed declined rather than increased, i.e. materials productivity has risen.[17] (Germany being a transit country, the European Single Market might possibly reverse the trend again and lead to a drastic increase in freight transport.)

Each of the sectors discussed above would of course need to be examined in greater detail, a step that cannot be undertaken here. One of the ensuing methodological questions is whether or not a different set of indicators would offer a more thorough understanding of environmentally relevant structural change in the economy.[18] The international comparison of the energy and materials side of nearly all the industrial countries, as well as the intention to establish a respective typology, however, seems to justify our concentration on the four indicators chosen for this study.

Environmental protection through resource economy

Figure 2 shows that some delinking was also taking place in the (former) German Democratic Republic (GDR), though it was different in scope and time.

Unlike the FRG, the GDR long continued to rely on the industrial sector, particularly on polluting heavy industry, as the main source of economic growth, while the development of the service sector was woefully neglected. Regarding energy and steel consumption, a slow process of delinking had begun in the early 1970s, but structural change in terms of a "materials economy" was modest. While, according to political rhetoric, increased energy and materials productivity was considered to be the "most important way of reducing

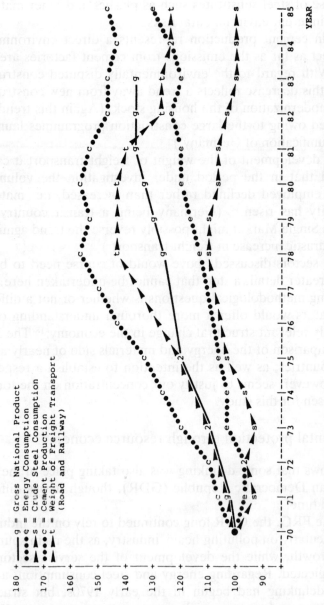

g = Gross National Product
e = Energy Consumption
s = Crude Steel Consumption
c = Cement Production
t = Weight of Freight Transport
    (Road and Railway)

YEAR

Fig. 2 Structural economic change in the German Democratic Republic, 1970–1985 (1970 = 100) (Source: Jänicke et al., note 8)

the burden on the environment,"[19] practice fell short in implementing this concept.

In addition, the genuine relief of environmental stress can occur only if an *absolute* reduction in the relevant energy and materials inputs is achieved. The reduction in the GDR was not very significant, even in relative terms.

Changes in structural environmental impacts: East-West comparisons

The differing scales of GDP and of energy and materials consumption within the national economies have not yet been considered in this chapter. This, however, is important since a process of active delinking would generally be achieved more easily where energy and materials consumption were already at a high level. For active delinking, three aspects (or types) of environmental impacts of production and consumption have to be differentiated: (a) absolute environmental impact; (b) impact per capita; and (c) impact per unit of gross domestic product (GDP).

With regard to the absolute impact (a), it is the change over time that is of interest. Without reference to the size of a country, its population and output, however, the absolute impact does not lend itself to international comparisons. Such comparisons only become feasible if one uses the per capita impact (b) and/or the impact per unit of GDP (c).

In a first round, we computed an aggregated environmental impact index, consisting of the per capita impacts of consumption of primary energy and crude steel, freight transport weight and cement production for all the countries under investigation. In computing the index, equal weight was given to the four indicators, marking the deviation from the mean value of all countries for 1970 and 1985. Thus the relative position and the patterns of change of the countries can be observed. The results of the computations are presented in figures 3, 4, and 5. (The abbreviations used are the international signs for motor vehicle licences.)

As figure 3 shows, in 1970 there was a significant relationship between a country's per capita GDP and the structural impacts on its environment regarding the four selected indicators (sectors). The correlation coefficient for the aggregated environmental impact index and the per capita GDP was 0.76 for all the countries considered. This means that around 1970 the national product of the industrial

41

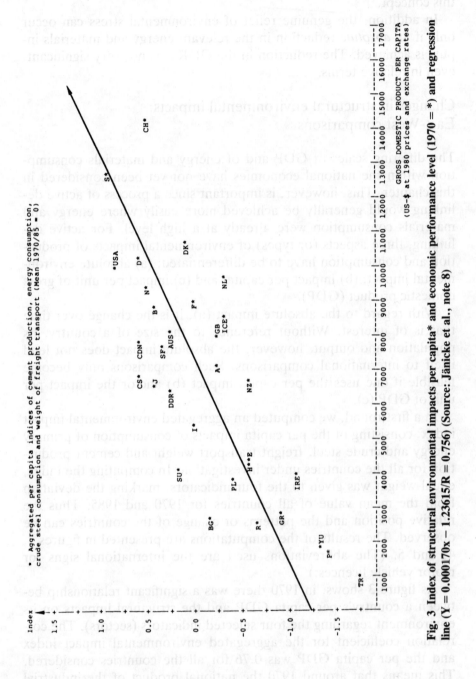

Fig. 3 Index of structural environmental impacts per capita* and economic performance level (1970 = *) and regression line (Y = 0.000170x − 1.23615/R = 0.756) (Source: Jänicke et al, note 8)

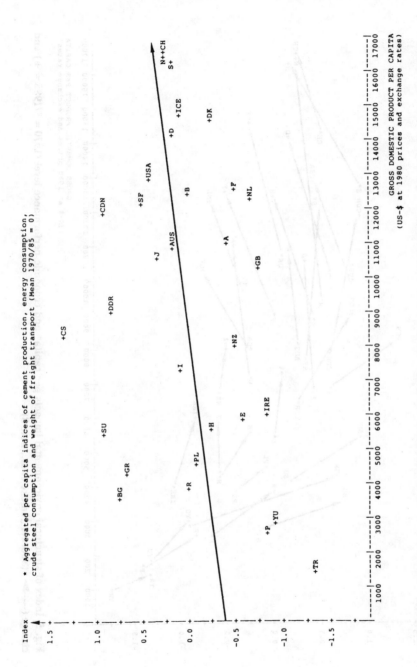

Fig. 4 Index of structural environmental impacts per capita* and economic performance level (1985 = +) and regression line (Y = 0.0000046x − 0.39506/R = 0.312) (Source: Jänicke et al., note 8)

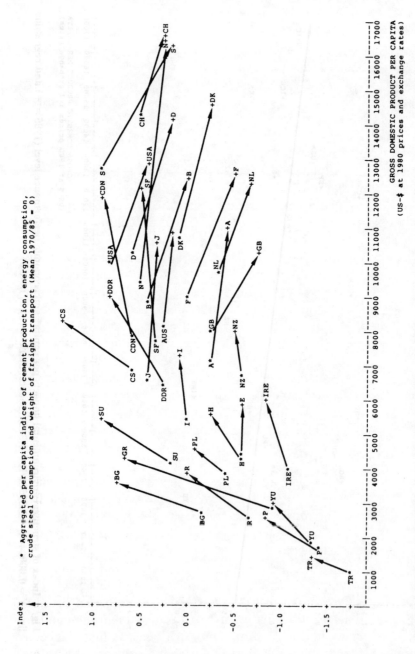

Fig. 5 **Index of structural environmental impacts per capita* and economic performance level (1970 = */1985 = +) and change (-----►) (Source: Jänicke et al., note 8)**

countries was still strongly based on "hard" production factors (high volume production).

Countries with high environmental impacts per capita (see figure 3) were Sweden (S), the United States (USA), the Federal Republic of Germany (D), Czechoslovakia (CS), Canada (CDN), Norway (N), Switzerland (CH), Japan (J), Belgium (B), and even Finland (SF). In the lowest third of the scale were Hungary (H), New Zealand (NZ), Romania (R), Spain (E), Greece (GR), Ireland (IRE), Yugoslavia (YU), Portugal (P), and Turkey (TR).

During the 1970s and the early 1980s, this relationship between economic performance (GDP) and structural impacts changed considerably. The correlation coefficient in 1985 was at only 0.31, significantly below that of 1970; figure 4 shows the new picture. This means that the process of structural change in several countries reduced the importance of the "hard" factors (high volume production) in the economy.[20]

Accordingly, the position of several countries has improved over time. This was especially true of Sweden, but also of the Federal Republic of Germany, France, the United Kingdom, and the United States. In contrast, the placing of several other countries has deteriorated. This was especially true of Greece, but also of Bulgaria, Romania, the USSR, and Czechoslovakia. The group with the highest structural environmental impacts by 1985 was led by member states of the (former) COMECON, namely Czechoslovakia, the USSR, the German Democratic Republic, and Bulgaria; Western industrialized countries showed up in the second (Canada), sixth (Greece), seventh (Finland), and eighth (USA) position, respectively. Japan, despite its improved position, was still in the top half of the scale.

The dynamics and the international pattern of structural change from 1970 to 1985 are indicated in figure 5, which is derived from figures 3 and 4. The main message here is the variation in the direction of change. In the group of low- and medium-income countries (among the industrial countries), two different patterns emerged: increasing environmental impacts, on the one hand, and stabilizing or decreasing environmental impacts on the other (see figure 5).

The fact that economically advanced Western industrial countries occupied leading positions as regards per capita environmental impacts in 1970 may not be so surprising as it seems at first glance. At that time, Sweden, the USA, and Japan, being confronted with high pollution loads and partly with environmental crisis, had to recognize the need for sweeping environmental protection measures. The fact (by contrast) that Czechoslovakia was "leading" in 1985 indicates the problématique of that country's economic structure. At that time, Czechoslovakia's energy consumption per unit of GDP was more than 50 per cent higher than in most other countries, and specific steel consumption was actually twice that of countries with comparable levels of GDP.

Typology of environmentally relevant structural change

As was explained above, the shifts in the international position of countries listed in figures 3 to 5 relate to structural per capita impacts only – i.e. no account is being taken of the individual country's economic growth rate. For example, the shift in Norway's position coincided with a high rate of economic growth (see table 2) so that the environmentally benign effects of structural change were partly neutralized. To be sure, the absolute (per capita) environmental impacts are of the utmost importance for the environmental policy debate. However, structural change in relation to the growth of the economy is also relevant for the environmental situation of a country. There may be no structural improvement in absolute (per capita) terms because high growth rates neutralize the otherwise positive effects of structural change.

To differentiate the patterns of change, the following typology may be useful:
1. Absolute structural improvement, i.e. an absolute (per capita) decline in production factors (sectors) causing high environmental impacts.
2. Relative structural improvement, i.e. a relative decline in production factors (sectors) causing high environmental impacts compared to the growth of the economy.
3. Absolute structural deterioration (which includes relative deterioration), i.e. a disproportional increase in production factors (sectors) causing high environmental impacts compared to the growth of the economy.

Environmental gratis effects may be defined as those effects that occur when (*ceteris paribus*) the rate of usage of those factors (sectors) having an impact on the environment remains (considerably) below the growth rate of the GDP (type 1 and 2).

In table 2 16 countries out of the whole sample of industrial countries investigated are grouped according to these three different de-

Table 2 Environmentally relevant structural change: percentage changes 1970/1985

Country	Consumption of Primary energy	Consumption of Crude steel	Cement pro-duction	Weight of freight transport	GDP[a]
Group 1: Absolute structural improvement					
Belgium	7.1	−24.5	−17.6	−2.2	42.7
Denmark	−2.7	−15.6	−33.2	20.1	40.8
France	30.3	−34.8	−23.4	−14.5	51.6
FRG	13.4	−26.3	−32.8	4.4	38.4
Sweden	26.4	−37.9	−41.2	−21.4	32.7
United Kingdom	−2.3	−43.5	−28.7	−18.2	32.4
Group 2: Relative structural improvement					
Austria	32.1	−33.9	−6.0	21.3	54.3
Finland	39.6	14.8	−11.2	12.2	65.7
Japan	37.3	−2.3	27.4	7.5	90.2
Norway	51.1	−21.6	−40.3	34.7	87.5
Group 3: Structural deterioration					
Bulgaria	74.9	24.9	42.3	77.5	37.3
Czechoslovakia	31.5	22.5	37.3	62.9	33.9
Greece[b]	119.3	67.3	162.9	43.1	69.1
Portugal[b]	89.0	34.2	133.1	27.4	69.0
Soviet Union	76.3	33.4	35.9	70.2	47.7
Turkey	218.8	184.4	173.2	118.6	118.2

Source: Jänicke et al. (note 8).

a. Calculation of the Gross Domestic Product percentage changes on the basis of constant (1980) US dollars. Bulgaria, Czechoslovakia, and Soviet Union data refer to percentage changes between 1970 and 1983 in the Gross National Product.

b. Transport data only take railway transport data into account.

velopment patterns. Again, we use here the above indicators of an energy- and materials-intensive mode of production, i.e. consumption of primary energy and crude steel, weight of freight transport, and cement production.

Of all the industrial countries studied, Sweden (see figure 6) is the environmentally most positive case. Although the growth rate of industrial production was very low after 1973, Sweden increased its GDP quite considerably, primarily through an expansion of the service sector. The drastic reduction in cement production (−41.2 per cent), the decreasing consumption of crude steel (−37.9 per cent), and the decrease in the weight of freight transport (−21.4 per cent) add up to notable overall environmental gratis effects.

Also in the United Kingdom, the four structural impact factors de-

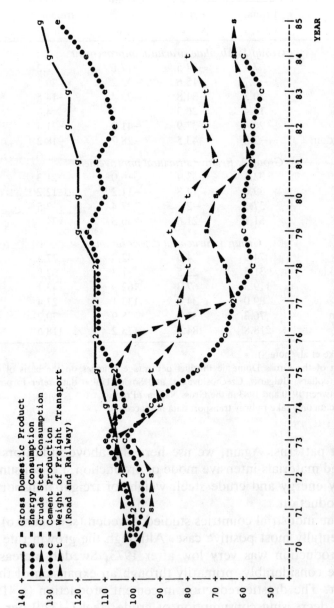

Fig. 6 Structural economic change in Sweden, 1970–1985 (1970 = 100) (Source: Jänicke et al., note 8)

g = Gross Domestic Product
e = Energy Consumption
s = Crude Steel Consumption
c = Cement Production
t = Weight of Freight Transport
    (Road and Railway)

YEAR

creased by between 2.3 per cent and 43.5 per cent but, in contrast to Sweden, these reductions were connected with, or induced by, high mass unemployment.

In Denmark, too, structural change in the economy decreased the importance of the energy- and materials-intensive sectors quite considerably. Between 1970 and 1985, the GDP grew by some 40.8 per cent, while three of the four impact factors decreased by between 2.7 per cent and 33.2 per cent.

In Japan (see figure 7), the process of delinking was partly neutralized by the rapid growth in overall industrial production and thus only resulted in relative structural improvement (see group 2 in table 2). The conclusion can be drawn that a forced rate of industrial growth interferes with the environmental relief of structural change. Countries with high growth rates must therefore undertake stringent remedial environmental protection measures in order to achieve a net relief for the environment.

In Czechoslovakia (see figure 8), no real delinking of economic growth from the four impact factors took place; some of them even increased. After the oil price hike of 1979 the economy entered a crisis. The development profile of Czechoslovakia, which had undertaken no structural change at the time under investigation, was representative of the economies of Eastern Europe. Group 3 of the countries (see table 2) consists for the most part of industrial latecomers, then in an early stage of industrialization. But Czechoslovakia was a relatively old industrial economy that (in 1985) ranked at the top among the countries suffering from high structural environmental impacts per capita.

This leads at least to two specific questions: (1) do all late-comers have to go through stages of increasing environmental impacts; and (2) what prevents old industrial countries from taking an environmentally friendly development path? A third, more general, question is, of course: What is to be learned from past experience, and under what conditions can economic restructuring become a strategic variable, or point of departure, for sustainable development?

Specific conclusions

First of all, the method used in this study leaves room for refinement.[21] Certain problems remain as regards data, particularly the differences in computing the national (domestic) product in East

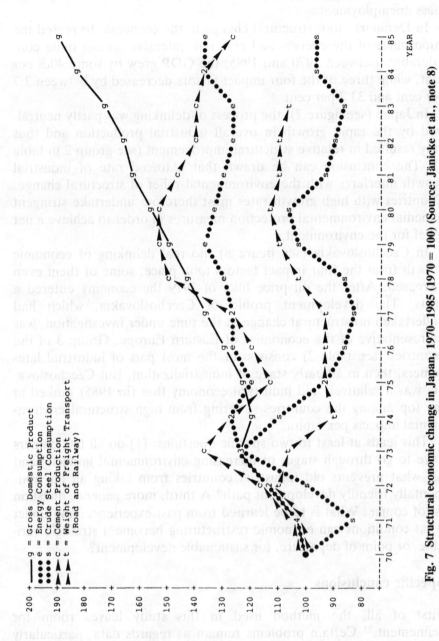

g = Gross Domestic Product
e = Energy Consumption
s = Crude Steel Consumption
c = Cement Production
t = Weight of Freight Transport (Road and Railway)

Fig. 7 Structural economic change in Japan, 1970–1985 (1970 = 100) (Source: Jänicke et al., note 8)

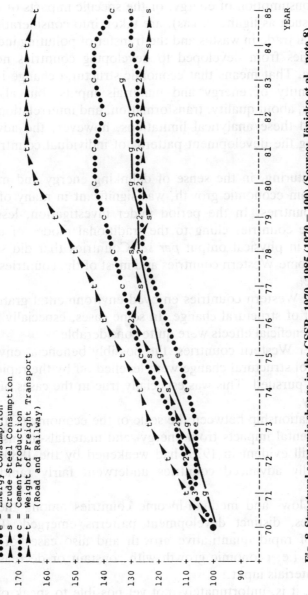

Fig. 8 Structural economic change in the CSSR, 1970–1985 (1970 = 100) (Source: Jänicke et al., note 8)

g = Gross National Product
e = Energy Consumption
s = Crude Steel Consumption
c = Cement Production
t = Weight of Freight Transport
(Road and Railway)

YEAR

and West. The question of substitution processes (steel/plastics, for example) is of high relevance and should be further investigated.[22] Additional information is needed if, for instance, *industrial* and not overall consumption of energy, or the specific impacts of energy *production* (such as lignite *v.* gas), are taken into consideration. The international trade in wastes and the transfer of polluting industries and technologies from developed to developing countries need further study, etc. That means that economic structural change is about not only quantity of energy and materials inputs, but also, and increasingly, about quality, transformation, and interrelations.

Beyond these analytical limitations, however, the advantages of comparing the development patterns of individual countries become evident:

– Restructuring, in the sense of delinking energy and materials inputs from economic growth, was significant in many of the industrial countries. In the period under investigation, less than half of these countries clung to the traditional modes of quantitative growth in physical output *per se*. Countries that did so were the low-income Western countries and most of the countries of Eastern Europe.
– Certain Western countries enjoyed environmental gratis effects as a result of structural change. In some cases, especially in Sweden, these beneficial effects were quite considerable.
– In other Western countries, the possibly beneficial environmental effects of structural change were levelled off by the rapid economic growth pursued. This was especially true in the cases of Japan and Norway.
– The relationship between the scale of the economy (GDP) and environmental impacts from energy- and materials-intensive production, still evident in 1970, had weakened by the 1980s. The economically advanced countries underwent fairly rapid structural change.
– In the low- and medium-income countries among the industrial countries, distinct development patterns emerged. There were cases of rapid quantitative growth and also cases of qualitative growth, i.e. economic growth with constant or decreasing energy and materials input.

All in all, it is, unfortunately, not yet possible to speak of *one* dominant development trend among the industrial countries towards dematerialization, recycling, improved industrial metabolism, or sustainable development.

General conclusions

The differences between these development patterns should be of particular interest for future environmental and economic policy in general, and structural policy in particular. It seems that the reasons for such differences and their consequences deserve further attention.

Economic or industrial restructuring is more than an economic phenomenon, particularly if it is understood to convey a break in energy and materials intensity and in pollution trends, that is, a shift towards a significantly different environmental impact pattern. Structure is the key to many theoretical problems; industrial restructuring can be a key to solving present and preventing future environmental problems. Structure is both a comforting and a disturbing notion; restructuring should be made a less uncomfortable, more environmentally friendly strategy.

By implication, the temporally uneven development of the economies studied (discontinuity and gradualism) manifests itself in uneven spatial and social patterns. Our concern here was with the environmental impacts involved in and induced by structural change. The better the environmental impacts of industrial structures are understood, and the earlier they are taken into consideration, the easier it should be to channel industrial development in a direction that is consonant with environmental protection, and thus to improve on industrial metabolism.[23]

In this sense, the "economic late-comers" need not fall into the environmental trap that most of the "economic forerunners" ended up in. By the same token, there is enough evidence that some of the "economic forerunners" could do more to escape from being "environmental late-comers." This, however, would require not only proactive structural change in the economy but also a preventative environmental strategy. This means that environmentally benign market forces would have to be stimulated by structurally innovative policies.

Notes

1. For instance, in the book *Restructuring the City* by Susan S. Fainstein et al., New York: Longman, 1986, the relationship between economic or industrial restructuring and the natural environment was not even mentioned, let alone elaborated.
2. The latter point generated some interest after the first, much-discussed report to the Club of Rome; see D. H. Meadows, D. L. Meadows, J. Randers, and W. W. Behrens, *The Limits to Growth*, London: Earth Island Limited, 1972.

53

Udo E. Simonis

3. For these and other approaches to the concept see R. A. Beauregard, "Space, Time, and Economic Restructuring," in Fainstein et al. (note 1 above), pp. 209–239.
4. World Commission on Environment and Development, *Our Common Future*, London: Oxford University Press, 1987.
5. This concept was well developed by R. B. Reich, *The Next American Frontier*, New York: Penguin, 1983.
6. See R.U. Ayres, "Industrial Metabolism. Theory and Policy," in this volume.
7. Ayres, note 6 above.
8. The following data and arguments rely on M. Jänicke, H. Mönch, T. Ranneberg, and U. E. Simonis, "Structural Change and Environmental Impact. Empirical Evidence on Thirty-one Countries in East and West," *Environmental Monitoring and Assessment* 12 (1989), no. 2: 99–114.
9. See W. Leontief, "Environmental Repercussions and the Economic Structure. An Input–Output Approach," *Review of Economics and Statistics* 52 (1970): 262–271.
10. See: OECD, *The State of the Environment 1991*, Paris: OECD, 1991; UNEP, *Environmental Data Report*, 3rd ed., Oxford: Basil Blackwell Ltd, 1991.
11. If one wished to include indicators on the agricultural sector (like fertilizers or pesticides), the service sector (computers or paper use), and other industries (the chemical industry), data availability and interpretation would, no doubt, become more complex.
12. See F. L. Pryor, "Growth and Fluctuations of Production in OECD and East European Countries," *World Politics* 2 (1985).
13. Particularly in German literature. See: H. H. Härtel et al., *Zusammenhang zwischen Strukturwandel und Umwelt*, Hamburg: Verlag Weltarchiv, 1987; and Rheinisch-Westfälisches Institut für Wirtschaftsforschung, *Strukturwandel und Umweltschutz*, Essen: RWI, 1987. See also: R. G. Healy, *America's Industrial Future. An Environmental Perspective*, Washington, D.C., 1982; J.G. Speth, *Needed: An Environmental Revolution in Technology*, Washington, D.C.: World Resources Institute, 1990.
14. OECD, *The State of the Environment*, Paris: OECD, 1985.
15. See Environment Agency, *Quality of the Environment in Japan 1982*, Tokyo, 1983, p. 52 ff.
16. See note 8 above.
17. Excluding local deliveries, in the early 1980s some 65 per cent of the weight of freight transport in the Federal Republic of Germany consisted of natural resources and materials. See Federal Ministry of Transport, *Verkehr in Zahlen*, Bonn, 1983, p. 175.
18. As indicated, the environmental relevance of the chemical industry could be considerable, changing somewhat the overall picture drawn in this chapter.
19. Translated from K. Steinitz, "Veränderungen in den Produktionsbedingungen der Volkswirtschaft der DDR," in W. Sydow, ed., *In die Zukunft gedacht*, Berlin, 1983, p.16.
20. One may call this the "dematerialization effect" of structural change. See: E. D. Larson, M. H. Ross, and R.B. Williams, "Beyond the Era of Materials," *Scientific American* 254 (1986), no. 6; and R. Herman, S. A. Ardekani, and J. H. Ausubel, "Dematerialization," in J. H. Ausubel and H. E. Sladivic, eds., *Technology and Environment*, Washington, D.C.: National Academy Press, 1989, pp.50–69.
21. Such a refinement, which takes the data and method used above further, is available now in German. See M. Jänicke and H. Mönch, in cooperation with M. Binder, *Umweltentlastung durch industriellen Strukturwandel*, Berlin: Sigma, 1992.
22. See note 20 above.
23. See Timothy O'Riordan, "The Precaution Principle in Environmental Management," in this volume.

4

Industrial restructuring in developing countries: The case of India

Rajendra K. Pachauri, Mala Damodaran, and Himraj Dang

Industrial metabolism and sustainable development

This chapter focuses on the attainment of energy conservation and efficiency as part of a process of industrial restructuring towards sustainable development. The specific case of Indian manufacturing industry is considered in some detail to show the potential for, and implications of, restructuring in industry in developing countries in accordance with the principles of "industrial metabolism."

Since the appearance in 1987 of the World Commission on Environment and Development's report *Our Common Future*, sustainable development has become the objective of development strategies and policies worldwide. Yet, six years later, the factors that would contribute to sustainable development and the methods to operationalize them are still undetermined. Without doubt, the need to minimize the throughput of resources while maintaining the system of production is central to any concept of sustainable development. However, the notion that the economic subsystem may have approached the finite biophysical limits of the global ecosystem has yet to gain currency, in spite of the writings of such prominent economists and scientists as Vitousek (1986), Daly and Cobb (1989), Goodland (1991), and Meadows et al. (1992).

Two answers emerged from *Our Common Future*. One was "growth as usual," albeit at a reduced rate. The other was to define sustainable development as "development without growth in through-put beyond environmental carrying capacity." Daly (1990), one of the pioneers of "steady-state economics," has provided an alternative definition of sustainable development, which we think may be useful for this chapter:

a process in which qualitative development is maintained and prolonged while quantitative growth in the state of the economy becomes increasingly constrained by the capacity of the ecosystem to perform over the long-run two essential functions: to regenerate the raw material inputs and to absorb the waste outputs of the human economy.

The recognition of an optimal scale of the economy is central to sustainable development as per Daly's definition. Beyond such an optimum, growth becomes "anti-economic growth." Goodland (1991) suggests that the environmental constraints to growth have already been reached: witness the high volume of human biomass appropriation (nearly 40 per cent), the looming threat of global warming, the rupture of the ozone shield, pervasive land degradation and the threat to the world's biodiversity from continued growth in the scale of the world economy . . .

The restructuring of industry towards sustainability in the developing countries would have simultaneously to take into account existing constraints and growth compulsions. For instance, for a number of reasons it may not be possible for a developing country to do away with aluminium production just because of energy scarcity, if all the other conditions requiring the establishment of the industry are satisfied. However, what may be possible is the achievement of higher energy efficiency levels in the industrial sector, reducing the through-put of raw materials and natural resources in general, and energy in particular, for a given level of output (Gross National/Domestic Product).

Industry and sustainable development

The industrial base of developing countries is undergoing diversification and moving into more capital-intensive areas such as metal products, chemicals, machinery, and equipment. Heavy industries, traditionally the most polluting, have grown in relation to light industries (World Commission on Environment and Development, 1987). The expected growth in these industries foreshadows rapid increases in pollution and resource degradation unless care is taken to control pollution and waste (especially hazardous wastes) and to increase re-cycling and re-use. However, these options have to be economically viable for them to be adopted. In several industrialized countries efforts at recycling have not been successful, because the large quan-tum of energy used and the other costs involved in the recycling proc-ess render these possibilities economically unattractive. This is in line with Georgescu-Roegen's view that since dissipated matter is in-evitably lost, only "garbo junk" is recycled (Georgescu-Roegen, 1980). Further, recycling tends to be labour-intensive, and for most industrialized countries labour costs are high. Also, pollution-control measures often require heavy capital investments at the initial stage. In most developing countries, with constraints in access to capital re-sources, these measures are often not acceptable even when they are economically viable.

Industry has an impact on the natural environment through the entire cycle of raw materials exploration and extraction, transforma-tion into products, energy consumption, waste generation, and use and disposal of products by the final consumers. If industrial growth is to be sustainable over the long run, it will have to change radically in terms of its quality. This does not necessarily suggest a quantita-tive limit to industrialization in developing countries. However, governments and international funding agencies could encourage those industries and industrial processes which are more efficient in terms of resource use, which generate less pollution and waste, which are based on the use of renewable rather than non-renewable re-sources, and which minimize irreversible adverse impacts on human health and the environment.

With the emergence of new process technologies that reduce the length of process chains, the possibilities of efficiency in resource use are enormous. The developing countries could take advantage of im-provements in the efficiency of resource use already achieved in in-dustrialized countries, and by adapting them to local conditions could not only reduce environmental costs but also "stretch" the resource base.

The increasing pressure on non-renewable resources (petroleum, copper, etc.), as well as the increasing constraints on sinks (ozone de-pletion, deforestation, dumping of solid wastes, etc.), suggest that throughput in the world economy has reached the global biophysical limits, and partially even surpassed them (Meadows et al., 1992). Yet it is neither ethical nor efficient from an environmental point of view to expect the developing countries to cut or arrest their industrial growth, which has the potential to absorb the large and growing population of the South. In the future, however, more growth for the poor must be balanced by negative throughput growth for the rich.

Resource utilization

While such a posture would address the political concern for development in the South, it does not address the problem of depletion of non-renewable natural resources. The concept of "sustainable development" does certainly not preclude the mining of non-renewables. A sustainable industrial policy for non-renewables, however, has to employ a different method of project appraisal. Since resource depletion may be treated as a social cost, a certain portion of the revenues from industrial projects should be invested in the creation of renewable substitutes, leaving aside an appropriate portion as disposable income. The income component would be higher either for a non-renewable asset with a longer life expectancy or for a faster growing substitute (higher discount rate).

This principle, enunciated by El Serafy, does not imply a rejection of the notion of income as defined by Hicks. The idea is that even for industrial projects the net present social value (NPSV) may be calculated to take account of the depletion of non-renewables (Mikesell, 1991). In fact, such a novel measure of appraisal of industrial projects is still in its infancy, though industrial strategy may be built around this principle in the future.

For renewable resources, industrial projects should seek to maximize productivity of resource stocks over the long run. This means, for instance, that, to sustain pulp and paper industries in the long run, in addition to well-managed forests reserves of pristine forest are essential as reservoirs of biodiversity. The same goes for industries based on fisheries and biotechnology, and so on. In sum, *sustainable societies would have to use the flows of resources rather than mine the stocks*. This would help delink economic growth from the intensive use of environmentally significant resources – a process that has begun in some industrialized countries like Sweden and Germany (see Udo Simonis, chapter 3 of this volume).

Industrial material recycling, as discussed above, can perhaps best be seen as a process wherein the short-term throughput of virgin raw materials is minimized without sacrificing output. In the following, we will concentrate on short-term measures that are feasible, of which improvement in energy efficiency is an important and representative example.

Energy efficiency: An overview

The interdependence between energy and industrial growth is crucial in formulating policies for sustainable development. Industry is a major market for energy, and the pricing and availability of energy closely affect industrial growth. Conservation of energy is possible through short-term measures in the industrial sector, but major changes in the structure and mode of transportation also become necessary if significant gains are to be made. But as the economic life of vehicles is relatively short, a transition in the road transport sector can be implemented more easily than in the case of rail transport, where replacement of existing capital stock is slower.

The major technical measures for energy conservation in industry include the recovery of heat from exhaust gases, the introduction of integrated energy systems, the recycling and re-use of materials, and automatic control, as well as the search for more advanced equipment and processes. Energy conservation in industry has led to improvements in overall energy efficiency in many countries over the last 15 years. In the United States, for instance, industrial energy use declined by 17 per cent between 1973 and 1986. This occurred in spite of a 17 per cent increase in industrial production during the same period. Structural changes and the replacement of open-hearth furnaces by more efficient basic oxygen furnaces has cut energy needs by half in the steel industries of most industrialized nations. Co-generation has grown rapidly in the United States and may surpass the share of nuclear energy by the end of the century.

Seen globally, these gains from decreased energy and materials intensity in the industrialized world may well be offset by the growing industrialization in developing countries. It is therefore imperative that the frontiers of technology shift along with the movement of many energy-intensive operations in the developing countries.

The iron and steel industry exemplifies the progress made in energy conservation and at the same time shows the potential for further improvements. With 6 per cent of the world's commercial energy consumption, the steel industry is a highly energy-intensive sector. Table 1 shows, however, that use of energy per ton of steel produced in India and China is more than twice as high as in Italy and Spain. The two latter countries have turned to the electric arc furnace,

Table 1 Energy use in steel manufacturing in major producing countries, ranked by efficiency, 1980

Country[a]	Production (MMT)[b]	Energy used per ton (gigajoules) GJ[c]
Italy	25	17.6
Spain	12	18.4
Japan	107	18.8
Belgium	13	22.7
Poland	18	22.7
United Kingdom	17	23.4
Brazil	14	23.9
United States	115	23.9
France	23	23.9
Soviet Union	150	31.0
Australia	8	36.1
China	35	38.1
India	10	41.0
World	700	26.0
Best technology		
Virgin ore		18.8
Recycled scrap		10.0

Source: Brown et al., 1985.
a. These 15 countries account for 84 per cent of world steel production.
b. Production figures represent averages for the years 1978–1981.
c. Energy totals are for crude steel-making, including ironmaking.

which uses 100 per cent scrap and as a result requires only two-thirds of the energy needed to convert the ore to the final product. The world recycling rate could easily be doubled or even tripled (Brown et al., 1985) from the present levels. In the United States, investments in energy conservation could cut the energy required per ton of steel by a third by the turn of the century. In China and India, investments to upgrade from the open hearth furnace would save at least 10 per cent of energy use. A World Bank study estimates that such investments could pay for themselves in less than a year (quoted in Brown et al., 1985). Further conservation could be effected in developing countries which plan to expand capacity, such as Brazil.

The aluminium industry provides another case of an energy-intensive industry where there is high potential for energy conservation. As table 2 shows, there are still wide disparities in electricity use for aluminium smelting. Energy intensity could be further reduced in this industry to 46.27 GJ/t, using currently available technology

Table 2 Electricity use in aluminium smelting in major producing countries, ranked by efficiency, 1981

Country	Share of world production[a] (thousand tons)	Electricity use per ton GJ
Italy	300	47.88
Netherlands	300	47.88
France	450	48.60
Brazil	300	50.40
Fed. Rep. Germany	800	52.24
Japan	700	53.64
United States	4,300	55.44
Australia	400	57.96
Norway	700	64.80
Soviet Union	2,000	64.80
Canada	1,200	72.00
World	15,900	59.40
Best technology		
Virgin ore		46.80
Recycled scrap		1,600[b]

Source: Brown et al., 1985.
a. Average primary production for years 1980–1982.
b. Electric energy equivalent.

(Brown et al., 1985). Recycling can cut energy requirements by over 90 per cent, but recycling rates worldwide averaged only 28 per cent in the early 1980s (Brown et al., 1985).

Energy use in Indian industry: A case-study

Structural change in the economy

An examination of trends in energy use in India may typify the trends in "industrial metabolism" in developing countries. When looking at structural change in industry, India differs markedly from countries like Austria, Belgium, Denmark, France, Germany, Finland, Norway, Sweden, the United Kingdom, and Japan. In these countries, economic growth after 1970 has, in absolute or relative terms, been progressively delinked from the use of natural resources (see Udo Simonis, chapter 3 of this volume). This process of delinking has been associated with:
– a decrease in resource depletion and environmental pollution;
– the use of *ex ante* environmental protection measures; and

61

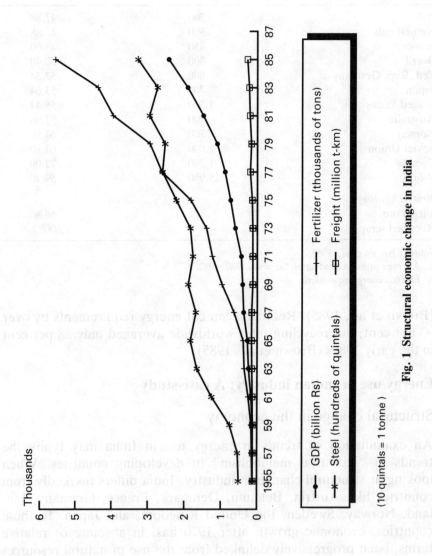

Fig. 1 Structural economic change in India

- the adoption of less polluting (cleaner) technologies in industry.
Structural change in India was different, as illustrated in figure 1:
- The growing consumption of primary energy has led to an increase in pollution.
- The increase in the production of steel and cement also represents an increase in pollution.
- The increase in the weight of freight transport indicates that material demands have increased.

The growth in factors with negative environmental effects in India occurred faster than the growth in GNP. This trend is without doubt contrary to recent experience in the more highly industrialized countries (see chapter 3).

In India, the annual average growth rate for energy production has exceeded 7.5 per cent since 1983, increasing to about 10 per cent in 1985. Gross domestic consumption has grown at a fluctuating rate, varying from 6 to 6.5 per cent. The higher growth rate of energy production suggests structural changes, with a build-up in energy-intensive sectors. This is a process which could continue into the next century, as per capita energy consumption in general is still rather low (9.8 TJ in 1989). For the Indian economy as a whole, energy demand has increased because of the increasing energy-intensity of production in both agriculture and industry.

Manufacturing industry

The manufacturing sector is the largest consumer of commercial energy in India. In producing about a fifth of India's GDP, this sector consumes about half the commerical energy available in the country. Six energy-intensive industries – aluminium, iron and steel, cement, pulp and paper, fertilizers, and textiles – that account for over 60 per cent of the energy consumed within this sector have been considered for this case-study.

Aluminium
The demand for aluminium is likely to increase in India owing to the rapid development of the electrical and transport sectors. On average, the specific energy consumption of the Indian aluminium industry is about 27 per cent higher than in industrialized countries, as table 3 reveals. In this case, measures of energy conservation offer the only possibility of restructuring, as there is no alternative to the Bayer-Hall process for primary aluminium reduction.

Rajendra K. Pachauri, Mala Damodaran, and Himraj Dang

Table 3 Comparison of energy consumption in the aluminium industry, 1984

Type of energy (GJ/T)	Indian industry (A)	Industry in industrialized countries (B)	B/A(%)
Thermal	46.73	34.25	36.4
Electrical	66.07	54.56	21.10
Total	112.80	88.81	27.0

Source: Tata Energy Research Institute, 1989.

Table 4 Energy consumption per unit output of the process centre and its variations for the period 1982/83 to 1986/87 *vis-à-vis* British steel plants' performance in 1986 (unit: GCAL/tp)

Sl. No.	Process centre consumption, 1982–1986/87	Variation of energy	Plant I	Plant II	Plant III	Plant IV	Plant V	Plant VI	British Steel 1986
1	Sinter	Max.	0.72	0.88	0.96	0.93	0.94	NE[a]	0.553
		Min.	0.68	0.74	0.85	0.91	0.96	NE	
2	Coke oven	Max.	2.16	2.35	2.31	3.5	2.28	2.5	1.549
	(net energy)	Min.	1.92	2.29	2.16	1.64	1.41	2.18	
3	Blast furnace	Max.	4.32	4.58	5.89	5.18	7.91	6.11	3.35
	(net energy)	Min.	3.98	3.95	5.39	4.59	6.1	4.43	
4	Open-hearth	Max.	1.1	1.28	—	NE	2.19	2.30	NE
	furnace	Min.	1.08	1.07	—	NE	1.88	1.86	
5	LD convertor	Max.	0.51	0.29	0.52	0.29	NE	NE	0.32
	(net energy)	Min.	0.39	0.38	0.39	0.26	NE	NE	

Source: Tata Energy Research Institute, 1989.
a. NE = Non-existent. There is no LD gas recovery except in Tata Iron and Steel Company.

Iron and steel

A high rate of growth for iron and steel is expected, as per capita consumption in India in 1986 was 19 kg of crude steel compared with 578 kg of crude steel per capita in Japan. Energy accounts for about a third of the total cost of finished steel. Specific energy consumption varies within a range of 36.4–62.8 GJ/T of crude steel. The comparable figure for industrialized countries is substantially lower, at 16.7–25.1 GJ/T. A comparison of the actual performance of Indian units with that of British steel is summarized in table 4.

64

Nearly 37 per cent of Indian steel is produced by the technically outmoded open-hearth furnace, which is no longer used in industrialized countries. Even in plants where the basic oxygen process is used, plant efficiencies are relatively low. Higher efficiencies are also possible through improvements in the quality of coking coal. Energy efficiency improvements of 20 to 30 per cent for fuel use and 12.5 to 22 per cent for electricity use are expected by 2025 in India.

Cement

Specific energy intensities for cement produced in India are 261 kg coal/tonne, and 406 kg coal/tonne for the dry and wet processes respectively. The dry process is more energy-efficient and a shift to this process would be profitable. If by the year 2010 either (a) more dry process operations and/or (b) more efficient (current world's best) techniques were chosen, total energy demand, and hence pollution, could be reduced drastically. Specific energy intensities for India and the world's best for the wet and dry processes are given in table 5.

Opting for the best available technology would lead to a reduction of around 12.0 tonnes of coal consumed per tonne of cement produced in the year 2010, i.e. from 48 to 36 tonnes. This defines savings in terms of both coal requirements and pollutant emissions. (The calculations are based on 0.18 kg/MJ coal consumption and a calorific value of 20.94 MJ.)

The above presentations serve as an indication of the extent of savings possible within an industry solely through energy-efficiency measures. Improvements in coal consumption rates would also reduce pollution. Further process improvements and a sectoral shift, i.e. from energy-intensive production to services, would have a bearing on the fuel mix and hence the energy consumption levels in the country. What becomes apparent is that energy-efficiency improvements are of great importance, although other improvements will be needed as well.

Table 5 Specific energy intensities for cement manufacturing

	Thermal GJ/T		Electrical GJ/T	
	World's best	India	World's best	India
West	5.0	7.0	0.25	0.41
Dry	2.9	3.7	0.39	0.55

Source: Tata Energy Research Institute, 1989.

65

Rajendra K. Pachauri, Mala Damodaran, and Himraj Dang

Table 6 Comparison of Indian and international specific energy consumption in the cement industry, 1983/84

	Electrical (KWh/tonne of OPC)		Thermal (Gcal/tonne of OPC)	
	Indian[a]	International	Indian[a]	International
Wet	0.41	0.25–0.37	6.9	5.0–5.4
Semi-dry	0.44	0.32–0.34	4.2	3.1–3.4
Dry	0.55	0.39–0.4	4.2	3.1–3.4

Source: Tata Energy Research Institute, 1989.
a. Weighted average, where weights used are actual production.

Table 7 Expected decline in energy intensities in the paper manufacturing industry (percentages)

	High-emission scenario	Low-emission scenario
Decline in fuel intensity	10	20
Decline in biomass intensity	5	5
Decline in electricity intensity	10	15

Source: Tata Energy Research Institute, 1989.

Significant energy savings are possible in the manufacture of cement in India, as shown in table 6. Technological innovations such as pre-calcination systems and suspension pre-heaters could be incorporated in the dry process which is currently used for the manufacture of over 64 per cent of the total cement production of India.

Pulp and paper
The installed capacity for paper production in India is 2.7 mt and is expected to rise to 4.25 mt by the turn of the century. In India, the energy efficiency of a typical large mill is much lower than that of its counterpart in an industrialized country. Even a relatively modern mill in India consumes 70 per cent more heat and 7 per cent more electrical energy to produce a tonne of paper than does a typical Scandinavian mill, for instance. Further, the Indian mill is likely to purchase more fuel and power since the co-generation potential of Indian units has not yet been exploited. As this industry will continue to grow, driven by increasing literacy and the demand of the packaging industry, energy intensity is likely to decline, as indicated by table 7.

66

Fertilizers

Chemical fertilizers have recorded a phenomenal increase in the past in India, and this growth might continue, driven by the demand for foodgrains. However, the efficiency of fertilizer use can be improved. Gas-based fertilizer plants are more energy-efficient than those based on naptha or fuel oil, and India is increasingly shifting to the natural gas option. It is estimated that energy efficiency per tonne of fertilizer produced could easily be raised by 20 per cent.

Textiles

Textile mills are major users of steam for washing, bleaching, and dyeing cloth. More than 50 per cent of the steam-generating systems in textile plants in India are over 35 years old, with "first law" efficiencies of only 50 per cent. "First law" efficiency is a single ratio of heat output to the heat value of fuel input. However, it is not a good measure of the potential for energy conservation. To estimate that potential, it is necessary to use "second law" efficiency. This is the ratio of fuel heating value needed to produce the end product (hot water for washing, in the case of textile mills) by the most efficient measure, to the amount of fuel actually used. One may suggest that the second law efficiency in this case is unlikely to be more than 10 per cent; but with basic retrofits fuel efficiency could be raised to 65 per cent.

Energy efficiency

In a recent study carried out by the Tata Energy Research Institute (TERI), the impact of restructuring in the industrial and transport sectors of the Indian economy was assessed against the overall background of energy sector developments up to the year 2010.

At the national level, one could project two future scenarios up to 2010: a business-as-usual (BAU) path, with the economy growing at an annual average rate of 5 per cent per annum, and an alternate path (ALT) in which strict energy conservation is pursued. The energy-by-fuel-type consumption estimates under these two alternate approaches are presented in table 8.

Under the ALT strategy, natural gas is the only energy source whose rate of growth is more or less constant. This is important from an environmental point of view, since natural gas emits the least CO_2 and particulates per unit combusted. Further, since combustion conditions can easily be regulated, NO_x formation is controlled. The

67

Table 8 Energy growth scenarios for India for the year 2010

	BAU	Rate(%)	ALT	Rate (%)
Electricity (PJ)	2.49	6.41	2.21	5.99
Coal (PJ)	13,516.3	6.01	11,338.88	5.08
Oil (PJ)	7,450.73	6.34	5,514.81	4.75
Natural gas (PJ)	2,290.52	10.03	2,286.85	10.02

Source: Tata Energy Research Institute, 1991.

most affected fuel source would be oil, whose rate of growth under an energy-conservation scenario would be 4.75 per cent as compared to 6.34 per cent under a BAU strategy; coal use would go down to 5.08 per cent from 6.01 per cent. Overall, the strategy has ramifications for the environment, given that coal is the most polluting energy source. Electricity also has an impact on the environment, depending on the fuel source of the electricity, i.e. coal, gas, or hydro. Accordingly, the environmental damage incurred would vary.

Under the ALT scenario, energy consumption in the transport and industrial sectors was considered. In the transport sector, all existing buses were assumed to be phased out with the introduction of new urban buses. The additional cost was taken as US$0.5 billion, with operation and maintenance (O&M) costs at 5 per cent of the capital cost and assuming a life of 20 years.

For the shift from road to rail, the investment of US$50 billion was assumed, in a manner similar to the strategy for road improvements. The life of the system was assumed to be 35 years and the O&M cost 2.5 per cent of the capital requirement.

The metro option supposes an average investment of US$1.3 billion for each city. Interest during construction was assumed to be 12 per cent. Further, the metro was assumed to start functioning in 2000 or 2001 and to displace 10 per cent of the cars and three-wheelers, 45 per cent of the two-wheelers and 35 per cent of the buses in each of the nine cities considered. The life of the metro was assumed to be 35 years, with O&M at 5 per cent of capital costs.

Given the above assumptions for the conservation measures to be implemented in the transport sector in the country, the annualized costs per unit of energy saved in the transport sector are as shown in table 9.

In all cases, the cost per unit of energy saved is lower than the economic cost of energy. Hence, they are all viable options.

In the industrial sector, conservation measures were considered for

Table 9 Annualized cost per unit energy saved in the transport sector

	5% of growth rate	
	Fuel saving (mtoe)	$/kgoe saved
Urban buses	140.81 (3.29)	
Road improvements	346.23 (8.107)	2.8×10^{-9} (0.118)
Shifts from road to rail	516.38 (12.091)	1.7×10^{-9} (0.072)
Metro system	116.12 (2.719)	2.5×10^{-9} (0.106)

Source: Tata Energy Research Institute, 1991.

Table 10 Cost of energy conservation investments per unit saved, in US$/joule

Iron and steel	Chemicals and petrochemicals	Cement
2.6×10^{-9} (0.11 $/kgoe)	2.6×10^{-9} (0.12 $/kgoe)	7.0×10^{-6} (0.03 $/kgoe)

Source: Tata Energy Research Institute, 1991.

the iron and steel, petrochemicals, and cement industries. O&M costs for process changes were assumed to be 2.5 per cent of capital costs, and the life was taken as 20 years. On the basis of these assumptions, the annualized cost per unit of energy saved in the industrial sector is as shown in table 10.

The incremental annualized investment for the transport and industrial sectors of India has been estimated at US$1,752.77 and 2,135.93 million (TERI, 1991).

In terms of energy savings, following from the various strategies outlined above, a brief summary is presented in table 11.

A further exercise was carried out on the basis of alternative locations for new industrial units and costs of pollution control related to these locations. The economic implications of these were evaluated accordingly. The major pollutants from industry are a function of the process employed, but owing to lack of data only air pollution resulting from the combustion of fuels was considered. Air pollution from the following Indian industries was examined: textiles, chemicals and petrochemicals, aluminium, integrated iron and steel, mini-mills steel, cement, fertilizers, paper, sponge iron, and machinery. Estimates of emissions from high-speed diesel, light diesel oil, fuel oil, low-stock high-sulphur fuel, coal, naptha, natural gas, and petroleum products used in the industrial sector are given. Emissions from the

Rajendra K. Pachauri, Mala Damodaran, and Himraj Dang

Table 11 Cost of industrial energy

	Business-as-usual (BAU)		Alternative path (ALT)	
Electricity (PJ)				
Industry	1,279.09	(359.4 TWh)	1,218.94	(342.5 TWh)
Transport	46.27	(13.0 TWh)	116.38	(32.7 TWh)
Coal (PJ)				
Industry	3,869.33	(184.9 Mt)	3,113.88	(148.8 Mt)
Transport	79.52	(3.8 Mt)	238.56	(11.4 Mt)
Oil (PJ)				
Industry	1,443.51	(33.8 Mt)	1,311.12	(30.7 Mt)
Transport	3,818.04	(89.4 Mt)	2,340.37	(54.8 Mt)
Natural gas (PJ)				
CNG			208.57	(5.7 BCM)
Industry	874.54	(23.9 BCM)	805.02	(22.0 BCM)

Source: Tata Energy Research Institute, 1991.

Table 12 Emissions from industrial sector in India

	SO_x (000 t)			CO (000 t)			NO_x (000 t)			TSP (000 t)		
	1	2	3	1	2	3	1	2	3	1	2	3
All India, 2010												
BAU scenario	1,216	274	180	31	6	4	1,113	154	134	28,820	1,692	1,298
HLT Scenario	1,134	148	221	28	3	5	1,063	105	140	27,954	1,658	862

Source: Tata Energy Research Institute, 1991.

industrial sector under the BAU and ALT scenarios are presented in table 12. Three zones were categorized: Zone I implies heavily polluted areas, Zone II moderately polluted areas, and Zone III relatively clean areas.

Under the ALT scenario, a deliberate attempt has been made to locate new projects in environmentally relatively clean regions, thereby alleviating/stabilizing the environmental stress that has emerged in the other areas. The newly declared industrial policy in India could result in a move to a more efficient utilization of energy, with optimization of material use as well as a reduction in waste generation, since it introduces greater competition through deregulation and opening of the public sector to private ownership. However, to ensure that the new industrial policy is successful, a pricing policy that reflects the true economic and environmental cost of production, an

70

Table 13 Levelized annualized cost of pollution control

	Discount rate (cost/unit in cents/J (cents/kWh)) pollutant					
	3%		5%		12%	
TSP	9.1×10^{-10}	(0.039)	1.1×10^{-9}	(0.047)	1.9×10^{-9}	(0.08)
NO$_x$	1.3×10^{-8}	(0.590)	1.4×10^{-8}	(0.600)	1.5×10^{-8}	(0.65)
SO$_x$	4.6×10^{-8}	(1.970)	4.7×10^{-8}	(2.010)	5.1×10^{-8}	(2.21)

Table 14 Some characteristics of different energy scenarios, 1985–2025

		Scenarios	
	1985	I (high)	II (low)
Population (millions)	766.1	1,691.6	1,691.6
GDP (1986 US$ million)	191,306	1,346,792	1,346,792
Industry sector share (%)	29	37	37
GDP per capita (1986 US$)	250	796	796
Primary energy supply (PJ)	9,055	42,505	33,911
Energy intensity (MJ/1986 US$)	47.3	31.6	25.2
Energy consumption per captia (GJ)	9.2	17.6	15

Source: Tata Energy Research Institute, 1989.

environmental policy that regulates without undue impediments, and a fiscal policy that induces the right kind of investments are essential. Tentative steps in this direction have been made, but a lot remains to be done.

Estimates of the levelized annualized cost of pollution control for some pollutants at various discount rates are given in table 13.

The control measures considered are electrostatic precipitators for particulate matter (TSP), selective catalytic reducers for NO$_x$, and flue gas desulphurizers for SO$_x$. The estimates have been made for thermal power plants only. They may, however, serve as an indicator of the costs involved in environmental protection, determined in terms of damage avoided.

Improvements in capacity utilization and the availability of power could greatly reduce the energy-intensity of all Indian industries. Long-term projections from the STAIR (Services, Transport, Agriculture, Industry, Residential) model suggest that even under the pursuance of a rather modest energy strategy, energy-intensity in India would decline drastically by 2025. The details of the projections are listed in table 14.

It has been estimated that India has an energy conservation potential of at least 10 per cent in the industrial sector during the course of the eighth Five-Year Plan, rising to 15 per cent in the next plan. The Interministerial Working Group on Energy has calculated that with the installation of new equipment the savings from coal-based, oil-based, and electric power-generation machines are approximately 20, 20, and 15 per cent, respectively.

Improved housekeeping in industries in the short-term, the training of personnel, and energy audits could save India some 151.61 PJ with an investment of only Rs. 4,000 million (approximately US$160 million). In the medium term, investments in installation for waste heat recovery systems, the replacement of inefficient boilers, the introduction of instruments and control systems, and better technology could save India 190.05 PJ with a financial investment of $1,150 million. In the long run, investments in co-generation, energy-efficient technologies, and computerization of process control operations could save India 132.39 PJ on a financial investment of $1,917 million (Government of India, 1983). Figure 2 shows the potential for energy conservation in various industries in India.

Conclusions

In this chapter we have looked at industrial restructuring options in terms of improving energy efficiency in a developing country. We have drawn largely from the example of India because it is not only a poor developing country but has a high rate of industrialization, and thus offers a wide spectrum of possibilities for improvement in efficiency and energy savings. One can assume that what is applicable to India will to a certain degree also hold for all other developing countries. Also, what is applicable to energy consumption in the industrial sector (including transport) will in some respects also be applicable to other raw materials and natural resources.

In general, energy-conservation measures have a positive environmental effect by reducing the volume of pollutants discharged from the energy-conversion process as well as by reducing the throughput of raw materials. However, their effect will depend on the type of measure, the type of industry, and the quantity of energy saved.

The qualitative environmental effects of energy conservation in four energy-intensive industries in India are presented in table 15. These measures have particular relevance for developing countries undertaking major industrial projects as, subject to financial con-

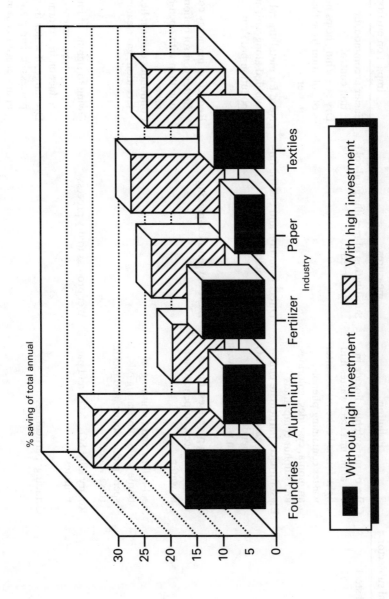

Fig. 2 Potential for energy saving, selected industries in India (Source: Energy Management Centre)

Table 15 Energy-conservation measures in major Indian industry subsectors and environmental impact

Industrial subsector	Pollution	Major energy-conservation measures	Impact on environment
Iron and steel	Coke ovens: sulphur dioxide in air; ammonia steel wastes and light-formed coke oil decanter wastes containing phenols, ammonia, cyanides, chlorides and sulphur compounds	Substitution of metallurgical coke by formed coke	Easier accommodation to pollution control Dry quenching helps in reduction of pollution from the quench tower
	Blast furnace: particulate emissions in off-gases; H_2S and SO_2 in air; suspended solids; cyanides, in water; a solid waste as slag	Direct reduction and electric furnace melting	Need for metallurgical coal is avoided along with attendant pollution problem
	Steel-making processes: fumes from furnaces; suspended soils in water	Basic oxygen steel-making	Reduction in energy consumption. Better control options on pollution than with open-hearth furnace
	Steel-rolling and furnishing: air-borne scale, lubricating oils, spent pickle liquor, and pickling rinse water		Continuous casting; heat conservation; gas cleaning
Cement	Rotary kiln: SO_2, NO_x, and particulates	Wet process to dry process	Owing to significant impact upon energy requirements, there is a reduction in airborne pollution
	Grinding: particulates		Discharge of water from wet-process cement plants is absent in dry-process cement manufacture

Precalciners		The generation of nitrogen oxides is reduced by both the low temperature and the short time the combustion gases stay in the burning zone, relative to conventional kilns.
	Use of pozzolanic cements and slag cement	The increased use of these cements would provide beneficial and economic use of such waste materials as blast furnace slag or fly ash, thereby tending to reduce the environmental problems associated with these waste materials
	Aluminium chloride electrolysis process	Reduction in electrial energy consumption by 30 per cent leads to coal saving and reduction-related coal-burning
Aluminium	Hard metal cathode made of titanium carbide or titanium dibromide replacing carbon cathode	Reduction in electrical energy is by 20 per cent, with attendant reduction in coal consumption and hence in pollution from coal-burning
	Pollution associated with burning of coal to raise steam for alumina plant and electricity for both alumina and aluminium plants. Fluoride emissions from electrolytic cells	

Source: Pachauri and Sambasivan, 1989.

straints, they can bypass outmoded technologies. This is what has been called the "advantage of the late-comers."

In summarizing, the policies of developing countries for the industrial sector should:

- increase awareness about the needs and benefits of energy conservation;
- develop technical expertise through training at various levels;
- provide fiscal incentives/disincentives to implement energy-saving schemes;
- institute a nodal organization to coordinate energy-conservation efforts in industry;
- encourage manufacturers to coordinate energy-conservation efforts in industry;
- encourage manufacture of energy-efficient equipment, devices, and instruments; and
- strike a balance between energy use, energy conservation, and pollution-abatement measures.

What applies to energy consumption naturally also applies to other material inputs, as well as to waste disposal. It seems to us that the pursuance of a conservation strategy such as the one outlined above, motivated by various environmental and economic incentives, constitutes the industrial restructuring agenda for a sustainable development path in developing countries.

The process of industrialization is far from satisfactory in developing countries. There are persistent shortages of basic industrial products such as iron and steel and low per capita availability of these products, in spite of an abundance of natural resources. This being the case, the consumption of raw materials and the production of wastes are probably going to increase further. However, industrial restructuring to reduce the throughput of energy and materials in the industrial system can also occur simultaneously with the process of industrial growth that is under way in developing countries. The potential for this restructuring and, implicitly, for an improved "industrial metabolism" is enormous, as the preceding sections should have demonstrated.

References

Ayres, R. U. 1989. "Industrial Metabolism." In: J. Ausubel and H. Sladovic, eds., *Technology and Environment*. Washington, D.C.: National Academy Press.

Brown, L. R., et al. 1985. *State of the World. A Worldwatch Institute Report on Progress toward a Sustainable Society*. Washington, D.C.: W.W. Norton & Co.

Daly, H. E. 1990. "Toward Some Operational Principles of Sustainable Development." *Ecological Economics* 2.

Daly, H. E., and J. Cobb. 1989. *Towards the Common Good: Redirecting the Economy towards Community, the Environment and a Sustainable Future*. Boston, Mass.: Beacon Press.

Georgescu-Roegen, N. 1980. "Energy, Matter and Economic Valuation: Where Do We Stand?" In: Daly and Umana, eds., *Energy, Economics and the Environment*. AAAS Selected Symposium 64.

Goodland, R. 1991. "The Case that the World Has Reached Limits." In: R. Goodland, H. Daly, and S. El Serafy, eds., *Environmentally Sustainable Economic Development: Building on Brundtland*. Washington, D.C.: World Bank.

Government of India. Interministerial Working Group on Energy. 1983. *Report on Utilization and Consumption of Energy*.

Meadows, D. H., D. L. Meadows, and J. Randers. 1992. *Beyond the Limits*. Post Mills, Vt.: Chelsea Green Publishing.

Mikesell, R. F. 1991. "Project Evaluation and Sustainable Development." In: Goodland, Daly, and El Serafy, eds., *Environmentally Sustainable Economic Development: Building on Brundtland*. Washington, D.C.: World Bank.

Pachauri, R. K., and G. Sambasivan. 1989. "Energy Conservation." In: UNDP, *Drylands, Wetlands, Croplands: Turning Liabilities into Assets*. New Delhi.

Tata Energy Research Institute. 1989. *Long-term Energy Scenario for India: Using the STAIR Model*. New Delhi.

———. 1991. *Environmental Considerations in Energy Development*. Report submitted to Asian Development Bank, Manila.

Vitousek, P. M., et al. 1986. "Human Appropriation of the Products of Photosynthesis." *BioScience* 34, no. 6.

World Commission on Environment and Development. 1987. *Our Common Future*. Oxford: Oxford University Press.

5

Evolution, sustainability, and industrial metabolism

Peter M. Allen

Introduction

Today many people realize and fear the possible impacts that past, current, and future industrial activities and technologies may have on the natural systems in which they are embedded.[1] Anthropogenic causes seem to be the main factor in widespread erosion and soil degradation, river, lake and oceanic pollution, the production of acid rain, and threats to groundwater quality through nitrate and pesticide leaching from farming and from the burying and dumping of toxic and radioactive wastes. The rate of extinction of numerous plant and animal species seems still to be accelerating and there is some consensus on the view that the increased levels of CO_2 resulting from man's activities may be causing drastic climatic change.

And all this is occurring as a result of the kind of economic growth that has characterized the West, and which by and large is the goal of most developing countries. It seems, therefore, that some major rethinking is required if industrialization is to occur throughout the world (Clark and Munn, 1986). Somehow, we must find ways of reducing the impacts of human activities on the environment, but of still maintaining and improving the quality of life, which is, after all, the avowed principal aim of development.

78

This book is part of this attempted rethinking. The title, *Industrial Metabolism: Restructuring for Sustainable Development*, suggests the important *process-based* vision of industry as part of an ecological structure. Traditionally, the view has been that industry takes high-grade resources and uses energy to transform them into products for human utilization, with of course some waste and pollution going into the "environment." However, this simple, traditional view is not sustainable. In reality, not only is one man's environment another man's system, but the global environment itself is being modified by the accumulation and build-up of wastes. The only sustainable systems that we so far know of are those which nature has evolved and which we call natural ecosystems. The crux of this chapter is, therefore, an examination of the underlying organizational principle of ecological structure.

As we shall see, this is related to the workings of the evolutionary process, and from this discussion we shall establish what is meant by sustainability in natural systems, and what the lessons of this are for mankind. In particular, it will be shown why the issues of adaptability and diversity are fundamental. Another critical idea that arises concerns the basic choice between the spatial dispersion of pollutants and wastes or their concentration. Again, the comparison with natural evolution will be made and the importance of recycling stressed.

In this chapter we trace the roots of our present environmental problems to the underlying concepts of traditional science. Its basic reductionist perspective is inappropriate for understanding the emergence and evolution of living systems, and has, therefore, tended to alienate us from nature. Next, a new perspective concerning evolutionary, open systems, which provides a deeper conceptual framework than the "mechanical system" for our understanding of the human condition, is set out. This new, evolutionary view shifts our focus from that of "maximized" exploitation to that of the maintenance of adaptability and diversity, and of framing legislation and policies to this end. It also provides a new basis for decision support tools, which help to explore possible futures, including the responses of the natural and human systems affected.

The new ideas explored here also concern the manner in which collective structure and conditions are affected by individual decision-making and values, and how in turn these are fashioned by evolution. Clearly, new issues of equity and responsibility arise between the aspirations of individuals, nations, and the global community. These are, of course, perennial problems that have always been present in social systems. How should the conflict between the rights and the responsibilities of individuals be resolved? There is no simple answer to this, nor any objective basis on which to formulate one. What must be worked out is a complicated compromise between the developed and the developing nations, such that the global situation is taken into account and given sufficient importance, that the future of the planet is not sacrificed by the selfish actions of its separate parts. As set out theoretically in the Brundtland Report, sustainability must be the aim for each region. But, as we shall see, the concept of sustainability is a complex one, and will require a change not only in environmental regulations but in the underlying values of our socio-economic systems.

The problem is urgent since levels of destruction of ecosystems and the exploitation of raw materials have reached record levels, reducing the biological potential and the capacity to sustain humans over large geographical areas. Anthropogenically modified ecological systems seem increasingly vulnerable and quite clearly unsustainable, with a strong possibility that as the intensity of exploitation of the remaining raw materials and areas of fertile land increases, so in turn the destruction of these will accelerate, leading to a potentially catastrophic runaway process.

These issues pose a tremendous challenge to us all. We must find ways of achieving a high quality of life using new approaches and technologies which do not lead to the irreversible consumption or destruction of their own input factors. In short, we must move away from a "slash-and-burn"" mentality to some greater vision of "cultivation."

The issue can no longer be avoided by simply talking about the need to limit population growth in developing countries, or by hoping that market prices reflecting progressive destruction will finally lead to some miraculous, technological response. Neither can we necessarily afford to wait for absolute scientific proof of the precise chains of causality that are involved. Wisdom is not identical to science. Instead it is related to how you choose to use the limited knowledge you have, and is clearly a mixture of caution and adventure.

Technical progress and reductionism

The first issue that it is important to reflect on is the underlying reason why the application of scientific knowledge to solve problems – the traditional view of technology – must inevitably create other problems in the process. The ultimate reason is the adoption of reductionist views and values in traditional science. This becomes clear if we consider carefully the proposition that before *any* deliberate action may be taken, it must be shown that the expected consequences will be *good* for the universe – the ultimate precautionary principle. Now, this would appear to outlaw any action at all, since one could not even define what "good" meant for the universe, let alone prove that good would follow from an action. But, if the "universe" is too large a sphere of evaluation, what is the right one? How do we justify our actions? What are the values that drive "improvements" in technology?

The answer is that we reduce the "system" we are considering until it can be interpreted as a *mechanism*. It has inputs, outputs, and some working parts. Within this narrow view, simple values can then be brought to bear on the problem. The mechanism can be said to "do something," that is, to transform inputs into outputs. We can then judge whether by some modification this "job" could be done more quickly, more cheaply, with less labour, less skill, fewer raw materials, etc. And so, technological progress leads to local, partial improvements of the system, based on narrow values and the roles and job descriptions of people within that system.

But, of course, the comfort obtained through wearing mental blinkers may be quite false. This is because only a small part of the whole system has been considered, and an individual with a particular role has used his own values to justify his action. In general the costs of any such action will necessarily be pushed out beyond whatever boundary marked the actor's concern. Inevitably, there will as a consequence be changes to and impacts on whatever was *not* included in the actor's evaluation, though it is in reality connected to his system. These could either be viewed as "unintended consequences" of his actions, or, perhaps more correctly, as "part of their consequences," and ones which follow naturally from his limited frame of reference.

In other words, many environmental problems are simply a necessary consequence of the myopic vision inherent in the roles that our system has allowed to evolve. That this has happened is, of course, partly due to their apparent short-term "effectiveness." Our system has evolved value systems and processes that not only degrade the environment but make it difficult for actors to do otherwise.

Such a *laissez-faire* attitude might possibly be justified if it could be shown that the continual improvement of the subsystems of a system would lead necessarily to an improvement of the whole system. This is the view put forward by Adam Smith, and clung to by most classical and neoclassical economists, whereby the separate pursuit of wealth by individuals is said to result in gain for the whole through the working of the "invisible hand." However, as we begin better to understand the behaviour and evolution of complex systems, this seems incredibly naive, or at best overoptimistic. It is just part of the ideology underlying Western economic thinking, and is, in reality, a myth.

However, such ideas are deeply rooted in the scientific rationality that has driven our thinking over the last few centuries. This is based on the view that understanding is arrived at by the study of *how* a particular set of mechanisms functions. And this merely requires analysis, which goes deeper and deeper into the underlying components of the system, creating disciplines and domains of expertise as it goes. Not only is reductionism the basis of traditional science, but it is also the basis of scientific credibility.

But if we are to deal successfully with the real world, the problem remains: What is the explanation of a particular system? Why is it as it is? And this is not at all the same question as: "How does it function?" The two questions only converge for *isolated* systems, or for systems that have reached an equilibrium with their environments. Prediction for such systems was remarkable, and this traditional scientific knowledge was used in the development of machines which characterized this new and powerful thing called technology.

But living systems are open to flows of energy, matter, and information. Living cells, organisms, people, populations, cities, and socio-economic and socio-technical systems are all open. That is why, as a metaphor, the "industrial metabolism" is more appropriate than the industrial machine.

The material realization and maintenance of such systems requires flows of energy and matter across the boundaries of whatever set of variables it is proposed to consider. Thus, the reductionist view which sees explanation in terms of functional mechanism is an incomplete description from which change, adaptation, and evolution are necessarily excluded. The initial (unnatural) interpretation of sustainable development, based on this false analogy, has been that of seeking a state of "maximum sustainable yield" for an exploited natural system, as if it were a "machine" that could be pushed to the limit, neglecting the adaptive responses that such evolved systems will have, and discounting the future according to the dictate of current interest rates.

In order to understand better the concept of sustainability, we must first show clearly the shortcomings of the mechanical vision characteristic of traditional science. Then, based on the manner in which evolutionary systems structure and organize themselves in nature, we can establish a new conceptual framework for the discussion.

The mechanical paradigm

The basis of scientific understanding has traditionally been the mechanical model (Prigogine and Stengers, 1987; Allen, 1985, 1988). In this view, the behaviour of a system could be understood, and anticipated, by classifying and identifying its components and the causal links, or mechanisms, that act between them. In physical systems, the fundamental laws of nature such as the conservation of mass, momentum, and energy govern these mechanisms, and determine entirely what must happen. This was such a triumph for classical science, that it was believed (erroneously) that analogous ideas must apply in the domains of biology, ecology, the human sciences, and particularly, of course, economics (Arrow and Debreu, 1954). It is exactly this vision that underlies Adam Smith's idea of an "invisible hand" working collective improvement through the self-seeking behaviour of individuals.

But in such a vision the problem of *change* remains unsolved. If we study a system over time, we find that its structure changes. Any system developed at a given time somehow transforms itself over time. In order to anticipate the changes that will occur in the system we must try to understand how this creative self-transformation can possibly occur. Obviously, it is not contained in the set of mechanical equations that characterize the system at any *one* time. It is clearly beyond the behaviour of a closed system.

In human systems what happens depends very strongly on what decisions are taken. Although, of course, the natural laws always work, they no longer suffice to determine what must occur. Systems open to flows of energy and matter can attain varying degrees of autonomy, where it is the interplay of non-linear interactions that decide how the system structures and evolves.

In the traditional scientific view, the future of a system is predicted from the mathematical equations which govern the "motion" of its components. But in order to write down the equations of motion for a real system it is always necessary to make approximations. The assumption that must be made is that the elements making up the variables (molecules in a structure, individuals within a population,

Peter M. Allen

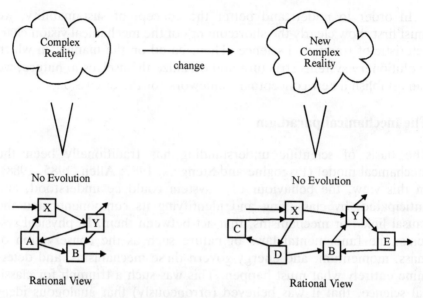

Fig. 1 At any different time we may analyse the components and functioning of the system, but this remains fixed while reality changes

firms in a sector, etc.) are all identically that of the *average* type. In this case, the model reduces to a "machine" which represents the system in terms of a set of differential (perhaps non-linear) equations which govern its variables.

This shows us the paradox underlying the scientific approach. At any given time, we can always analyse a system, and imagine that we have "understood" its structure and constituent mechanisms. From this, we may feel that we can even make predictions, and use it as a base for our policies and actions. However, the very act of formulating the structure as a set of mechanisms actually excludes the non-average individual microdiversity, which will be responsible for structural change and the qualitative evolution of the system.

In other words, the elements that will lead to invention and innovation are precisely what is excluded from the traditional scientific description of an economic or even an ecological system. The interactions of economic sectors, described through input–output relations, are comparable to the interacting population dynamics of an ecosystem, but neither contain the mechanisms of their own self-transformation. This is the paradox: in order to know the future, we use an analytic tool that throws away the factors that are important in creating that future.

84

The attraction of rational analysis is strong, and the scientific reader will certainly be using it in order to assimilate this paragraph and chapter, but clarity is bought at the expense of vital details, and it is the dialogue between the apparent structure and the deviations from it that provides the power of self-transformation and emergence in systems. The Newtonian vision of the world as a collection of "clockwork mechanisms" that can be laid out and examined is fine for the actual machines that humans produce, but is an inadequate representation of the world in which these are embedded. Real systems are in fact coupled in a multiplicity of ways with factors in their environment, through flows of matter, energy, and information, and although *in vitro* experiments can be useful in understanding some simple physical systems, the essential behaviour of ecosystems arises *in vivo*, through the visible and invisible dialogue with their environment. It is this science-inspired tendency to separate the "inside" of a system from its "outside" that is at the root of environmental problems.

Equally, it is this separation of inside from out, together with the mechanical description, that has produced a methodology in technology and engineering which is often characterized by "optimized" solutions under fixed conditions. But this fails to allow for the fact that information flows, learning, and change are all taking place and that in the real world the inside is co-evolving with the outside.

From the discussion we see that evolutionary change must result from what has been removed in the reduction to the deterministic description, that is, the *non-average*. Systems evolve through the interplay of two kinds of terms. First there are deterministic average mechanisms operating between typical components, whose identity and nature are revealed by rational, scientific analysis. Second, however, there is what has been suppressed in the rational picture, the non-average behaviour and detail which probes the stability of the existing structure and on occasions can be amplified and lead to qualitative structural changes and a reorganization of the average mechanisms.

The evolution of ecological structure

In recent years there has been some talk about the ecological restructuring of industry. But before we can discuss this coherently, we need to know what precisely ecological structure is. What is the organizational principle which underlies it? If we cannot answer this, then we surely cannot hope to organize human systems in an "ecological" manner. So, first, let us consider the only example that we have of sustainable structure: an ecosystem.

The key issues concern such questions as *why* the ecosystem is as it is. Why this number of populations? Why not more or less? Why these connections and not others? What would happen if we interfered with the system? Are the feeding relationships necessary, or do they merely reflect proximity and convenience?

None of these questions can be answered from the flow diagram of figure 2. Not only that, but, if we build a model based on the appropriate mechanisms of birth and death which change the numbers of each population, we might imagine that we could then use a computer to *predict* the behaviour of the system and perform simulations for policy analysis.

Unfortunately, this is not the case. When we run our computer model, it simplifies down to just a few species, because there are parallel paths through the system. Some of these are more "effective" than others; this leads to the elimination of apparently inferior paths through the action of (un)"natural selection."

But, in reality this does not occur. The system remains complex. Some source of diversity successfully opposes the tendency to simplify down that is apparent in our computer simulation. And this is the key to the understanding of ecological structure, the evolutionary process, and sustainability itself. The organizing principle that underlies sustainable systems is the presence, the maintenance, and the production of microscopic diversity in the system! These ideas have been developed in a series of recent papers (Allen and McGlade, 1987a, 1989; Allen, 1990; Allen and Lesser, 1991).

Ecological structure results from the working of the evolutionary process, and this in turn results from the nature of ecological structure. We can understand the ecological structuring of human activities by considering a "possibility space" representing the technologies and options that could potentially arise. In practice, of course, this is a multidimensional space of which we would only be able to anticipate a few of the principal dimensions. Ecological structure emerges over time, as the types of behaviour present in our possibility space increase and become more complex over time, and this is what we have successfully modelled.

The possibility space will be explored if the methods or techniques that firms use are influenced by new scientific knowledge and new ideas or by information and perceptions concerning others. New no-

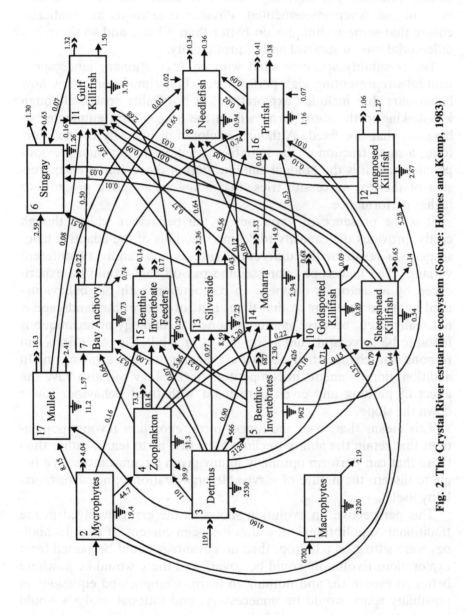

Fig. 2 The Crystal River estuarine ecosystem (Source: Homes and Kemp, 1983)

tions must be either generated within a company or may be copied or miscopied from others. Either way, cost and effort are expended in finding, filtering, and adapting ideas. New ideas still involve an element of risk when implemented. Physical constraints automatically ensure that some techniques do better than others, and so there is a differential rate of survival and of profitability.

The possibility space is filled with an "evolutionary landscape," with hills representing high performance. Our simulations show how behaviours that include "exploration" in possibility space, although loss-making in the short term, will in the longer term eliminate behaviours that are fixed. Although exploration is costly in the short term, a small fraction of the initiatives tried are better then previous practice, and it is the gradual amplification of these, and the suppression of the less successful tries, that allow an adaptive progress to higher performance.

It is the presence of variations in the behaviour which, though costly, provides the capacity to "climb" the hills of the adaptive landscape as a result of the differential success and failure of different variants. The landscape expresses the pay-off that would be experienced by an actor or company in competition with the behaviours used by its competitors at that time. But, of course, the landscape is not really fixed, because as soon as a new technology or technique is found to be successful, and a firm moves up a hill, the other firms will respond and change their behaviour, moving the hill away again. In addition, improvements in competitors' technology will also have the effect of pushing any given participant with fixed behaviour lower down the slope.

This means that, over the longer term, evolution favours populations that retain the ability to climb hills, that is, to learn, rather than those that can perform optimally in any given circumstances. We begin to discern the nature of survivable organizations, and of sustainability itself..

This perspective on evolution shows us the error involved in the traditional "equilibrium" view that has been current. If each technology were sitting on a hilltop, then no advantage could be gained from exploration. Evolution would be "over" and there would be nowhere better to evolve to, and nothing to learn. Complicated equations in possibility space would be unnecessary, and rational analysis would be able to optimize a firm's behaviour without evolutionary adaptation. In short, life would be simple but boring.

Fortunately, or unfortunately, we need not worry about this possibility, because this would only be true if evolution were really over. In the real world, competitors, allies, clients, technologies, raw materials, costs, and skills all change. Any group or firm that fixed its behaviour would sooner or later be eliminated, having no adaptive or learning capacity with which to respond.

The landscape in possibility space reflects the advantage to be gained from any particular option, and depends on the techniques and behaviours that happen to be present at a particular moment. The peaks of the landscape represent the present performance goals of the firm or group in question, whose decisions and innovations will try to move up the slope. However, the other actors of the system will continue to modify the landscape as they also adapt and change in pursuit of their goals. The goals of each type of actor co-evolve with those of the others present.

These experiments show that a mixture of exploratory diffusion paths in some behaviour or technology space, and their differential success, makes the difference between what is merely mechanical and what, on the contrary, contains the capacity for adaptation and creativity. It is the latter that might be called "organic." It is this vision of ecological structure as a temporary balance between exploration and constraint that is at the core of our new understanding.

Computer models have been developed that show explicitly how these adaptive landscapes are generated by the mutual interaction of behaviours or technologies. In the space of possibilities, closely similar products are mostly in competition with each other, but there is some "distance" in this space, some level of dissimilarity, at which two products or technologies do not compete with each other.

If we begin with a single type of product, then it will grow until it reaches the limits set by the competition either for underlying resources or for customers. At this point, the pay-off for explorers and entrepreneurs switches from negative to positive, as they can now escape somewhat from competition. We see that any successful behaviour eventually digs a hole in the landscape, until there is a hill to climb on either side and exploration is rewarded. Growth is restricted initially because of the "competitive shadow" of the original behaviour, but at a certain distance the products are sufficiently different from the original type; they begin to reach another market and require different resources.

In its turn, this new behaviour or product increases in volume until it too is limited by internal competition for the limiting resource; and once again there is a pay-off for innovation, particularly for those on

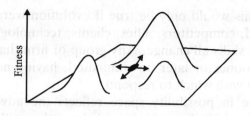

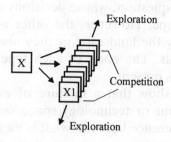

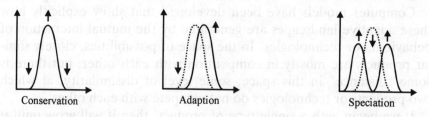

Fig. 3 The evolutionary landscape of untried options. Costly experimentation leads to better performance

the outside of the distribution, as they climb another slope towards new regions of possibility space. An evolutionary tree develops, branching as it grows. However, there are also moments when completely novel options emerge spontaneously during the simulation, and an ecology of interdependent behaviours emerges.

The ecology that emerges is dynamic, since the identity of each behaviour is maintained by the balance between a continual diffusion of innovators outwards into the space of untried options and the competitive field that exists around it owing to the others. In fact, it would not be possible to anticipate the final range of technologies or

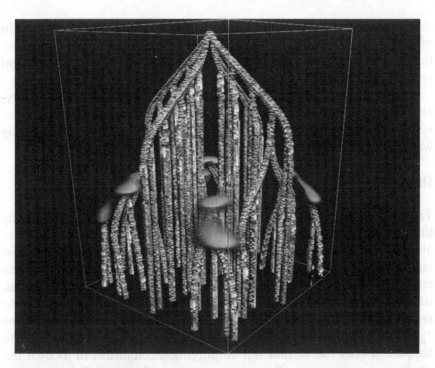

Fig. 4 A 3D visualization of our mathematical model of emergent evolution. An ecology of interdependent behaviours emerges

products that will inhabit the system, because random events which occur during the "filling" process will affect the emerging pattern of new technologies or products. Instead of the system simply filling pre-existing market niches, the whole process is a creative one, which would be different if repeated from the same initial conditions.

This model offers us a non-reductionist, scientific basis for discussing the interaction of individuals and their collective structures. Such a system operates beyond the mechanical paradigm, because its response to external interventions can involve changes in structure and in the nature of the behaviours or technologies in the system. Suppressing particular components of such a system, perhaps as a result of changing market conditions or environmental regulations, will provoke a complex response from the system, as other behaviours adjust.

Although the "inventiveness" of the system is constantly present, as there is diffusion into the possibility space, it is fascinating to see that our research shows that only at certain moments in time does this lead to structural change. In other words, the system evolves in phases of apparent stability, separated by periods of instability and fairly rapid reorganizations, although the pressure of exploration and creativity is relatively constant.

Such a picture may eventually explain such phenomena as the cycles of growth and stagnation that seem to characterize our economic systems, a phenomenon that has been linked to "economic long waves" and the patterns of innovation and change.

Discussion

The evolutionary models described above tell us that change is really the result of non-average behaviour exploring untried options, which, at certain moments, encounters mechanisms of positive feedback that lead to its amplification and self-reinforcement. Once a new option emerges it drives the system in the direction of its own amplification, irrespective of the objective or external value of these changes *for the system as a whole*. In other words, something doesn't have to be "good" for the overall system, or the environment, in order for it to happen; it only has to find self-amplifying mechanisms in its own immediate surroundings. Clearly, this exposes the root of the problem concerning the balance between collective and individual responsibilities and rights. The survival of the whole system may depend on the system's effective adaptation to external events, while the survival of the individuals of which it is comprised may require success in the internal adaptive processes.

As evolution proceeds, it gradually switches from introducing adaptations which deal with the external world to adaptations which succeed within the internal environment. The landscape of advantage ceases gradually to reflect the technology of the primary sector, dealing with the extraction and treatment of raw materials and energy, and gradually becomes increasingly concerned with techniques within techniques, with services to these and then to themselves. This is just the normal process of the development of ecological structure. And this principle applies not only to the balance of internal and external relations, but also to each organization within that structure.

Our evolutionary simulations begin to reveal the universality of myopic values in complex systems, whether they be natural or man-made. In natural ecosystems, each species too will be concerned with the solving of problems of its own, local survival and will not be thinking about planetary good. But if our situation is not intrinsically different from that of natural evolutions, why should we worry, and why should we change? The answer is that natural systems have taken a long time to evolve and explore the coexistence of different populations, and have suffered many local catastrophes and extinctions in the process. We should not forget that more than 90 per cent of species that have existed on the earth have become extinct. Throughout the millions of years of evolution, most of the forms that nature has tried have flowered briefly and then disappeared. We should, therefore, be most wary about assuming that nature's way is the best for us. We now have a conceptual framework of evolutionary systems which allows us a new basis of reflection, even upon the wisdom of nature itself!

The Industrial Revolution only started in earnest some 300 years ago, and was based on technologies that were clearly unsustainable. Despite our capacity to switch our appetite for fossil fuels and raw materials from one source to another, the growth in world population and in material expectations makes the present trajectory still quite clearly unsustainable. What mankind must do is to attempt to substitute reflection and anticipation for the actual experience of catastrophe, in order to learn about the obvious. This book is a step in this direction.

Quite naturally, then, self-amplifying mechanisms within industrial and post-industrial societies take the focus of evolution in human systems away from adaptations concerning the harmony of man and nature, and the sustainable use of the environment and natural resources, towards a multitude of ephemeral values and ends, whose consequences and effects for the collective system are largely unknown.

Many examples of these kinds of positive feedback "attractors" exist in the history of industrial development (Arthur, 1988), starting with the use of steam power to drive pumps in coal mines in order to provide coal for steam power. Similarly, the growth of industrial complexes required the development of railways and roads, while the development of the latter required industry. So, positive feedback loops led to the emergence of spatial concentrations of complementary activities, of pools of skilled labour. They also led to cities, where the different and multiple factors – from technology, through public infrastructure, to finance and investment – were available and working together in an emergent evolutionary "complex." Simulation models exploring the working of such structuring principles on settlement patterns, urban form, market systems, and learning processes

93

have been developed over the past 15 years or so (Allen, 1985, 1988, 1990; Allen and Sanglier, 1978, 1979, 1981).

As this evolution progresses, additional technologies are developed to cope with the unintended consequences of existing technologies which "create" markets through environmental damage. This process of technological "fix" is a measure of the hidden inefficiency of the short-term optimization of industry. A recent comparison of UK and German industrial development shows the Germans to be much more successful in industrial restructuring that begins to address sustainability, in part because of the longer time-scales that are acceptable in decision-making.

Instead of regarding human progress as following some steady path towards a better quality of life, meaning the gradual improvement of man's relationship with the natural world, we see the emergence of change driven by the values of an internal game. Imitation, economies of scale, learning by doing, perceived complementarities of behaviour, and the growth of interdependences all lead to the emergence of an artificial world, cut off from nature and yet of course embedded within it, and therefore potentially ripe for environmental catastrophe.

In human society, fashions, styles, and cultures may rise and fall without necessarily expressing any clear functional advantages with respect to the natural world in which they reside. Indeed, it may be informative to view culture not so much as being the best way of doing things somewhere, but more as resulting from the exclusion of knowledge concerning other ways of doing things. Ritual and shared ideology emerge and serve as the identity and focus of a social group, irrespective of the precise merits or truth of the ideology itself. So much of human attention is focused on playing a role in groups where values are generated internally, and the physical world outside is largely irrelevant.

It is therefore naive to believe that underneath the rich tapestry of life there is a rational scheme within which the complexities of the world would appear as being necessary and unavoidable. Instead we have what Margalef has called "the baroque of nature," but here we would include man. Evolution is creative beyond reason, and in that lies its resilience, since it is not framed to respond to any particular limited scheme.

In Europe, from initially agricultural societies, through the various accidents of history and the ebb and flow of ideas, religions, and authority, evolution moved away from its concerns with crops and livestock and developed new, internal and local values with which to define "successful" technologies and processes. Greatly increased scientific knowledge, together with urban growth and the gradual isolation of the bulk of the population from the realities of their relationship with natural resources, meant that the external consequences (ecological and social) of progress gradually dropped out of the consciousness of society.

Indeed, it became something of a new dogma that if something could be produced and sold at a sufficient profit, then it should only be suppressed if it were contrary to the law. The "burden of proof" has rested with the public or public authorities, and it was rather glibly assumed that the "law" would somehow know what it was wise to inhibit. But this is obviously not the case. Once we begin to understand how complex systems evolve, we see that we can only have an imperfect understanding of the consequences of our actions.

This brings us to the "precautionary principle." If it is difficult to prove that some product or technology is causing harm, then it is probably equally difficult to prove the contrary. But both positions reflect a view based on the concepts of traditional science, that such propositions have definite answers. Despite the attraction of a clear and definite stance, we must try instead to recognize the real complexity of such matters, and move to a new position, involving a mixture of both caution and risk. However, it appears clear that we should at least examine the size of the risk involved, and shift the debate from one in which "scientific proof" is the central focus, to one in which the gains and risk to society are assessed. To destroy mankind for the sake of some new ice-cream or cosmetic would seem to most people to be too high a price to pay, even for the upholding of the principle of individual freedom.

To achieve sustainability we need to understand what the implications of the proposed ecological restructuring of industry might be. The first point concerns the short- and the long-term view. As we have shown above, the qualities which are good in the short term for optimal efficiency are not those which lead to long-term survival. Indeed, they are the opposite. It is equally true, however, that failure in the short term will preclude the chance to show how good something would have been in the long term. In any case, "optimality" can only be defined if measured in certain terms; the measurement system of efficiency is in reality quite complicated, and judgement and wisdom often feature more than economists would suggest. Actual decision-making processes in industry are a curious mixture of formal economic accountability to the external capital system and what might be called common sense, much of which reflects human centred, long-term views and sensitivity to environmental issues. The role of government in determining the shape of the external environment is therefore absolutely crucial to sustainable industrial structures.

In general, then, sustainability will result from a balanced strategy corresponding both to fairly efficient average behaviour and to a permanent exploration of possibility space. The adaptability of the whole system results from the adaptability of its component parts, and instead of simply trying to outcompete others in a given domain, creativity and originality can allow a company to move into new areas with less competition. And the power to do this resides in the microscopic diversity of the system, which now can be seen to be vital for two reasons. First, it is the motor of creativity and adaptation, and, second, cultural and technological diversity tend to encourage a wide range of different activities and requirements and hence spread the stress on natural resources and the environment.

However, sustainability also requires that we affect local internal value systems and decisions so as to make them take into account their externalities and their collective effects. Mathematical models capable of providing real information about the evolution of the system as a whole will therefore be valuable in bringing the unconsidered consequences of a decision into view, and making them part of an evaluation. They can also provide vital information concerning the kinds of attributes that are related to survival and sustainability.

Another important point concerns the other properties of ecological systems that we observe. In mature ecosystems, for example, recycling is a major phenomenon, so that a carbon atom, in entering the ecosystem of figure 2, is actually recycled about 15 times as it goes through the system. This clearly is related to sustainability, as the evolutionary principle has a tendency to englobe and then recycle the factors that it requires as inputs. In other words, it evolves in such a way as to expand the organic, living, organized parts into the physical boundaries of the system, and then to retain and re-use materials in the system. At every stage, outputs are being tested as potential inputs for new processes.

This brings us to an important underlying principle in our whole thinking about industrial metabolism, the ecological restructuring of industry, and the problems of waste and pollution. Our evolutionary model shows us that when some successful innovation occurs in the system, some new source of positive feedback has been discovered. Now, in natural ecosystems, this would result in the "success" of some population for a time, during which its prey would decline in numbers and its wastes would build up. However, in the natural example, after some time, some variant of another population would discover that it could "use" this newly successful population and its accumulations of waste. This is because any spatial concentrations of matter having high free energy are potential sources of food for other populations. After a further period, the initial innovative population would have been reincorporated into the ecosystem, and the challenge that it offered initially would have been met from the internal diversity of the populations of the ecosystem.

In the case of the human population, why therefore are our wastes not recycled as part of the ecosystem? Why are we worrying so much about protecting the environment?

The first reason may simply be one of time. There simply is not sufficient time for an ecological response, particularly as we keep changing what we are dumping on the environment. The second reason, however, is that we are tending to use dispersion as our method of getting rid of wastes. So, instead of accumulations building up and becoming a potential source of raw material for some unknown future process, we are dispersing our wastes into the soils, the oceans, and the atmosphere. Clearly, part of the solution to such problems would be for each new technology to be obliged to provide the "antidote" to itself, that is, the mechanisms necessary to break down the new wastes that have been created. The stimulation both of clean technologies and of recycling should therefore be considered along with such ideas as a carbon or raw materials tax.

This does raise a very general point. Obviously, there are two choices in dealing with wastes: one is dispersion, and the other is concentration. While concentration can appear to be very dangerous in the case of toxic wastes and should require special costly permits, this approach does offer the future possibility that new processes or organisms may be found which can use waste materials, so that they will then become part of an ecological recycling process. In the longer term dispersion may be far more dangerous, since it gradually leads to a shift in the basic parameters of the biosphere, and to a potentially irreversible global change.

The new vision of an industrial metabolism requires not only that we control dispersion as a means of waste treatment, but that mechanisms should be foreseen for making concentrations of wastes part of an alternative ecology. Instead of disrupting the ecological structure and producing zones of accumulation with no known outlets, we must try only to allow technologies that can demonstrate how they can fit within an ecological pattern of flows.

Such changes, however, require vision. And the existence of a strong need for a radical shift in the functioning of the industrial system does not guarantee at all that industry itself will respond. Indeed, the internal games played within the various large companies, often multinationals, that dominate most markets today may well mean that once again concern for the external world will always in fact be a secondary matter.

New taxes on environmental damage, carbon, or raw materials, for example, may well lead to shifts towards more sustainable behaviour, but it may also require quite a sophisticated study for the real effects to be anticipated. In reality, we do not know the environmental damage that we are doing when we destroy some local ecosystem, since we do not understand precisely the source of its resilience and adaptability. Merely setting a price on such actions may therefore simply allow the wealthy to continue to do whatever they like.

There is, however, a place for governmental and international action. It is up to the political process to set the framework within which industry should operate. When Voltaire visited England in the eighteenth century, he remarked that political considerations had been subordinated to commercial ones in England, contrary to the case elsewhere in Europe, and that this was the reason for English prosperity. Perhaps it is time now to re-examine this idea, and to subordinate commercial interests at least to some restrictions concerning the natural environment.

We must begin to face up to our responsibilities, and consider the whole metabolism of modern society and its industrial motor. We must set about the difficult task of finding policies and regulations that will lead to the evolution of "earth-friendly" technologies and industry. One important strength in this is that the nations and companies that stimulate this kind of technological evolution will become the new industrial leaders, since environmental concern and regulation can only grow over the next decades as increasing cognizance is given to the external effects of internal processes.

The question is *how* we can change industrial culture, and again we may see what evolutionary theory and ecology have to suggest. This transition requires that we step outside any narrow disciplines and try to understand the overall evolution of the physical, socio-economic, demographic, technological, and cultural systems that are the objects of concern. It is not sufficient to ask "experts" what to do, since in some ways they are already part of the problem. It is the narrow values of experts that we are attempting to escape from. We need to construct a systemic view of our society, using as a basis the kind of evolutionary models referred to in this chapter, which can be used quantitatively to integrate the information of experts in the different fields.

This chapter is really about a research agenda concerning the implications for mankind of the conceptual framework of evolutionary processes and ecological structure. The identification of attributes related to survivability and adaptiveness is clearly key, and the links to cultural and social diversity require examination. The development of holistic methodologies and respective tools for policy evaluation and decision support seem also to be urgent. Similarly, methods with which to assess the size and scale of risks involved in the growth or continuation of technological processes seem equally pressing, together with drafting of some precautionary principle that will limit the possibility of trivial aims putting large parts of humanity at risk. In short, our research agenda is one which tries to reintegrate creativity and adaptability into scientific thinking, and man back into nature, providing thereby the understanding necessary to mankind for the development of sustainable strategies.

Note

1. The author would like to thank Roger Seaton for his most helpful discussion, suggestions, and comments on the draft version of this chapter.

References

Allen, P. M. 1985. "Towards a New Science of Complex Systems." In: E. Ploman, ed., *The Science and Praxis of Complexity*. Tokyo: UNU.

———. 1988. "Evolution: Why the Whole is Greater than the Sum of Its Parts." In: E. Ploman, ed., *Ecodynamics*. Berlin: Springer Verlag.

———. 1990. "Why the Future Is Not What It Was." *Futures*, July/August, pp. 555–570.

Allen, P. M., and M. Lesser. 1991. "Evolutionary Human Systems: Learning, Ignorance and Subjectivity." In: P. Saviotti and S. Metcalfe, eds., *Evolutionary Theories of Economic and Technological Change*. Chur: Harwood, pp. 160–171.

Allen, P. M., and J. M. McGlade. 1986. "Dynamics of Discovery and Exploitation: The Scotian Shelf Fisheries." *Can. J. of Fish. and Aquat. Sci.* 43, no. 6: 1187–1200.

———. 1987a. "Evolutionary Drive: The Effect of Microscopic Diversity, Error Making and Noise." *Foundations of Physics* 17, no. 7: 723–738.

———. 1987b. "Managing Complexity: A Fisheries Example." Report to the United Nations University, Tokyo.

———. 1989. "Optimality, Adequacy and the Evolution of Complexity." In: P. L. Christiansen and R. D. Parmentier, eds., *Structure, Coherence and Chaos in Dynamical Systems*. Manchester: Manchester University Press.

Allen, P. M., and M. Sanglier. 1978. "Dynamic Models of Urban Growth." *Social and Biological Structures* 1: 265–280.

———. 1979. "A Dynamic Model of Growth in a Central Place System." *Geographical Analysis* 11, no 3: 258–272.

———. 1981. "Urban Evolution, Self-Organization and Decision Making." *Environment and Planning A* 21: 167–183.

Arrow, K., and G. Debreu. 1954. "Existence of an Equilibrium for a Competitive Economy." *Econometrica*.

Arthur, B. 1988. "Self-reinforcing Mechanisms in Economics." In: Anderson, Arrow, and Pines, eds., *The Economy as an Evolutionary Complex System*. New York: Addison-Wesley.

Clark, W. C., and R. E. Munn. 1986. *Sustainable Development for the Biosphere*. Cambridge: Cambridge University Press.

Gleick, J. 1987. *Chaos*. New York: Penguin Books.

Nelson, R., and S. Winter. 1989. *An Evolutionary Theory of Economic Change*. Cambridge, Mass.: Belknap Press.

Nicolis, G., and I. Prigogine. 1977. *Self-organization in Non-equilibrium Systems*. New York: Wiley Interscience.

Prigogine, I., and I. Stengers. 1987. *Order Out of Chaos*. New York: Bantam Books.

Part 2
Case-studies

6

Industrial metabolism at the national level: A case-study on chromium and lead pollution in Sweden, 1880–1980

Ulrik Lohm, Stefan Anderberg, and Bo Bergbäck

Introduction

In many countries, estimations of annual emissions of chemicals from point sources are now being regularly presented for the nation as a whole. For Sweden, the figures show that the emissions have been decreasing since the mid-1970s. This is, of course, encouraging with regard to environmental protection objectives. Unfortunately, however, these figures do not present a complete picture. Nor do they provide sufficient information to evaluate human impact on the environment systematically, especially in a long-term perspective. There are two major shortcomings of the standard estimates:

1. Lack of a spatial dimension; a nationwide scale is hardly satisfactory to assess impacts (or the value) of reduced industrial emissions.
2. Lack of a temporal dimension; to evaluate present pollution loadings, knowledge about the dimension and localization of past emissions is needed.

The development of industry in Sweden has led to an increased use of chemicals and other materials. In this study we want to approach the environmental problems of tomorrow that will arise from the use of various materials, from a historical standpoint. This type of study could be used as an argument for what has recently been called the precautionary principle of environmental management (see O'Riordan, chapter 12 of this volume). The purpose is to develop methods to reconstruct the flows of materials and estimate the emissions over time. This is done through studies of the development of production, technology, trade, and the longevity of products in society. This last part in the chain will form the "consumption emissions."

The concept of industrial metabolism suggests that we should seek to estimate the total load of toxic substances in soils and sediments, i.e. to describe and assess the development of a new "immission landscape." In this chapter industrial metabolism is illustrated in terms of the total flow and accumulation of chromium (1920–1980) and lead (1880–1980) in Sweden (Anderberg et al., 1989, 1990; Bergbäck et al., 1989, 1992).

The method of analysis is based on a simplified flow scheme: Various substances enter the economy either through imports or domestic production. Production of goods and extraction of primary materials result in "production emissions." The main part of these emissions is found in the products themselves, and is accumulating in the "anthroposphere." Depending on the type of product, large amounts may remain for a long time. Some parts are recycled after use. However, a significant quantity is sooner or later spread to the environment through consumption emissions, dissipative losses (see Ayres, chapter 1 of this volume), consumer-related emissions, or emissions from diffuse sources.

This materials' balance approach method (inspired by Ayres and Kneese, 1969; Ayres, 1978; Ayres and Rod, 1986; Tarr and Ayres, 1990) consists, in somewhat simplified form, of the following steps:
1. Construction of flow schemes for various substances.
2. Collection of data concerning production, trade, and technology with the aim of filling the boxes in the flow schemes and creating a base for assumptions concerning emissions.
3. Estimating the emissions over time, using the net surplus and the flow scheme of the substance; emission coefficients concerning consumption are based on "life-expectancy" of the product in the technosphere.
4. Calculation of the anthropogenic amounts of stable substances in the soil and sediments per region and decade, i.e. the immission landscape.

The use of chromium and lead in Sweden

In Sweden, the use of chromium has been quite extensive owing to the historic importance of steel alloy production. As there are no chromium mines in Sweden, the import of chromium ore has long made up more than half of total Swedish ore imports. These imports have increased dramatically during this century. Imported chromium ore is mainly used for the production of ferrochrome. Since 1920, the Swedish iron and steel industry has been the major user of chromium, particularly for stainless steel. The use of chromium in the leather-tanning and textile industries was once important, but with the decline of these industries and the introduction of synthetic materials for tanning and dyeing, this use has decreased rapidly. The chemical industry and anti-corrosion treatment have replaced these industries as the major users of imported chromium compounds.

Lead mining has a long history in Sweden, but it is only since the Second World War that it has really been important; Sweden has become a major lead producer and ore exporter in Europe. Still, imports of various lead products have also been quite significant, particularly between 1945 and 1980. Traditionally, pigments and metal products were the most important uses, but since 1920 the electrical industry (cables and batteries) has been the dominant user, with 70–80 per cent of total consumption.

Calculation of emissions

Production emissions

Production emissions of chromium have been estimated for the ferrochrome alloy and steel industries and for leather tanneries. These activities contributed more than 90 per cent of the chromium emissions to water, and almost 100 per cent to the air in the late 1970s, according to estimates by the Swedish Environmental Protection Board.

For lead, the emissions have been calculated for metalworks, the iron and steel industry, glassworks, the rubber industry, and battery manufacturing. These branches were responsible for approximately 95 per cent of the emissions to air and water in the late 1970s.

The method for calculating time series for production emissions has been to use the best available single-year estimate of uncontrol-

105

led emissions for the various branches. We then let the emissions follow the development of production and/or use of lead/chromium backward in time. The emissions from a particular branch of industry were distributed between the individual factories according to the number of workers employed, or the production figures at different periods in time (10-year periods, except for the first and last periods, where five years were used). Finally, the total emissions per time period and region were summed up.

Consumption emissions

For consumption emissions, specific factors for various products have been used (see below). Here, the emissions were distributed between regions according to the distribution of population, except in the case of gasoline, where sales statistics were used.

The diffusion of lead or chromium from a certain use was calculated as follows

$$A \times E \times T$$

where A is the share of total lead/chromium consumption for the particular use, E is the assumed emission factor, and T is net consumption, from which the consumption of lead in gasoline and ammunition has been subtracted. The emission factor (see table 1) is defined as the part of the product that is mobilized in the environment within a decade. (Here we have used the factors given by Tarr and Ayres, 1990.) The emissions from gasoline and ammunition have been calculated separately, assuming that 80 per cent and 100 per cent of the lead content, respectively, will reach the environment.

Table 1 Emission factors for calculation of consumption emissions

	Chromium	Lead
Metallic uses	—	0.005
Alloys	0.001	—
Lead oxides	—	0.1
Other pigments	0.5	0.5
Batteries	—	0.01
Cables	—	0.01
Leather	0.05	—
Anti-corrosion	0.02	—
Other uses	0.05	0.01

Source: Tarr and Ayres, 1990; Ayres and Ayres, in this volume.

The development of emissions over time

In Sweden, the production emissions of chromium increased drastically in the period 1910–1970. Until the 1950s, tanning (see table 2) was the main source of chromium pollution, while steel and ferrochrome plants (see table 3) dominated the emissions after 1960. Despite a continued increase in chrome alloy steel production, the emissions drastically decreased in the 1970s, owing to an increasingly effective control programme.

The use of chromium in Sweden has increased constantly since the

Table 2 Calculated chromium emissions from tanneries in Sweden, 1910–1980

Year	Number of tanneries	Number of workers	Production of leather (T/yr^{-1})	Emissions to water $(t/10\ yr)$
1910	279	2,050	250	230
1920	177	2,580	1,330	1,220
1930	72	1,940	1,960	1,800
1940	48	2,850	2,740	2,520
1950	37	2,690	3,070	2,820
1960	24	1,640	1,750	1,600
1970	13	1,070	650	600
1980	7	719	3	225

Source: Swedish Industrial Statistics, various years.

Table 3 Calculated chromium emissions from ferrochrome alloy and steel plants in Sweden, 1920–1980

	Ferrochrome alloy plants			Steel plants		
	Ferrochrome production $(10^3\ t\ yr^{-1})$		Chromium emissions to air $(t\ 10\ yr^{-1})$	Purchase of FeCr $(10^3\ t)$	Chromium emissions $(t\ 10\ yr^{-1})$	
Year	FeSiCr	FeCr			Air	Water
1920		2	58	0.5	10	41
1930		10	422	2	66	267
1940		14	594	7	171	696
1950		12	984	12	322	1,360
1960	44	12	3,150	30	861	3,660
1970	64	54	4,470	79	1,340	5,900
1980	152	28	1,050	85	338	1,710

Source: Swedish Industrial Statistics, various years.

Table 4 Total consumption emissions in Sweden, 1920–1980 (calculated from import surplus)

Year	Import (t yr^{-1})	Export (t yr^{-1})	Consumption emissions (t/10 yr)
1910	175		
1920	1,573	16	497
1930	8,224	2,889	643
1940	8,120	5,846	1,560
1950	17,837	3,224	3,990
1960	52,258	11,172	8,290
1970	79,818	17,114	11,200
1980	117,360	60,860	12,300

Source: Swedish Trade Statistics, various years.

beginning of the century. Between 1950 and 1980, imports increased more than sixfold (see table 4). Most of the chromium will end up in the technosphere in numerous products. Even if only very small quantities are assumed to reach the environment, in the long run these emissions will be most significant. As consumption emissions are still increasing, leaching from chromium products appears to be a major future source of pollution.

For lead, production emissions culminated in the 1970s, but owing to improved production control are now relatively limited. The total production emissions to air in the period 1880–1980 (see table 5) have been dominated by one particular metalworks (Rönnskär), with a percentage of up to 57 per cent. Other contributors have been iron and steel production (16 per cent), rubber (12 per cent), glass (11 per cent), and battery manufacture (2 per cent). The major sources of total emissions to water (see table 6) have been metalworks (47 per cent), iron and steel (39 per cent), mining (9 per cent), and crystal glass production (5 per cent).

The consumption of lead in Sweden increased drastically in conjunction with rapid industrialization, by more than 40 times between 1880 and 1960. But since then it has decreased because of the stagnation in some of its major areas of use, and also because of increased recycling. The shares of the various uses have changed significantly over the hundred years. By the end of the last century, metal products and chemicals, mostly white and red lead used in paint, were dominant. Since around 1920, most of the lead has been used for

Table 5 Calculated lead emissions to air in Sweden, 1880–1980 (based on production figures), in tonnes per year

Year	Coal	Oil	Metal, non-ferrous	Iron and steel	Battery	Glass	Rubber	Total
1880	1		1	4		1		7
1885	1		3	6		1		12
1890	2		3	7		2		13
1895	2		6	10		3		21
1900	3		5	12		4		34
1905	4		7	15		4		30
1910	5		5	18		5	1	33
1915	5		14	18		3	1	41
1920	3	<1	17	18	1	7	4	50
1925	4	<1	4	11	2	9	4	33
1930	6	<1	3	15	2	10	8	44
1935	7	<1	33	16	3	14	9	81
1940	6	<1	77	24	3	9	13	131
1945	0	<1	96	28	5	13	9	152
1950	7	1	77	29	7	20	45	187
1955	6	4	239	47	9	27	53	384
1960	4	6	250	71	10	40	56	436
1965	3	10	385	99	15	63	65	640
1970	3	14	427	89	20	74	77	704
1975	2	11	427	69	10	100	76	695
1980[a]	2	10	245	50	1	30	60	398
Total (1880–1980)	400	300	11,700	3,300	400	2,200	2,400	20,600

Source: For production figures: Swedish Industrial Statistics, various years.
a. Estimated by the Swedish Environmental Protection Board.

Table 6 Calculated lead emissions to water in Sweden, 1880–1980 (based on production figures), in tonnes per year

Year	Metal, non-ferrous	Iron and steel	Ore production		Glass	Total
			Laisvall	Other		
1880	1	4		<1	<1	5
1885	2	6		<1	<1	8
1890	2	9		<1	<1	11
1895	3	11		<1	1	15
1900	8	13		<1	1	22
1905	4	14		<1	1	19
1910	3	16		<1	1	20
1915	7	19		<1	1	27
1920	9	18		<1	1	28
1925	2	11		1	2	15
1930	2	15		2	2	19
1935	11	16		3	3	30
1940	25	24		3	2	51
1945	32	28	2	5	3	63
1950	25	29	4	5	4	58
1955	78	47	7	4	5	130
1960	82	71	14	4	8	161
1965	126	99	19	4	13	238
1970	140	82	21	6	15	237
1975	140	52	23	5	20	212
1980[a]	15	20	24	6	6	41
Total	3,600	3,000	500	200	400	7,700

Source: Swedish Trade Statistics, various years.
a. Estimated by the Swedish Environmental Protection Board.

cables and batteries, while metal products and chemicals have kept stable shares of 10–15 per cent each (see table 7).

After the Second World War tetraethyl lead was introduced as an additive to gasoline. Around 1970 this use reached over 2,000 tonnes, or 3.5 per cent of total consumption. Even though this share is rather small, it has by far been the most important emission source during the latter half of the century. The production and import of lead shot and cartridges have fluctuated considerably throughout the century, but ammunition has always been a significant source of lead emissions. The total amount of lead emissions calculated from both production and consumption was approximately 190,000 tonnes between 1880 and 1980. The share of consumption emissions was 85 per cent, with about one-fourth each from both ammunition and gasoline, and

Table 7 Calculated consumption emissions of lead in Sweden, 1880–1980

Year	Metal	Alloys	Battery	Cable	Lead oxides	Other pigments	Other uses	Total (t y⁻¹)	Total (t 10 y⁻¹)
1880	3				15	142	3	160	800
1890	7				33	147	6	189	1,980
1900	8				63	157	8	235	2,350
1910	8				87	207	16	318	3,180
1920	8		20	34	122	470	9	663	6,630
1930	12		18	76	144	519	20	790	7,900
1940	18		32	131	156	430	37	804	8,040
1950	12	4	45	174	187	980	30	1,432	14,320
1960	11	10	78	219	429	181		928	9,280
1970	8	6	91	117	399	231		852	8,520
1980	11	6	110	54	351	104		637	3,185
Total (1880–1980)									66,000

Source: Swedish Trade Statistics, various years.

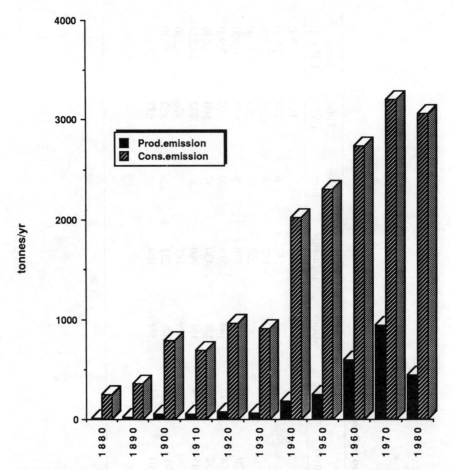

Fig. 1 Calculated emissions originating from production and consumption of lead in Sweden, 1880–1980

one-third from other consumer uses (e.g. lead pigments, cables, and batteries). The emissions from consumption have dominated for the whole period studied (see figure 1).

When comparing different sources of lead emissions over time, the significance of automobiles and trucks is particularly striking. Over a period of less than four decades, automotive emissions of lead far exceed total industrial emissions for the whole century.

The emerging immission landscape

In order to describe the immission landscape at different times, a simple flow model was used, where emissions to land and water,

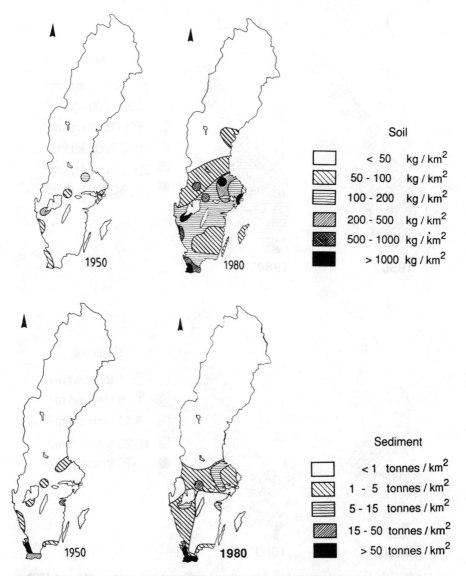

Fig. 2 Calculated amounts of chromium in soil and sediment in Sweden, 1950 and 1980

flows from soil to water, and, finally, accumulation in sediments and soils were considered. Detailed maps of chromium and lead loads in Sweden from 1880 to 1980 have been published elsewhere (Bergbäck et al., 1989, 1992). In figures 2 and 3 a comparison is made for accumulated amounts of chromium and lead in soils and sediments between 1950 and 1980.

113

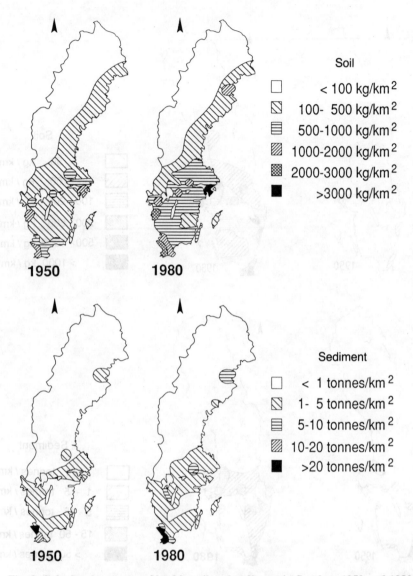

Fig. 3 Calculated amounts of lead in soil and sediment in Sweden, 1950 and 1980

These calculated amounts of metals in soils in Sweden correspond to measurements taken during the 1980s, particularly in areas where high production emissions had taken place. Exact comparisons, however, are difficult to make, as our calculations represent mean loads in administratively defined areas. Comparisons with monitoring data reveal similarities but also discrepancies in the patterns, and the

114

latter could in some cases be explained by the composition of the bedrock. (Uncertainties in the calculations are further discussed in Bergbäck et al., 1989, 1992.)

The present rate of lead consumption in Sweden is approximately 25,000 tonnes per year, excluding ammunition and gasoline . If this rate were to remain constant between 1980 and 2080, another 2.5 million tonnes would be added to the 2 million tonnes already accumulated in the last 100 years, giving a total of 4.5 million tonnes of lead in the anthroposphere.

It would also be relevant to compare the anthropogenic release of lead into the environment with the mobilization of lead from the bedrock during the weathering cycle. Weathering mobilization may be calculated by using average trace metal concentrations in soils and the suspended sediment flux in rivers. According to Nriagu, the global weathering rate for lead is approximately 180,000 tonnes per year (Nriagu, 1990). In Sweden's case, this would mean about 500 tonnes per year. Thus, 50,000 tonnes might have been released by natural weathering processes within the last 100 years. This amount should be compared with our calculations of *total* emissions, which are approximately four times higher.

The rate of emissions (see figure 4) and accumulation of chromium is higher than for lead. The use of chromium products in Sweden (e.g. stainless steel) has increased dramatically since the Second World War. As long as consumption emissions remain at a high level, chromium will have a strong impact on the environment in the future.

In figure 5 the emission rates of lead, chromium and cadmium are compared, with a roughly calculated weathering rate for these metals. Obviously, the anthropogenic contribution is significant, especially for lead.

Conclusions

Even though production emissions in Sweden have decreased during the last few decades, the accumulation of lead and chromium in soils and sediments will continue owing to the dissipative consumption losses of various products. To give an example: Suppose consumption emissions remain on the 1970–1980 level while production emissions are assumed to be low or even negligible; then the calculated amounts of chromium in the soils of some urban areas (e.g. Stockholm) will be as high as they are in the most polluted industrial regions today within only a few decades (Bergbäck et al., 1989). Thus,

Ulrik Lohm, Stefan Anderberg, and Bo Bergbäck

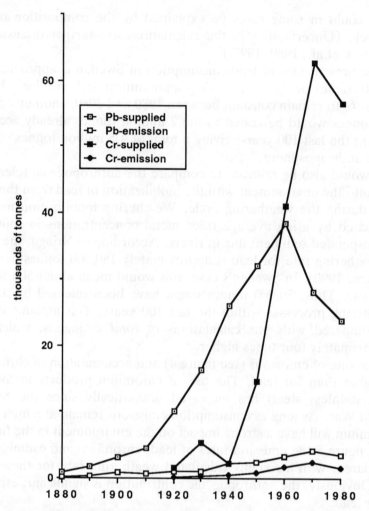

**Fig. 4 Chromium and lead emissions in Sweden compared with supply (imports −
export + production) in thousands of tonnes per year**

urban environments can be regarded as ecological "hot spots" for
toxic metals. Also, in the future agricultural soils in suburbanized
areas may be close to exceeding their carrying capacity for trace
metal pollution.

The changing spatial pattern of heavy metal loads in Sweden
reflects the dynamics of industrialization. The first industrial revolution was based on local resources, such as raw materials and energy
sources. Later, with greater affluence and mobility, an "urban world"
developed. Consequently, the pollution load in soils and sediments

116

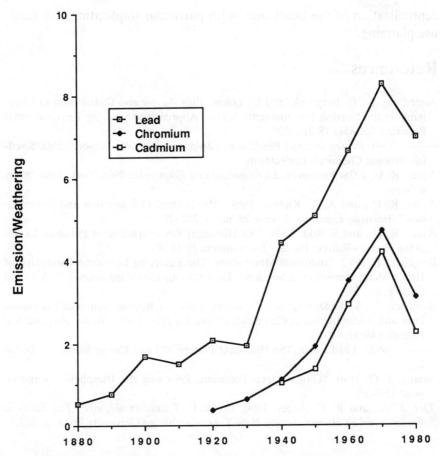

Fig. 5 The ratio between total emissions and weathering for lead, chromium, and cadmium in Sweden

has altered from being a "defined pollution problem" within certain industrial regions to a situation where the end-use of products, together with the mobility pattern of goods, define the pollution problem.

In a general sense, our results illustrate a new dimension of the landscape. Industrial and urban areas often have soils and sediments with a higher recognized level of heavy metals. In these areas the "societal weathering rate" exceeds the natural one. In rural areas, with a more natural background dominated by the average bedrock composition, the pollution load of heavy metals is still less pronounced. The consequences of this development are difficult to predict, but it is obvious that a new dimension will be added to the conceptualization of the landscape, with particular implications for land-use planning.

References

Anderberg, S., B. Bergbäck, and U. Lohm. 1989. "Flow and Distribution of Chromium in the Swedish Environment: A New Approach to Studying Environmental Pollution." *Ambio* 18:216–220.

———. 1990. *Pattern of Lead Emissions in Sweden 1880–1980*. Report 13/90. Swedish National Chemicals Inspectorate.

Ayres, R. U. 1978. *Resources, Environment and Economics*. New York: John Wiley & Sons.

Ayres, R. U., and A. V. Kneese. 1969. "Production, Consumption and Externalities." *American Economic Review* 59, no. 3: 282–296.

Ayres, R. U., and S. Rod. 1986. "An Historical Reconstruction of Pollutant Levels in the Hudson-Raritan Basin." *Environment* 28:14–43.

Bergbäck, B. 1992. "Industrial Metabolism. The Emerging Immission Landscape of Heavy Metal Immission in Sweden." Dissertation. Linköping Studies in Arts and Science, no. 76.

Bergbäck, B., S. Anderberg, and U. Lohm. 1989. "A Reconstruction of Emissions, Flow and Accumulation of Chromium in Sweden 1920–1980." *Water, Air, and Soil Pollution* 48:391–407.

———. 1992. "Lead Load: The Historical Pattern of Lead Use in Sweden." *Ambio* 21.

Nriagu, J. O. 1990. "Global Metal Pollution. Poisoning the Biosphere." *Environment* 32:7–33.

Tarr, J. A., and R. U. Ayres, 1990. In: B. L. Turner et al., eds., *The Earth as Transformed by Human Action*. New York: Cambridge University Press, p. 623.

7

Industrial metabolism at the regional level: The Rhine Basin

William M. Stigliani and Stefan Anderberg

Introduction

In November 1986 an accident at a pharmaceutical company located on the River Rhine at Basel, Switzerland, resulted in the inadvertent release of 33 tons of toxic materials.[1] The effects were immediate and dramatic: half a million fish and eels died and local residents could not use the river as a source of drinking water for about a month. This accident, highly publicized in the world press, raised a major public outcry calling for an action plan for reducing the risks of such accidents in the future.

Historically, however, the impact of chemical accidents on the overall pollutant load to the river has been relatively minor. For example, in 1980 about 27 tons of toxic materials daily (10,000 tons per year) were transported by the Rhine into the Dutch Delta and the North Sea. This toxic load was the result not of accidents but, rather, of normal industrial, commercial, agricultural, and urban activities conducted within the Rhine Basin on a routine basis.

The effects of such chronic pollution are not as obvious or spectacular as those occurring after industrial accidents. Much of the daily input ends up in sediments of the Dutch Delta, and the rest is washed out to the North Sea. Even today the sediments in the delta are so

119

polluted that the spoils, collected during dredging operations to keep navigation lanes open, are too toxic to be applied to polder lands in the Netherlands, as was the practice in the past.On the other hand, the River Rhine today transports far fewer pollutants to the Netherlands than it did in 1980, even though the level of economic activities in the basin has not changed very much since then.

Analysing the history of pollution in the Rhine Basin, including the recent clean-up, can provide valuable insights into the linkages between economic activities and chemical pollution, and the opportunities for decoupling economic growth from environmental degradation. The research described in this chapter, while not addressing all possible aspects of this history, will, we hope, provide a basis for improved policy-making.

Geographic features of the Rhine basin

The Rhine Basin extends over five European nations (fig. 1). Included are most of Switzerland, the north-east corner of France, Luxembourg, most of the south-western *Länder* (provinces) of Germany, and most of the Netherlands. The population of the basin is about 50 million and the area is about 220,000 km². About half of the land is used for agriculture, one third is forests, and the remainder is urban and suburban areas.

The basin is perhaps the most heavily industrialized in the world. Although the stream flow of the Rhine comprises only about 0.2 per cent of the flow of all rivers, about 10 to 20 per cent of the total Western chemical industry (OECD countries) is located in its basin. Industry is particularly concentrated in the catchment areas of the Ruhr, Neckar, Main, and Saar tributaries. Little net sedimentation of heavy metals occurs until the flow reaches the Dutch Delta, which extends from the German-Dutch border to the North Sea. About 75 per cent of the metals are deposited in the sediments of the delta, and the remainder disperses into the North Sea.

Methodology

Our study analyses the entire system by which resource inputs to the industrial economy are converted into outputs that must be absorbed and processed by the environment. For analysing a given chemical, this systems approach can be divided into three steps:
1. Identification of materials in which the chemical is embodied, and the pathways by which they flow through the industrial economy.

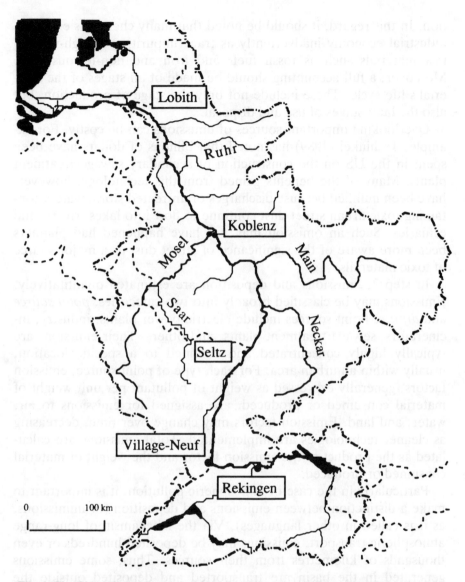

Fig. 1 The Rhine Basin. Place-names in boxes signify locations of monitoring stations of the International Commission for the Protection of the Rhine

2. Estimation of emissions and deposition to air, water, and soil for each material at each stage of its life cycle.
3. Construction of a basin-wide pollution model for assessment of proposed emission reduction policies, environmental impacts, or other relevant issues related to the chemical in question.

In step 1, it is essential not to miss any important source of pollution. In this regard, it should be noted that many chemicals enter the industrial economy inadvertently as trace impurities of high-volume raw materials such as fossil fuels and iron and non-ferrous ores. Moreover, a full accounting should be made of all stages of the material's life cycle. These include not only the stage of production, but also the later stages of use and disposal.

Overlooking important sources of emissions can be costly. For example, Tschinkel (1989) has noted that billions of dollars have been spent in the US on the construction of secondary sewage treatment plants. Many of the benefits gained from this technology, however, have been nullified because discharges of untreated storm waters containing toxic urban street dust continue to flow into lakes, rivers, and estuaries. Such an omission may not have happened had planners been more aware of the significance of street dust as a major source of toxic materials.

In step 2, emissions and deposition are estimated quantitatively. Emissions may be classified broadly into two categories: *point source* and *diffuse*. Point sources include electric power plants, industry, incinerators, sewage treatment plants, and others. Their emissions are typically highly concentrated and confined to a specific location, usually within an urban area. For each type of point source, emission factors, generally expressed as weight of pollutant per unit weight of material consumed or produced, are assigned for emissions to air, water, and land. Emission factors may change over time, decreasing as cleaner technologies are implemented. Total emissions are calculated as the product of the emission factor and the weight of material consumed or produced.

Particularly in the case of atmospheric pollution, it is important to make a distinction between emissions and deposition (or immissions, as it is called in other languages). Via the mechanism of long-range atmospheric transport, emissions may be deposited hundreds or even thousands of kilometres from their sources. Thus, some emissions generated in the basin are transported and deposited outside the basin, and some emissions from outside the basin are transported into it. A long-range atmospheric deposition model has been developed at IIASA (Alcamo et al., 1992) for estimating deposition in the basin.

In contrast to point-source emissions, diffuse emissions are generally less concentrated, more dispersed spatially, and dependent on land use, which can be broadly categorized as forests, agricultural lands (both arable and grassland), and urban areas. The only inputs to forested lands are assumed to be atmospheric deposition via long-

122

range transport. Chemical inputs to agricultural soils include not only long-range atmospheric deposition, but also agrochemicals, manure, and sewage sludge. Diffuse emissions from these two land uses are determined using a run-off export model (Jolankai et al., 1991).

Transport of pollutants to surface and ground waters is much greater from agricultural lands than from forested areas. Transport occurs via storm run-off, erosion, and vertical seepage. The relevant parameters to be determined are the rates of applications of particular chemicals, expressed as weight per hectare, and the partition coefficient, which determines the fraction of chemical that is mobilized and transported and the fraction that remains bound in the soil. Even if only a small percentage of the chemicals is mobilized, total emissions can be significant because of the enormous chemical inputs and the large spatial coverage of agricultural lands.

Another important source of diffuse emissions is transport of pollutants from paved urban areas to surface waters. This occurs by the build-up of toxic materials in street dust during dry periods, and the washing out of the dust during storm events. The pathways by which the transport may occur are shown in figure 2. There are three main sources of toxic materials in urban dust: corrosion of building materials (particularly for heavy metals such as zinc, used in galvanizing and surface materials), exhausts and tyre wear from automobiles and other road vehicles (important for lead and zinc), and local and long-range atmospheric deposition (a dominant source of cadmium).

When storm sewers are separate from municipal sewers (path SSS in figure 2), the pollutants are transported directly to surface waters. Alternatively, storm sewers may be connected to municipal sewers that discharge to surface waters without treatment (path CSSW in figure 2), or they may be connected to municipal sewers in which the effluents are treated (path WWTP in figure 2). In sewage treatment plants with primary and secondary treatment, typically 50 per cent or more of input heavy metals are trapped in sewage sludges. Even when the storm sewers are connected to sewage treatment plants, however, some fraction of the polluted street dust may be transported to the river unabated if the volume of storm flow exceeds the flow capacity of the sewage treatment plant (path CSO in figure 2), which is often the case. Another important source of pollution, also indicated in the figure, is the atmospheric deposition on unpaved urban areas, with subsequent seepage to ground waters and transport to the river.

To calculate emissions from corrosion, it is necessary to determine

123

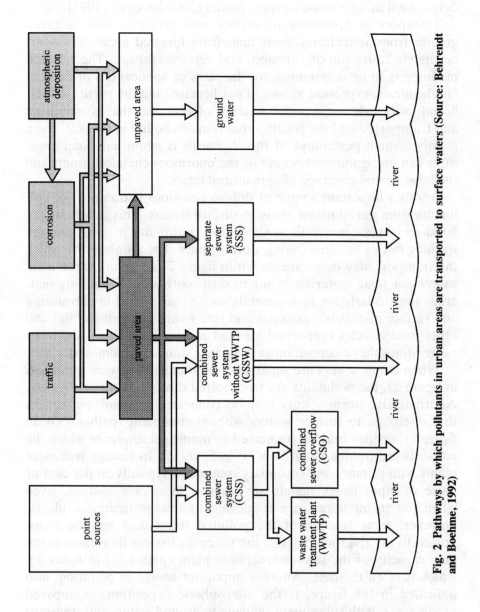

Fig. 2 Pathways by which pollutants in urban areas are transported to surface waters (Source: Behrendt and Boehme, 1992)

rates of corrosion per unit surface of the corroded material and the total surface coverage of the material in question. For instance, rates of zinc corrosion are strongly linked to urban SO_2 concentrations and will decrease over time as SO_2 levels are lowered. The following equation (ECE, 1984) shows the empirical relationship between SO_2 concentration and the rate of zinc corrosion from galvanized steel:

$$Y = 0.45 * [SO_2] + 0.7,$$

where Y = annual corrosion rate of galvanized steel ($g/m^2/yr$), and $[SO_2]$ = concentration of SO_2 in air (mg/m^3)

Emissions from road traffic owing to tyre wear may be estimated by determining emission rates per vehicle km, and multiplying this rate by vehicle km per year and the number of vehicles per year.

Lead emissions from combustion of gasoline may be calculated by multiplying lead emitted per unit of gasoline burned and multiplying by annual gasoline consumption. The emissions are allocated spatially by apportioning them according to traffic density.

In urban areas, local atmospheric emissions are particularly important, since a significant fraction, typically around 10 per cent of the total emissions, are deposited within 10 to 20 kilometres of the source. Factors affecting the proportion of local to long-range emissions include smokestack height, velocity of the gases and particulate matter leaving the stack, meteorological conditions, and particle size of emitted pollutants. The IIASA study includes an analysis of trends in local emissions as affected by changes in the above-mentioned factors (Hrehoruk et al., 1992).

Lastly, it is necessary to employ an urban hydrology model that estimates the fraction of street dust that flows to the river. Even though urban and suburban areas occupy only about 15 per cent of total surface area in the basin, their contribution to the total diffuse load of aqueous emissions is significantly higher. This is because of the prevalence of hard, impermeable surfaces in urban lands (typically around 33 per cent of total urban area), from which run-off and transport of pollutants can be as high as 90 per cent, compared to a maximum of about 25 per cent for agricultural lands (Ayres and Rod, 1986).

Completion of steps 1 and 2 for a given chemical provides a pollution model of the basin, including inputs and outputs for the chemical, its flows through the industrial economy over time, and its spatial allocation for each time period of interest. The model can be used for

William M. Stigliani and Stefan Anderberg

various purposes. For example, a historical analysis of pollution can provide information on changing trends in pollution sources. In the case of pollution in the River Rhine, the IIASA analysis indicates that since the mid-1970s diffuse sources of emissions of heavy metals have become increasingly important relative to point sources. Another useful application of the historical analysis is the possibility for estimating the cumulative build-up of toxic materials in soils and sediments. Currently, hardly any information exists on the rates of accumulation of toxic chemicals over wide spatial regions, or on the evaluation of resulting impacts to the environment and human health. (For a comprehensive discussion of cumulative chemical loading and potential environmental impacts see Stigliani, 1988, and Stigliani et al., 1991.)

The pollution model can also be used to test the effectiveness of proposed policy options for reducing emissions of toxic chemicals. Because the model is based on mass balance analysis, all material flows to air, water, and land within the basin must be taken into account. The model will thus expose options that would not reduce overall emissions in the basin, but, rather, would transfer them from one pollution pathway to another.

The example of cadmium

Step 1: Identification of materials containing cadmium and their pathways through the industrial economy

As an example of the approach taken in our study, the discussion focuses on the industrial metabolism of cadmium (Cd). Primary materials containing cadmium and its range of concentrations are shown in table 1.

Table 1 Natural occurrence of cadmium

Material	Typical range (ppm)
Soils, global average	0.01–0.7
Zinc ore concentrates	1,000–12,000
Lead ore concentrates	3–500
Copper ore concentrates	30–1,200
Iron ore	0.12–0.30
Hard coal	0.50–10.00
Heavy oil	0.01–0.10
Phosphate ore	0.25–80

Source: Boehm and Schaefers, 1990.

126

Cadmium enters the industrial economy inadvertently as a trace impurity of high-volume raw materials. The most important of these are phosphate ores, coal, oil, and iron ore. The production of phosphate fertilizer is a major source of aqueous cadmium pollution in the Rhine Basin (Elgersma et al., 1991), and fertilizer application is now the major source of cadmium pollution in agricultural soils. Combustion of coal and oil are major sources of atmospheric cadmium pollution. Iron and steel production results in the generation of large volumes of solid wastes contaminated with cadmium, as well as atmospheric and aqueous cadmium emissions. An added source of cadmium pollution in steel production is the input of steel scrap treated with cadmium as a surface coating.

The cadmium contained in zinc ores is generally of sufficiently high concentration that separating and refining it as a by-product of zinc refining is economically feasible. In fact, it is via this route that all primary cadmium is produced. There is some mining of Zn/Cd ores within the basin, but most of the ores, in the form of zinc concentrates, are imported. Inputs of cadmium to the Zn/Cd refinery are transformed into three outputs: refined cadmium metal; refinery emissions (to air, water, and soil); and a trace component in refined zinc metal (0.15–0.50 per cent in zinc produced at thermal refineries, and 0.02 per cent or less in zinc produced at electrolytic refineries). Cadmium is also present in lead and copper ores but, as shown in table 1, the concentrations are much lower than for zinc, and the production and use of lead and copper in the Rhine Basin is not an important source of cadmium pollution.

As shown in figure 3, cadmium and zinc pollution are linked for at least two zinc-containing products, automobile tyres and galvanized metals, which are significant sources of emissions, particularly in urban areas. Tyre wear and corrosion of galvanized zinc cause the release of zinc and associated cadmium. The deposited metals accumulate in street dust and may be transported as aqueous emissions during storm run-off or dispersed as wind-blown dust. The amount of cadmium contained as an impurity in finished zinc metal has been decreasing since the 1960s, as electrolytic refineries have accounted for an increasingly greater share of zinc production. Nevertheless, even in recent decades significant quantities of cadmium have entered the economy by this route.

For the Federal Republic of Germany in the period 1973–1986, it is estimated that 40 tons of cadmium per year on average (560 tons over the entire period) were contained in zinc products for domestic

127

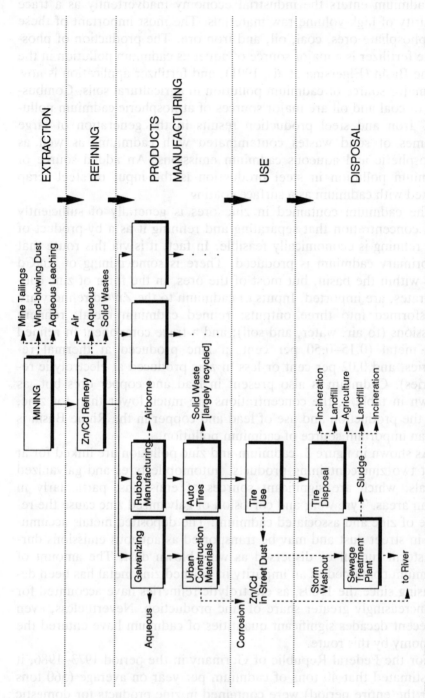

Fig. 3 The coupling of zinc and cadmium pollution caused by the presence of cadmium as a trace impurity in zinc-containing products

consumption (Rauhut and Balzer, 1976; Rauhut, 1978a, 1981, 1983, 1990; Balzer and Rauhut, 1987). Since the population of the West German part of the Rhine Basin comprises about one-half of the total West German population, and assuming an equal per capita distribution of zinc products, it is estimated that about 280 tons of cadmium entered the basin by this route from the Federal Republic of Germany alone. When account is taken of the rest of the population in the basin, a total of about 467 tons of cadmium is estimated to have been associated with zinc products over the 14-year period.

The largest inputs of cadmium to the Rhine Basin are not from inadvertent trace impurities, but rather through the refining of cadmium metal, and the production, use, and disposal of cadmium products. As shown in figure 4, cadmium metal, some of which is pro-

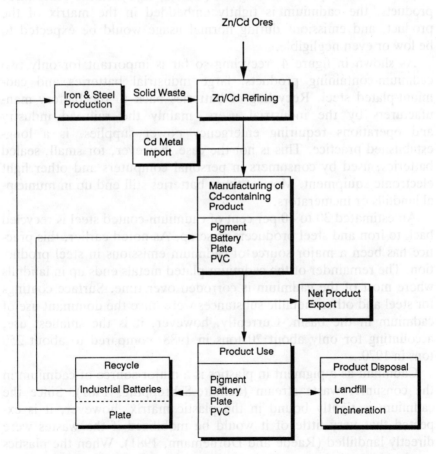

Fig. 4 The flow of cadmium-containing products through the industrial economy

129

duced at the basin's zinc refineries and some of which is imported, is the input to plants that manufacture cadmium-containing products. The four major products are pigments (mostly for plastics), nickel-cadmium (Ni-Cd) batteries, plate (for surface protection of steel and other metals), and stabilizers (in PVC plastic). Emissions of cadmium occur for each of these manufacturing sectors.

The next stage in the material flow is the use of cadmium in the basin. Ayres et al. (1988) have noted the importance of dissipative emissions, referring to emissions that may occur during the normal use of products. Such emissions are important, however, only when the chemical is easily mobilized during use. Of the four major cadmium-containing products, only cadmium plate might be expected to generate emissions to the environment via corrosion when exposed to polluted atmospheres during use (Carter, 1977). In the other three products, the cadmium is tightly embedded in the matrix of the product, and emissions during normal usage would be expected to be low or even negligible.

As shown in figure 4, recycling so far is important for only two cadmium-containing products, large industrial batteries and cad-mium-plated steel. Recycling of batteries back to the battery man-ufacturers by the industrial users, mainly the railroad industry and operations requiring emergency power supplies, is a long-established practice. This is not the case, however, for small, sealed batteries, used by consumers in personal computers and other light electronic equipment. Most of these batteries still end up in municip-al landfills or incinerators.

An estimated 30 to 40 per cent of cadmium-coated steel is recycled back to iron and steel producers as scrap. As noted earlier, this prac-tice has been a major source of cadmium emissions in steel produc-tion. The remainder of the cadmium-plated metals ends up in landfills where most of the cadmium is corroded over time. Surface coatings for steel and other metallic substances were once the dominant use of cadmium in the basin. Currently, however, it is the smallest use, accounting for only about 20 tons in 1988, compared to about 250 tons in 1970.

Cadmium as a pigment in plastics is a major source of cadmium in the consumer waste stream (Schulte-Schrepping, 1981). Since the cadmium is tightly bound in the plastic matrix, however, it is ex-pected that very little of it would be mobilized if the wastes were directly landfilled (Raede and Dornemann, 1981). When the plastics are incinerated, however, they constitute a major source of atmospheric cadmium emissions, as well as cadmium concentrated in the residue incinerator ashes.

Cadmium as a stabilizer in PVCs is used particularly in outdoor window frames. As with cadmium-pigmented plastics, cadmium in this form is not likely to be appreciably mobilized, either during use or after disposal to landfills. Very little of the disposed PVC is incinerated, since most of it ends up in landfills with other debris from demolition of old buildings.

Step 2: Estimation of cadmium emissions and deposition to air, water, and solid wastes

Atmospheric emissions and deposition
ATMOSPHERIC EMISSIONS WITHIN THE RHINE BASIN. Because atmospheric pollutants may be transported over long distances, a substantial fraction of emissions generated in the basin are transported and deposited out of the basin and, conversely, some fraction of emis-

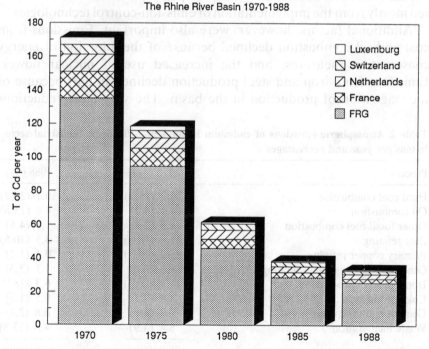

Fig. 5 In-basin atmospheric emissions of cadmium

sions generated out of the basin are transported and deposited in the basin. Therefore, the calculation of cadmium deposited in the basin from the atmosphere requires the incorporation of emission sources both inside and outside the basin.

Such a European-wide database was provided by Pacyna (1988) and Pacyna and Munch (1988) for the early 1980s. Historical emissions were calculated using available production statistics for the relevant sectors generating the emissions, and estimations of the evolution of emission factors per sector since the 1950s (Pacyna, 1991). Deposition was calculated using the TRACE 2 model developed at IIASA and described in detail in Alcamo et al. (1992). The model employs "transfer matrices" which convert emission inputs into deposition outputs.

Figure 5 shows the in-basin atmospheric emissions of cadmium for selected years in the 1970s and 1980s. The Federal Republic of Germany has been the predominant source of emissions, accounting for between 75 and 80 per cent of total emissions over the entire period. Table 2 shows the distribution of emissions by sector for 1970 and 1988. One may observe that over the 18-year period there was an overall reduction in air emissions of 87 per cent. This decrease occurred mostly from the implementation of emission-control technologies.

Additional factors, however, were also important. Emissions from coal and oil combustion declined because of the adoption of energy conservation measures, and the increased use of nuclear power. Emissions from iron and steel production declined in part because of the stagnation of production in the basin. The very large reductions

Table 2 Atmospheric emissions of cadmium in the Rhine Basin by industrial sector, in tons per year and percentages

Process	1970 (%)	1988 (%)
Hard coal combustion	26.2 (15.3)	10.1 (30.2)
Oil combustion	14.1 (8.2)	4.6 (13.8)
Other fossil fuel combustion	4.7 (2.8)	1.5 (4.5)
Zinc refining	31.6 (18.5)	3.5 (10.5)
Primary copper refining	25.2 (14.7)	0.4 (1.2)
Other non-ferrous metal refining	4.1 (2.4)	1.1 (3.3)
Iron and steel production	44.9 (26.3)	6.3 (18.9)
Coke production	3.9 (2.3)	0.5 (1.5)
Cement manufacturing	7.8 (4.6)	0.8 (2.4)
Waste incineration	8.4 (4.9)	4.6 (13.8)
Total	171.0 (100)	33.5 (100)

in non-ferrous metal production (zinc, copper, and others) were in part the result of the closing down of large pyrometallurgical smelters. Another significant trend was the increase in the relative share of emissions from incinerator wastes. In 1970 these emissions only accounted for about 5 per cent of the total; by 1988 they already accounted for 14 per cent of total emissions.

ATMOSPHERIC DEPOSITION IN THE RHINE BASIN. Table 3 lists total atmospheric deposition in the basin, and the calculated contributions to the deposition by countries inside and outside the basin. One may

Table 3 Atmospheric deposition of cadmium in the Rhine Basin – contribution by country, in (tons per year and percentages)[a]

Country	1970	1975	1980	1985	1988
Federal Republic of	55.3	41.2	23.6	13.9	11.7
Germany	(39.4)	(46.8)	(43.4)	(40.3)	(39.3)
France	8.5	5.7	3.9	2.4	1.8
	(6.1)	(6.4)	(7.1)	(6.9)	(6.2)
Netherlands	14.6	2.5	1.9	1.2	0.9
	(10.4)	(2.9)	(3.5)	(3.4)	(2.3)
Switzerland	1.4	1.1	0.9	0.7	0.5
	(1.0)	(1.2)	(1.7)	(1.9)	(1.6)
Luxembourg	1.2	0.8	0.4	0.2	0.2
	(0.9)	(0.9)	(0.7)	(0.6)	(0.6)
Belgium	35.5	15.3	7.1	3.6	3.5
	(25.3)	(17.4)	(13.1)	(10.5)	(11.8)
United Kingdom	6.0	3.8	2.5	1.7	1.6
	(4.3)	(4.3)	(4.6)	(5.0)	(5.3)
Italy	1.4	1.3	0.9	0.7	0.6
	(1.0)	(1.4)	(1.6)	(2.0)	(2.1)
German Democratic	5.1	5.4	4.8	3.9	3.5
Republic	(3.6)	(6.2)	(8.8)	(11.3)	(11.7)
Poland	4.2	5.3	4.1	3.1	2.8
	(3.0)	(6.1)	(7.5)	(9.0)	(9.4)
Czechoslovakia	0.9	1.0	0.8	0.6	0.6
	(0.7)	(1.1)	(1.5)	(1.9)	(2.0)
Soviet Union	1.8	2.1	1.8	1.4	1.2
	(1.3)	(2.4)	(3.4)	(4.0)	(3.9)
Other	4.2	2.7	1.6	1.1	0.9
	(3.0)	(3.0)	(3.0)	(3.1)	(3.1)
Total	140.3	87.9	54.4	34.6	29.8
	(100)	(100)	(100)	(100)	(100)

a. Percentages in parentheses.

133

observe that there was a 79 per cent decline in deposition over the 18-year period, which is obviously strongly related to the decline in emissions within the Rhine Basin, as well as in the Western European nations in close proximity to it. Deposition in the basin contributed by the formerly socialist countries of Eastern Europe also declined during this period, although the decrease was not nearly as large as in the Western European countries.

The share of total deposition attributed to the five Rhine Basin countries showed a slight but continuous decline, beginning in 1975, when they accounted for about 58 per cent of the total deposition, until 1988, when they comprised about 50 per cent. The share of total deposition from the three Western European nations Belgium, the United Kingdom, and Italy dropped by about 37 per cent between 1970 and 1988. In fact this trend was dominated by large decreases in Belgium's contribution, which was reduced from 25 per cent in 1970 to about 12 per cent in 1988. Belgium is one of the leading producers of zinc/cadmium in the world. Until the early 1970s, cadmium was produced solely at thermal zinc refineries with large atmospheric emissions of cadmium. During the 1970s, the thermal smelters were phased out, in some cases by closures and in others by a switch to electrolytic zinc/cadmium production with greatly reduced air emissions.

The opposite trend is shown for the Eastern European countries. Emissions from the German Democratic Republic, Poland, Czechoslovakia, and the Soviet Union contributed only about 9 per cent of the total deposition in 1970, but the share increased to about 27 per cent in 1988. This occurred not because emissions from Eastern Europe increased so much, but rather because total deposition in the basin decreased so rapidly, thus increasing the shares of contributions from Eastern Europe. These shifts in percentage shares reflect regional differences in efforts to limit air pollution. While Western European nations, beginning in the 1970s, were able to reduce their emissions mainly through the extensive application of air pollution control equipment, emissions in Eastern Europe remained largely unchanged during this time.

The estimated distribution of cadmium deposition among the three major land uses (agriculture, forests, and urban areas) in the basin is given in table 4. About 44 per cent of the total deposition goes to agricultural lands, 31 per cent to forests, and about 25 per cent to urban areas. Relative to their spatial coverage in the basin (about 15 per cent of the total land), urban areas receive *more* cadmium than

Table 4 Distribution of atmospheric deposition of cadmium in the Rhine Basin according to land use, in tons per year

Year	Agriculture	Forests	Urban areas	Total
1970	61.6	43.1	35.6	140.3
1975	38.0	26.6	23.2	87.8
1980	24.1	16.9	13.4	54.4
1985	15.4	10.7	8.5	34.6
1988	13.2	9.3	7.3	29.8

forests or agricultural lands. This is particularly so because most point sources are located in urban areas, and about 10 to 15 per cent of atmospheric emissions are deposited locally within a radius of up to 20 km from the point source. (As will be discussed below, urban atmospheric deposition constitutes a major source of diffuse cadmium loading to surface waters in the basin.)

Figure 6 shows the estimated annual loads of cadmium for the time periods 1973–1977, 1978–1982, and 1983–1987 at various monitoring stations on the Rhine and some of its tributaries. The station at Lobith is on the German-Dutch border. Since there is no net sedimentation of cadmium on an annual basis in the River Rhine[2] before the Netherlands border, the load represents the total inputs to the river from all upstream sources. The analysis was conducted by Behrendt and Boehme (1992) and is based on monitoring data provided by the International Commission for the Protection of the Rhine in Koblenz, Germany. The analysis also included a disaggregation of the total load into point and non-point (diffuse) loads by a methodology developed by Behrendt (1992).

One may observe the emergence of two major trends during this 14-year time period. Firstly, the cadmium load at Lobith decreased significantly over time, from 145 tons per year during the first period, to 96 tons per year in the second period, to 26 tons per year in the third period. Secondly, the relative contribution to the total load from point sources decreased from 82 per cent in the first period, to 79 per cent in the second period, to 42 per cent in the third period, while the contribution from diffuse sources increased from 18 to 21 to 58 per cent.

Aqueous emissions
INDUSTRIAL SOURCES. Table 5 lists estimated aqueous emissions of cadmium in the Rhine Basin during the 1970s and 1980s according to

135

Table 5 Aqueous emissions from industrial point sources in the Rhine Basin[a]

Activity	1970–72	1973–77	1978–82	1983–87	1988
Zinc production (primary and secondary)	74.0	63.9	40.4	2.8	0.1
Cadmium production (secondary)	3.0	3.0	1.2	0.0	0.0
Lead production (primary and secondary)	3.7	4.3	1.6	0.1	0.0
Coke production	10.7	9.5	4.3	1.0	0.9
Iron and steel production	21.4	21.4	19.5	8.5	2.1
Pigment manufacturing	13.4	7.0	1.3	0.3	0.1
Stabilizer manufacturing	1.3	0.6	0.0	0.0	0.0
Battery manufacturing	2.4	1.5	1.1	0.6	0.3
PVC manufacturing	1.4	1.2	0.9	0.4	0.1
Phosphate manufacturing	27.9	26.9	15.2	15.1	9.8
Total	159.2	139.3	85.5	28.8	13.4

Source: Elgersma et al., 1991.

a. The emission values listed here are somewhat higher than the values for point sources shown in figure 6 because not all the aqueous emissions within the basin end up in the River Rhine. Some are trapped in sediments of tributaries. Also, this table includes point source emissions in the Netherlands, while figure 6 includes emissions only up to the German-Netherlands border.)

industrial sector (Elgersma et al., 1991). The estimates for a given point source were calculated by multiplying plant production by an assumed emission factor. Historical emissions were derived from production statistics for the various industrial sectors, together with an appraisal of changes in emission factors over time owing to the implementation of regulatory standards and the adoption of water-pollution control technologies. The assumptions applied in these estimations were calibrated by comparison with the estimates shown in figure 6.

One may observe that during the 1970s primary and secondary production of zinc was by far the most important source of aqueous cadmium pollution, accounting for more than 45 per cent of all emissions. Most of the pollution from this sector can be attributed to two thermal zinc smelters that did not refine cadmium, but, rather, treated it as a disposable waste. Reductions in emissions from these plants in the late 1970s and 1980s were achieved in part by recycling the wastes to an electrolytic zinc/cadmium refinery located in the basin. Further reductions were achieved when one of the smelters ceased refining zinc ore in the early 1980s.

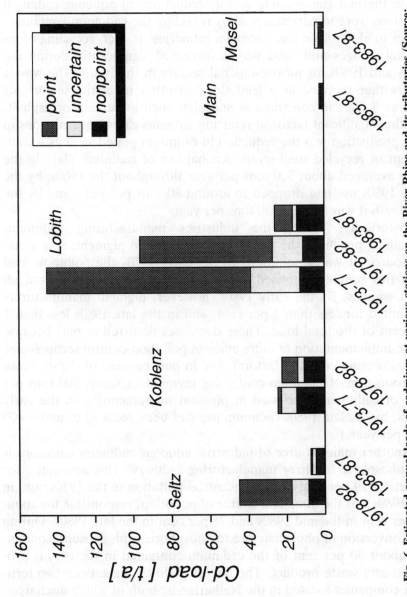

Fig. 6 Estimated annual loads of cadmium at various stations on the River Rhine and its tributaries (Source: Behrendt and Boehme, 1992)

The second-largest polluting sector was the iron and steel industry, including coke production, which accounted for between 20 and 33 per cent of the emissions during the 1970s and 1980s. As in the case of the thermal zinc-refining sector, reductions in aqueous cadmium emissions were in part achieved by recycling the cadmium-containing wastes to electrolytic zinc/cadmium refineries. In fact, recycling of industrial sludges and solid wastes increased significantly during the 1970s and 1980s for most industrial sectors in the basin. The wastes were either recycled as a feed stock to other industrial sectors, or used as a filler in construction materials such as cement or asphalt. Another significant factor in reducing aqueous cadmium emissions in steel production was the reduction in cadmium-plated steel as a component of recycled steel scrap. Annual use of cadmium plate in the basin averaged about 300 tons per year throughout the 1960s; by the early 1980s use had dropped to around 80 tons per year, and by the late 1980s it was less than 30 tons per year.

Historically, among the industries manufacturing cadmium-containing products, the production of cadmium pigments was a major source of water pollution. In the early 1970s the pollution load from this source comprised about 8 per cent of the total from all point sources. By the early 1980s, however, pigment manufacturers accounted for less than 2 per cent, and in the late 1980s less than 1 per cent of the total load. These decreases occurred in part because of the implementation of more efficient pollution-control technologies (thus lowering emission factors), and in part because of the decrease in production of cadmium-containing pigments. (Nearly 900 tons per year of cadmium were used in pigment manufacturing in the early 1970s; by the late 1980s cadmium use had been reduced to under 400 tons per year.)

Another major source of industrial aqueous cadmium emissions is the phosphate fertilizer manufacturing industry. This accounted for about 17–19 per cent of total industrial pollution in the 1970s, and in the 1980s was the dominant source of pollution, responsible for about 50 per cent in the mid 1980s and 75 per cent in the late 1980s. During the conversion of phosphate ore to phosphoric acid, gypsum, containing about 30 per cent of the cadmium contained in the ore, is produced as a waste product. The largest polluters have been two fertilizer companies located in the Netherlands, both of which discharged the gypsum directly to the Rhine. It is the intention of these companies, however, to limit their combined emissions to less than one ton by 1993 (Elgersma et al., 1991).

Table 6 Aqueous emissions of cadmium from municipal sewage: households and plating works, in tons per year

Country	1970	1975	1980	1985	1988
Federal Republic of Germany					
Households	1.0	0.8	0.7	0.6	0.5
Plating works	6.8	3.2	1.5	0.2	0.0
France					
Households	0.1	0.1	0.1	0.1	0.1
Plating works	1.8	1.3	0.7	0.1	0.0
Netherlands					
Households	0.4	0.3	0.3	0.2	0.2
Plating works	1.4	0.7	0.1	0.0	0.0
Switzerland					
Households	0.1	0.1	0.1	0.1	0.1
Plating works	0.0	0.0	0.0	0.0	0.0
Luxembourg					
Households	0.0	0.0	0.0	0.0	0.0
Plating works	1.5	0.7	0.1	0.0	0.0
Totals					
Households	1.6	1.3	1.2	1.0	0.9
Plating works	11.5	5.9	2.4	0.3	0.0
Grand total	13.1	7.2	3.6	1.3	0.9

EMISSIONS TO MUNICIPAL SEWERS. The two major point sources of cadmium emissions to municipal sewers are waste waters from households and small cadmium-plating operations. The contribution of these two sources during the 1970s and 1980s is shown in table 6. The table takes into account the evolution of primary and secondary sewage-treatment plants in the basin over this time period. In 1970, only about 33 per cent of the population in the basin was connected to secondary treatment plants. By the end of the 1980s, this percentage had increased to about 84 per cent (OECD, 1991). The introduction of secondary treatment has resulted in large reductions in aqueous cadmium emissions, since about 70 per cent of the cadmium inputs are trapped in digested sewage sludges generated during treatment, and about 30 per cent leave the plant as an aqueous effluent.

DeWaal Malefijt (1982), in a comprehensive study of the sources of heavy metals in sewers, estimates the cadmium load from household waste waters to be 45 mg Cd per inhabitant per year. About 20 mg is directly from human wastes, another 20 mg is from corrosion of sewer pipes, and 5 mg is present in the waste water from other sources.

As shown in table 6, aqueous plating wastes were a major source of cadmium to sewers in the 1970s. In the 1980s, however, cadmium emissions were virtually eliminated. One reason for this was that production of plate decreased by more than 80 per cent over this time period. Another reason was the implementation of strict regulations on emissions as required by the German Waste Regulation Act of 1978, and the EC Directive of 1983, which called for reduction in three steps up to 1986. To comply with these regulations, aqueous emission factors were reduced from about 0.0250 tons Cd/(ton plate produced) in 1970 to about 0.0003 tons Cd/(ton plate produced) by the mid 1980s. These laws caused a rapid restructuring in the plating industry, forcing small firms that could not afford to conform to these regulations to cease production of cadmium plate.

Solid wastes and application of agrochemicals

INDUSTRIAL AND MUNICIPAL WASTES. Solid wastes constitute by far the largest disposal pathway of cadmium in the Rhine Basin. The following are the four major source categories of wastes containing cadmium:
– Fly ash from coal combustion.
– Flue dusts and slag from iron and steel production.
– Wastes from manufacture of cadmium plate.
– Disposal of consumer and commercial wastes to landfills, including fly ash from incineration of consumer wastes.

It should be noted that thermal zinc smelting plants also generate substantial amounts of solid cadmium waste. Estimates of inputs and outputs of cadmium in the two thermal smelters in the Rhine Basin indicate, however, that in the 1970s their solid wastes were discharged directly to the river. This practice, in large part, accounts for the very large aqueous emissions from the smelters given in table 5. By the early 1980s one smelter stopped producing zinc altogether and the other recycled most of its solid wastes to an electrolytic smelter.

Table 7 provides estimates of cadmium contained in solid wastes disposed in the basin by sector. For most of the categories listed in the table, the tonnage of solid wastes declined appreciably over time. One exception was waste from coal combustion. The increase in this case resulted from increasing reductions in air emissions and concomitant increases in the collection of cadmium-containing dusts and particles. Most of this waste was fly ash from combustion of lignite

140

Table 7 Cadmium in solid wastes sent to landfills in the Rhine Basin, in tons per year and percentages

Activity	1970	1975	1980	1985	1988
Coal combustion					
Tons per year	9.9	12.6	15.6	17.9	19.2
Percentage of total	(1.2)	(1.6)	(2.0)	(3.6)	(5.0)
Iron and steel production					
Tons per year	68.3	67.0	51.9	18.5	14.0
Percentage of total	(8.6)	(8.4)	(6.8)	(3.7)	(3.7)
Cd plate manufacture					
Tons per year	50.4	39.6	26.8	18.2	11.5
Percentage of total	(6.4)	(5.0)	(3.5)	(3.6)	(3.0)
Municipal waste disposal					
Tons fly ash (incineration)[a]	100.2	112.3	124.3	89.8	53.2
Tons direct landfill[a]	340.8	338.0	335.1	252.7	169.5
Tons Cd plate[b]	216.0	223.3	205.2	100.2	112.0
Tons sewage sludge	4.1	3.7	3.1	1.9	1.7
Total tons per year	661.1	677.3	667.7	444.9	336.4
Percentage of total	(83.7)	(85.0)	(87.6)	(89.1)	(88.3)
Grand total					
Tons per year	789.7	796.5	762.0	499.5	381.1
Percentage of total	(100)	(100)	(100)	(100)	(100)

a. Sources of cadmium in fly ash and direct landfill are small consumer Ni-Cd batteries, and plastics containing cadmium pigments. Cadmium used as stabilizer in outdoor PVC window frames is not included here, since disposal of this source (in building demolition debris) is not likely to be mixed with municipal wastes.
b. Includes cadmium plate *not* recycled to steel refineries. Most cadmium plate, used in automobiles, machinery, and electronic equipment, is disposed of in repositories with other hard goods and generally not mixed with municipal wastes. They are listed here because of their importance as a source of cadmium emissions.

coal. With regard to fly ash generated from combustion of hard coal, recycling became increasingly important. In 1970, about 50 per cent of the fly ash was recycled. The percentage increased to about 65 per cent in 1980 and about 90 per cent in 1990 (Risse et al., 1991).

Wastes from cadmium plate manufacturing decreased by nearly 80 per cent, mostly because of large reductions in production, which declined from nearly 600 tons in 1970 to about 280 tons in 1980 and about 100 tons in the late 1980s. About half of the production was used in the basin, with the balance being exported. Thus, disposal of cadmium plate to municipal landfills also decreased substantially. The declining trend not only reduced the volume of cadmium waste in plate manufacturing and municipal wastes: as was the case for

141

aqueous cadmium emissions, it also resulted in a substantial reduction of cadmium in solid wastes from steel production.

Cadmium-coated scrap steel, although constituting only a small fraction of the total scrap, has been identified as the major source of cadmium pollution in steel production (Hutton, 1982). Assuming a ten-year lifetime of steel products coated with cadmium plate, and a recycling rate of about 40 per cent, it is estimated that about 125 tons of cadmium per year entered steel production from inputs of cadmium-coated scrap in the 1970s. By the late 1980s, however, the inputs had decreased to around 50 tons per year. Two other factors contributing to the decline of cadmium in steel wastes were a 20 per cent reduction in steel production and a significant increase in the recycling of cadmium-containing flue dusts and slags generated in production processes.

Municipal wastes landfilled in 1988, including fly ash from municipal incinerators, were about half of the quantity landfilled in 1970. These reductions occurred mainly because of large reductions in the consumption of cadmium-containing products over this time period. Of particular importance was the drastic decrease in the use of cadmium in pigmented plastics, formerly the major source of cadmium in domestic wastes (Schulte-Schrepping, 1981). Use of cadmium pigments in the basin in 1988 (about 200 tons) was less than half the use in 1970 (about 440 tons). This trend was somewhat offset, however, by the increased use of small, sealed consumer Ni-Cd batteries, the cadmium content of which increased from less than 20 tons in 1970 to about 125 tons in the late 1980s.

Recycling of solid wastes ("secondary materials") in the Rhine Basin has emerged as the major alternative to land disposal and incineration. The evolution in recycling noted above for fly ash from hard-coal combustion is typical for other industrial solid wastes as well. Fly ash from coal combustion and slags from iron and steel production are used as feed stocks in the manufacture of bricks, cement, concrete, and asphalt road foundation. Flue dusts from iron and steel production and thermal zinc refining are recycled as inputs to non-ferrous electrolytic metal refineries.

Recycling serves three major purposes. First, it replaces primary materials, thus conserving scarce resources. Secondly, it reduces the volume of solid wastes, thus reducing the amount of land that otherwise would have to be set aside for landfills. Thirdly, and most important from the environmental perspective, recycling the wastes into new products that effectively immobilize the cadmium may reduce the potential availability of leachable cadmium to the environment.

Some research has been conducted for testing the leaching behaviour of recycled products (Goumans et al., 1991). It appears that the recycling option may offer a viable alternative for managing cadmium-containing solid wastes, although more research is needed to determine the long-term leaching behaviour (30 or more years) of recycled products.

An important factor that needs to be taken into account when assessing the environmental impacts of disposed solid wastes is the potential for the chemical in question to leach from the waste material in which it is embodied. The concentration of the toxic material in the waste is *not* a good index for such an assessment, since it is not necessarily proportional to the fraction of toxic material susceptible to leaching. Very few data are available that allow for assessment and comparison of the long-term "leaching potentials" of different solid wastes under field conditions. There is, however, information from standardized laboratory leaching tests which provide estimates of leaching of heavy metals from waste materials under varying chemical conditions (Van der Sloot, 1991). The waste material is ground to a specified particle size and then subjected to an acidic solution (pH 4) at a liquid/solid ratio of 100. The amount of heavy metal leached under these conditions is defined as the "maximum availability," which refers to the total leaching that may occur over a period of 30 to 50 years.

Table 8 lists values of maximum availability of cadmium in the four major categories of cadmium-containing wastes. The table illustrates the wide variation in maximum availability among the various kinds of wastes. There is, for example, a striking difference between fly ash from coal combustion, with a maximum cadmium availability of 10 per cent, and fly ash from incineration of municipal waste, with a maximum availability of 90 per cent. The reason for the difference is the presence of chlorine in municipal wastes (from plastics and other consumer products), and the lack of chlorine in coal (Van der Sloot, 1991). During incineration the chlorine forms complexes with cadmium that are appreciably soluble in water.

Table 8 probably overestimates somewhat the availability of cadmium under field conditions. This is particularly true of recent decades, during which solid wastes in the Rhine Basin have been increasingly disposed of in landfills engineered to restrict their mo-

143

Table 8 Estimated maximum availability of cadmium in various solid wastes (over 30- to 50-year time period)

Activity generating waste/ type of waste	Maximum availability of cadmium in waste (%)
Coal combustion	
Fly ash	10[a,b]
Iron and steel production	
Flue dust	50[b]
Slag	100[b]
Cadmium plate manufacturing	
Plating residues	100[c]
Municipal waste disposal	
Incineration	
Fly ash	90[b]
Bottom ash	25[b]
Direct landfill	
Pigments (in plastics)	1[c]
Pigments (surface coatings)	20[c]
PVC	1[c]
Batteries	30[c]
Cadmium plate	90[c]
Sewage sludge	90[c]

a. Van der Sloot et al., 1985.
b. Versluijs et al., 1990.
c. IIASA, 1992.

bilization by controlling the chemical conditions within the waste site, by the use of impermeable linings, and by treatment of drainage waters.

Table 9 provides an estimate of the availability of cadmium from solid wastes, taking into account the introduction of modern, safer landfills. For the new industrial landfills, it was assumed that the availability of industrial wastes was only 10 per cent of the maximum availability given in table 8. For municipal landfills, however, the maximum availability was assumed, even for new landfills. This assumption appears justifiable because the pH of wastes in municipal landfills is typically in the range of 4 to 5. (The maximum availability is based on leaching at pH = 4.) Moreover, municipal wastes contain high concentrations of organic acids which can form complexes with heavy metals and increase their mobility.

Two trends are evident from table 9. Firstly, there has been a better than 50 per cent reduction in the availability of cadmium. Secondly, municipal waste disposal has been the major source of available

Table 9 Estimated actual availability of cadmium contained in solid wastes generated in the Rhine Basin, in tons per year[a]

Activity	1970	1975	1980	1985	1988
Coal combustion					
Tons per year	1.0	1.1	1.1	0.9	0.7
Percentage of total	(0.2)	(0.3)	(0.3)	(0.4)	(0.4)
Iron and steel production					
Tons per year	52.4	43.3	27.0	6.5	3.5
Percentage of total	(12.7)	(10.7)	(7.4)	(3.1)	(2.0)
Cd plate manufacture					
Tons per year	50.4	33.1	18.0	8.0	3.5
Percentage of total	(12.2)	(8.2)	(4.9)	(3.8)	(2.0)
Municipal waste disposal					
Tons incineration (fly ash)	84.4	95.3	106.0	77.1	45.8
Tons direct landfill	27.4	25.9	24.5	25.7	22.1
Tons Cd plate	194.4	201.0	184.7	90.5	100.8
Tons sewage sludge	3.7	3.3	2.8	1.7	1.5
Total tons per year	309.9	325.5	318.0	195.0	170.2
Percentage of total	(74.9)	(80.8)	(87.3)	(92.7)	(95.7)
Grand total					
Tons per year	413.7	403.0	364.1	210.4	177.9
Percentage of total	(100)	(100)	(100)	(100)	(100)

a. Availability for a selected year is defined as the total amount of cadmium that may be leached to the environment over a 30- to 50-year period after the initial disposal.

cadmium, and its share of the total available cadmium has increased over time, from about 75 per cent in 1970 to about 96 per cent in 1988.

The data given in table 9 assume that the new landfills function without leaks or mechanical failures. In actuality this is not always the case, as leaks from presumably safe landfills have been reported in the literature (Hjelmar et al., 1988). Moreover, in the long term (more than 30 years) even correctly functioning safe landfills may begin to leak (Foerstner, 1991), resulting in emissions of toxic materials accumulated over previous decades. In addition, complex chemical reactions can occur in landfills, resulting in the generation, *in situ*, of toxic chemicals such as benzene, phenols, and vinyl chloride (Fleming, 1992). Hence, constructing the "ideal landfill" that is completely safe for current and future generations is a daunting, if not impossible, task. Clearly, more research is required to understand the complex chemistry of landfills leading to the generation and mobilization

145

Table 10 Comparison of annual and cumulative annual availability of cadmium in solid wastes in the Rhine Basin, in tons per year

Year	1970	1975	1980	1985	1988
Annual availability	13.8	13.4	12.1	7.0	5.9
Cumulative annual availability	218.0	267.8	307.7	323.1	320.5

of toxic chemicals, and more thought must be given to engineering design for containing the chemicals over the long term.

As noted earlier, *availability* corresponds to the fraction of heavy metals that may leach from the solid waste over a 30- to 50-year time period. An important consequence of this long-term leaching behaviour is that the waste may continue to be a source of toxic emissions for decades after it is deposited on the land. Thus, when assessing the total availability of a heavy metal for a given year, one must consider the *cumulative* availability of wastes deposited over the previous 30 to 50 years. Accounting for historical wastes is particularly important because until the 1970s most solid wastes were dumped on the land without precautions being taken to ensure their containment.

Table 10 compares the estimated annual availability, obtained by dividing the sums given in table 9 by 30, with the estimated cumulative availability, obtained by the following calculation for a given year = x:

$$i = x$$

Cumulative availability (year = x) = S (availability)/30

$$i = x - 30$$

Table 10 reveals a 15-year time-lag between the year with maximum annual availability (1970) and the year of the maximum cumulative availability (1985). This result demonstrates the importance of considering the long-term cumulative effects of toxic chemicals in the environment. It suggests that measures for reducing solid wastes may not always lead to immediate improvements because of the legacy of toxic materials deposited in past decades that are still environmentally active. (For a more detailed discussion of the impacts of cumulative chemical inputs, see Stigliani, 1988.)

Table 11 Inputs and outputs of cadmium to agricultural soils, in tons per year

Source	1970	1975	1980	1985	1988
Atmospheric deposition	+61.6	+38.0	+24.1	+15.4	+13.2
Phosphate fertilizer	+47.7	+43.0	+43.7	+38.0	+35.9
Sewage sludge	+2.2	+2.3	+1.8	+1.1	+1.0
Plant uptake	−2.2	−2.7	−3.3	−4.0	−4.1
Run-off	−6.8	−4.2	−2.6	−1.7	−1.4
Erosion	−2.0	−2.1	−2.3	−2.3	−2.4
Net input	+100.5	+74.3	+61.4	+46.5	+42.2

APPLICATION OF AGROCHEMICALS. Three major inputs of cadmium to agricultural lands are via atmospheric deposition, application of phosphate fertilizer, and the spreading of sewage sludge. Once the cadmium is in the soil, it can be transported out of the soil by plant uptake, surface run-off, and erosion. The net accumulation of cadmium in agricultural soils can be determined by accounting for inputs and outputs, as shown in table 11.

In the Rhine Basin, net cadmium inputs to the soil have been reduced by more than 50 per cent between the early 1970s and the late 1980s. The most significant reduction has been in atmospheric deposition, which decreased by nearly 50 tons per year (80 per cent) over this time period. In addition, there were more moderate reductions in inputs from phosphate fertilizer (25 per cent reduction) and sewage sludge (about 50 per cent reduction). Whereas atmospheric deposition was the largest source of cadmium to agricultural lands in 1970, by the mid-1970s phosphate fertilizer became the dominant source. By the late 1980s it accounted for more than 70 per cent of the total inputs.

Plant uptake of cadmium increased mainly because of increases in crop yields over the 18-year period. (The yield of cereal crops in the basin is estimated to have increased from about 2.7 tons per year in 1970 to about 5.6 tons per year in the late 1980s; WRI, 1988.) Surface run-off of cadmium decreased because of decreases in the concentration of cadmium in wet deposition. Erosion of cadmium increased slightly, reflecting the slow increase in the total soil cadmium content over time.

An important question is whether the cumulative cadmium inputs to agricultural soils are causing significant increases in the soil con-

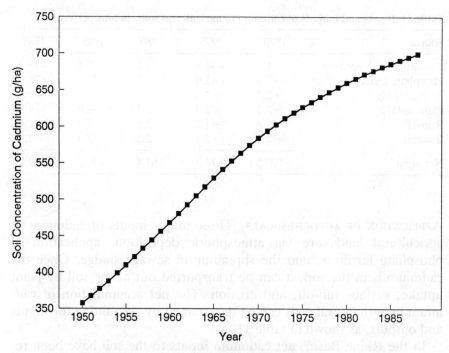

Fig. 7 Estimated build-up of cadmium concentration in agricultural soils in the Rhine Basin, 1950–1988 (Source: Stigliani and Jaffe, 1992)

centrations of cadmium above background levels, and, if so, whether these increases could lead to unacceptably high levels of cadmium in the crops grown in the basin. With this question in mind, the net inputs of cadmium to agricultural soils since 1950 were estimated, using available information on historical phosphate use (Behrendt, 1988) and calculating atmospheric deposition.[3] The net inputs were converted into soil concentration units, and the calculated increase in concentration was plotted over time as shown in figure 7. Under the assumptions of the model, the average cadmium concentration in agricultural soils has risen from approximately 360 g/ha in 1950 to about 700 g/ha in 1988, corresponding to an increase of 94 per cent in the 38-year period. (A later section discusses the possible implications of this increase for crop uptake of cadmium and human health.)

Eventually, a steady state will be reached between inputs and outputs, and soil concentrations of cadmium will level off. Hutton (1982) has calculated a likely steady state concentration for the EC agricultural lands to be between 1,400 g/ha and 2,900 g/ha, for annual inputs of 8 g/ha of cadmium. If this value pertains to the Rhine Basin as well, then the current concentrations are still far from equilibrium, and soil concentrations will continue to rise well into the next century if current annual inputs continue in the future.

Diffuse sources of aqueous emissions

Diffuse sources of emissions may be differentiated from point sources in at least three ways. First, the emissions occur at random, intermittent intervals; secondly, emissions can vary by several orders of magnitude from one event to another; and, thirdly, the emissions are usually closely related to meteorological variables such as precipitation. The load of diffuse sources to the River Rhine was estimated in two ways. The analysis of extensive river-monitoring data by Behrendt and Boehme (1992) provided annual estimates of the diffuse load during the 1970s and 1980s. Their results were shown graphically in figure 6. As a second approach, annual loads from the sources of diffuse emissions were estimated independently of the monitoring data. The results of the two approaches were then compared.

As was shown in figure 2, in urban areas four major sources of diffuse emissions have been identified: atmospheric deposition, corrosion, traffic in paved areas, and atmospheric deposition and landfills in unpaved areas.

Given that most of the population in the Rhine Basin is concentrated close to the river or its tributaries, it may be expected that a relatively high percentage of the cadmium deposited from these sources will enter the river. Atmospheric deposition (wet and dry) on paved surfaces accumulates as street dust, is washed off during storm events, and is conducted to the river through storm sewers or municipal sewage-treatment plants. Cadmium emissions from corrosion occur mainly via the corrosion of galvanized zinc, in which cadmium is present as an unwanted impurity. The corroded material accumulates in street dust and is washed out through the same pathway as atmospheric deposition. The main source of cadmium from traffic is automobile tyres. Zinc oxide is used in tyre manufacturing, and a small fraction of cadmium is present with the zinc as an impurity. The fragments from tyre wear collect in street dusts and are transported to surface waters along with other cadmium dusts.

Unpaved urban areas have been the recipient of high loads of cadmium from both short-range and long-range atmospheric deposition. The cumulative load to all unpaved urban soils over the period 1950–1988 is calculated at about 830 tons. In addition, solid waste landfills are concentrated in unpaved urban areas. As was shown in table 10, the cumulative leaching potential during the 1970s and 1980s is estimated to have been between 200 and 300 tons of cadmium per year. During storm events, cadmium stored in unpaved areas may be transported horizontally by surface run-off or vertically through seepage to ground waters, where it may be transported to the river via subsurface flow. Leaching from landfills is more problematic for the older sites, which were not constructed to contain the wastes. In the case of the new, safer landfills, drainage waters are collected and treated at municipal sewage treatment plants. Even so, the plant may only remove 50–70 per cent of the cadmium. The balance of the cadmium leaves the plant in the aqueous effluent.

There are three major sources of diffuse emissions from agricultural areas. One is surface run-off during heavy storm events. It is estimated that 10 per cent of the river flow is contributed by such run-off. Cadmium, as wet deposition, is deposited during the storm and enters the river as a component of run-off. The second source is erosion of a thin layer of the surface soil. Cadmium contained in the layer is transported with the eroded soil. The third source is through subsurface groundwater flow. In this case, the source of the cadmium is from natural geological deposits. Most of the cadmium enters the river during heavy storm events, when run-off and erosion are accelerated.

Table 12 gives estimates of the diffuse loads of cadmium to the River Rhine from urban and agricultural areas during the 1970s and 1980s. The total load decreased by more than 60 per cent during the two decades. The most important factor determining this trend was the reduction in atmospheric emissions, which led directly to reductions of atmospheric cadmium inputs to paved urban surfaces and agricultural run-off. Moreover, the reduction of SO_2 concentrations in urban centres greatly reduced the corrosion rate of galvanized zinc and its cadmium impurity (Hrehoruk et al., 1992).

During the early 1970s, paved urban areas are estimated to have been the most important source of diffuse cadmium emissions, responsible for more than 40 per cent of the total load. In subsequent years this share declined sharply – 36 per cent in 1975, 27 per cent in 1980, 22 per cent in 1985, and 20 per cent in 1988. In addition to reductions in air emissions, another mitigating factor was the reduction in the concentration of cadmium impurity in zinc owing to the increase in the production of zinc from electrolytic refineries. The latter produce a much purer zinc than do the thermal refineries. Despite

Table 12 Diffuse sources of aqueous emissions of cadmium from urban and agricultural areas, in tons per year

Source	1970	1975	1980	1985	1988
Urban areas					
Paved areas					
Atmospheric					
deposition	9.9	6.0	3.2	2.0	1.6
Corrosion	4.1	3.0	1.6	0.7	0.5
Traffic	0.4	0.4	0.5	0.6	0.6
Unpaved areas					
Run-off and leaching[a]	8.5	7.3	6.2	4.8	3.6
Agricultural areas					
Run-off	6.8	4.2	2.6	1.7	1.4
Erosion	2.0	2.1	2.3	2.3	2.4
Groundwater	3.2	3.2	3.2	3.2	3.2
Total calculated diffuse					
emissions	34.9	26.2	19.6	15.3	13.3
Estimates of Behrendt					
and Boehme (1992)		73–77	78–82	83–87	
Range		12.7–38.5	11.2–27.1	14.4–16.4	
Mean		26.2	19.6	15.3	

a. Determined as difference between sum of paved and agricultural areas and mean values determined by Behrendt and Boehme (1992).

this factor, cadmium emissions from traffic increased slightly because of the large increase in traffic in the 1970s and 1980s.

The estimated cadmium loads from unpaved surfaces are highly uncertain because no data are available for making direct calculations. Nevertheless, the estimates appear to be reasonable. As noted by Stigliani and Jaffe (1992), the vertical leaching velocity of cadmium is very much influenced by soil acidity. At a pH of 6, cadmium leaches at a rate of about 0.3 cm/yr. The rate increases to about 1.2 cm/yr at a pH of 5, and about 5.7 cm/yr at a pH of 4. Given that urban soils have received high loads of acidic deposition for many decades, a substantial fraction probably have pH values of between 4 and 5. Thus, it is most likely that shallow urban groundwaters have been contaminated to some degree, and that transport of these groundwaters to the Rhine is a significant source of cadmium pollution in the river.

Assuming that half of the cadmium originates from the cumulative loading of atmospheric deposition on unpaved areas and half from cadmium-containing solid wastes, each source contributed between 2 and 4 tons/yr. With respect to solid wastes, this amounts to about 1 per cent of the total cumulative annual availability given in table 10. The fact that the load from unpaved areas appears to be decreasing may be due to both reduced atmospheric deposition of cadmium and better containment of solid wastes in new landfills. Because of the cadmium already present in unpaved urban soils, however, it is possible that leaching to the River Rhine will continue for decades into the future.

With regard to agricultural soils, run-off of cadmium decreased because of reduced cadmium concentrations in wet deposition. Erosion of cadmium increased slightly, because the soil concentration of cadmium continued to increase over this time period, albeit at a slower rate than in previous decades. Cadmium inputs from groundwaters were assumed to be constant, because their origin is from natural geochemical sources unaffected by anthropogenic activities.

Step 3: Construction of a basin-wide pollution model for assessment of proposed emission reduction polices, environmental impacts, or other issues related to the chemical in question (in our case, cadmium)

The result of completion of steps 1 and 2 is a basin-wide pollution model which provides an enhanced understanding of the "industrial metabolism" of cadmium in the Rhine Basin. Inputs and outputs have been quantified over time, and changing trends in the sources of pollution have been identified. The pathways by which cadmium moves from its introduction into the economy of the Rhine Basin to its final destination in the environment have been delineated to the extent possible from available data.

Impacts of cumulative loading
One use of the model is to determine the long-term environmental impacts of the cumulative loading of toxic chemicals in the soils and sediments of the Rhine Basin. From 1950 to 1988, it is estimated that cumulative inputs of cadmium in unpaved urban areas, agricultural lands, and forests in the basin have been 830 tons, nearly 4,000 tons, and about 1,500 tons, respectively. Stigliani and Jaffe (1992) have examined the effects of cadmium accumulation in agricultural soils. According to this research, crop lands are particularly vulnerable to cumulative loading for two reasons. First, inputs of toxic materials from application of agrochemicals and atmospheric deposition have

Table 13 Estimated average intake of cadmium (μg/week) at different values of pH in agricultural soils in the Rhine Basin

Year	pH = 6.0	pH = 5.5	pH = 5.0
1960	140	300	660
1970	200	440	940
1980	230	500	1090

Source: Stigliani and Jaffe, 1992.

been historically high. Secondly, the pH of the soils has been artificially maintained at around 6 by the addition of lime. Soils at a pH of 6 have a much higher capacity to adsorb heavy metals and pesticides than do more acid soils. Thus, in contrast to the situation for acidified urban soils in which cadmium is rapidly leached out, the metal essentially accumulates in agricultural soils. (The history of this accumulation was discussed previously with regard to figure 7.)

The next step in the analysis is to estimate the impact of the increased soil concentrations on plant uptake and food consumption. These aspects are discussed in detail in Stigliani and Jaffe (1992). Table 13 presents estimates of the average cadmium intake in mg/week per capita in the Rhine Basin, assuming that *all* of the diet is obtained from food grown in the basin. The World Health Organization (WHO) recommends that maximum cadmium intake should not exceed 400 to 500 mg/week. The table shows that cadmium intake is still below the recommended maximum, but *only* under the condition that the pH of the soils is maintained at 6 or above. If the pH were to shift from 6 to 5.5 (more acid), the increased uptake of cadmium in the food supply could lead to levels that exceed the WHO-recommended threshold standard for human consumption. Such a shift is quite feasible, particularly in areas affected by acid deposition and given the fact that lime is often not applied continuously on an annual basis.

The most important point of the analysis is that in 1960 a shift to a soil pH level of 5.5 would have resulted in consumption levels still well below the WHO standard. Thus, the major impact of the cumulative loading of cadmium in agricultural soils since 1950 has been a loss of resilience with respect to cadmium uptake during random fluctuations in pH. The safe functioning of the agricultural system now requires tighter constraints on the range over which such fluctuations may occur.

153

Testing the effectiveness of proposed pollution reduction policies
One important application of the "industrial metabolism" approach
is testing possible pollution-reduction strategies within the context of
systems analysis. Because this approach is based on mass balance,
policies that do not reduce overall emissions but, rather, merely shift
them from one pollution pathway to another can be readily exposed.
By way of example, a policy for reducing inputs of cadmium to the
environment via the banning of cadmium-containing products will be
discussed here. (Although no such ban is yet in effect, perhaps the
anticipation that it will be implemented has already resulted in a
marked decline, since the early 1980s, in the production and use of all
cadmium-containing products, with the exception of Ni-Cd batteries.)

Let us assume that the policy under consideration would be the
banning of all cadmium products in the Rhine Basin except for Ni-Cd
batteries, for which there is a growing market and for which suitable
substitutes have not yet been developed. Furthermore, it is proposed
that by the late 1990s at least 50 per cent of the small sealed consumer Ni-Cd batteries entering the domestic disposal stream will be recycled. To what extent would this policy serve the purpose of reducing
cadmium emissions?

The first step in the analysis is to determine the flow in the production, use, and disposal of cadmium products in the basin. Figure 8 de-
picts this flow for the mid-1980s.[4] Also shown are the emissions of
cadmium to air, water, and solid wastes. The numbers in brackets
beside the solid wastes are the estimated availabilities, as previously
defined. The sum of the availabilities of cadmium provides an appro-
ximate index by which the effectiveness of control strategies can
be appraised. In the mid-1980s, this sum was 204 tons, with waste
disposal the largest contributor at 195 tons.

Figure 9 is a flow diagram depicting the situation in the late 1990s,
assuming that the proposed mitigation strategy has been implemented. It is assumed that the use of small, sealed consumer batteries will double relative to the mid-1980s. This represents a
moderately reduced growth rate relative to the 1980s, when consumer
use doubled within ten years.

One positive effect of the product ban would be a drastic decrease
in availability from solid waste disposal, from 195 tons in the mid-
1980s to 49 tons in the late 1990s. A problem still remains, however,
because the supply of cadmium entering the basin is essentially in-
elastic, since it is a by-product of zinc production. The production of
zinc in the basin has been quite stable, averaging about 185,000 tons

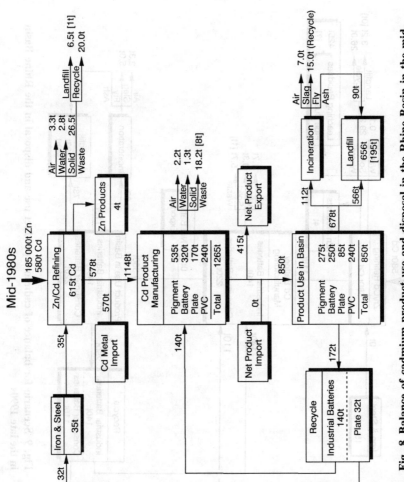

Fig. 8 Balance of cadmium product use and disposal in the Rhine Basin in the mid-1980s

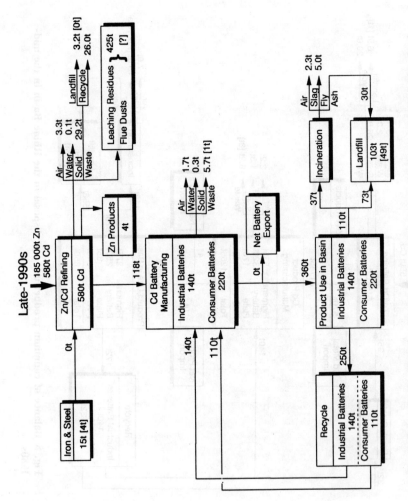

Fig. 9 Scenario for balance of cadmium product use and disposal in the Rhine Basin in the late 1990s

per year since the late 1960s. It is not likely that there will be any drastic reductions or increases in zinc production in the late 1990s. Thus, it seems reasonable to assume that about 600 tons of cadmium will be separated from zinc at the refineries. In contrast to the mid-1980s, with an import of 570 tons of cadmium metal, according to the scenario only 118 tons of cadmium will be required for battery production, resulting in a surplus of about 425 tons of cadmium at the zinc refineries. These will be in the form of flue dusts at the thermal refinery and leaching residues at the electrolytic refinery. There are no data on the availabilities of cadmium in these wastes. It appears that they may be considerable, however, since cadmium in most solid wastes is appreciably soluble in acids, as well as in the presence of commonly occurring complexing agents such as ammonia (Rauhut, 1978b). In recent decades the flue dusts from the thermal smelter have been sent to the electrolytic refinery for processing into cadmium metal. (As noted earlier in the discussion, until the late 1970s these flue dusts were discharged into the Rhine, and constituted the largest source of water pollution.) About 95 per cent of the cadmium in the leaching residues generated at the electrolytic refinery were refined to cadmium metal in the mid-1980s. Moreover, the iron and steel industry sent solid wastes containing about 35 tons of cadmium to the electrolytic refinery.

Under the scenario shown in figure 9, there will be a very low demand for recycled cadmium-containing wastes from the metallurgical industries. EC regulations regarding the disposal of solid wastes will require that they be stabilized, i.e. they must be treated to ensure a low cadmium availability. Stabilization of wastes is expensive and not always effective in reducing availability (Kosson et al., 1991). So, the ultimate effect of banning cadmium products and recycling 50 per cent of the disposed consumer batteries may be to shift the pollution load from the product disposal phase to the zinc/cadmium production phase. This does not imply that banning cadmium-containing products is not a wise strategy; rather, it indicates that if such a ban were to be implemented, special provisions would have to be made for the safe handling of surplus cadmium wastes generated at the zinc refineries!

One possible option that would reduce the volume of surplus cadmium at the refinery would be to allow the production and use of cadmium-containing products with inherently low availability for leaching. The other option, depositing the cadmium-containing refinery wastes in safely contained landfills, has other associated risks,

157

as noted above. What is certain is that as long as zinc is produced in the Rhine Basin, cadmium will be introduced as either a desired or an unwanted by-product.

Conclusions

Analysis of the chemical "metabolism" of modern industrialized societies is very complex, requiring a sophisticated systems approach. Nevertheless, studies tracking the flow of toxic materials through the economy and into the environment can be an indispensable tool for environmental management.

Studies of the Rhine Basin are of particular interest because the region has passed through the phase in which high productivity is associated with correspondingly high levels of polluting emissions, into a phase where production has been partially decoupled from pollution. Understanding the societal, economic, and technological driving forces that stimulated this transition could provide a blueprint for the clean-up of river basins that are currently trapped in the coupled production-pollution syndrome – and there are many of them in the world today. The insights provided by our study, together with studies of the industrial metabolism of highly polluted regions such as Eastern Europe, could provide a basis for the rational prioritization of actions required for restoring the environment to an acceptable level.

Furthermore, the Rhine Basin study has demonstrated that even regions in a more advanced stage of environmental management could benefit from such studies. Indeed, "input management" (e.g. Odum, 1989), rather than "fire brigade actions," will be of increasing importance in formulating action alternatives that are better integrated and more directed toward the goals of long-term economic and ecological sustainability.

Finally, it should be noted that one of the most useful functions of soils and sediments is their ability to serve as a "sink" for the retention of toxic chemicals. This sink, however, usually has a finite sorption capacity, the size of which is governed by fundamental chemical properties such as pH, organic matter content, etc. So far, hardly any information is available regarding the long-term, broad-scale cumulative loadings of toxic chemicals into the environmental sinks, and on whether, and under what conditions, the sorption capacity might be transgressed beyond a threshold value considered safe for the environment and for human health. We believe that the analysis presented in this chapter illustrates the usefulness of our approach in evaluating long-term environmental impacts.

Notes

1. The material presented in this chapter is taken from a larger ongoing study being conducted at the International Institute for Applied Systems Analysis (IIASA) at Laxenburg, Austria. Both authors are staff members. IIASA's Rhine Basin Study includes analysis of seven chemicals: cadmium (Cd), lead (Pb), zinc (Zn), nitrogen (N), phosphorus (P), lindane, and polycyclic chlorinated biphenyls (PCBs). The time horizon is the period from 1950 to 2010. All sources of pollution are considered, including atmospheric and aquatic emissions from point sources, generation of industrial and municipal solid wastes, application of agrochemicals, sewage effluents, corrosion of materials, and traffic-related emissions. The major output of the study will be basin-wide deposition maps portrayed in decade time slices for each chemical. Estimated inputs of pollutants to the river from point sources and terrestrial run-off are being computed with the assistance of the Research Centre for Water Resources Development (VITUKI), Budapest, Hungary. These estimates have been calibrated in accordance with the statistical analysis of Behrendt and Boehme (1992), by which point and diffuse loads to the river can be calculated from river-monitoring data. In-stream transport and ecological effects in the Dutch Delta are being modelled by scientists from the National Institute for Public Health and Environmental Protection (RIVM) in Bilthoven, Netherlands, and Delft Hydraulics, in Delft, Netherlands. Major funding for the project has been provided by RIVM.
2. This is not so for the tributaries of the Rhine, however, where significant sedimentation does occur.
3. Historical atmospheric deposition was calculated from the TRACE 2 model (Alcamo et al., 1992), using historical emissions as input. Emissions were estimated from historical levels of production for the major industrial sectors and historical trends in emission factors for these sectors as determined by Pacyna (1991).
4. Disposal, as indicated in figures 8 and 9, is actually the "disposal commitment" for the given years. Because the life cycle of cadmium-containing products varies from a few years (for cadmium pigments) to several decades (for cadmium in PVC), the numbers in the figures represent the disposal over years to decades in the future, from the products that entered the industrial economy in the years indicated.

References

Alcamo, J., J. Bartnicki, K. Olendrzynski, and J. Pacyna. 1992. "Computing Heavy Metals in Europe's Atmosphere: Part I. Model Development and Testing." (Submitted to *Atmospheric Environment*.)

Ayres, R. U., L. W. Ayres, J. A. Tarr, and R. C. Widgery. 1988. "An Historical Reconstruction of Major Pollutant Levels in the Hudson-Raritan Basin: 1880–1980." NOAA Tech. Memo. NOS OMA 43. Rockville, Md.: National Oceanic and Atmospheric Administration, US Department of Commerce. 3 vols.

Ayres, R. U., and S. R. Rod. 1986. "Patterns and Pollution in the Hudson-Raritan Basin." *Environment* 28: 14–20, 39–43.

Balzer, D., and A. Rauhut. 1987. "Verbrauch und Verbleib von Cadmium und seiner Verbindungen in der Bundesrepublik Deutschland (1981–1983)." LGA-Rundschau 87-3, Nürnberg.

William M. Stigliani and Stefan Anderberg

Behrendt, H. 1988. *Changes in Nonpoint Nutrient Loading into European Fresh-waters: Trends and Consequences since 1950 and Not-impossible Changes until 2080.* Laxenburg, Austria: International Institute for Applied Systems Analysis. (WP-88-026.)

———. 1992. "Estimation of Point and Diffuse Loads of Pollutants Using the Dependencies of Load and Concentration on Discharge." (In preparation.)

Behrendt, H., and M. Boehme, 1992. *Point and Diffuse Loads of Selected Pollutants in the River Rhine and Its Main Tributaries.* Research report. Laxenburg, Austria: International Institute for Applied Systems Analysis.

Boehm E., and K. Schaefers. 1990. "Massnahmen zur Minderung des Cadmiumeintrags in die Umwelt." Prepared by Fraunhofer-Institut für Systemtechnik und Innovationsforschung für Bund/Länderausschuss Umweltchemikalien (BLAU). Karlsruhe.

Carter, V. E. 1977. *Metallic Coatings for Corrosion Control.* London: Butterworth, pp. 111–112.

DeWaal Malefijt, A. J. W. 1982. "Cadmium, chroom, koper, lood, nikkel en zink in huishoudelijk afvalwater en in af te voeren neerslag." H_2O 15: 355–361.

ECE (Economic Commission for Europe, Geneva, Switzerland). 1984. *Air Pollution Studies 1. Air-borne Sulphur Pollution, Effects and Control.* Report within framework of Convention on Long-range Transport of Air Pollution. New York: United Nations.

Elgersma, F., B. S. Anderberg, and W. M. Stigliani. 1991. *Aqueous Emission Factors for the Industrial Discharge of Cadmium in the Rhine River Basin in the Period 1970–1990: An Inventory.* Laxenburg, Austria: International Institute for Applied Systems Analysis.

Fleming, G., ed. 1992. "Waste and Spoils: Examples of Chemical Time Bombs." Report of expert meeting of Land Disposal and Chemical Time Bombs, University of Strathclyde, Glasgow, Scotland, 12–14 December 1991. (In preparation.)

Foerstner, U. 1991. "Long-term Changes of Acidity and Metal Chemistry in Landfills." Report submitted to expert meeting on Land Disposal and Chemical Time Bombs, University of Strathclyde, Glasgow, Scotland, 12–14 December 1991.

Goumans, J. J. J., H. A. van der Sloot, and T. G. Aalbers, eds. 1991. *Waste Materials in Construction.* Amsterdam: Elsevier.

Hjelmar, O., E. Aagaard Hansen, and A. Rokkjaer. 1988. "Groundwater Contamination from an Incinerator Ash and Household Waste Co-disposal Site." Paper presented at UNESCO Workshop on Impact of Waste Disposal on Groundwater and Surface Water, Copenhagen, Denmark, 15–19 August 1988.

Hrehoruk, J., H. Modzelewski, and B. Frydzynska. 1992. *Deposition of Zinc, Cadmium and Lead to the Rhine Basin due to Emissions from Local Sources and Corrosion Caused by SO_2.* Research report. Laxenburg, Austria: International Institute for Applied Systems Analysis.

Hutton, M. 1982. *Cadmium in the European Community: A Prospective Assessment of Sources, Human Exposure and Environmental Impact.* MARC Report, no. 26. London: Monitoring and Assessment Research Centre, Chelsea College, University of London.

IIASA. 1992. "Report of the Expert Work Group on Emission Factors for Cadmium, Lead, and Zinc from Solid and Aqueous Wastes." Working paper. Laxen-

160

burg, Austria: International Institute for Applied Systems Analysis. (In preparation.)

Jolankai, G., I. Biro, and R. Ajkay. 1991. *Computer Analysis of the Balance of Point and Diffuse Source Loading of Heavy Metals in the Rhine Basin*. Phase II Interim Report. Budapest:VITUKI.

Kosson, D. S., H. van der Sloot, T. Holmes, and C. Wiles. 1991. "Leaching Properties of Untreated and Treated Residues Tested in the USEPA Program for Evaluation of Treatment and Utilization Technologies for Municipal Waste Combustor Residues." In: J. J. J. M. Goumans, H. A. van der Sloot, and T. G. Aabers, eds., *Waste Materials in Construction*. Amsterdam: Elsevier, pp. 119–134.

MHPPE. 1988. *Memorandum on the Prevention and Recycling of Waste*. The Hague: Ministry of Housing, Physical Planning and Environment.

Novotny, V. 1988. "Diffuse (Nonpoint) Pollution – A Political, Institutional, and Fiscal Problem." *Journal of Water Pollution Control Federation* 60: 1404–1413.

Odum, E. P. 1989. "Input Management of Production Systems." *Science* 243: 177–182.

Organisation for Economic Co-operation and Development. 1991. *OECD Environmental Data: Compendium 1991*. Paris: OECD Publication Services.

Pacyna, J. M. 1988. *Atmospheric Lead Emissions in Europe in 1982*. Lillestrom: Norwegian Institute for Air Research. (Report no. NILU OR: 18/18.)

———. 1991. *Emission Factors of Atmospheric Cd, Pb, and Zn for Major Source Categories in Europe in 1950 through 1985*. Lillestrom: Norwegian Institute for Air Research. (Report no. NILU OR: 30/91.)

Pacyna, J. M., and J. Munch. 1988. *Atmospheric Emissions of Arsenic, Cadmium, Mercury and Zinc in Europe in 1982*. Lillestrom: Norwegian Institute for Air Research. (Report no. NILU OR: 17/88.)

Raede, D., and A. Dornemann. 1981. "Migration Studies on Cadmium Pigments in Plastics." In: *Cadmium 81: Edited Proceedings, Third International Cadmium Conference, Miami, USA, 3–5 February 1981*. London/New York/New York: Cadmium Association/ Cadmium Council/International Lead Zinc Research Organization, pp. 37–40.

Rauhut, A. 1978a. "Verbrauch und Verbleib von Cadmium in der Bundesrepublik Deutschland im Jahr 1974 und 1975." *Metall* 32: 947–948.

———. 1978b. "Industrial Emissions of Cadmium in the European Community: Sources, Levels and Control." European Community Study Contract, no. ENV/ 223/74E.

———. 1981. "Cadmium-Bilanz 1976/77 und Cadmiumverbrauch bis 1979." *Metall* 35: 344–347.

———. 1983. "Cadmium-Bilanz 1978–1980." *Metall* 37: 271–275.

———. 1990. "Cadmium-Bilanz 1984–1986." Unpublished manuscript. Nürnberg.

Rauhut, A., and D. Balzer. 1976. "Verbrauch und Verbleib von Cadmium in der Bundesrepublik Deutschland im Jahr 1973." *Metall* 30: 269–272.

Risse, F., J. Jacobs, W. vom Berg, and K.-H. Puch, 1991. "Nebenprodukte aus Kohlekraftwerken und Rückstände aus Müllverbrennungsanlagen in der Bundesrepublik Deutschland." *VGB Kraftwerktechnik* 71: 504–508.

Schulte-Schrepping, K. H. 1981. "Emission of Cadmium from Refuse Incineration Plants." In: *Cadmium 81: Edited Proceedings, Third International Cadmium Conference, Miami, USA, 3–5 February 1981*. London/New York/New York: Cadmium Association/ Cadmium Council/International Lead Zinc Research Organization, pp. 60–63.

Stigliani, W. M. 1988. "Changes in Valued 'Capacities' of Soils and Sediments as Indicators of Nonlinear and Time-delayed Environmental Effects." *Environmental Monitoring and Assessment* 10: 245–307.

Stigliani, W. M., P. Doelman, W. Salomons, R. Schulin, G. R. B. Smidt, and S. E. A. T. M. van der Zee. 1991. "Chemical Time Bombs: Predicting the Unpredictable." *Environment* 33:4–9, 26–30.

Stigliani, W. M., and P. F. Jaffe. 1992. *Industrial Metabolism: A New Approach for Analysis of Chemical Pollution and Its Potential Applications*. Research report. Laxenburg, Austria: International Institute for Applied Systems Analysis.

Tschinkel, V. J. 1989. "The Rise and Fall of Environmental Expertise." In: J. H. Ausubel and H. E. Sladovich, eds., *Technology and Environment*. Washington, D.C.: National Academy Press.

Van der Sloot, H. A. 1991. "Systematic Leaching Behaviour of Trace Elements from Construction Materials and Waste Materials." In: J. J. J. M. Goumans, H. A. van der Sloot, and T. G. Aabers, eds., *Waste Materials in Construction*. Amsterdam: Elsevier, pp. 19–36.

Van der Sloot, H. A., E. G. Weyers, D. Hoede, and J. Wijkstra. 1985. Physical and Chemical Characterization of Pulverized-coal Ash with respect to Cement-based Applications. Contract 11.9.1 with the Bureau of Energy Research Projects (BEOP). Petten, Netherlands: Netherlands Energy Research Foundation.

World Resources Institute. 1988. *World Resources 1988–89*. New York: Basic Books, p. 273, table 17.1.

8

Industrial metabolism at the regional and local level: A case-study on a Swiss region

Paul H. Brunner, Hans Daxbeck, and Peter Baccini

Introduction

One of the most outstanding features of modern man is the capability to exploit, refine, and consume large masses of raw materials. During the development of mankind from neolithic tribes to highly structured urban societies, the total flow of goods used to support human activities increased by two orders of magnitude (fig. 1).[1] Today, in densely populated areas, the fluxes of many anthropogenic materials surpass natural material fluxes.The main reason for this result is the continuous development of the art and technology of prospecting, extracting, upgrading, and designing new and existing materials. In addition, the population growth of the last few centuries has accelerated the flux of anthropogenic materials (fig. 2).

The huge increase in the consumption of goods has several implications: On one hand, it causes a quantitative problem, since the large mass of used goods has to be recycled or disposed of as waste, and thus financial and natural resources (land, water, and air for dissipation) are required for its management. On the other hand, there is a qualitative challenge: the growth in the consumption of materials such as heavy metals or organic compounds leads to large stocks of potentially hazardous materials in the anthroposphere, and to in-

163

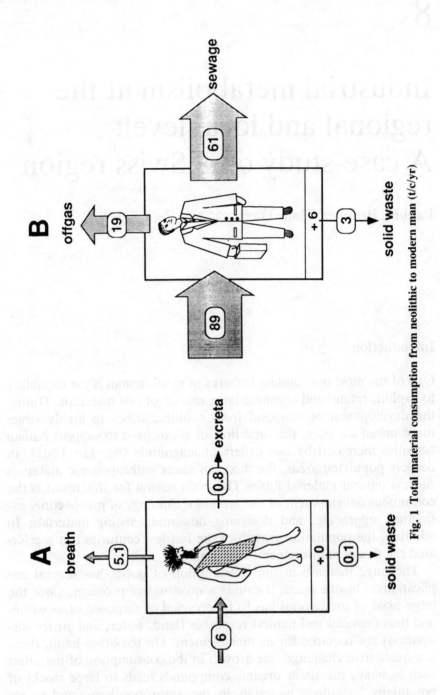

Fig. 1 Total material consumption from neolithic to modern man (t/c/yr)

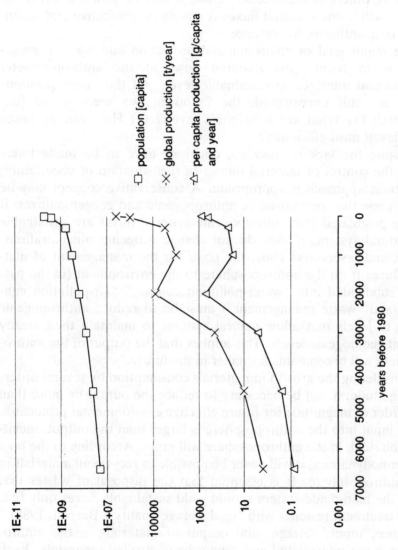

Fig. 2 Increase in global and per capita production of lead for the last 7,000 years
(Source: Brockhaus, 1967; Settle and Patterson, 1980)

creased fluxes of materials detrimental to the environment. The data contained in figures 1 and 2 show that the consumption of total goods has increased by about two orders of magnitude, and that the consumption of many trace materials such as lead has increased by six and more orders of magnitude.[2] Thus, it may be concluded that the past growth in the material fluxes is mainly of qualitative and secondarily of quantitative importance.

The major goal of environmental protection and waste management is to reduce the material flows at the anthrosphere/environment interface to sustainable levels. Of the many questions which are still unanswered, the following two seem to be fundamental: (1) What are sustainable levels? (2) How can we reach these levels most efficiently?

Despite the lack of answers, decisions have to be made today about the control of material fluxes. In this situation of uncertainty, a cautious approach is appropriate. A conservative concept may be based upon the comparison of anthropogenic and geogenic fluxes: it can be postulated that anthropogenic material fluxes are sustainable for natural systems *if* they do not change geogenic concentrations, fluxes, and reservoirs. Thus, the goals for the management of material fluxes from the anthrosphere to the environment (in the past often subdivided into "water-pollution control," "air-pollution control," and "waste management") must be to reduce anthropogenic fluxes to levels that allow natural systems to maintain their steady state at geobiogenic levels. This implies that the output of the anthrosphere will become much smaller in the future.

Considering the growth in materials consumption by several orders of magnitude, it will be necessary to reduce the output by more than one order of magnitude for future effective environmental protection. If the input into the anthrosphere is larger than the output, inevitably the stock in the anthrosphere will grow. According to the laws of thermodynamics, it will never be possible to recycle all materials in the anthrosphere. It is essential that the disposal of wastes that leave the man-made system should yield sustainable fluxes only (c.f. waste treatment residues with "final storage quality": Baccini, 1988).

Hence, input, storage, and output of materials in the anthrosphere are interrelated and cannot be controlled separately. Each measure to control the flux of materials has impacts on all three processes. This is true for global, national, and regional economies. In the future, it will be necessary to answer the question of how to control "industrial metabolism" on all levels in view of regionally and globally sustainable fluxes. In this chapter, we will focus on the regional level, which is the level where most control decisions are made: cities and communities plan and regulate their anthroposphere; people decide to move to a region; companies are attracted by regional advantages; the specific resources of regions offer particular opportunities, etc.

In order to assess and control regional industrial metabolism, a three-step procedure is proposed. The first – scientific and technical – step consists of a *regional material balance*. It includes the assessment of imports, exports, and internal fluxes of goods and materials in the anthroposphere and environment, and emphasizes the growth and/or depletion of natural and anthropogenic reservoirs. In the second – technical and economic – step, the most efficient *means to control* anthropogenic material fluxes are determined. The third – political and social – step consists of the *implementation* of the measures to control industrial metabolism.

The emphasis of this chapter is on step 1, and the objective is to present a methodology for the establishment of regional material balances, using a case-study on a Swiss region. The main question is how to determine the important processes and fluxes in a region consisting of thousands of anthropogenic and natural processes. The work focuses on fluxes of goods and includes two examples of materials such as lead and phosphorus. The results are used to discuss part of step 2, means to control selected materials in a given region. Economic, political and social issues (steps 2–3) are not treated here. Although the region investigated is located in Switzerland, and the concepts discussed here have been developed there, we believe that the approach and methodology chosen can be applied anywhere.

Methodology

First, a set of definitions is given to describe the material fluxes through a regional anthroposphere. Next, these definitions are used for a systems analysis of a region. Third, field data are collected for the flux of selected materials through the most important processes. Finally, material fluxes through the region are calculated, and two examples of how to use these results for the control of material fluxes in the anthroposphere are given.

Definitions

In order to investigate the flow of materials through a regional economy systematically, and to use this information for control pur-

167

Table 1 Terms used for the analysis of the anthroposphere

Notion	Definition	Conventional discipline	Method
Material	Chemical element or its compounds	Physics, chemistry	Physical and chemical analysis
Good	Material or material mixture	Economics	Market analysis, economics
Process	Transport, transformation, and storage	Engineering, biology, economics	Materials accounting, material balancing
Activity	Set of processes and fluxes of goods, materials, energy, and information	Cybernetics, anthropology	Systems analysis

Source: Baccini and Brunner, 1991.

poses, we use the following definitions, summarized in table 1 (Baccini and Brunner, 1991):

A *material* is a chemical element (e.g. lead, carbon) and its compounds (lead chloride, benzene). Material flows are measured in mass per time units, material fluxes in mass per time and area. The "area" can be an entire region, a household, or a person; hence the flux unit may be in kg/capita and year.

A *good* consists of one or many materials, such as a pipe made of lead, or gasoline containing benzene. A good has a negative or positive economic value. In the economic sense, goods can also be energy, information, or services. In this work, we apply the term to material goods only, such as cars, water, or municipal solid wastes.

A *process* is defined as a transport, transformation, or storage of goods, materials, energy, and information. A transport often involves a change in the value of a good. There are processes possible on all levels: a car engine may be looked at as a process, in same way as a private household, a waste incinerator, a branch of a regional economy, or an entire region.

An *activity* can be defined as a set of processes and fluxes of goods, materials, energy, and information serving a certain purpose, such as to nourish, to clean, or to transport. The concept of "activities" allows one to evaluate different strategies of control. For example, the activity "to nourish," comprising the production, upgrading, storage, distribution, preparation, and consumption of food, involves large fluxes of nitrogen and phosphorus, which may eventually have a

168

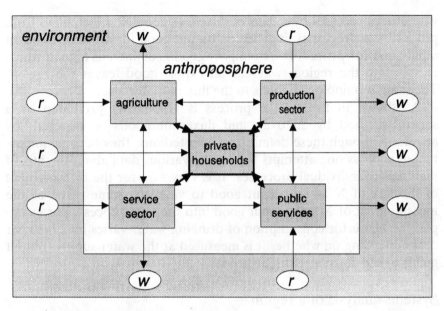

Fig. 3 The anthroposphere as a man-made system (r = resources, w = wastes)

negative impact on water, air, and soil. A material flux analysis of the activity "to nourish," from the fertilizer to the edible meal, will thus reveal the most effective measures for the control of these fluxes.

The anthroposphere is the field where human activities take place; it is embedded in the environment (fig. 3). Sometimes called the man-made biosphere, it can be envisaged as a living organism. It has its own metabolism consisting of the uptake, transformation, storage, and discharge of energy, matter, and information. The anthroposphere can be described as a system of processes, and fluxes of goods, materials, energy, and information (see table 1). There are many regional varieties of the anthroposphere, since it is highly influenced by such parameters as the climate, the topography and geology, the native population and its values, the neighbouring regions, and others. The main goal of the metabolism of the anthroposphere is to supply private households with energy, consumer goods, and information; the target process of all anthropogenic activities is the household. All other processes have merely a supporting function.

The method developed to describe the system "region" is based on processes and fluxes of goods and materials (Baccini and Brunner, 1991). Each flux has a "process of origin" and a "process of destination" and thus is precisely defined. Equally, each process is linked with other processes by means of fluxes. A good X, which flows from process A to process B, is called an output good for process A and an input good for process B. An import good is defined as a good which crosses into the region, whereas an export good leaves the region. The same terminology applies to the flux of materials.

As shown in figure 3, a process is graphically presented by a square, a good by an oval, and fluxes of goods or materials by arrows. Although these definitions seem tedious, they become important as soon as one attempts to link the various data about the flux of materials of individual processes. It is very rare for the measurement of the flux of X as an output good to yield the same result as the measurement of X as an input good into the next process. For example, the figure for consumption of drinking water varies by 20–30 per cent depending on whether it is measured at the water supply (output good) or the consumer (input good).

Systems analysis of a region

Description of the region

The region investigated in this work is the Untere Bünztal (Lower Bünz Valley). This broad valley, which is located approximately 400 m above sealevel, covers 66 km², and is limited on both sides by rolling wooded hills. It forms a single watershed, containing two major but small rivers with a water flow of about 0.5–2 m³/sec. Fifty-six per cent of the land area is used for agriculture, 30 per cent is forested, and 13 per cent represents urban areas. The average precipitation amounts to 1,100 mm, and the average temperature is 8–9 °C. The valley may be called representative for regions in Western and Central Europe as well as for the north-eastern United States.

There are 28,000 persons living in the region, in 9,300 private households located in 12 communities. The average per capita purchasing power of US$30,800 (1986) matches that of other regions in Europe. Fifty-nine per cent of the 11,000 employees work in the production sector, 35 per cent in the service and public sector, and 6 per cent in the primary sector (agriculture). Some 55 per cent of the 1,400 enterprises in the region belong to the service sector, and the remaining 45 per cent are equally divided between production and agriculture. Of the 19 branches present in the production sector, the metal industry branch just dominates with 17 per cent of all employees, followed by the plastic and the construction industries with 13 per cent. Other important branches are the electric/electronic industries (11 per cent), textiles (9 per cent), and others (for details see Rist et al., 1989).

The region may be described as a well-mixed economy with an important fraction of its employees working in a few large companies in the production sector, such as a steel mill and a chemical company.

Analysis of the system

Establishing a systematic and comprehensive regional material balance is a comparatively new undertaking. Hardly any methods and data exist for materials accounting on the local level. For the time being, it is beyond the capacity of any research project to investigate the *total* material flow of a region; the number of goods and materials (elements and compounds, especially of organic carbon), as well as the number of processes, is far too large. Thus, the art of regional materials accounting is to find the few processes and goods which determine the overall flux of a particular material. The following approach was taken in order to simplify the system "region."

As a first step in designing the systems analysis on a general level, the region can be divided into eight major processes. The next step is a more detailed investigation and a subdivision of each of these processes into subprocesses.

A rough assessment of the most abundant fluxes of goods through private households reveals that about 80–100 t/c/yr of goods flow through an average household (see fig. 1; Brunner and Baccini, 1992). Most of these goods originate from the public services (water, natural gas) and the service sector. The production sector supplies the matrix of the regional anthroposphere, such as buildings, roadways, and the nutrients (food) and energy (fuel) to be distributed by the service sector. A few companies with either a large number of employees or a high (financial) turnover are expected to be important for the flux of goods in and through the region. In order to find these important companies, a detailed knowledge of the region is indispensable.

A valuable tool for this work was an existing database about the places of work and the businesses for each sector and branch in the region. When this database was combined with information about the average financial turnover of places of work, a rank order of the importance of the 1,400 businesses in the region became possible. Of course, a rank order according to such economic criteria is not congruent with a ranking based on the fluxes of goods or materials. In the absence of any such information in the production sector, the

171

economic ranking was useful as a first approach – somewhere to start the survey. One advantage of including economic information in this study was that it opens up the possibility of combining material flux data with net product data, and thus serves as a first approach to the problem of linking ecology and economy.

On the basis of this preliminary investigation, the following five most important processes have been defined in the regional anthroposphere.

PRIVATE HOUSEHOLDS. This process stands for the many processes which take place in a private home in relation to the activities "to breathe," "to nourish" (e.g. shopping, preparation, and consumption of food), "to reside" (construction and maintenance of buildings, heating, purchase and maintenance of furniture, carpets, curtains), "to clean" (laundry, dishwasher, toilet, shower, car wash, cleaning), and "to communicate" (transport of persons, goods, energy, and information). Included are processes (and goods) which serve exclusively the private household but which take place outside of it, such as the use of a motor vehicle for shopping, the use of a sewerage system to collect sewage from households, or part of the telecommunication network for TV and phone. The process "private households" comprises all 1,300 households in the region.

SERVICE SECTOR. This sector includes all the businesses engaged in trade and commerce (e.g. shopping centres, retailers, grocery stores), financial and personal services (banks, insurance companies), the catering trade (hotels, restaurants), transportation, and others. Its main purpose is to serve the private individuals in households.

PRODUCTION SECTOR. This process comprises all businesses which produce machinery, metals, chemicals, food, textiles, furniture, shoes, vehicles, etc., and includes the construction business. The goods of the production sector are mainly delivered to the service sector. A detailed list is given in Rist et al. (1989).

PUBLIC SERVICES. In economic classifications, the public sector is usually included in the tertiary (= service) sector. For this work, a separate process, "public services," was chosen for the following reasons: In the region investigated, public services are responsible for the largest fluxes of goods, namely the supply of water, the collection and treatment of sewage, and the collection of solid wastes. Also, public utilities supply electricity, natural gas, and telephone services. For all these subprocesses, there are extensive and reliable databases available. Thus, the flux of goods between the "public services" and the "private households" is important and well documented, justifying a separation from other, less comprehensively investigated processes.

AGRICULTURE. This term stands for the processes which are necessary to plant, grow and harvest plants and to raise animals. In a separate project, subprocesses of the process "agriculture" were linked with the processes "atmosphere" and "soil" in order to determine the contribution of the agricultural practice to the material fluxes in the soil system. These results have been published before and are not included in this work (Von Steiger and Baccini, 1990).

In order to fulfil the requirements for processes of "origin" and "destination," three synthetic processes were introduced: man-made import and export processes in the neighbouring regions, and a process "environment." These are composed of many subprocesses. For simplification, they have not been included in figure 4.[3]

The following illustrates some of the subprocesses. Private households use the good "air" for the activities "to breathe," "to reside" (heating), and "to communicate" (transportation). The process of origin for "air" is the Planetary Boundary Layer (PBL), which is a subprocess of the process "environment." The process of destination for the offgases is again the PBL. The source of drinking water is the subprocess "groundwater" in the environment; a subprocess "distribution of drinking water" in the public services supplies private households with drinking water. The collected and treated sewage is finally transferred to the subprocess "River Bünz" in the environment.

The most general list of fluxes of goods consists of the ten good categories represented by bold arrows in figure 4. A category of goods may contain a few single goods (such as the flux from the public services to private households, consisting of drinking water, natural gas, and a few more items) or several hundred to several thousand goods (such as the flux from the production to the service sector, or from the service sector to private households). (A complete list of goods is given in Rist et al, 1989.)

Initially, 12 materials were selected for this study. Two elements were chosen for detailed investigations: lead (Pb), which is still used

173

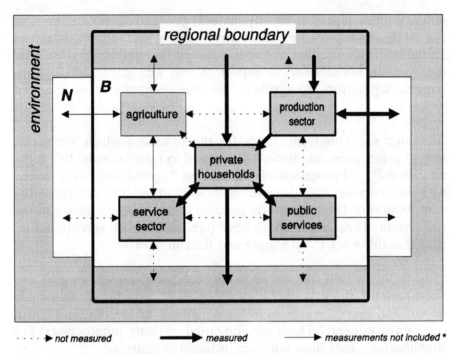

Fig. 4 Systems analysis of the region Unteres Bünztal (B = Anthroposphere of region, N = Anthropospheres of neighbouring regions)

partially as an additive in gasoline, and which is contained in many consumer products such as cars, batteries, curtains, ties, corks, and construction materials; and phosphorus (P), which is an essential nutrient for the biosphere, a widely used ingredient in cleaners and dishwashing liquids, and an important agent to prevent boiler scale and corrosion.

Assessment of fluxes of goods and materials

In order to determine the flow of goods through the anthroposphere of the region, two kinds of methods were used. The process "private households" was characterized by results from existing market research studies, and the other processes were analysed by individual surveys of the most important companies and public utilities. These techniques yield sufficient information about the flux of goods, but are in general not applicable to the collection of data about the flux of materials, since neither private households nor many businesses know the material composition of the goods they use. Thus, information about materials was collected from other sources, such as general tables (Ciba-Geigy, 1977) or specific articles about the content of, say, phosphorus in goods like detergents and fertilizers.

Private households
There is abundant information from market research on the average consumption of most goods in private households in many regions. These data cover short-lived goods such as food, cleaning agents, and newsprint, as well as goods with longer residence times (e.g. appliances, furniture, textiles). However, there was no market research information about the Bünztal available. Hence, data were used from regions with similar per capita income and similar household size, two properties which are known to be significant for the comparison of the consumption in households. The projection for the entire region was made by multiplying the number of inhabitants with the average per capita consumption. The hypothesis that the use of figures from other regions may be applied to the Bünztal was tested by comparing data on basic foodstuffs from various regions; deviations were between 5 and 15 per cent and are considered acceptable.

The example of phosphorus (P) in table 2 illustrates the procedure

Table 2 Assessment of the P-flux through the average private Swiss household

Goods	Flux of goods (kg/capita/year)	Concentration of P (g P/kg good)	Flux of P (g P/capita/year)
Milk and milk products	109	0.9	98
Dishwashing detergents	2	31.6	63
Bread	24	1.8	43
Vegetables	30	1.2	36
Cheese	8	3.9	31
Meat	16	1.9	31
Fruits	41	0.7	28
Cleaning detergents	9	2.0	18
Cereals	5	2.9	15
Sausages	10	1.4	15
Eggs	6	2.0	12
Pasta	5	2.0	10
Meals consumed out of house	216	0.6	124
Rest (41 goods with P < 10 g/c/y)	439	n.d.	86
Total	920		610

Source: Brunner et al., 1990.

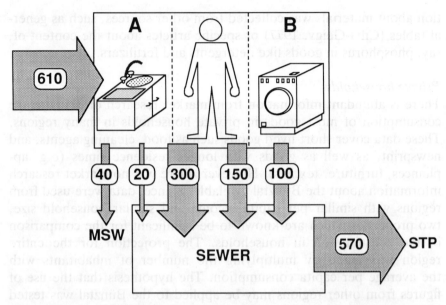

Fig. 5 Flux of phosphorus through the process "private household," in g P/c/yr (A = Process kitchen, B = Process dishwashing and cleaning, MSW = Municipal solid waste, STP = Sewage treatment plant)

for determining the material flux through the household. Data about the flux of 54 goods was supplied by a market research firm (IHA); the concentration of P was taken from Ciba-Geigy (1977), and the P-fluxes were calculated by multiplying the flux of goods with its P-concentration.

The results on P-input obtained by this procedure were successfully cross-checked with available data on P-output from waste and sewage management (fig. 5).[4] The P-flux of all the households in the entire region was obtained by multiplying the per capita flux with the 28,000 inhabitants of the region.

Production sector, service sector, and public sector

For each of the three sectors, branches such as "production of food and drinks," "manufacturing of chemicals," and "public water supply" were defined according to BAS (1985). The number and size (given as number of employees) of the businesses in each branch were taken from BAS (1987). The largest companies of each branch were selected and asked for interviews. This allowed us, as a first step, to reduce the 1,377 businesses to 102 enterprises with more than 20 employees, comprising 6,632 workers, or 64 per cent of the total of the three sectors. In a second step, 29 enterprises were excluded from the survey because, on the basis of their field of business, their material flux appeared to be rather small.

With the support of the local chamber of commerce 73 enterprises were individually approached and asked to participate in the project. Of these, 38 companies participated fully, and 11 were eliminated because they had very small fluxes of goods, or could not supply the necessary information in time. Of the remaining 24 businesses, 10 construction companies were included as an entity (see below), and 12 were not surveyed because of the limited manpower available for this research. Only two did not wish to participate in the study. As a rough assessment showed the importance of one of these companies (a car-shredder), indirect methods were used to estimate the contribution of the shredder to the regional material flux. (This indirect method is based upon the assessment of the material balance before and after a particular process: information about the manufacturing of cars, a material balance of a similar car-shredder in another region, and information about the amount and composition of the automobile scrap metal treated in a regional smelter permits a rough estimate of the flow of goods and materials through the car-shredder.)

In addition to the survey of individual companies, comprehensive data about all construction businesses in the region were obtained from the regional market leader of the construction branch. Detailed information about water consumption, waste-water treatment, waste management, and energy consumption was supplied by the public utilities of the 12 regional communities; it was fortuitous that the systems boundary coincides with the boundaries of the communities. Thus, it was possible to cross-check the figures on overall water consumption against waste-water production, the data on individual waste production against the global figure on waste collection and treatment, etc. By such cross-checking, gross errors can be detected.

Table 3 summarizes the fraction of businesses, employees, and material turnover covered for each branch in the survey. Despite the fact that only a few percentages of all businesses were investigated, it was possible to include a large percentage of all employees and a very high percentage of the total turnover of goods.

The participating companies were interviewed by an engineer and an economist. In addition to questions regarding the business structure (field of activity, employees, most important processes of origin, and destination for the goods used/produced), the following specific data were collected:

Table 3 Fraction of businesses, employees, and turnover of goods included in the survey (percentage surv.)

Branch	Number of businesses		Number of employees		Goods turnover[a]	
	Total	% surveyed	Total	% surveyed	1,000 t/yr	% surveyed
Food/beverage	18	22	442	73	93	73
Textiles/clothing	18	17	598	29	7	16
Leather/shoes	3	33	249	98	0.07	98
Chemicals	5	20	409	95	25	97
Plastics	10	70	849	98	18	96
Sand/gravel/stones	8	13	351	68	127	68
Metal-processing	57	14	1,136	51	180	96
Electro-technics	15	13	682	55	4	68
Watches/jewellery	14	7	65	51	0.1	
Construction	31	32	845	89	478	100
Trade/commerce	50	4	348	34	190	90
Storage/transport	5	20	15	40	16	100
Other (farming, etc)	1,070	0	5,010	0	N.d.	N.d.
Total	1,377	3	11,000	52	1,140	90

Source: Own research.

a. In this table, "good" stands for output goods only, and does not include wastes such as municipal solid waste, sewage, or offgas. For most branches turnover was calculated on the assumption that each branch has a specific turnover per employee, but that in some branches (e.g. metal-processing, trade/commerce) the total turnover is heavily influenced by a few companies; cf. Rist et al., 1989).

- List and annual flux of input goods, including energy.
- List and annual flux of output goods, including wastes such as municipal solid waste (MSW), production of waste, waste water, and flue gas.

The information collected varied in its preciseness. In most cases, it was sufficiently detailed to be directly included in the total regional flux of goods. For instance, a chemical company supplied very elaborate data, including hundreds of raw materials and many output goods. Such data have to be aggregated, however, before they can be used. Most companies also provided information about financial turnover, cash flow, and net product.

Calculation method

The information about the fluxes of goods of the "average" private household and of each business was used to calculate a list of the most important processes and of the most important goods in the region (tables 4 and 5). These calculated figures, however, have errors of +/− 20 per cent: some information is missing (not all processes have been surveyed), the information does not cover the same time period for all businesses, and the data collected are not always accurate because making measurements or calculations is difficult (solid waste) or impossible (flue gas).

The flux diagrams of lead[5] and phosphorus[6] (figs. 6 and 7) were calculated as follows: A material flux balance was established for

Table 4 Important processes and total flux of goods through the region, including private transportation

	Flux of goods in kt per year and branch			
Branch	Total good	Water	Offgas	Solid waste
Private households[a]	2'56	1'84	630	9.2
Production of chemicals	1'91	1'88	75	4.5
Production of food	600	534	19	0.4
Construction	480	N.d.	N.d.	N.d.
Metal-processing (incl. shredder)	430	60	130	40
Rest	690	280	150	N.d.
Total	6'70	4'60	1'000	54

Source: Rist et al., 1989.
a. Including private transportation.

179

Table 5 Most important fluxes of goods (in t/c/yr) and their fraction flowing through private households of the region

Good	Flux in t/c/yr	
	Total	$ through household
Water	164	41
Air	36	60
Construction materials	18	N.d.
Metals/scrap	12	N.d.
Food/drinks	4	21
Fuel	2	55
Rest	2	26
Total	238	38

Source: Brunner et al., 1990.

each process, using measured and estimated flux and concentration data. As not all fluxes through a process were known, some fluxes had to be calculated as difference of inputs and outputs. When all fluxes through a process are measured, it is often not possible to balance inputs and outputs. The balancing period was one year. The change of reservoirs was taken into account for soils and landfills only; annual inputs and outputs of all other processes were considered in equilibrium. The material balance of each single process was then linked to all other processes, yielding an overall regional balance. This procedure required careful validation of the material fluxes through most processes, since the output fluxes of one process and the input fluxes of the following process do not always correspond. In general, most emphasis was put on those large fluxes that are measurable with the least error.

Results

Methodology

Systematology
In order to establish a regional material balance, engineers, scientists, and economists have to work together, develop a common language, collect data from most different sources, and combine these data to reveal regional fluxes. Such cooperation would be facilitated if the same systems analysis approach and a common terminology were

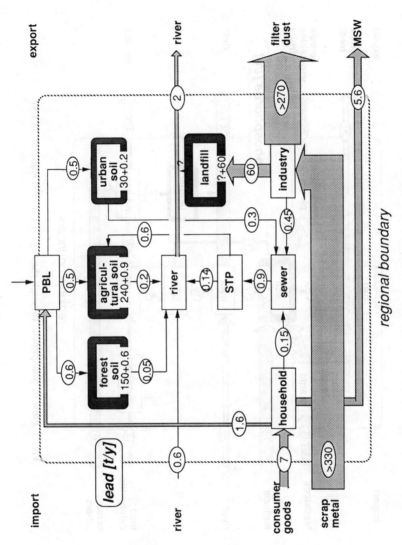

Fig. 6 Flow of lead through the region Unteres Bünztal, in t/yr

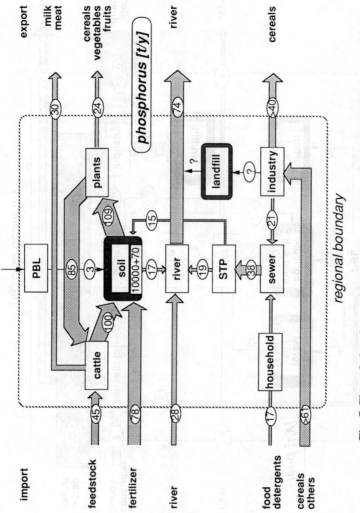

Fig. 7 Flow of phosphorus through the region Unteres Bünztal, in t/yr

182

used. It is an important future task to educate experts from various fields in the techniques of materials accounting.

The terms developed and the approach taken in this work are based on four steps. The basis – the first step – is a comprehensive systems analysis of the region, defining the region, the boundaries, the processes, and the link between processes by means of fluxes of goods and materials. This is followed by a rough assessment of the importance of the fluxes of goods, carried out with available or easily accessible information. On the basis of this estimation, those fluxes that have to be measured and assessed in more detail are selected. The last step consists in calculating and validating the regional material fluxes.

The Bünztal project has shown that this procedure is feasible if these four steps are taken as an iterative rather than as a consecutive process: the initial systems analysis may have to be expanded or reduced according to the first assessment of the fluxes, or because of the impossibility of balancing a process or process chain. The calculation of the final results may display a large deficit in a process, thus making it necessary to add supplementary measurements to the third step. Even with heavy expenditure, it may not be possible to balance a process (as in the case of lead in the process "river").

The experience in the Bünztal shows that methods have to be developed to take into account the uncertainty of the individual fluxes for regional material balances. These would allow one to quantify the probability that a deficit or a surplus in a regional balance is not an analytical artefact and that additional fluxes have to be looked for.

Materials accounting
The most demanding task in regional materials accounting is to reduce the very many processes and fluxes of goods to a number that is small enough for analysis and still contains the gross of the fluxes of goods and materials. To achieve this, detailed knowledge of the region is necessary. Thus the cooperation of the region itself is important, and should include the public sector as well as private institutions.

The method applied in this study yields abundant information about the flux of goods through the various sectors and branches of a region. The data about these fluxes can easily be verified by comparing the output and input fluxes of consecutive processes, or entire process chains. The method also yields satisfactory results for materials if the concentration of materials in the goods used is known.

183

This is often not the case. The assessment of the fluxes of Pb and P, as displayed in figs. 6 and 7, requires a detailed analysis of many processes (private households, detergent manufacturing, sewage treatment, waste management, car manufacturing, scrap processing, agricultural practice, and others) and involves laborious and costly investigations. But the main obstacle for regional materials accounting is the lack of information about the composition of today's intermediate and consumer goods. While the producer of the primary raw material still knows the composition of his raw iron, zinc, or ethylene, this information is soon lost on the way to the intermediate manufacturer, and particularly when it reaches the final consumer; end-users buy goods and not materials!

For future regional materials accounting, it is indispensable that the information about the material composition of a good should flow parallel to the information about, say, the price or the weight of a good. And this information should be passed from the process of origin to the next process of destination. This appears to be the only way to collect reliable information about the material make-up of today's complex goods, such as refrigerators, motor vehicles, or houses. Technically, with the data-bank management systems now available, it should pose no problem to carry such information from its origin, through the chain of processes, to the end-user.

Regional fluxes of goods and materials

Flux of goods
The overall anthropogenic flux of goods through the Bünztal is given in figure 8. The most important single good is water, which amounts to 69 per cent of the total flux and is mainly used to transport materials and energy in households and industrial processes. Air, utilized in combustion processes such as heating and motor vehicles, comes second with 15 per cent of the total flux. Construction materials account for 8 per cent, scrap iron and junk cars for 5 per cent, and other import goods for 3 per cent.

Of all aggregated processes, private households have the largest turnover, consuming more than one-third of all goods. The branch "production of chemicals" utilizes 29 per cent of the goods, "food and drink" 9 per cent, construction business 7 per cent, metal processing 6 per cent, and the remaining branches 10 per cent.

The fraction of goods which remains in the region is comparatively small and amounts to less than 10 per cent of the import. It consists

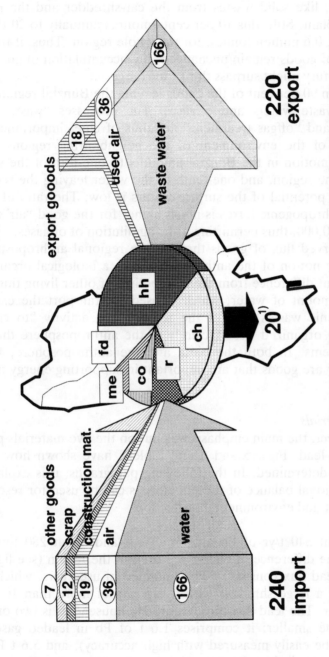

Fig. 8 Regional flux of goods through the anthroposphere, in t/c/yr (HH = Private households, CH = Production of chemicals, ME = Metal processing, FD = Processing of food and drink, R = Others)

185

chiefly of solids to build the matrix of the anthroposphere like construction materials, and goods from processes which are specific to the Bünztal, like solid wastes from the car-shredder and the metal processing plant. Still, this 10 per cent amounts annually to 20 t/c, or 10 kg/m^2, or 0.6 million tonnes, for the whole region. Thus, if the future fluxes of goods remain unchanged, the accumulation of goods in the next century might surpass the 1 t/m^2 range.

More than 90 per cent of the goods leaving the Bünztal region (export) are waste waters and offgases. The processes "waste-water treatment" and "offgas treatment" are thus of chief importance for the quality of the environment of the neighbouring regions. The water consumption in the Bünztal amounts to one-fifth of the water input into the region, and one-tenth of the water leaving the region; the dilution potential of the surface waters is low. The ratio of geogenic to anthropogenic fluxes is much higher for the good "air"; it is around 1:500,000, thus permitting a strong dilution of offgases.

The observed flux of goods through the regional anthroposphere supports the notion of the anthroposphere as a biological organism. An important difference from the metabolism of other living things is the large amount of water, which is used to transport the excreta (anthropogenic wastes) out of the region. The activity "to clean" seems to be organized less efficiently in the anthroposphere than in natural systems. In both the biota and the anthroposphere, food, fuel, and air are goods that are important in supporting energy metabolism.

Flux of materials

In this project, the main emphasis was put on the two materials phosphorus and lead. Figs. 5 and 6 and table 2 have shown how such fluxes were determined. In the following paragraphs, it is explained how the regional balance of these materials can be used for resource management and environmental protection.

LEAD. About 340 t/yr of Pb are imported, and about 280 t/yr are exported; the difference of 60 t/yr is stored in the region (see fig. 5). The main lead flux consists of Pb contained in used cars, which are shredded in a large shredder with a capacity of more than 100,000 cars per year. The lead flux through private households is two orders of magnitude smaller; it comprises 1.6 t of Pb in leaded gasoline (which can be easily measured with high accuracy), and 5.6 t Pb in household goods (which have been determined from the Pb concentration in MSW, and thus do not represent the actual consumption of lead in households).

Much of the lead from the car-shredder is processed in a steel mill within the region, which produces iron rods for construction, filter ash from a baghouse, and furnace slag. Owing to the chemical/physical behaviour of lead, most of the lead (200 t/yr) is concentrated in the filter ash, and some is contained in the mild steel (70 t/yr). These goods are exported and re-used; thus about 80 per cent of the lead imported into the region leaves the region again. The non-metallic shredder residue contains about 60 tons of lead; at present, this residue is landfilled.

RESOURCE MANAGEMENT. The landfill of the non-metallic shredder residue is the largest sink for lead in the region. It can be assumed that after a decade of landfilling this stock is the most important regional reservoir of lead. Therefore, the careful management of this stock is or will become extremely important. On the one hand, the lead in the landfill poses a threat to the hydrosphere. On the other hand, it may be an important resource for the future.

Following the goals introduced in the Introduction, the shredder residue should be transformed into a good which releases sustainable fluxes only. In addition, the objectives of resource conservation require that the material be in a concentrated and re-usable form. Unfortunately, the good "shredder residue" is far from attaining these two goals, since the lead is highly diluted with organic matter and may be mobilized during landfilling. A possible solution is to treat the shredder residue thermally, thus removing the organic matter and concentrating lead in the fly ash. Further treatment is required to render the fly ash immobile; since solidification with binders like cement dilutes the potential resource of lead and makes it more difficult to re-use, other techniques such as vitrification should be attempted. The final residue should preferably be disposed of in monofills, which contain one type of mixture of concentrated materials only. (Of course, if cars were designed with sustainable development in mind, direct recycling of single car parts might become possible, which would make the shredder in the region obsolete. Direct recycling, however, seems only to be a future option.)

ENVIRONMENTAL PROTECTION. The regional lead balance allows the setting of limits for the leaching of lead from the wastes as well as for emissions from the thermal treatment of wastes and goods. The

187

largest regional sink of lead is the landfill. The good which contains the largest fraction of lead is the residue from the car-shredder. This waste does not yet have "final storage" quality; when it is landfilled, long-term biogeochemical reactions occur, which may mobilize the lead and other materials contained in the landfill. The geogenic flux of lead through the River Bünz is about 30 kg/yr. If the landfill releases about 1 kg/yr of lead, the geogenic flux will be changed less than by its natural variations. This means that, of the total content of about 1,000 tons of Pb in the landfill (corresponding to 10–20 years of landfilling), only about 1 ppm may be mobilized per year. Thus, the future regional goal for the treatment of shredder wastes can be defined as the production of a residue that releases not more than about 10 ppm of the mass of lead when landfilled. (Of course, other materials have to be considered as well).

One technical option for producing a residue with "final storage" quality would be incineration, followed by immobilization of the incineration residues. During thermal treatment, between 40 and 60 per cent of the lead is transferred to the flue gas. Air-pollution-control techniques allow the removal of most, but not all, of the lead from the gas stream. If the lead flux in the filtered flue gas is below 5 kg/yr, the incinerator emissions will not markedly change regional lead concentrations in the soil. A load of 5 kg Pb for 1,000 years in the soil reservoir of ~400 t equals an increase of about 1 per cent, if it is assumed that 80 per cent of the lead is retained in the soil. The flux of 5 kg/yr corresponds to 0.02 mg(Pb)/Nm^3. Considering the lead in the raw gas as about 30 t/yr, a removal efficiency of more than 99.98 would be required – a value that can be achieved only if the best available air-pollution-control technique is applied. (A similar calculation for lead fluxes from the incineration of municipal solid wastes demonstrates that the allowable emissions are about five times higher (0.1 mg(Pb)/Nm^3). The reason for this is the lower overall flux of MSW and lead when compared to the shredder residue).

PHOSPHORUS. The main import goods for P in the Bünztal region are fertilizers and feedstock, the main internal P-fluxes are the agricultural cycle soil-plant-animal-soil, and the main export pathway is the River Bünz (see fig. 7). Most of the P-input into the process industry is from cereals, which are stored temporarily in a large industrial stock. The import flux (229 t/yr) surpasses the export flux (168 t/yr); thus, about 60 tons of P are accumulated annually in the region, and the stock of P in the soil of the region is increasing.

The amount of P in the River Bünz is mainly determined by three processes. The soil, as a result of surface run-off, erosion, and leaching, contributes ~17 t/yr, the sewage-treatment plant (STP) 19 t/yr, and unknown processes such as landfills or illegal effluents 10 t/yr. In this study, the fluxes from the third category were not investigated. The River Bünz receives ~46 t P/yr, which is about 1.6 times more than the initial load when entering the region. If the elimination of P in the sewage-treatment plant were maximized, about 13 t/yr could easily be eliminated from the river. By contrast, it is not possible to influence the fluxes due to erosion and leaching from the soil in the short term; as long as the reservoir soil is increased, the flux from this process will increase even more. Owing to the high input of P from past and current agricultural practice, the flux of P to the surface waters also will remain high in the future.

The accumulation of P in the soil cannot be detected in the short term by soil analysis (this is true for heavy metals and trace substances in general): because of the heterogeneity of the soil, as well as the limited accuracy of sampling and laboratory analysis, a change in the soil concentration becomes significant only after decades. The material balance approach, however, allows the detection of a potential accumulation before large reservoirs have been developed, and thus can serve as an early-warning system. According to the values given in figure 7, the concentration of P in the soil of the Bünztal increases by about 1 per cent per year and thus will double within roughly 70 years. (In the past, the stock of lead in the soil grew annually by 0.5–1 per cent owing to the use of leaded gasoline.)

Regional materials accounting may be used as a powerful tool for soil protection: the most efficient means of decreasing the P-load of the soil can be assessed using figure 7. The flux of P is mainly due to the two activities "to nourish" and "to clean." It was recognized several decades ago that P can be the limiting factor for the eutrophication of surface waters. In areas where eutrophication of lakes is a serious problem, the time-span between scientific recognition of its cause and preventative action was about two decades. Most actions concerned the replacement of phosphate-based detergents, that is, processes and goods involved in the activity "to clean." In the region investigated, the turnover of P resulting from the activity "to nourish" is nearly one order of magnitude larger than that from cleaning purposes (see table 2 and fig. 7). In future it will be of great importance to reduce in time the material fluxes for the activity "to nourish" to regionally balanced levels. This suggests that regional

Table 6 Results and consequences

Result	Consequences
1. Anthropogenic fluxes > geogenic fluxes	Short-term increase in concentrations in air and waste water, long-term accumulation in soil and sediments
2. Import in region > export from region	Accumulation in the anthroposphere, accumulation in landfills → future resource potential
3. Private household as chief process of regional metabolism	Importance of municipal solid waste (MSW); management for the control of material fluxes at the anthroposphere/environment interface; final storage concept; products from MSW treatment as new intermediate and long-term resources
4. New strategy of regional material management replaces end-of-pipe environmental protection	Materials accounting on all levels; efficient control of material fluxes; design for multiple and long-term re-use

Source: Own design.

materials accounting should be applied as an early-warning tool, and that strategies should be developed which allow a decrease in the time-lag between the recognition of a problem and the implementation of measures to control it (table 6).

Conclusions

1. If the goal of environmental protection is to conserve the quality of water, air, and soil for a long period of time, the contribution of anthropogenic materials must not change geogenic fluxes and reservoirs beyond their natural variations. This means that measures to limit the flux from the anthroposphere to the environment have to be based on regional characteristics: the area of a region, its geology, climate, reservoirs of water, air and soil, population density, the activities of the population, etc., determine which fluxes from the anthroposphere fulfil the above criteria. If the geogenic material flux is relatively small, as in the case of the water flux of the Bünztal, the admissable per capita level of anthropogenic material fluxes is much lower than in a region with abundant geogenic resources. Owing to the large population density and the high per capita turnover of the region investigated, both the sink "soil" and the relatively small conveyer belt "surface water" receive large anthropogenic inputs. The concentrations of metals and phosphorus in the soil are constantly in-

creased; the concentrations and fluxes of many materials in the River Bünz are enlarged on their way through the valley. Regional material balances allow us to identify the most effective measures for the control of material fluxes in a region.

2. In general, the material imports and exports of modern urban regions are not in equilibrium. In the case under consideration, nearly 10 per cent of the total material flux remains in the region and is accumulated, particularly in the anthroposphere (infrastructure) and in the soil (landfills, topsoil). In fact, if imports of solid goods and fuels are considered alone, the accumulation amounts to 50 per cent of the import flux. Hence, the stock of materials is increasing. In future, this stock has the potential for becoming the region's largest waste problem, as well as serving as its major resource. As a new goal of resource management, it is suggested that materials should be kept within the anthroposphere; thus, resources should be conserved by multiple re-use, and the flux of materials to the environment (landfills, soil, and sediments) should be minimized. Engineers and designers should make sure that the material composition of a good is such that the re-use of all materials becomes possible for consecutive life cycles. Mining should be replaced by recycling. If materials are efficiently managed, the re-use of anthropogenic materials requires less energy than primary production from ores (steel, paper, glass, aluminium). However, this strategy will be successfully implemented only if the designing process is supplemented by the new objectives of a long-term sustainable metabolism of the anthroposphere.

3. In urban areas, the key processes for material fluxes are private households. They are characterized by a large turnover and a growing stock of materials. Hence, the management of wastes from households is an important part of regional material management. Recently developed integrated concepts are based on the principle that waste treatment should minimize long-term risks, and that it should produce only three kinds of residuals: (1) goods with final storage quality; (2) goods with adequate properties and markets for recycling; and (3) sustainable emissions (Brunner and Baccini, 1992).

4. A strategy for limiting inputs and outputs at the anthroposphere/environment interface, and for controlling materials within the anthroposphere itself, will replace the present practice of end-of-pipe oriented environmental protection. In order fully to exploit the potential of materials management for efficient resource conservation and environmental protection, it is essential to identify the key processes within a region and to establish their annual mat-

erial balance. Study of the Untere Bünztal has shown that data on the flux of goods are abundant and readily available; but for most materials, there is not enough information to establish a regional balance. Therefore, traditional financial bookkeeping has to be supplemented by material bookkeeping on all levels, such as those of private and public households, primary production, agriculture, trade and commerce, waste-treatment facilities, etc. Such accounting is not totally new: it is already customary for materials like gold, plutonium, and morphine-based drugs, and is well established in the banking sector, the nuclear industry, and in health care. In the case of private households or small and medium-sized enterprises, it could be delegated to specialized institutions while large enterprises could do it for themselves. If the information about material fluxes from the processing of ores to the manufacturing and distribution of goods can be linked to an overall material flux, regions will have an important tool to maximize the use of their resources and to minimize environmental impacts. In the future, regions which use materials accounting for their planning and management may gain considerable economic advantages (see table 6).

Notes

1. The total material consumption has increased by between one and two orders of magnitude from neolithic to modern man. The values given comprise the materials consumed in private households and the materials used for private transportation. The most important goods are water and air, used to transport wastes and offgases, followed by fuel for power, heating/ cooling, and transportation, and earth crust materials to construct the matrix of the anthroposphere. For details see Brunner and Baccini, 1992.
2. The *input* of lead into the anthroposphere has grown by between six and seven orders of magnitude. Owing to the lack of data about the *output*, the storage of lead in the anthroposphere cannot be estimated. If efforts to protect the environment are successful (i.e. if future fluxes to the environment are minimized), the stock in the anthroposphere will eventually become an important future resource of lead. Brockhaus (1967) and Settle and Patterson (1980), who provide the data for figure 2, attribute the peak to the extensive use of lead during the Roman Empire.
3. The system (fig. 4) comprises the anthroposphere of the region (B), the environment, and the regional boundary. For simplification, the anthrospheres of the neighbouring regions are treated as one single anthroposphere (N), containing the two processes "import" and "export" only. The bold arrows and boxes indicate the fluxes and processes which have been assessed in this work. The three processes "production sector," "service sector," and "public services" have been subdivided into 19 branches, and in each branch the most important businesses were identified and included in the assessment of the flux of goods.
4. Seventy-five per cent of the P consumed in households (including out-of-house meals) is ingested by man and discharged with urine and faeces. The sewers system is by far the most important transport vehicle for P contained in wastes. The difference between the input of P

in the process "private household" and the output of P measured in municipal solid waste and sewage was found to be <15 per cent.

5. Import and export are not in equilibrium; about 15 per cent of the lead imported in the region is stored in landfills and the soil. The two main processes for the lead flux are a shredder for used cars and a smelter for scrap iron. Since the landfill of the residue from the shredder and smelter is rapidly becoming the largest regional stock of lead, the quality of the waste products of these two processes is important for environmental protection (low mobility), as well as for use as a future resource (high concentration).

6. The main imports due to agricultural goods exceed the main export (River Bünz) by 35 per cent. The concentration of P in the soil increases annually by about 1 per cent. In the future, this reservoir may become the chief source of P for the River Bünz. In order to balance the input and output of P in the soil, the application of fertilizer should be reduced by more than 50 per cent. (Not all processes have been balanced: cf. STP, river.)

References

Baccini, P., ed. 1988. *The Landfill, Reactor and Final Storage*. Lecture Notes in Earth Sciences, 20. Berlin, Heidelberg, and New York: Springer Verlag.

Baccini, P., and P. H. Brunner. 1991. *Metabolism of the Anthroposphere*. Heidelberg and New York: Springer-Verlag.

Brunner, P. H., and P. Baccini. 1992. "Regional Materials Management and Environmental Protection." *Waste Management and Research* 10, no. 1.

Brockhaus, F. A. 1967. *Brockhaus Enzyklopädie*, vol. 2. Wiesbaden: ATF-BLIS, p. 655.

BAS Bundesamt für Statistik. 1985. *Allgemeine Systematik der Wirtschaftszweige 1985* [General Systematology for Economic Sectors 1985]. Bern: Federal Office of Statistics.

―――. 1987. *Die eidgenössische Betriebszählung 1985* [Swiss Federal Census of Places of Work 1985]. Bern: Federal Office of Statistics.

Ciba-Geigy. 1977. *Wissenschaftliche Tabellen Geigy* [Scientific Tables Geigy]. Basel: Ciba-Geigy Ltd.

Rist, A., H. Daxbeck, and P. H. Brunner. 1989. *Überblick über den Güterumsatz in Industrie und Gewerbe des 2. Sektors im Unteren Bünztal* [Survey of the Material Turnover in the Production Sector of the Lower Bünz Valley]. EAWAG Project no. 300712. Dübendorf, Switzerland: EAWAG.

Settle, D. M., and C.C. Patterson. 1980. "Lead in Albacore: A Guide to Lead Pollution in Americans." *Science* 207: 1167–1176.

Von Steiger, B., and P. Baccini. 1990. *Regionale Stoffbilanzierung von landwirtschaftlichen Böden mit messbarem Ein- und Austrag* [Material Balances of Agricultural Soils]. Liebefeld-Bern, Switzerland: Nationales Forschungsprogramm "Nutzung des Bodens in der Schweiz."

9

A historical reconstruction of carbon monoxide and methane emissions in the United States, 1880–1980

Robert U. Ayres, Leslie W. Ayres, and Joel A. Tarr

Introduction

In this chapter we attempt to reconstruct the historical emissions of two major atmospheric pollutants in the United States during the century 1880–1980: carbon monoxide (CO) and methane (CH_4).[1] Both are involved, directly or indirectly, in the creation of urban "smog" conditions, environmental health problems, acid rain, climate warming, or all of these. We approach the problem of historical reconstruction by identifying the main anthropogenic sources of each of the major emissions separately. This requires a discussion of a number of major industrial metabolic processes, as well as a review of some economic history. In preparing this chapter, a variety of historical and contemporary sources were used in order to produce a series of back-casts, since no direct measurement of these emissions took place until recent decades.

The methodology illustrated in this chapter (and also in chapter 11) is applicable in many other cases. Historical *ex post* reconstructions are of importance in calibrating more recent observational data. Such calibrations, in turn, are important for the purpose of developing viable long-term environmental forecasting models, and for a better understanding and validation of the concept of "industrial metabolism."

The chapter is divided into two sections.

Carbon monoxide (CO)

Carbon monoxide combustion sources

Carbon monoxide is produced by incomplete combustion of carbon-based fuels. This occurs when a carbonaceous fuel is burned in a *rich* mixture, i.e. in a *reducing* atmosphere.[2] In recent years, by far the greatest tonnages of CO in the United States, as elsewhere, have been produced by the automobile; hence we consider this source first. Emissions depend on certain driving conditions, as shown in figures 1 and 2. In particular, uncontrolled emissions decrease with average speed. National average CO emissions for urban driving prior to the adoption of emission controls for automobiles (*c.* 1965) were estimated to be about 3.1 per cent by volume, or 31,000 ppm. (Hurn, 1968). More recent revised (1986) EPA estimates have reduced this by 33 per cent. It is now thought that uncontrolled CO emissions from automotive vehicles amount to 2 per cent of exhaust gases by volume.

The composition of gasoline is approximately C_8H_{18}, with a molecular weight of 114. In the fuel/air mixture corresponding to average engine conditions during the pre-control era (i.e. resulting in 2 per cent CO in the exhaust), approximately 43 molecules of atmospheric nitrogen (N_2), and slightly less than 12 molecules of oxygen (O_2) combine with 1 "molecule" of gasoline. The exhaust mixture contains about 43 molecules of nitrogen, 9 molecules of water vapour (H_2O), 6.8 molecules of CO_2, and 1.2 molecules of CO, plus very small amounts of oxygen, unburned fuel, etc. Note that about 2 out of 13 of the carbon atoms in the fuel are not fully oxidized. In terms of weight, uncontrolled automotive CO emissions were equivalent to the ratio of molecular weights $(1.2*28)/114 = 0.295$. In other words, for each ton of gasoline consumed, nearly 0.3 tons (295 kg) of toxic CO was emitted.

Emissions of CO in 1970, from automotive vehicles, were originally estimated by EPA (1969) to be 100 teragrams, or Tg. Controls introduced in new automobiles cut motor vehicle emissions from motor vehicles by about 50 per cent per unit of fuel consumed. In absolute

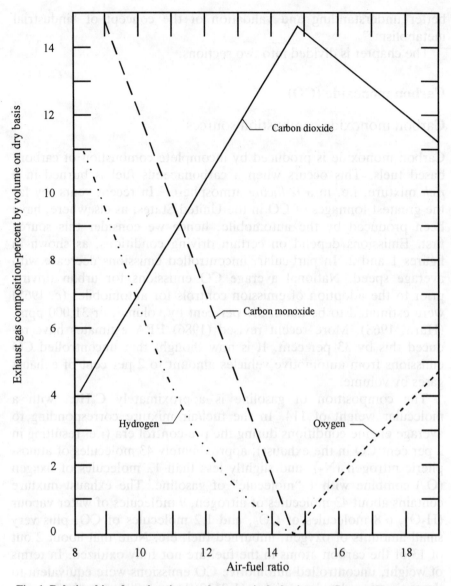

Fig. 1 Relationship of combustion products to air-fuel mixture (Source: Hurn, 1968)

terms, the reduction was from 62.7 teragrams in 1970 (peak) to 52.7 teragrams in 1980 (and 48.5 in 1984). This relatively minor decrease is in sharp contrast to the 90 per cent reduction in emission that was set as a goal of air-pollution-control efforts in the late 1960s.

The slowness of the change is partly due to the fact that cars re-

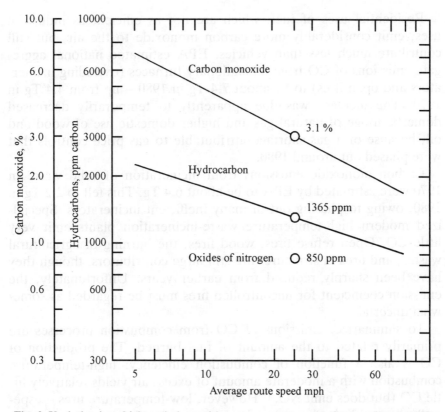

Fig. 2 Variation in vehicle emissions with average route speed (Source: Hurn, 1968)

main in use for more than a decade on average. Thus changes in the emissions characteristics of new cars are not reflected in overall fleet emissions for many years. However, it is also evident that the current automotive emissions control technology is less effective on older cars.

Motor vehicle engines are not the only combustion process where CO is generated. However, by comparison, most enclosed stationary combustion processes utilize enough excess air to reduce sharply the amount of unburned hydrocarbons and CO. Old coal-burning industrial boilers, for instance, generated apparent CO emissions in the range of 0.1 to 0.55 kg (CO) per metric ton of coal. This corresponds to an emission coefficient in the range 0.0001 to 0.00055. More recent boilers tend to be at the lower end of the range.[3] By comparison with automobiles, however, electric power generating facilities and large industrial boilers are not significant sources of CO.

Residential uses of fuel, which are not as efficient as industrial uses, emit considerably more carbon monoxide to the air, but still contribute much less than vehicles. EPA estimated national aggregate emissions of CO from all stationary furnaces (excluding incinerators and open fires) to be about 7.4 Tg in 1980 – up from 4.4 Tg in 1970. The increase was due apparently to temporarily decreased domestic usage of natural gas and higher domestic use of wood and oil, because of a gas shortage attributable to gas price controls that were phased out around 1980.

Carbon monoxide emissions from incineration of solid waste in 1970 were estimated by EPA to be about 6.4 Tg. This fell to 2.2 Tg in 1980, owing to phasing out of many inefficient incinerators. Specialized modern high-temperature waste-incineration plants emit very little CO. Open refuse fires, wood fires, the burning of agricultural wastes, and fires in structures are still large contributors, though they have been sharply reduced from earlier years. Unfortunately, the emission coefficient for uncontrolled fires must be regarded as somewhat uncertain.

To summarize, emissions of CO from combustion processes are primarily related to the amount of fuel burned. The production of CO is also a function of combustion efficiency: high-temperature combustion with a moderate amount of excess air yields relatively little CO (but does emit NO_x). However, low-temperature fires – especially "smouldering" ones – do generate significant emissions. For this reason, it can safely be assumed that the *average* CO output per unit of fuel consumed was somewhat greater in the past than it is today. We justify this statement in detail later. However, the main cause was greater dependence on solid fuels (wood, then coal) for domestic and residential heating purposes.

Up until the late nineteenth century, wood was the most important type of fuel used by Americans. In 1850 it supplied over 90 per cent of fuel supplies and in 1870 it still supplied 75 per cent. The peak of physical consumption was reached with the consumption of nearly 140 million cords in the latter year. After this point, the use of wood for fuel gradually declined, reaching 2.6 per cent of total energy consumption in 1955 (Schurr and Netschert, 1960).

Wood was used preferentially as long as it was abundant, in spite of the fact that it had several disadvantages. Its preparation was relatively labour-intensive compared to coal production. Wood also has less heat value than coal; a cord of dried hardwood weighs twice as much as a ton of coal but only contains 80 per cent of its heat value. Because of its inefficient use, dependence on wood fuel contributed to energy intensiveness. In 1850 households consumed 90 per cent of all wood fuel, with 75 per cent burned for space heating in large open fireplaces that operated at low thermal efficiency. Little wood fuel was utilized to generate mechanical energy outside the transportation sector (Greenberg, 1980).

During the decades after 1850, wood was increasingly replaced as a fuel in all sectors by anthracite and then bituminous coal. Per capita consumption of fuel wood dropped from 3.51 net tons in 1850 to 2.17 tons in 1880, and then to 1.01 tons in 1900. In 1879, about 95.5 per cent of fuel wood was consumed by households and about 4.5 per cent for industrial purposes. In eastern cities such as Philadelphia, and in some western cities such as Pittsburgh with good access to coal supplies, mineral fuels began to replace wood in the 1820s. In rural areas, however, and in cities without good access to coal, wood remained the primary fuel throughout the nineteenth century. In regard to industry, railroads were the heaviest users of wood fuel in manufacturing and transportation up to about 1870. After this date, however, mineral fuels (first anthracite but later mainly bituminous coal) rapidly replaced wood. By 1880, mineral fuels, mostly bituminous coal, already constituted more than 90 per cent of locomotive fuel (Schurr and Netschert, 1960; Tarr and Koons, 1982).

For our purposes it is necessary to estimate the past emissions of CO from fuel wood and coal combustion for residential heating and cooking. Even as late as 1910, the equipment used for these purposes was very inefficient. This is easily confirmed by direct evidence. (Ashes collected in New York City were found to consist of 55 per cent carbon by weight; Hering and Greeley, 1921.) When wood or lump coal is burned in fireplaces, kitchen stoves, or domestic furnaces (as much of it was), combustion tends to be incomplete. This is because the first stage of low-temperature combustion produces mainly CO. The CO only ignites and oxidizes to CO_2 in air at temperatures above 1191–1216 °F, and at concentrations above 12.5 per cent by volume.

Thus, without mechanical fuel-air mixing (or convective mixing in large furnace volumes), the production of a significant amount of unburned CO is almost inevitable. In wood stoves, CO emissions range from 0.083 to 0.37 ton per ton of wood (0.16 average), while in open fireplaces emissions range from 0.011 to 0.04 tons/ton (0.022 average). In the case of anthracite coal, burned mostly in stoves or furnaces, we assume slightly greater combustion efficiency (higher temperature), corresponding to the low end of the range of wood (0.08 tons/ton), and we assume that the proportion of wood burned in stoves or furnaces was 20 per cent in 1800, rising to 50 per cent in 1860, then declining gradually to 10 per cent in 1950. We also assume that the proportion of wood burned in stoves had risen to 30 per cent by 1980, owing to the revival of wood-burning as a source of residential heat.

The burning of trash and refuse is still a major source of CO emissions, but emission coefficients for earlier methods are difficult to estimate. Municipal batch-type incinerators (since 1945) were mostly built to a design that resulted in CO emissions of about 0.055 per cent (520–570 ppm), compared to 12 per cent CO_2. Since each molecule occupies the same volume regardless of weight, this means that about 1 molecule of CO is created for every 21 molecules of CO_2. Assuming that dry combustible refuse – mostly paper – has a carbon content of 39 per cent by weight (similar to cellulose), we infer that about 0.0325 tons of CO are emitted per ton of refuse burned. Unfortunately, we lack statistics on the tonnage of refuse that has been incinerated over the last century.

Emissions of CO from industrial processes

The other significant sources of past and present CO emissions (see table 4) are (or were) industrial processes, primarily in the metallurgical and petrochemical industries. In particular, the reduction of iron ore to metallic iron is a process requiring the manufacture of carbon monoxide in large amounts.[4] This takes place in a blast furnace; the carbon is supplied from coke (nowadays supplemented by other hydrocarbons). However, until the coking process was developed, the source of carbon for smelting was charcoal, made from wood. The resulting pig iron is a solid solution of iron carbide (Fe_3C) in a matrix of iron (Fe). Further refining to pure iron or steel requires that most of this carbon be oxidized. Both smelting and refining result in the production of large quantities of carbon monoxide.

Other metals are reduced by similar carbothermic smelting processes, also yielding CO as a by-product. In the case of aluminium, reduction takes place in an electrolytic cell, and the carbon is supplied by anodes made from petroleum coke. Again, the carbon combines with the oxygen in the alumina, yielding pure aluminium and CO.[5]

200

On deeper reflection, much of the apparent complexity of the chemistry is irrelevant. Each atom of oxygen originally combined with a metal as ore is subsequently combined with an atom of carbon as CO. The amount of carbon monoxide *created* in metallurgical smelting/refining processes is thus exactly proportional to the amount of the metal that is *reduced* from ore. Thus, in the case of iron, hypothetical production of 50 million metric tons of pig iron (94 per cent Fe by weight) corresponds to a production of 47 million tons of pure Fe. This, in turn, implies an input of 67.14 million tons of Fe_2O_3, of which 20.14 million tons are oxygen. When the reduction processes are complete, it follows that exactly 35.24 million tons of CO must have been produced. The "bottom line" is that 0.75 tons of CO are produced within the blast furnace or steel furnace for each ton of iron (Fe) reduced from iron ore. (This relationship is universal, so it applies to all ores and all furnaces.) By a similar calculation, each ton of virgin aluminium generates 1.555 tons of CO.[6] Under modern conditions, of course, most of this CO is either captured and utilized as fuel (called blast furnace gas) or it is flared. However, in earlier periods of industrial history this was not the case.

As noted above, the theoretical ratio of CO to Fe is 0.75. This corresponds to a C:Fe ratio of 0.43. That is, at least 0.43 tons of C are needed in principle to produce a ton of iron. Assuming that all this carbon is derived from coke, this would correspond to a blast furnace "coke rate" of 0.404 tons of coke per ton of pig iron (94 per cent Fe). As a matter of fact, according to the Office of Technology Assessment, the coke rate in Japan in 1976 was 0.43, as compared to 0.48 in the Federal Republic of Germany, 0.52 in France, and 0.60 in the United States and the United Kingdom.[7]

As already noted, until the 1850s iron-making in the United States was based on charcoal. The making of charcoal is a very old process dating back at least 2,000 years, and remained relatively unchanged until the eighteenth century. In that century and into the nineteenth, its greatest use was in regard to the production of iron. Charcoal was an ideal furnace fuel because it was relatively free from sulphur or phosphorus impurities and because its ash had properties that were helpful in smelting the ore.

Essentially, the making of charcoal involved the controlled burning of wood in the location of an iron furnace. In the north-eastern United States, these furnaces were located on so-called "iron plantations" situated within large wooded areas. The availability of a flowing stream was also a necessity. In 1830, there were a number of iron plantations of 10,000 or more acres. Normally, the tasks of woodcutting and charcoal-making demanded more workers than any other task at the ironworks: it sometimes required as many as 12 colliers to keep a single furnace working.

Because dry weather was necessary, most charcoal was made during the late spring, summer, and early autumn. The process followed was to stack bundles of cord wood in 6- to 10-foot lengths in a cone with a base of about 25 feet in diameter, cover it with damp leaves and turf, and burn it for between three and ten days. No attempt was made to condense any of the by-product wood chemicals or impurities vented from the chimney during the charcoaling process.

As suggested already, early charcoal (and iron) furnaces were not thermodynamically efficient. Charcoal iron furnaces utilized huge amounts of fuel. Peter Temin has calculated that since one acre of timber provided an average of about 30 cords of wood and each cord of wood produced 40 bushels of charcoal, an acre of timber supplied 1,200 bushels of charcoal. In 1840, a ton of pig iron required 180 bushels of charcoal, so that the wood from one acre of land would supply fuel to make 6⅔ tons of pig iron.[8] Factors such as wood quality and labour quality could make a difference in production.

From the late eighteenth century up until the 1820s, there was little change in the technology of production in the charcoal iron industry. Production was largely a function of oven size, and furnaces stayed stable in shape until the 1820s. The typical blast furnace of the older type had constricted internal dimensions and a narrow top diameter, so that total height might be only three or four times the interior width. The furnaces were open at the top, permitting carbon monoxide, heat, and smoke to escape. The furnace was charged with alternate layers of charcoal, ore, and limestone. As the air blast was applied, the ore melted at the air inlet (*tuyere*) of the furnace and dropped to the hearth, while the floating slag was drawn off from the top of the molten iron pool. When the charge was exhausted, the molten pig iron was run into a casting bed of sand about twice a day (Bining, 1973; Paskoff, 1983).

In the years after 1840 and especially after the Civil War, technological improvements resulted in a reduction of charcoal consumption per ton of iron smelted. New blast furnaces were built that reached a height of 40–45 feet in the 1840s, while after the Civil War they reached 65 feet. These new furnaces used higher temperature air blasts and were built with narrower internal dimensions and more vertical walls. They were located only in the immediate vicinity of ore beds and generally along canals and navigable rivers. This suggests that proximity to ore and transportation, rather than to timber for charcoal, were the critical factors in the location of charcoal iron furnaces (Schallenberg and Ault, 1977). Such furnaces had much higher rates of production than those in the antebellum years. One Michigan furnace produced a ton of iron with about 81.5 bushels of charcoal, or less than half the amount estimated to have been necessary in the 1840s (Schallenberg and Ault, 1977).

There were continuous improvements in the technology of charcoal-making during the second half of the nineteenth century. Charcoal kilns were introduced in the 1850s and were adopted throughout the industry after the war. The kiln was a permanent shell built of masonry, brick, or sheet iron and had vents to control the rate of carbonization. The maximum production of kilns was between 45 and 50 bushels of charcoal per cord. A few such kilns had gas by-product collection pipes for the production of wood chemical distillates, but this was rare (Schallenberg and Ault, 1977). In the 1870s and 1880s, the retort method of making charcoal was adopted, with wood being carbonized by external heat. Output of these retorts was 60–65 bushels of charcoal per cord of wood. With this technology, the methanol, tar, and other volatile by-products were passed into an integral chemical plant for condensation and separation and eventual sale. These plants were highly mechanized and capital-intensive but had much lower labour costs than previous methods of charcoaling (Schallenberg and Ault, 1977). These improvements, however, took place in the context of a relatively static market for charcoal iron and a dramatic increase in the use of mineral fuels, especially bituminous coal and coke, in iron production.

By 1854, the first date for which comparative figures are available, charcoal fuel was used to produce 306,000 tons of pig iron, 303,000 tons of anthracite and coke, and 49,000 tons of bituminous coal. By 1870, charcoal was used in the production of 326,000 tons of pig iron, 830,000 tons of anthracite and coke, and 509,000 tons of bituminous coal and coke. By 1905, bituminous coal and coke had taken a dramatic lead, producing 20,965,000 tons, against 1,644,000 tons of anthracite and coke, and only 353,000 tons of charcoal.

"Best practice" charcoal-based iron furnaces built in the 1880s – competing with less efficient coke-based technologies – achieved a conversion rate of about 1.0 (tons carbon/tons pig iron). This became the *average* for charcoal-based iron furnaces by 1919, when average coke-based iron still required 1.2 tons/ton. However, by that time, the best practice coke-based iron-making was as efficient as the remaining few charcoal furnaces. The coke rate is still regarded as a primary measure of efficiency. The overall average C:Fe ratio can be assumed to have declined almost linearly from about 1.9 in 1840 to its 1976 value of 0.6, as shown in figure 3.

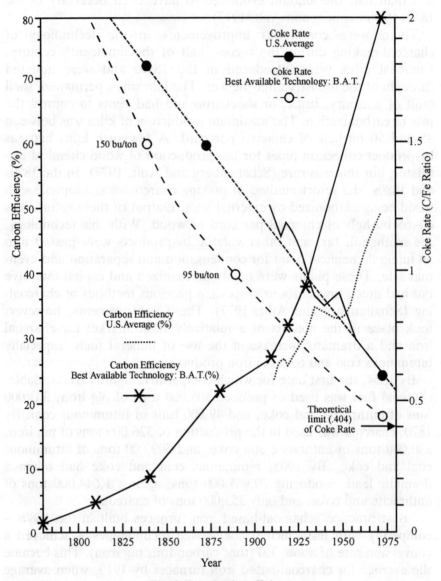

Fig. 3 Fe reduction efficiency

Table 1 Imputed efficiency of charcoal conversion (percentages)

	Reported conversion rates[a]		
Assumed weight of 1 cord	c. 1840 35–40 bu/cord (700–800 lb charcoal/cord)	c. 1875 45–50 bu/cord (900–1,000 lb charcoal/cord)	c. 1910 60–65 bu/cord (1,200–1,300 lb charcoal/cord)
2,500 lb (Ayres and Scarlott, 1952)	70–80	90–100	120–130[b]
3,000 lb (Riegel, 1937)	58.3–66.7	75–87.5	100–130[b]
4,000 lb (Schurr and Netschert, 1960)	43.8–50.0	56.3–62.5	75.0–81.2

a. Assuming 12 per cent moisture.
b. These figures are physically impossible.

The total amount of carbon monoxide produced per unit of iron has dropped even more drastically, since charcoal manufacture a century or more ago was an inefficient process. Assuming cordwood to be 12 per cent moisture (H_2O) and 88 per cent cellulose ($(C_6H_{10}O_5)_n$), an ideal carbonization process would yield 0.39. (about 0.4) tons of charcoal (C) per ton of wood, with no emission of CO. However, in practice the yield of charcoal in the nineteenth century was less than this. A by-product wood distillation plant operated by the Ford Motor Co. (1936) yielded 649 lb of charcoal per (short) ton of dry scrap wood, or 0.3245 tons C per ton Fe (Riegel, 1937). In terms of charcoal output, this corresponds to an efficiency of 0.32/0.39, or 82 per cent, probably the highest level practically achievable. Yield efficiencies are calculated in table 1 for several different charcoal yields and wood density assumptions.

On the basis of these calculations it is fairly clear that the lower weight estimates are inconsistent with the higher estimates of charcoal output. This reduces the uncertainty. If conversion rates as high as 60 bu/cord were ever achieved the wood must have been both dry and unusually dense. We note that an average of 3,500 lb/cord (12 per cent H_2O) and a maximum conversion efficiency of 82 per cent would imply a charcoal output of $0.82 \times 1,400 = 1,148$ lb or 57.4 bushels of charcoal. This appears to be a reasonable figure. The 35–40 bu/cord conversion rate was reported as typical of current practice in the 1840s. Average yield in 1879 was 49 bu/cord, according to one source (Schurr and Netschert, 1960). Known technological improvements in the 1890s presumably increased the average yield to some degree. All

Table 2 Comparison of charcoal processes

Year	Charcoal conversion rate (bu/cord)	Charcoal conversion efficiency (%)	Ratio of carbon input (in wood) to carbon output (in charcoal)
1840	35–40	50–57	1.75–2.0
1879	49	70	1.43
1937	57.4	82	1.22

things considered, we therefore adopt 3,500 (3,250–3,750) lb/cord as the "best guess" of average wood density. This implies the historical trend in efficiency shown in table 2.

Extensive use of anthracite as a substitute for charcoal in the iron industry came in the 1840s; it was made possible by the application of the hot blast to the iron-making process. Anthracite reduced fuel costs by almost half compared to charcoal, leading to its rapid adoption. Anthracite furnaces sprang up along the established coal trade routes close to urban areas, with the Lehigh Valley of Pennsylvania becoming the centre of the anthracite industry. By 1846, there were 43 anthracite blast furnaces in Pennsylvania and by 1856 there were 92. In the latter year Pennsylvania produced three times as much anthracite pig iron as charcoal iron, or approximately 300,000 tons (the national total was 394,509 tons) (Binder, 1974; Chandler, 1972).

According to historian Alfred D. Chandler, the combination of iron and coal "encouraged large-scale manufacturing of iron products for the first time. . ." (Chandler, 1972). Factories appeared for wire products, railway tracks, wheels, locomotives, steam engines, stoves, and agricultural equipment such as harvesters and ploughs.

Anthracite was also used in other industries requiring heat in the manufacturing process, such as glass and paper, baking, sugar-refining, and brewing, as well as in the processing of earthenware, plated ware, and chemicals (Chandler, 1972). While anthracite was to retain its importance in general industrial use and domestic heating for generations, its importance in the making of iron products was relatively short-lived, as shown in figure 4. Once the railroads had crossed the Appalachian Mountains in the 1850s, thereby making bituminous coal readily available, anthracite was rapidly displaced as a source of carbon in iron-making.

Combining all the above factors, we can now estimate the total production and emissions of carbon monoxide per ton of iron.

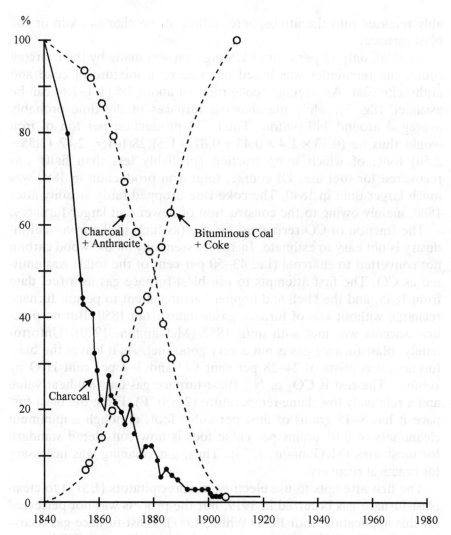

Fig. 4 Substitution of anthracite and coke for charcoal in iron-making in the US (Source: Temin, 1964)

In 1840, all iron was made with charcoal. The average consumption was 180 bushels (1.8 tons) of charcoal per ton of pig iron (94 per cent Fe), and each atom of carbon embodied in charcoal was accompanied by between 0.86 and 1.0 atoms of carbon in waste carbon monoxide: we assume the median value of 0.93. A ton of pig iron, therefore, required the production of $1.8 \times 0.93 \times 28/16 = 2.93$ (2.71–3.15) tons of carbon monoxide. Essentially, all of this was presumably released into the atmosphere, either at the charcoal kiln or the blast furnace.

By 1880, only 13 per cent of US pig iron was made by the charcoal route; the remainder was based on coke or a mixture of coke and anthracite coal. An average "coke rate" of about 1.5 (1.4–1.6) can be assumed (fig. 3), while the charcoal furnaces of the time probably averaged around 140 bu/ton. Total CO production per ton of iron would thus be $(0.13 \times 1.4 \times 0.43 + 0.87 \times 1.5)(28/16) = 2.42$ (2.35– 2.50) tons, of which some fraction (probably less than half) was recovered for fuel use. Of course, total iron production in 1880 was much larger than in 1840. The coke rate dropped fairly steadily after 1880, mainly owing to the construction of newer and larger furnaces.

The fraction of CO recovered for use (as fuel) in the iron/steel industry is not easy to estimate. In 1840, essentially all the wood carbon not converted to charcoal (i.e. 43–50 per cent of the total) was emitted as CO. The first attempts to use blast-furnace gas as a fuel date from 1845, and the "bell and hopper" arrangement to permit furnace recharge without loss of furnace gases dates from 1850. But no practical success was met with until 1857 (McGannon, 1970). Unfortunately, blast-furnace gas is not a very good fuel. As it leaves the blast furnace, it consists of 24–28 per cent CO and 3–4 per cent H_2O by volume. The rest is CO_2 or N_2. Blast-furnace gas has low heat value and a relatively low flame temperature (2,650 °F). From the blast furnace it has 8–15 grains of dust per cubic foot, although a minimum cleanliness of 0.01 grains per cubic foot is now considered standard for most uses (McGannon, 1970). Thus, gas cleaning was necessary for practical recovery.

The first attempts to use electrostatic precipitators (ESPs) to clean blast-furnace gas occurred in 1919, but the process was not perfected for this application until 1930 (White, 1957). Blast-furnace gas recovery for in-plant fuel use can be assumed to have been negligible up to 1910, and no more than modest until after gas-cleaning technology had been perfected. However, with the availability of cost-effective technology, carbon monoxide recovery within large integrated iron and steel works was well advanced by 1937 and essentially complete by 1955. However, recovery is far less efficient in smaller specialty plants or other industries.

Hence, in the absence of better data it seems safe to suggest that most of the carbon monoxide produced in the iron/steel industry was not recovered until well into the twentieth century. We assume an increasing recovery fraction of around 20 per cent (15–25) in 1920, rising to 45 per cent (35–50) by 1937, reaching 75 per cent (60–80) by 1950 and 85 per cent (80–90) in 1960 (fig. 5). Even today, a considerable amount of CO is vented without flaring, principally by iron foundries, although the overall percentage of emissions is now rather low.

Petroleum refineries were also major sources of carbon monoxide at one time, mainly from catalyst regeneration (after 1900) and decoking of thermal distillation, cracking, and reforming units. In the 1950s, uncontrolled Los Angeles refineries generated about 20 kg of CO per ton of crude oil processed (Elkin, 1968) or a coefficient of 0.02. However, controls introduced by 1966 cut this down to about 1.2 kg/ton (0.0012). Most US refineries have since introduced even more rigorous controls, not so much to eliminate CO emissions as to eliminate the associated hydrocarbons, especially toxic PAHs. We assume that CO emissions per ton of crude oil processed in 1920 were significantly higher (0.05 to 0.10 tons/ton), mainly as a result of the decoking of batch-type thermal crackers.

The EPA attributes around 6.3 Tg of CO annually (1980) to industrial offgases, down from 9.0 Tg in 1970 (USEPA, 1986). However, a comprehensive survey of industrial sources of by-product CO carried out in 1977 indicated a total production of 142 million tons (128 Tg), of which 117 million tons were attributable to iron and steel manufacturing, and 14.5 million tons were generated by the petroleum industry (Rohrmann et al., 1977). Only 63 million tons were actually recovered as fuel (see table 3). Of the remainder, 57 million tons were classed as "not recoverable," on the grounds that it was largely oxidized to CO_2 at furnace walls prior to emission, and 22 million tons were identified as "flared or exhausted." As of the mid-1970s, some 17.8 million tons were still flared by the iron and steel, petroleum and carbon black industries (Rohrmann et al., 1977).

These figures imply that 4.2 million tons were vented by these three industries. It is virtually certain that some of the 57 million tons "not recoverable" was actually vented as CO, though in dilute form. The question is: how much? If 10 per cent of the "not recoverable" fraction were emitted, it would mean total industrial offgas emissions of 9.9 million tons. This is close to the EPA estimate, and seems plausible. However, if 20 or 30 per cent of the "unrecoverable" CO were actually emitted as such, a much larger total would result. Thus, the EPA emissions estimates are more likely to be too low than too high.

It is evident that emissions from two major industrial CO sources

ing to 45 per cent (35–50) by 1957, reaching 75 per cent (60–80) by 1980 and 85 per cent (80–90) in 1984 (fig. 5). Even today, a considerable amount of CO is vented without flaring, principally by iron foundries, although the overall percentage of emissions is now rather low.

Petroleum refineries were also major sources of carbon monoxide, at one time mainly from catalyst regeneration (after 1900) and decoking of thermal distillation, cracking, and reforming units. In the 1950s, Southern California Angeles refineries generated about 30 kg of CO per ton of crude oil processed (Elkin, 1968), or a coefficient of 0.02. However, emissions were reduced by 1966 or this down to about 1.2 kg/ton (0.0008?). Petroleum refineries have since introduced even more rigorous controls to eliminate CO emissions as to eliminate the associated hydrocarbons, especially toxic PAHs. We find that CO emissions per ton of crude oil processed in 1920 were significantly higher (0.3 to 0.10 tons/ton, mainly as a result of the older batch-type thermal crackers.

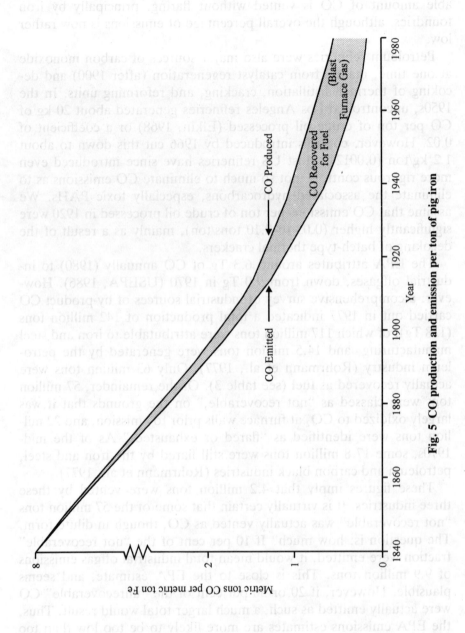

Fig. 5 CO production and emission per ton of pig iron

Table 3 Estimated annual production of by-product CO, 1975

	1,000 tons/yr/no. of sites				CO content vol (%)
	Produced theoretically	Recoverable from process	Used entirely as fuel at present	Flared or exhausted	
Iron and steel					
Sinter	1,090 (41)	1,090 (41)	0	1,090 (41)	0.35
Blast	58,280 (53)	58,280 (53)	43,898 (53)	12,382 (53)	22.5
BOF[a]	28,126 (36)	527 (36)	0	527 (36)	30
BOF[b]	3,781 (2)	3,781 (2)	3,781 (2)	0	50
Electric	25,751 (125)	294 (125)	0	294 (125)	0–6
Ferroalloys					
FeMn	976 (9)	617 (1)	543 (1)	617 (1)	40
FeCr	413 (10)	NA	0	NA	
FeSi	1,484 (15)	300 (3)	78 (1)	300 (3)	90
SiMn	148 (8)	44 (9)	0	44 (1)	
Other alloys	250 (11)	NA	0	NA	65
Coke ovens	2,439 (63)	2,439 (63)	2,439 (63)	0	6
Silicon products	370 (10)	NA	0	NA	
Aluminium	1,695 (32)	244 (5)	0	224 (5)	30
Phosphorus	1,316 (9)	1,316 (9)	1,184 (9)	132 (9)	98
Titanium dioxide	275 (8)	275 (8)	0	275 (8)	15
Carbon black	2,275 (29)	2,275 (29)	33 (1)	2,242 (29)	6
Calcium carbide	183 (5)	165 (3)	65 (2)	100 (3)	75
Lead and tin	363 (7)	363 (7)	0	363 (7)	<1
Zinc (thermal)	162 (2)	162 (2)	142 (2)	20 (1)	80
Petroleum refining	14,561 (149)	14,561 (149)	10,921 (112)	3,640 (37)	8
Kraft paper pulping	160 (116)	160 (116)	160 (116)	160 (116)	<1
Total	142,098	84,893	63,084	21,709	

NA = negligible CO available for recovery under present process conditions.
a. Without suppressed combustion.
b. With suppressed combustion.

(iron and steel, petroleum) have dropped sharply in recent decades. This is partly due to increased process efficiency and partly to concern for emissions control *per se*. Emissions from the paper and pulp, carbon black, petrochemical, ferroalloy, and non-ferrous metals industries have also dropped, though probably not as dramatically, since these industries are less concentrated. We can say, however, that in comparison with the petroleum and iron and steel sectors, they have not, until recently, contributed more than a small fraction of the total industrial emissions.

One other historical, but not contemporary, source of industrial CO emissions is worth mentioning: manufactured or "town" gas. Although the production of manufactured gas began early in the nineteenth century, it reached its peak from about 1880 to 1950, when it was largely displaced by natural gas. Manufactured gas was most widely used for lighting, as a cooking fuel, and for heating.

An authoritative study of the manufactured gas industry estimates that approximately 15 trillion cubic feet of gas was manufactured in the United States from 1880 to 1950. The number of sites in the nation during this period ranged from a high of about 1,000 in 1890 to a low of 200 in 1950. Size of plant increased considerably during this period, with the highest gas production of 365,000 million cubic feet occurring in 1930, from 737 plants, and the second highest in 1950, with 331,000 million cubic feet of gas from 194 plants. These plants were widely distributed throughout the nation, although New York, New Jersey, Massachusetts, and Pennsylvania had the highest production.

Manufactured gas was produced from coal by a variety of methods. The most common form of manufactured gas was so called water gas or "blue gas," produced by reacting coal or coke with steam at 1,000 to 1,400 °C, yielding a gas rich in hydrogen and carbon monoxide with a heating value of about 300 BTU per cubic foot.[9] On the West Coast manufactured gas was generated from petroleum in a process that thermally cracked the oil into a gaseous product known as "oil gas" (ERT, 1984).

This process was a major user of coal and coke in the United States, especially during the period 1900–1950. Losses of CO in the manufacturing process and in distribution were never accurately assessed, but could scarcely be much less than 2–3 per cent, and probably reached 5 per cent or more. Thus, in comparison with other industrial sources of CO at the time, this contribution was rather low.

Carbon monoxide emissions coefficients and estimates

Table 4 gives the USEPA (1986) estimates of CO emissions for the United States by decade from 1940 to 1980, by source category. As noted in the table itself, some of the earlier industrial estimates seem likely to be significantly too low, for reasons discussed in the text. Our estimates are based on known characteristics of combustion processes and metallurgical reduction processes and (admittedly crude) estimates of CO recovery/disposal efficiency in the past. However, we

Table 4 EPA estimates of CO emissions 1940–1980 (teragrams/yr)

Source	1940	1950	1960	1970	1980
Highway vehicles	22.0	33.1	46.5	62.7	45.3
Aircraft	0.0	0.8	1.6	0.9	1.0
Railroads	3.7	2.8	0.3	0.3	0.3
Vessels	0.2	0.2	0.6	1.1	1.4
Off-highway	3.4	6.7	8.0	6.8	4.7
Mobile source total	29.3	43.6	57.0	71.8	52.7
Electric power	0.0	0.1	0.1	0.2	0.3
Industrial boilers	0.4	0.5	0.6	0.7	0.6
Commercial/institutional heat	0.1	0.1	0.0	0.1	0.1
Residential heat	15.4	10.7	6.3	3.4	6.4
Stationary combustion total	15.9	11.4	7.0	4.4	7.4
Chemicals	3.8	5.3	3.6	3.1	2.0
Petroleum	0.2[a]	2.4[a]	2.8	2.0	1.6
Iron and steel mills	1.5	1.1[a]	1.3	1.6	0.9
Primary aluminium	0.0	0.1	0.3	0.6	0.8
Iron foundries	1.0	1.4	1.0	1.1	0.3
Pulp mills	0.1	0.2	0.3	0.6	0.7
Industrial total	8.6[a]	10.5[a]	9.3	9.0	6.3
Incineration	2.0	2.5	2.5	2.7	1.2
Open waste burning	1.3	1.8	2.6	3.7	1.0
Forest fires	22.8	12.8	6.7	5.1	6.9
Other burning	3.7	3.7	3.3	2.1	0.7
Waste and miscellaneous total	29.8	20.8	15.1	13.6	9.8
Grand total	81.6	86.3[a]	88.4[a]	98.8	76.2

Source: USEPA, 1986.
a. Almost certainly too low (see text).

Table 5 CO emission coefficients (tons CO/ton fuel)

Process	Fuel	1800	1860	1890	1920	1950	1980
Stationary fuel combustion for residential heating and cooking	Wood	0.05	0.09	0.072	0.054	0.036	0.063
	Anthracite coal	0.08	0.08	0.08	0.08	0.08	0.08
	Distillate						
	Natural gas						
Boiler fuel (all kinds)	Coal and oil	0.005	0.005	0.005	0.004	0.003	0.002
Petroleum refining runs to stills		—	—	—	0.02	0.02	0.023
Auto transportation	Gasoline	—	—	—	0.34	0.34	0.16
Iron and steel manufacturing (inc. charcoal)		8.11	2.15	1.10	0.25	0.10	0.02

conclude that the EPA estimates for uncontrolled industrial emissions are more likely to be too low than too high and that their historical estimates are certainly too low. Table 5 gives our assumed emissions coefficients.

Methane (CH$_4$)

Methane sources

Methane is emitted to the atmosphere primarily by anaerobic micro-organisms that obtain their metabolic energy from carbohydrates by fermentation, yielding methane as a waste product. Such organisms are found in wet soils, especially in swamps and flood-irrigated fields (e.g. rice paddies). They also live in the guts of termites and other wood-eating insects, and in the intestines of most herbivorous animals, especially cattle and sheep, where they assist with the digestion of cellulose.

These sources are anthropogenic to the extent that humans alter natural patterns, for example by deforestation to facilitate cattle-grazing, by draining wetlands, or by irrigation of drylands. However, because the methane production associated with various land uses and animal husbandry practices are not yet well understood, we have not quantified these changes in methane emissions for the United States over the past century. Our focus here is on methane emissions from fossil-fuel production and use, that is, coal-mining, coking, oil and gas drilling, and natural gas distribution. We discuss these four sources in this order.

Coal-mining

Coal is a porous carbonaceous material in which substantial quantities of gas (mainly methane) are typically found in cracks or adsorbed on the surfaces. The coal gas contains upward of 90 per cent methane – a typical figure would be 95 per cent. As the coal is broken up in the drilling and mining process and later crushed for use, most of this adsorbed methane is released into the atmosphere. This is the source of methane seepage into coal mines, which has resulted in many explosions and fires.

There is enormous variability between coal seams with regard to adsorbed methane, but for a given rank of coal the major variable is depth. Deeper coals contain more adsorbed gas than surface coals,

215

probably owing to the higher pressure. The US Bureau of Mines has developed an empirical equation relating gas volume (in litres/kg or m³/tonne) with depth:

$$V = k_0(0.096h)n = -b\frac{1.8h}{100} + 11$$

where h is depth in metres, k_0 and n_0 are parameters depending on the rank of the coal, and b is a function of density. Both are related to the ratio of fixed carbon to volatile matter, as shown in figure 6. Adsorptive capacity v. depth is plotted in figure 7.

From figure 7 we can estimate that the gas content of anthracite (from underground mines) ranges between 15 and 20 litres/kg (or cubic metres per metric ton). Appalachian bituminous coals average

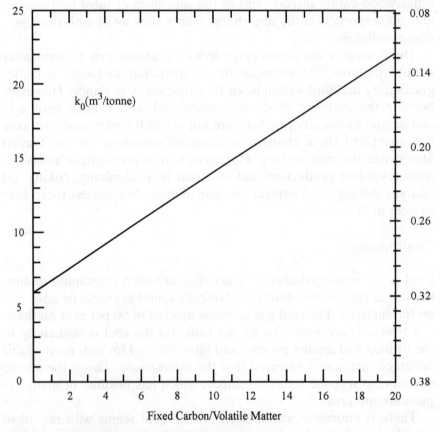

Fig. 6 Constants k_0 and n_0 as a function of fixed carbon/volatile matter ratio (Source: US Bureau of Mines)

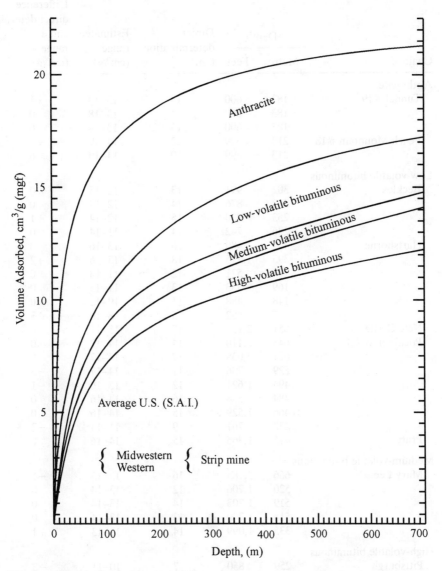

Fig. 7 Adsorptive capacity of coal as a function of rank and depth (Source: US Bureau of Mines)

10–15 litres/kg. Data for a number of mines in the Pittsburgh area are shown in table 6. Midwestern and Western strip-mined medium or low volatile coals would cluster generally in the range 5–10 litres/kg. The national average for all bituminous and anthracite coals has been estimated to be 6.25 or 7.0 litres/kg (SAI, 1980). Emissions

217

Table 6 Comparison of estimated and direct determination of methane content of coal

Coalbed	Depth Metres	Depth Feet	Direct determination (cm³/gᵃ)	Estimated range (cm³/g)	Difference direct deter. and est. range (cm³/g)
Anthracite					
Tunnel #19	183	600	19	13–18	+1
	183	600	14	13–18	0
	183	600	13	13–18	0
Peach Mountain #18	213	699	22	14–19	+3
	213	699	19	14–19	0
Low-volatile bituminous					
Beckley	302	991	13	12–15	0
	267	876	14	12–14	0
	253	830	15	12–14	+1
	236	742	14	11–14	0
Hartshorne	451	1,480	16	13–16	0
	395	1,295	18	13–16	+2
	174	571	12	11–13	0
	169	533	13	11–13	0
	148	488	11	10–12	0
	77	252	5	8–10	−3
New Castle	651	2,137	17	15–17	0
Pocahontas #3	643	2,110	14	14–17	0
	621	2,038	17	14–17	0
	529	1,736	11	14–17	−3
	494	1,621	12	13–16	−1
	484	1,588	16	14–16	0
	466	1,529	15	14–16	0
	232	761	9	11–14	−2
Pratt	416	1,365	15	14–16	0
Medium-volatile bituminous					
Mary Lee	666	2,185	16	13–15	+1
	520	1,706	12	13–14	0
	519	1,703	14	13–14	0
	518	1,700	13	13–14	0
	335	1,099	14	12–13	+1
High-volatile bituminous					
Pittsburgh	259	850	7	10–11	−3
	235	771	6	9–11	−3
	206	676	5	9–10	−4
	130	427	3	8–9	−5
	95	312	2	5–6	−3
Redstone	225	747	4	9–11	−5
Sewell	207	679	9	9–10	0
Sewickley	205	675	5	9–10	−4
Waynesburg	122	402	3	8–9	−5

Source: US Bureau of Mines.

a. 1 cm³/g = 1 litre/kg = 1 m³/mt.

218

from sub-bituminous coals and lignite are smaller (2.8 litres/kg and 1.4 litres/kg, respectively) and can probably be neglected for our purposes, since the quantities of these fuels mined in the United States are small.

The earliest coal mines in the United States were in Virginia. However, Pennsylvania and West Virginia soon became dominant sources and remained so until the last quarter of the nineteenth century, when the Illinois coal fields were opened. Western coals were extensively exploited even later. Utah, Wyoming, and Montana have large deposits of low-sulphur, high-ash coals relatively near the surface and accessible to large-scale strip-mining techniques. Meanwhile, some of the older Eastern mines have been largely exhausted (especially in the so-called Pittsburgh seam) and Eastern coals are increasingly from deeper mines. Nevertheless, coking coal used in the steel industry is still obtained mainly from the Appalachian mines.

Two long-term trends are apparent:
1. Eastern coal mines have become continuously deeper, on average, over time, with a corresponding gradual increase in associated methane release per ton of coal output to the present level.
2. Most of the increased total production since the late nineteenth century is due to the opening of shallower mines – mostly strip mines – in the Midwest and Far West. Western coals yield less methane per ton than Appalachian coal, but have increased as a fraction of total output.

Taking these two change factors into account we assume a slight increase in methane emissions from Eastern coals but a constant average for the United States as a whole. These contrary trends result in relatively constant average emission rates, as reflected in our historical emission coefficient estimates (table 7) at the end of this chapter.

Coking

Coke is the solid residue produced from the carbonization of bituminous coal after the volatile matter has been distilled off. The main object of coking is to free the bituminous coal from impurities – water, hydrocarbons and volatilizable sulphur – leaving in the coke fixed carbon, ash, and the non-volatilizable sulphur. The suitability of a coal for conversion to coke is determined by its "coking" properties. Coke is used primarily as a reducing agent for metal oxides in metallurgical processes and secondarily as a fuel. It was first used in

219

Table 7 Methane emissions coefficients (metric tons CH$_4$/metric ton of fuel)

	1800	1860	1890	1920	1950	1980
Anthracitea[a]	—	0.005	0.006	0.007	0.007	0.007
Appalachian bituminous (underground)[a]	0.005	0.005	0.005	0.005	0.005	0.005
Bituminous, US average	—	—	0.005	0.005	0.005	0.005
Coking[b]	—	—	0.270	0.054	0.030	—
Gas[c]	—	0.30	0.25	0.22	0.20	—
Gas distribution[d]	—	—	0.03	−0.02	0.01	0.01

a. Emissions coefficients for coal are calculated on the basis of an assumed density of 0.714 kg/m^3 for methane, and gas adsorption of 10 l/kg for anthracite and Appalachian bituminous coals, and 7 l/kg for average US bituminous coals.
b. Based on coal used for coking.
c. Based on unaccounted potential production of associated gas.
d. Based on gas marketed.

the iron-making process in Great Britain in the early 1750s as a replacement for charcoal. The primary factor driving the change was the costs – the cost of producing charcoal pig iron greatly increased in the latter half of the eighteenth century while the costs of coke pig iron fell sharply. By the end of the century, coke pig iron provided some 90 per cent of the total iron industry production in Great Britain (Hyde, 1977).

This substitution took place about a century later in the United States because of the greater availability of wood for charcoal manufacturing in the eastern US, as discussed previously. Before the 1830s, almost all pig iron was made with charcoal. In the 1830s, ironmakers began using mineral fuel in the iron-making process, but it was primarily anthracite rather than bituminous coal. By 1854, the first year for which aggregate statistics are available, pig iron made with anthracite constituted 45 per cent of the total pig iron produced in the country, while that made with bituminous coal only furnished 7.5 per cent. By 1880, however, the percentage of pig iron made with bituminous coal and coke had reached 45 per cent, mixed anthracite and coke provided the fuel for 42 per cent, while the remaining 13 per cent was made with charcoal. One state alone, Pennsylvania, provided 84.2 per cent of US coke production in that year. By 1911, bituminous coal and coke provided the reducing agent for 98 per cent of the pig iron manufactured (Temin, 1964; Warren, 1973).

The first method of making coke was copied from that used to prepare charcoal. Coal was heaped in piles or rows on level ground and covered with a layer of coal dust to minimize airflow. Once the process had been started (with the help of wood), the heat drove off the volatile gases, consisting of methane and ethane plus some ammonia and hydrogen sulphide (H_2S). These gases burned at the surface of the pile, which provided heat to keep the process going. When the gaseous matter had been used up, the heap was smothered with a coating of dust or duff, then cooled by wetting, leaving a silvery white residue high in carbon. If a higher, dryer heat was applied, the hydrogen sulphide gas was driven off but the sulphur remained and combined with the carbon. No attempt was made to capture any of the escaping gases. The time necessary for coking a heap was usually between five and eight days. The coke yield was approximately 59 per cent of the original mass (Binder, 1974). However, no information is available concerning the total amount of coke produced by this crude process.[10]

By the late nineteenth century, coke was produced mainly in the so-called beehive coke oven. Beehive coke was supposedly first made in western Pennsylvania in 1817; coke iron was produced for the first time in 1837, also in western Pennsylvania, from high-quality coking coal from the Connellsville seam (Warren, 1973). Extensive use of coke in the iron-making process, however, did not begin until after the Civil War. In 1855, there were 106 beehive ovens in the country; by 1880 there were 12,372 ovens in 186 plants, and by 1909 the maximum was reached with 103,982 ovens in 579 plants. By 1939, the number of beehive ovens had shrunk to 10,934 in 76 plants. In terms of their distribution, initially almost all of the beehive ovens were in the so-called Pittsburgh coal bed area located in western Pennsylvania and northern West Virginia. As late as 1918, over half the ovens in the country were still in this region (Eavenson, 1942).

Beehive ovens were arranged in single stacks or in banks of single or double rows. Most late-nineteenth-century ovens were charged from coal delivered by a car running on tracks above the wagon. Before charging, the ovens were preheated by a wood and coal fire. After the coal had been charged, the front opening was bricked up, with a 2- or 3-inch opening left at the top.

The coking process proceeded from the top downward, with the required heat for the coking process produced by the burning of the volatile by-products escaping from the coal. When no more volatile matter was escaping, the coking process was complete. The brickwork was removed from the door, and the coke was cooled with a water spray and then removed from the oven by either hand or

221

mechanical means (Wagner, 1916). The yield of high-class Connell-sville coal coked in beehive ovens in 1875 was 63 per cent (Platt, 1875); in 1911 the US Geological Survey reported that the average yield nationally for beehive ovens was 64.7 per cent (Wagner, 1916).

Still, no attempt was made to capture and utilize the valuable by-products resulting from the beehive coking process. The maximum tonnage of coal utilized in the beehive process was 53 million tons in 1910. If it is assumed that 10,000 cubic feet of gas can be produced from each ton of bituminous coal, then a potential of 530 billion cubic feet of gas that could have been utilized for various heating and light-ing processes was theoretically available from the beehive ovens. (Only a fraction of this was needed to provide heat for the process.) In addition, it is estimated that 400 million gallons of coal tar, nearly 150 million gallons of light oils, and 600,000 tons of ammonium sul-phate – an important fertilizer – were also wasted. Of course, captur-ing these by-products depended on the availability of a feasible and economical technology as well as on markets for the products (Schurr and Netschert, 1960).

There were some limited attempts to recapture by-products in the years before the Civil War. The so-called Belgian or retort oven re-sulted in the recovery of some by-products and was utilized primari-ly for low-volatile or "dry" coals. It had been pioneered by Belgian, German, and French engineers and the technology was gradually ap-plied in the American coal fields. Retort ovens generated a higher coke yield per ton of coal than the beehive ovens (average 70 per cent), produced valuable by-products, and provided for more rapid coking. However, the process was much more expensive than the beehive oven since the coals used had to be crushed, sorted, and cleaned before coking. A number of retort ovens were used by the Cambria Iron and Steel Works at Johnstown, Pennsylvania, in the 1870s. But the extensive adoption of the by-product oven in the United States did not occur until after 1900 (Warren, 1973).

By-product coke ovens constructed during the first decades of the twentieth century were of two types: the horizontal flue construction of Simon-Carves or the vertical flue of Coppee. In both cases the coking chamber consisted of long, narrow, retort-shaped structures built of firebrick and located side by side in order to form a battery of ovens. The retorts were usually about 33 feet long, from 17 to 22 in-ches wide, and about $6\frac{1}{2}$ feet high. The oven ends were closed by fire-brick-lined iron doors luted with clay to form a complete seal. The heat required for distillation was supplied by burning a portion of the gas evolving from the coal in flues which surrounded the oven. Some types of ovens constructed at the beginning of the century employed the recuperative principle for preheating the air for combustion, but most used a regenerative chamber to conserve heat better. The yield of by-products was determined by the quality and quantity of coke desired (Wagner, 1916).

The use of the by-product oven was originally limited by undeveloped markets for by-products to balance the higher costs of the capital equipment used by the process. Thus, beehive coke produced from high-quality Connellsville coal long maintained a cost advantage for local iron smelters. Utilization of some of the by-products, especially the high-calory coke-oven gas, to provide supplementary heat (e.g. for "soaking" pits or rolling mills) in the integrated iron and steel works themselves finally reduced the costs associated with the coking process below that required to produce beehive coke (Meissner, 1913). The result was a large expansion of the use of by-product ovens located at or near integrated steel mills, especially after the First World War (Warren, 1973). Fractional by-product recovery from all coking operations in the United States is shown in figure 8.

Emissions of methane to the atmosphere from by-product ovens can be assumed to be rather low. Emissions from beehive ovens can be presumed to correspond more or less to the methane content of coke-oven gas that was recovered from by-product ovens. The methane content of coking coal (based on average recovery from by-product ovens) can be taken as 27 per cent of the weight of the original coal.

Oil and gas drilling

Natural gas is found in distinct gas reservoirs or is present with crude oil in reservoirs. Two types of gas can be distinguished on the basis of their production characteristics: (1) non-associated gas, which is free gas not in contact with crude oil, or where the production of the gas is not affected by the crude oil production; (2) associated gas (also called "casinghead" gas), which is free gas in contact with crude oil that is significantly affected by the crude oil production; it occurs either as a "gas cap" overlying crude oil in an underground reservoir or as gas dissolved in the oil, held in solution by reservoir pressure (Schurr and Netschert, 1960).

Natural gas was encountered in the United States early in the nineteenth century in the drilling of water wells and brine wells. It

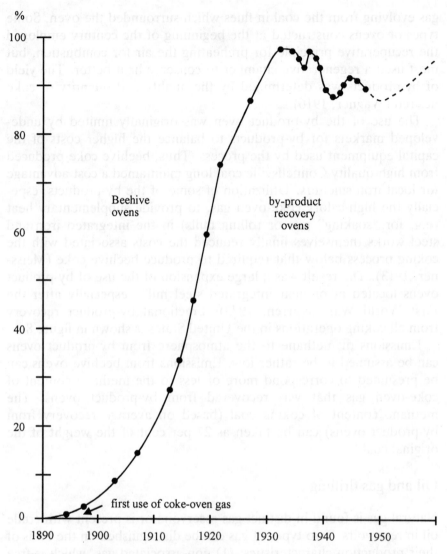

Fig. 8 By-product recovery from coke in the US (Source: US Bureau of Mines)

was not put to any practical use until 1824, when it was utilized for illumination and other purposes in Fredonia, New York. Systematic exploitation of the resource, however, whether for domestic or industrial purposes, did not occur until after the middle of the century and primarily in connection with drilling for oil (Stockton et al., 1952). Oil was first discovered in sizeable quantities in 1859 in western Pennsylvania, and the oilfields of the Appalachian area in the

224

states of New York, Ohio, Pennsylvania, Indiana, Kentucky, and West Virginia were the first to be developed. Natural gas was "associated" with these oilfields, but "non-associated" gas wells were also regularly discovered in these areas (Henry, 1970). Other nineteenth-century discoveries of oil and natural gas were made in California, Kansas, Arkansas, Louisiana, Texas, and Wyoming.

Statistics on sources of gas (gas wells and oil wells) have been kept in the United States only since 1935. The fraction attributable to gas wells producing no oil (non-associated gas) has been rising almost continuously since the statistics have been kept. Fitting a logistic curve to the data and extrapolating backward in time suggests that the "non-associated" fraction might have been about 10 per cent in 1860 when oil production began (see figure 9). It is clear from anecdotal evidence that some wells at least were producing gas alone as early as 1870 (Henry, 1970).

Oilfield gas was first put to use in the areas around the wells, where it lighted the oil derricks and raised steam for the well-pumping engines. This utilization was dependent on the invention of separators or gas traps to separate the oil from the gas. These were first developed in about 1865, with the subsequent invention of a

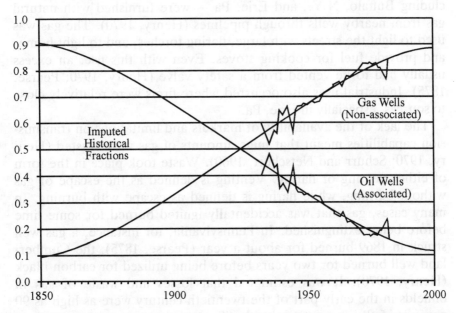

Fig. 9 Natural gas production from oil and gas wells (Source: Nakicenovic and Gruebler, 1987)

225

variety of separators (Kiessling et al., 1939). As late as 1950, the largest single class of natural gas consumption was in gas and oilfield operations (18.9 per cent or 1,187 billion cubic feet) (Stockton et al., 1952).

After field use, another important industrial use of natural gas that did not require transmission over long distances was the manufacture of carbon black. Carbon black plants were located near the wells where they took advantage of large volumes of cheap gas not usually tapped by transmission lines. Carbon black manufacture (for ink) began in Cumberland, Md., in 1870 (Henry, 1970). It was widespread in the Appalachian fields during the late nineteenth century, although most plants were gone by 1929 (Thoenen, 1964). In 1950, about 93 per cent of the industry was located in the south-western states of Texas, Louisiana, New Mexico, and Oklahoma. An upsurge in demand for carbon black occurred after 1915, when it was found that by adding carbon black to natural latex the structure and durability of rubber products such as tyres was greatly increased (Stockton et al., 1952).

Where municipal markets were relatively close, the gas was piped to them. As early as 1873, for instance, several towns in the oil region of New York State, Pennsylvania, Ohio, and West Virginia – including Buffalo, N.Y., and Erie, Pa. – were furnished with natural gas from nearby wells through pipelines (Henry, 1970). The gas was used to light the streets with large, flaring torches, and to light homes and provide fuel for cooking stoves. Even with this use, an excess usually had to be vented from a safety valve (Henry, 1970; Pearse, 1875). Industrial uses also occurred where firms were relatively close to sources, especially in Erie, Pa.

The lack of the availability of markets and limitations on transmission capabilities meant that huge amounts of gas were wasted (Henry, 1970; Schurr and Netschert, 1960). Waste took place in the form of either venting or flaring. Venting is defined as the escape of gas without burning, while flaring is defined as escape with burning. In many cases, gas that was accidentally ignited burned for some time before being extinguished. In Pennsylvania, for instance, a gas well struck in 1869 burned for about a year (Pearse, 1875); the Cumberland well burned for two years before being utilized for carbon black (Henry, 1970). It was estimated that losses and waste of gas in oilfields in the early part of the twentieth century were as high as 90 per cent of all gas associated with oil production.

Many gas wells were left to "blow," especially because of the expectation that oil would flow when the gas head had gone (Stockton et al., 1952; Williamson and Daum, 1959). West Virginia was an important oil and gas producer at the turn of the century and in 1903 it was estimated that during the previous five years 500 million cubic feet of gas had been "allowed to escape into the air" each day from the state wells (Thoenen, 1964). In Illinois, in 1939, it was estimated that 95 per cent (134 billion cubic feet) of the gas associated with the new Salem oilfield in the state was flared. From 1937 to 1942 it was estimated that 416 billion feet of gas were flared in Illinois (Murphy, 1948). In other cases, discovery wells in gas fields were capped or plugged and "forgotten." In the case of the early fields, many wells were inadequately plugged (Thoenen, 1964; Prindle, 1981). Losses from such wells cannot be estimated with any accuracy, although the quantity lost was probably quite small by later standards.

The best-known example of waste was in the Texas fields in the 1930s. When the natural gas in an unassociated well is allowed to expand rapidly or is cooled, somewhat less than 10 per cent of the gas condenses into a liquid (natural gasoline) suitable for use in vehicles. The phenomenon had first been observed around the turn of the century in the Appalachian fields, where so-called "drip" or casinghead gasoline was often considered a nuisance. The invention of the internal combustion engine, however, provided a market for such "natural" gasoline, and a number of small gasoline plants were established starting in 1910 in the producing fields. In West Virginia, the utilization of natural gas in the making of casinghead gasoline was viewed as a "great force in the conservation of natural gas" (Thoenen, 1964).

In Texas in the 1920s and 1930s, when markets for natural gas were still quite limited, natural gasoline became a most valuable product. The process used in Texas to produce gasoline from natural gas wells was known as stripping gas, and numerous companies engaged in the practice of marketing the stripped condensate and then venting or releasing the remaining 90 per cent to the atmosphere or flaring it (Prindle, 1981). One historian estimated that in 1934 approximately a billion cubic feet of unassociated gas was stripped and released or flared daily in the Texas Panhandle alone (Prindle, 1981).

The possibilities of recovering and marketing even a small part of the associated gas were small in cases where the rate of production could not be controlled. The gas from these wells was almost invariably flared. Waste was probably most severe in the East Texas oilfields. During the early 1940s it was estimated that one-and-a-half billion cubic feet of casinghead gas was flared each day from the larger fields. Motorists could supposedly drive for hours at night near the Texas fields without ever having to turn on their automobile lights because of the illumination from the casinghead flares (Prindle, 1981).

State legislation was an obvious approach to the conservation of natural gas. At one time or another almost all states involved in petroleum and natural gas production passed conservation laws (Murphy, 1948). Pennsylvania had the first legislation, passed in 1868, and West Virginia had a law in 1891. The West Virginia law, for instance, applied to all wells producing petroleum, natural gas, salt water, or mineral water. In regard to natural gas, owners were required to "shut in and confine" the gas and to plug the well after exhaustion. There was no provision, however, to prevent venting or flaring (Thoenen, 1964). In Texas, an 1899 law prohibited the flaring of unassociated gas. A 1925 law, however, specifically permitted the flaring of associated gas from an oil well (Prindle, 1981). But since it was often difficult to define clearly the difference between a gas and an oil well, enforcement was difficult. It was not until the middle 1930s that the Texas law was successfully enforced through the reclassification of hundreds of oil wells as gas wells and the prohibition of flaring (Prindle, 1981). Still a few states that had major oil fields, such as Illinois, had no gas and oil conservation legislation as late as the Second World War (Murphy, 1948).

Considerable amounts of natural gas were conserved and utilized by technological developments. Methods of capturing associated natural gas, for instance, were developed and the gas used to run pumps and lights at the works. Other developments, such as the Starke Gas Trap to purify wet gas, occurred over the years, and also led to conservation (White, 1951). An important development was the application of high-pressure compressors to the extraction of gasoline from casinghead natural gas. These compressors made it possible for field operators to develop small gasoline plants on their producing fields. After 1913 the absorption process increasingly replaced the compressor-condensation system as a means of extracting gasoline from both dry and wet natural gases. Between 1911 and 1929 (the peak year), the volume of natural gas liquids produced increased from 3,660,000 gallons to 72,994,000 gallons (Thoenen, 1964).

The most important factor reducing the waste of natural gas has been the development of long-distance pipelines to available markets. The first major attempt was by the Bloomfield & Rochester Gas Light Co. in 1820, which organized the piping of gas 40 km from a

well in Bloomfield, N.Y., to the city of Rochester. The gas was pronounced inferior by consumers, however, resulting in the failure of
the company. The first successful cast-iron gas transmission pipeline
in 1872 linked a well in Newton, Pa., with nearby Titusville (about 9
km). In 1875, natural gas was piped 27 km from a well near Butler,
Pa., to ironworks at Sharpsburg and Allegheny, near Pittsburgh
(Pearse, 1875). In 1883, the Chartiers Valley Gas Co. was formed to
supply the city of Pittsburgh with gas from wells near Murraysville –
about 25 km. By the following year 500 km of pipelines were in
place, supplying natural gas to the city. The field, however, was exhausted in little more than a decade and natural gas was replaced by
coal in the city's growing steel industry (Tarr and Lamperes, 1981).

High-pressure technology was first used in 1891 by the Indiana
Natural Gas and Oil Company to bring gas 120 miles from northern
Indiana gas fields to Chicago. By the 1920s, integrated companies
that combined production, transmission, distribution, and storage
facilities had been developed in the Appalachian area, in the Midwest, and in California, Oklahoma, and Texas. By 1925, pipelines as
much as 300 miles in length had been constructed and were serving
3,500,000 customers in 23 states (Stockton et al., 1952). Most of the
interstate movement of natural gas took place in the north-eastern
United States, where densely populated urban areas were located
nearby the Appalachian fields. In 1921, 150 billion cubic feet of gas
moved interstate, of which approximately 65 per cent was produced
in West Virginia and flowed mostly into Pennsylvania and Ohio. Less
than 2 per cent of the total interstate movement of gas originated in
Texas (Sanders, 1981).

During the late 1920s, important metallurgical advances as well as
improvements in welding and compression methods resulted in the
possibility of constructing much longer and bigger pipelines. Most critical was the development of continuous butt-welding and of seamless
tubes made of steel with greater tensile strength. Also important
were improvements in methods of compression, which made it possible to move higher volumes of gas without recompression. By 1934,
approximately 150,000 miles of field, transmission, and distribution
lines existed in 32 US states, with some transmission lines of as long
as 1,200 miles (Sanders, 1981; Stockton et al., 1952; Schurr and Netschert, 1960).

The post-Second World War period saw a great expansion of long-
distance pipelines, with 20,657 miles of natural gas lines constructed
between 1946 and 1950. Probably most significant was the conversion

229

to natural gas transmission of two long-distance pipelines ("big" inch and "little" inch), built during the war by the government to transport petroleum. These pipelines were the first connecting the East Texas field through the Midwest to Appalachia and the Atlantic seaboard. By 1949, gas from the Southwest was supplying 60 per cent of the Columbia Gas Company's 2 million customers in Pennsylvania, Ohio, and West Virginia. Markets for gas clearly meant the reduction of waste and increased resource utilization. At the end of 1946, 39 per cent of Texas gas wells were shut because of the lack of pipelines, but by 1951 this number had been reduced to 25 per cent (Sanders, 1981; Stockton et al., 1952; Schurr and Netschert, 1960).

An important method of dealing with the problem of seasonal peaks in regard to natural gas utilization has been the development of storage facilities. The first successful storage facility was developed in Ontario in 1915 and applied in a field near Buffalo, New York. Large-scale underground storage was initially developed in the Manifee field of eastern Kentucky and its use has spread since then. In 1940, there were only 19 underground storage pools in operation, but by the mid-1950s the number had grown to nearly 200. To a large extent, storage took place in consumer rather than producer states. Storage was especially important for states that had developed a dependence on natural gas through local supplies that had later become depleted. In 1949, for instance, Pennsylvania, Ohio, Michigan, and West Virginia were the leading states in terms of amount of gas stored and withdrawn from storage (Stockton et al., 1952; Schurr and Netschert, 1960).

With regard to methane emissions, two questions now arise:

1. How much natural gas was potentially recoverable from oil (or gas) wells that were opened prior to the development of significant markets for the gas?

2. How much of this gas was vented or flared? (As already explained, flaring converts most methane to harmless carbon dioxide and water vapour.)

As noted previously, the discovery of natural gas was a by-product of petroleum exploration. Gas was not sought independently until 20 years or so ago. Although the gas content of petroleum varies widely from field to field, it is likely that the potential gas output of petroleum wells is, on average, proportional to the petroleum output.

The "proportionality" hypothesis above implies that the gas/oil recovery ratio should, on average, have gradually increased over time approaching a limit as gas increased enough in commercial value to

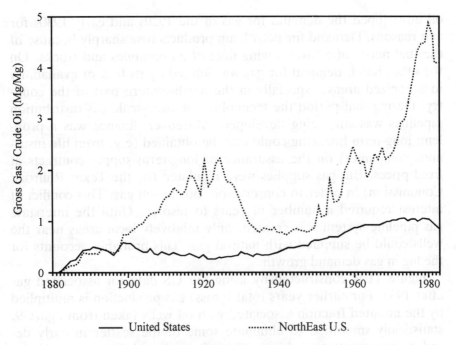

Fig. 10 Gas/oil production ratios, US and Northeast US

justify its complete recovery. One would also expect the relative quantity of natural gas recovered to increase, relative to oil, as markets for gas developed. A gas pipeline distribution system was an essential precondition for an increasing demand for gas. In actuality, the gas/oil output ratio has increased, on average, since 1882 – when recovery began – but has done so quite unevenly (fig. 10).

In the Northeast (mainly Pennsylvania), the gas/oil ratio rose gradually to about 2:1 in the early 1920s, then moved down to a trough in the 1930s, followed by a second, higher peak in the late 1950s and a still higher peak in 1980 of nearly 5:1. In the case of the United States as a whole, the initial peak recovery rate was earlier (*c.* 1900) and lower (around 0.4), and was followed by a trough in the 1930s and 1940s.

The troughs between the first and second peaks are difficult to explain in terms of the proportionality hypothesis. It is hard to believe that the troughs are accidental or that a physical phenomenon (such as declining pressure) could be responsible. Instead, an economic explanation for the troughs seems to be most plausible. The demand for oil outstripped the demand for gas in the 1920s and early 1930s for two reasons. Demand for petroleum products rose sharply because of the fuel needs of a fast-growing fleet of automobiles and trucks. On the other hand, demand for gas was limited by its lack of availability in urbanized areas, especially in the north-eastern part of the country. During that period the technology of large-scale gas distribution pipelines was still being developed. Moreover, finance was a problem: long-term financing could only be obtained (e.g. from life insurance companies) on the assurance of long-term supply contracts at fixed prices. But gas supplies were regulated (by the Texas Railroad Commission) in order to conserve oil, not to sell gas. This conflict of interest required a number of years to resolve. Until the interstate gas pipeline system was created, only relatively local areas near the wells could be supplied with natural gas. This probably accounts for the lag in gas demand growth.

Figure 11 is constructed by using the US data for associated gas after 1935. For earlier years total (gross) gas production is multiplied by the imputed fraction associated with oil wells taken from figure 9, statistically smoothed to eliminate some of the scatter in early decades. It suggests two things. First, it implies that most of the increase in the gas/oil extraction ratio (after 1935 at least) is attributable to non-associated gas wells. Second, it implies that the ratio of associated gas to oil production peaked around 1900 (at about 0.35, plus or minus 0.10). The dip in apparent associated gas/oil ratio after 1960 coincides with the period of gas scarcity due to low (regulated) prices.

A modified "proportionality" hypothesis seems to fit the facts best, that is, that the (average) potential production of associated gas is roughly constant over time for a given area. The difference between (imputed) output of associated gas and "potential" output of associated gas is unaccounted for. This must have been used on site (e.g. for carbon black), vented or flared. Actually, use of gas to manufacture carbon black is roughly equivalent to flaring, in the sense that combustion is deliberately inefficient to maximize soot (unburned carbon) production. We can assume that unaccounted-for gas was mostly (90 per cent) flared for safety and/or economic reasons or used on site, but that flaring (including gas used in carbon black production) was only 90 per cent efficient in terms of methane oxidation.

This suggests a total emission factor of 20 per cent, although this estimate must be regarded as somewhat uncertain. The 20 per cent

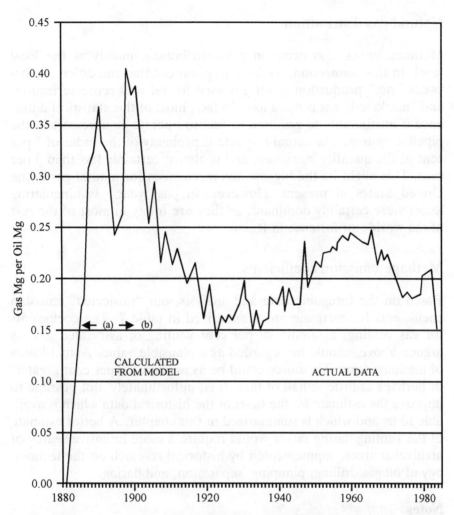

Fig. 11 Ratio of associated gas to crude oil, US: raw data compared to model
(Sources: (a) data on gas marketed 1882–1889 based on estimates of coal replacement,
originally by USGS, cited in Schurr and Netschert, 1960; (b) data 1990–1904 cited by
Schurr and Netschert, 1960, and attributed to *Minerals Yearbook*, but disagrees with
figures in *Historical Statistics*, also attributed to *Minerals Yearbook*.)

(give or take 10 per cent) of associated gas that is assumed to be
vented comes from three sources: (1) blowouts and "gas volcanoes"
(occasionally large) and "gushers"; (2) leaks; and (3) small "stripper"
wells, for which gas recovery is uneconomic and flaring is unnecessary or impossible.

Natural gas distribution

Methane losses also occur in gas distribution, mostly at the local level. In this connection, we have to point out that the difference between "net" production (after gas used for oil well repressurization) and "marketed" gas is not a loss. In fact, most of this statistical difference is attributable to gas used as fuel to operate compressors in the pipeline system. The actual loss rate is probably of the order of 1 per cent of the quantity marketed, and is almost certainly less than 3 per cent. This might be the biggest loss mechanism for natural gas in the United States at present. However, in past years, venting/flaring losses were certainly dominant, as they are today in most of the rest of the world, for instance in Russia.

Methane emission coefficients

Based on the foregoing data and analysis, our "projected" emission coefficients for methane are summarized in table 7. The coefficients for gas venting, assuming 20 per cent venting of associated gas, as argued above, should be regarded as a plausible value. Actual losses of methane from this source could be as much as 50 per cent greater, or perhaps as little as half of that. It is, unfortunately, not possible to improve the estimate on the basis of the historical data which is available to us and which is summarized in this chapter. A better estimate of the venting/flaring factor would require a more intensive search of archival sources, supplemented by historical research on the technology of oil/gas drilling, pumping, separation, and flaring.

Notes

1. This chapter is adapted (and considerably reduced) from a technical report prepared in collaboration with Resources for the Future, Inc., for the US Department of Energy. The data are published here for the first time.
2. A mixture which is neither "rich" nor "lean" is called *stoichiometric*. The stoichiometric mixture for typical hydrocarbon fuels requires 14.6 g of air per g of fuel. A 12:1 ratio is quite "rich," while a 17:1 ratio is "lean." In a typical driving cycle, ratios may fluctuate between these limits. For a rich mixture, CO concentrations will be as high as 7 per cent of exhaust gas volume, while for a lean mixture it will fall below 1 per cent.
3. However, EPA national emission estimates (USEPA, 1986) apparently assume higher emissions coefficients, closer to 0.002.
4. The basic chemical reactions in iron-smelting are as follows:

$$3Fe_2O_3 + 11C \rightarrow 2FE_3C + 9CO$$

Further refining in steel-making furnaces reduces the iron carbide to pure iron. This is done either by directly oxidizing the carbon to CO by passing oxygen through the molten metal, as in the exothermic Bessemer or basic oxygen processes:

$$2Fe_3 + O_2 \rightarrow 6Fe + 2CO$$

or by adding a controlled amount of oxygen in the form of iron oxide (ore), as in the endothermic open-hearth process:

$$3Fe_3C + Fe_2O_3 \rightarrow 5Fe + 3CO$$

5. In this case the smelting reaction is similar, that is,

$$Al_2O_3 + 3C \rightarrow 2Al + 3CO$$

although the reaction is driven not by heat but by an electric current. The source of carbon in an electrolytic cell is a carbon electrode (the anode), made from petroleum coke. Non-ferrous metals are also smelted by a similar process, except that most non-ferrous metal ores are initially sulphides. These are first converted to oxides by a process known as "roasting," which emits the sulphur as SO_2, unless it is captured and made into sulphuric acid or is otherwise disposed of.

6. Actually, the above estimate is a lower limit on CO generation per ton of metal, since it assumes the production process to be thermodynamically efficient. That is, it does not count carbon monoxide resulting from the combustion of fuel needed to satisfy the requirement for exothermic heat to raise the temperature of the ore/coke/limestone mass to reaction temperature. Even if all of the blast furnace gas is successfully captured and burned to preheat blast air and/or reaction mass, a lot of the process heat is lost, along with substantial amounts of unburned CO, because of incomplete combustion.

7. Part of this difference reflects different relative costs of coking coal *vis-à-vis* other fuels, since there is some tendency to substitute coke-oven gas or oil for coke (mainly by injection through the *tuyeres*). The advantage of substitution – assuming equal cost per BTU – would be that hydrogen oxidizes only to H_2O and yields a much larger exothermal heat energy than does the partial oxidation of carbon to CO. Thus, an "ideal" blast furnace would utilize only 0.404 tons of coke (carbon) per ton of pig iron, while obtaining heat for the endothermal reduction process from hydrogen injection.

8. Assuming that the average production of a charcoal furnace was 1,000 tons a year (accurate for the 1850s), 150 acres were necessary to supply a furnace for one year. Since a stand of timber could regenerate itself in 20 years, approximately 3,000 acres of woodland were needed, as well as land for other plantation requirements (Temin, 1964). Various woods were used to make charcoal, with hickory being preferred, but black oak most commonly used (Temin, 1964). Great areas of timber were clear-cut for iron production. In 1862, for instance, a low-production year, 25,000 acres (39 square miles) were cleared, while in 1890, the peak year of charcoal-iron production, the figure was 94,000 acres (147 square miles) (Williams, 1989). Without significant technological change, charcoal dependence meant that increased iron production would make deeper and deeper inroads into the timber supply (Bining, 1973; Paskoff, 1983).

9. The reactions when the hot carbon or coke reacted with steam in the water gas process were:

$$C + O_2 \rightarrow CO_2 \text{ exothermic}$$
$$2C + O_2 \rightarrow 2CO \text{ exothermic}$$
$$C + CO_2 \rightarrow 2\,CO \text{ endothermic}$$
$$C + H_2O \rightarrow CO + H_2 \text{ endothermic}$$
$$CO + H_2O \rightarrow CO_2\,H_2 \text{ endothermic}$$

The last three endothermic reactions utilize heat released by the first two exothermic reactions. In balance, all the CO_2 that is produced is reduced to CO in the presence of the red-hot carbon. Thus, the product is a variable mix of CO, H_2 and N_2, with a heating value

235

in the range of 10.4–11.3 x 106 Joules/m³ (as compared with 38.3 x 106 Joules/m³ for natural gas). The main pre-war process used coke and air (not pure oxygen), so the fuel gas was considerably diluted with atmospheric nitrogen. In a practice known as carburetion, town gas was commonly upgraded in heating value by the injection of oil into the reactor, which pyrolysed hydrocarbons and yielded additional hydrogen. In a typical town gas plant, 13 kg of coke (C) and 19 kg of water (steam) plus 68 kg of air are converted to 100 kg of gas product, of which 23 kg, or 23 per cent by weight, consists of carbon monoxide (CO) (ERT, 1984).

10. However, as late as 1875 it was still utilized by the Cambria Iron Company at two Pennsylvania locations, Bennington and Broad Top.

References

Ayres, E., and C. A. Scarlott. 1952. *Energy Sources – The Wealth of the World.* New York: McGraw-Hill.

Binder, Frederick Moore. 1974. *Coal Age Empire: Pennsylvania Coal and Its Utilization to 1860.* Harrisburg, Pa.: Pennsylvania Historical Commission.

Bining, A. C. 1973. *Pennsylvania Iron Manufacture in the Eighteenth Century.* Technical report. Pennsylvania Historical and Museum Commission.

Chandler, A. D., Jr. 1972. "Anthracite Coal and the Beginnings of the Industrial Revolution in the United States." *Business History Review* XLVI, no. 2 :141–181.

Eavenson, H. N. 1942. *The First Century and a Quarter of American Coal Industry.* Baltimore, Md.: Waverly Press Inc.

Elkin, Harold F. 1968. "Petroleum Refinery Emissions." In: H. Stern, ed., *Air Pollution: Sources of Air Pollution and Their Control.* 2nd ed. New York: Academic Press, chap. 34.

Environmental Research and Technology, Inc., and Koppers Co. 1984. *Handbook on Manufactured Gas Plant Sites.* Pittsburgh, Pa.: ERT and Koppers Co.

Greenberg, Dolores. 1980. "Energy Flow in a Changing Economy, 1815–1880." In: Frese and Judd, eds., *An Emerging Independent American Economy, 1815–1875.* Tarrytown, N.Y.: Sleepy Hollow Press, pp. 28–58.

Henry, J. T. 1970. "The Early and Later History of Petroleum." In: *Western Pennsylvania.* New York: Augustus Kelley. (Reprint of original 1873 edition.)

Hering, Rudolph, and Samuel A. Greeley. 1921. *Collection and Disposal of Municipal Refuse.* New York: McGraw-Hill.

Hurn, R. W. 1968. "Mobile Combustion Sources." In: Stern, ed., *Air Pollution: Sources of Air Pollution and Their Control.* 2nd ed. Environmental Sciences Series, 3. New York: Academic Press, pp. 55–95.

Hyde, Charles K. 1977. *Technological Change and the British Iron Industry, 1700–1870.* Princeton, N.J.: Princeton University Press.

Kiessling, O. E., et al. 1939. *Technology, Employment, and Output Per Man in Petroleum and Natural-gas Production.* WPA Report E-10. Philadelphia, Pa.

McGannon, Harold. 1970. *The Making, Shaping and Treating of Steel.* 9th ed. Technical report. Pittsburgh, Pa.: US Steel Corporation.

Meissner, C. A. 1913. "The Modern By-product Coke Oven." In: McCleary, ed., *Year Book of the American Iron and Steel Institute, 1913.* New York: American Iron and Steel Institute, pp. 118–178.

Murphy, B. M. 1948. *Conservation of Oil and Gas: A Legal History, 1948*. Technical report. Washington D.C.: American Bar Association.

Nakicenovic, Nebojsa, and Arnulf Gruebler. 1987. *The Dynamic Evolution of Methane Technologies*. Working paper WP-87-2. Laxenburg, Austria: International Institute for Applied Systems Analysis.

Paskoff, P. F. 1983. *Industrial Revolution: Organization, Structure, and Growth of the Pennsylvania Iron Industry, 1750–1860*. Baltimore, Md.: Johns Hopkins University Press.

Pearse, J. B. 1875. "On the Use of Natural Gas in Iron Working." In: F. Platt, ed., *Special Report on the Coke Manufacture of the Youghiogheny River Valley. 2nd Geological Survey of Pennsylvania:1875*. Harrisburg, Pa.: Board of Commissioners, pp. 173–214.

Platt, Franklin. 1875. *Special Report on the Coke Manufacture of the Youghiogheny River Valley. 2nd Geological Survey of Pennsylvania: 1875*. Technical report. Harrisburg, Pa.: Board of Commissioners.

Prindle, D. F. 1981. *Petroleum Politics and the Texas Railroad Commission*. Technical report. Austin, Tex.: University of Texas Press.

Riegel, E. R. 1937. *Industrial Chemistry*. New York: Reinhold Publications.

Rohrmann, C. A., et al. 1977. *Chemical Production from Waste Carbon Monoxide*. Technical report. Richland, Wash.: Battelle NW Laboratories.

Sanders, M. E. 1981. *The Regulation of Natural Gas: Policy and Politics, 1938–1978*. Technical report. Philadelphia, Pa.: Temple University Press.

Schallenberg, R. H., and D. A. Ault. 1977 "Raw Materials Supply and Technological Change in the American Charcoal Iron Industry." *Technology and Culture* 18, no. 3: 436–466.

Schurr, Sam H., and Bruce C. Netschert. 1960. *Energy in the American Economy, 1850–1975*. Baltimore, Md.: Johns Hopkins University Press.

Science Applications Inc. (SAI). 1980. *Overview of Unconventional Natural Gas R&D Activities*. McLean, Va.: Science Applications Inc. (NTIS PB 80–227 986.)

Stockton, J. R., R. C. Henshaw, Jr., and R. W. Graves. 1952. *Economics of Natural Gas in Texas*. Technical report. Austin, Tex.: University of Texas Press.

Tarr, Joel A., and K. E. Koons. 1982. "Railroad Smoke Control: The Regulation of a Mobile Pollution Source." In: Daniels and Rose, eds., *Energy and Transport: Historical Perspectives on Policy Issues*. Beverly Hills, Calif.: Sage Publications, pp. 71–94.

Tarr, Joel A., and B. C. Lamperes. 1981. "Changing Fuel Use Behavior and Energy Transitions: The Pittsburgh Smoke Control Movement, 1940–1950." *Journal of Social History* 14, no. 4: 561–588.

Temin, Peter. 1964. *Iron and Steel in Nineteenth-century America: An Economic Inquiry*. Cambridge, Mass.: MIT Press.

Thoenen, E. D. 1964. *History of the Oil and Gas Industry in West Virginia*. Charleston, W. Va.: Education Foundation.

US Bureau of Mines. 1975. *Mineral Facts and Problems*. Washington D.C.: US Government Printing Office.

———. 1985. *Mineral Facts and Problems*. Washington D.C.: US Government Printing Office.

US Environmental Protection Agency Office of Air Quality Planning and Standards

(USEPA). 1986. *National Air Pollution Emission Estimates, 1940–1984*. Technical report. Research Triangle Park, N.C.: USEPA. (EPA-450/4-85-014.)

Wagner, F. H.. 1916. *Coal and Coke*. New York: McGraw-Hill.

Warren, Kenneth. 1973. *The American Steel Industry, 1850–1970: A Geographical Interpretation*. Oxford: Clarendon Press.

White, Gerald T. 1951. *Formative Years in the Far West: A History of Standard Oil Company of California and Predecessors through 1919*. New York: Appleton-Century-Crofts.

White, H. J. 1957. "Fifty Years of Electrostatic Precipitation." Paper presented at the Golden Jubilee Meeting, Air Pollution Control Association, Pittsburgh, Pa., 2–6 June 1957.

Williams, Michael. 1989. *Americans and Their Forests: A Historical Geography*. New York: Cambridge University Press.

Williamson, Harold F., and Arnold R. Daum. 1959. *The American Petroleum Industry*. Evanston, Ill.: Northwestern University Press.

10

Sulphur and nitrogen emission trends for the United States: An application of the materials flow approach

Rudolf B. Husar

Introduction

Among the substances metabolized by industrial activities, fossil fuels are the most significant, both in quantity and by the variety of chemicals that are mobilized. Industrial consumers take fuels as inputs and exhaust residue products to air, land, and water. Sulphur and nitrogen compounds are major fossil fuel residues that are released primarily into the air and subsequently deposited to land and water bodies.

The elements redistributed by the "industrial metabolism" of fossil fuels are carbon, sulphur, and nitrogen, as well as crustal and trace metals. In fact, these are the main chemicals of which living matter is composed. As such, they are the key nutrients for the plants on earth. However, these substances may be either beneficial *or* harmful to the receiving ecosystem, depending on their quantity, rate, and chemical form.

In order to assess the possible harm or benefit of fossil fuel residues and the possible remedying actions, it is helpful to construct a complete material flow scheme that describes the end-to-end transfer of these materials as they pass from one long-term geochemical reservoir to another.

In order to construct such a flow model, it is helpful to utilize the ecosystem analogue for the human-induced material flow, which has producers, consumers, and receptors (recyclers) as the key players. A general description and mathematical formulation of the ecological analogue is given elsewhere (Husar, 1986; also see chapter 2 of this volume). The purpose of this chapter is to illustrate the application of the producer, consumer, receptor method to the construction of a sulphur and nitrogen flow scheme for the United States. The essence of the approach is that one follows the path of the fuel or nitrogen from "production," i.e. mining, through the consumers to the environmental receptors. (More details on the methodology can

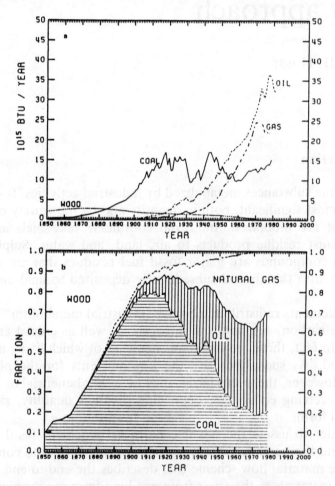

Fig. 1 Trend for US fossil fuel consumption since 1850: (a) consumption by fuel type; (b) fraction of total energy by fuel type (Source: Husar, 1986)

be found in Husar, 1986.) In constructing the materials flow model emphasis was placed on obtaining the relevant data from the measurement records of various US agencies. Also, data were sought for the term trends in order to illuminate the dynamics of the producer-consumer-receptor system.

In the following, the presentation of the fuel production and consumption data sets is accompanied by a discussion of the technological trends for different industrial sectors; the changes in technology were taken mostly from Darmstadter et al. (1987).

Combustion of coal and oil products, along with the smelting of metals, produces the bulk of the anthropogenic sulphur and nitrogen emissions to the atmosphere. The driving force for fuel production is the consumption of energy by different sectors.

From the turn of the century to the 1970s, US energy consumption has been characterized by a steady increase in total consumption and shifts from one fuel to another (fig. 1). From 1850 to about 1880, wood was the primary energy source. By 1900, and during the first quarter of this century, rising energy demand was matched by the increasing use of coal. The depression years of the early 1930s are reflected in a sharp drop in coal consumption, which increased again during the war years in the early to mid 1940s. Coal consumption declined to another minimum in 1960, because the increasing energy demands were supplied by cleaner fuels, natural gas and petroleum. Accelerated oil and gas consumption began in the late 1930s and 1940s, such that by 1950 the energy supplied by oil exceeded that of coal and maintained its rise up to the early 1970s. By 1960, natural gas surpassed coal as an energy source.

Sulphur emissions

Figures for the mobilization of sulphur(s) can be derived by quantifying fuels and minerals production, the concentration of sulphur in fuels and minerals, and the transfer from producers to consumers.

Sulphur in fossil fuels is mostly in the form of organic compounds that constitute the biomass. A fraction of the S in coal is also in inorganic, pyritic form. Following combustion, sulphur is oxidized to SO_2 and a small fraction to SO_3. The environmental impact of metabolized S begins at the mine, owing to acid mine drainage, and continues to the atmosphere as regional sulphurous haze. Further damage may occur following its deposition to the human lung and to human-made materials, as well as to aquatic and forest ecosystems.

241

However, sulphur deposition to sulphur-deficient agricultural land may induce crop growth.

Coal production

In the United States, coal is mined in three regions: Appalachia, the Midwest (Interior), and the West. The coals in the regions differ in their quality and concentration of impurities such as sulphur. Figure 2 shows the time-dependent contributions of the three regions to the national production of coal. The output of the Appalachian districts from Pennsylvania to Alabama has remained at about 300 million tons a year since about 1920. The production in the Western region was rather small until around 1970. These curves reveal that a major shift in coal production occurred in around 1970, when the output of Western coal became significant. Remarkably, within the span of a decade or so, low-sulphur Western coal captured a quarter of the United States coal market.

The significance of these shifts for sulphur emissions is that each coal-producing district has its own range of sulphur content: a shift in the relative production rate thus results in a change of the average sulphur content and sulphur production. (The coal-production data

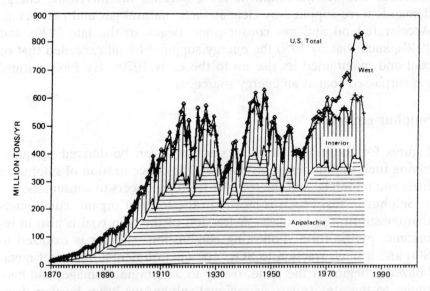

Fig. 2 Coal production in the three US coal-producing regions: Appalachian, Interior, and West. (Sources: *US Geological Survey Yearbooks*, 1880–1932; US Bureau of Mines, *Mineral Yearbooks*, 1933–1980; Energy Information Administration, 1983)

242

described above define the raw material production rate P_i defined in figure 2.)

Coal sulphur content
The next parameter that will be examined is c_i, the concentration of the contaminant sulphur for each coal-producing region. Knowing

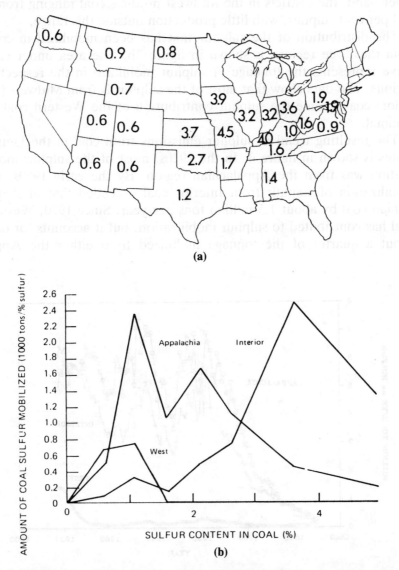

Fig. 3 Sulphur content of coals: (a) spatial distribution; (b) distribution function for each coal-producing region (Source: Energy Information Administration, 1981)

243

the production rate P_i and concentration c_i permits the calculation of the mass of contaminant, $M_i = c_i P_i$ that is mobilized by each producer.

Each coal-producing district has a geologically defined range for the sulphur content of its coal (fig. 3a). Western coal, for instance, is low in sulphur, since it contains less than 1 per cent of S. On the other hand, the districts in the Midwest produce coal ranging from 2 to 4 per cent sulphur, with little production outside this range.

The distribution of the sulphur that has been mobilized in coals from the three regions is shown in figure 3b. The area under each curve represents the tonnage of sulphur mobilized in the respective regions. The data show that most of the sulphur is from Midwest (Interior) coals, while the sulphur contribution of the Western coals is minimal.

The resulting trend in sulphur emissions from coal in the United States is shown in figure 4. In the 1920s, most of the sulphur mobilization was from the Appalachian region. By the early 1980s, the mobilization of sulphur from Interior coal exceeded that of Appalachian coal by about 1.5 million tons per year. Since 1970, Western coal has contributed to sulphur mobilization, but it accounts for only about a quarter of the tonnage mobilized from either the Appa-

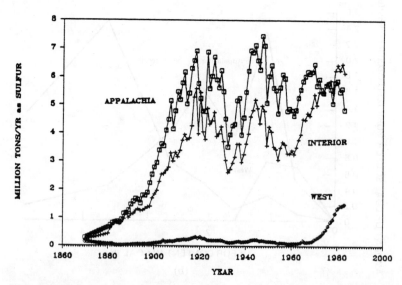

Fig. 4 Trends in coal sulphur emissions for the Appalachian, Interior and Western coal-producing regions

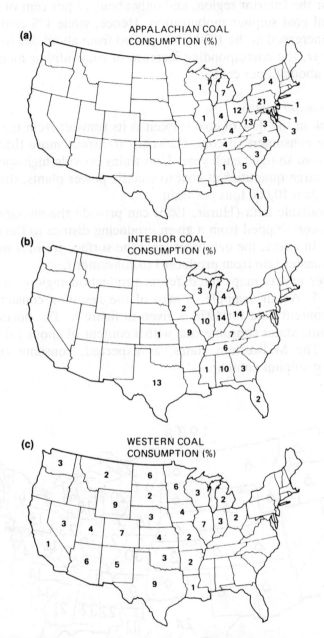

Fig. 5 Normalized surface transfer maps of shipment to consumer states from coal-producing regions. The numbers assigned to the states represent the percentages of total production consumed by the states: (a) Appalachia; (b) Interior; (c) the West

lachian or the Interior region, and only about 12 per cent of the total amount of coal sulphur mobilization. Hence, while US coal production has increased in the 1970–1980 period from about 500 to 800 million tons/yr, the corresponding increase in coal sulphur mobilization was only about 12 per cent.

Surface transfer matrix
A key link in the flow of coal sulphur is its transfer from the producers to the consumers of coal. Railroads transport more than half of the total coal shipped each year. Unit trains provide high-speed shipments of large quantities of coal to electric power plants, often hauling more than 10,000 tons per train.

The available data (Husar, 1986) can provide the amount of coal that has been shipped from a given producing district to the consuming state. In effect, the databases yield the surface transfer matrix s_{ij}, i.e. the transfer rate from producer i to consumer j.

Transfer matrix maps for different production regions are shown in figure 5. As an example, a map of the resulting consumed coal sulphur content data for 1978 is given in figure 6. The northern and mid-Atlantic states consume coal with a content of about 1.4 per cent sulphur. The Midwestern states, as expected, consume coal with the highest sulphur content.

Fig. 6 Estimated average sulphur content of coal consumed in the United States, 1978

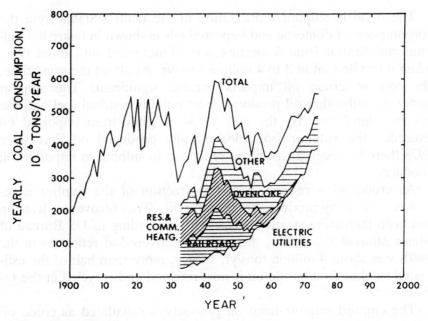

Fig. 7 Trend of US coal consumption by consuming sector (Source: Husar, 1986)

Coal consumption

In 1975, coal consumption was about 550 million tons/yr, roughly the same as in around 1920 and 1943 (fig. 7). However, since the 1930s there has been a total transformation in the economic sectors that consume coal. Before 1945, coal consumption was divided among electric utilities, railroad, residential and commercial heating, oven coke, and other industrial processes. The railroad demand was particularly high during the war years of the early to mid 1940s. Within one decade, the 1950s, coal consumption by railroads and by the residential-commercial sector essentially vanished. Currently, electric utilities constitute the main coal-consuming sector, and the trend of total coal use in the United States since 1960 has been determined by the electric utility coal demand.

Oil production

Sulphur mobilization from the combustion of oil products can be estimated from either production or consumption data. Detailed state-by-state data for oil production were not available for this report. Therefore, the estimates below were based on state-by-state data for oil consumption and sulphur content.

247

The trend in sulphur mobilization in the United States from the consumption of domestic and imported oils is shown in figure 8a. Sulphur mobilization from domestic crude oil increased until about 1960, when it levelled off at 3 to 4 million tons/yr. At about the same time, the role of crude oil imports became significant. The sulphur imported with other oil products, most notably residual fuel oil, also became significant. By the late 1970s, sulphur from imported oil exceeded the sulphur from domestically produced oil, but since 1978 there has been a significant reduction in sulphur in imported oil products.

As crude oil is refined, a certain fraction of the sulphur is recovered as a by-product, sulphuric acid. The recovered fraction has been increasing steadily since 1950. According to US Bureau of Mines *Mineral Yearbooks*, the sulphur recovered at refineries in the 1980s was about 4 million tons/yr. Hence, more than half of the estimated sulphur from crude oil is now retained and recycled at the refineries.

The emitted sulphur from oil products is calculated as crude oil sulphur content minus recycled sulphur. As shown in figure 8b, the oil sulphur emissions estimated in this manner ranged between 3 and 4 million tons/yr for the period 1950 to 1978. Since then, there has been a significant decrease, caused primarily by declining imports and the increasing fraction of recycled sulphur. For 1982, emissions of sulphur from oil consumption were about 2 million tons/yr, which is less than 20 per cent of the sulphur emissions from coal.

Copper and zinc smelting

Significant production of copper began in the United States in about 1895 and reached approximately 1 million tons annually by 1920. For the next 40 years copper production fluctuated at that level, with no significant trend. During the 1960s smelter copper production again increased, reaching a peak of over 2 million tons in around 1970, followed by a decline in the 1970s.

Virtually all copper ore is treated at concentrators near the mines. Concentrates are further processed at smelters. Production of sulphuric acid is the main process for removing sulphur oxides from smelter gases. However, acid production is practical only from converter gases. With tightly hooded converters, 50 to 70 per cent of the sulphur oxides can be removed; removal of additional sulphur oxides requires scrubbing, and thus is more costly.

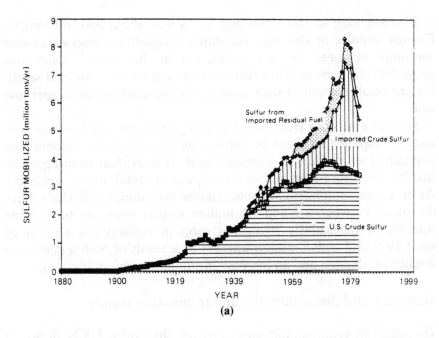

(a)

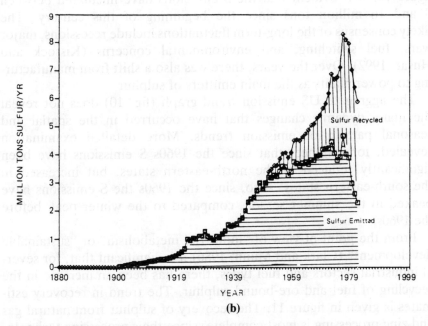

(b)

Fig. 8 (a) Trend in sulphur mobilization, before recycling, from domestic and imported oils; (b) trends in sulphur recycling during petroleum processing and sulphur emissions from petroleum consumption in the United States (Source: Husar, 1986)

Zinc smelting in the 1960s and 1970s was about 800,000 tons/yr. Foreign imports of zinc ores constitute a significant fraction of zinc consumption. Lead smelter production in the United States was about 700,000 tons/yr. However, sulphur emissions from lead smelting are small compared with those from the smelting of copper and zinc.

Sulphur emissions from metal smelting are estimated from the tonnage of sulphur mobilized by mining the ore, minus the sulphur that is retained at smelters as sulphuric acid. It is evident from figure 9a that by 1980 more than half of the sulphur in metal ore was recycled. As a result, sulphur emissions (mobilized minus recycled) have fluctuated between 0.5 and 1.5 million tons/yr since the turn of the century. A particularly significant drop in emissions has occurred since 1970 (1.5 to 0.5 million tons/yr) as a result of both a decline in smelter production and an increase in sulphur recovery (fig. 9b).

Summary and discussion of sulphur emission trends

The trend in total sulphur emissions for the entire US is shown in figure 10. It is evident that the S emissions have fluctuated between 8 and 16 million tons since the beginning of this century. The likely consensus of the long-term fluctuations include recessions, major wars, fuel switching, and environmental concerns (Kissock and Husar, 1992). Over the years, there was also a shift from manufacturing to power plants as the main emitters of sulphur.

The aggregate US emission trend graph (fig. 10) does not reveal the many dynamic changes that have occurred in the spatial and seasonal pattern of emission trends. More detailed examination revealed, for instance, that since the 1960s S emissions have been significantly reduced in the north-eastern states, but increased in the south-eastern states. Also, since the 1960s the S emissions have peaked in the summer season, compared to the winter peak before the 1960s.

From the point of view of "industrial metabolism" or "sustainable development" (Clark and Munn, 1986) it is significant that, for several industrial sectors and fuel types, there has been an increase in the recycling of fuel and ore-bound sulphur. The trend in recovery estimates is given in figure 11. The recovery of sulphur from natural gas and zinc processing is most complete, since their processing technologies allow easy separation and re-use. It is also encouraging that the recovery from copper and lead ores, as well as from oil products, is

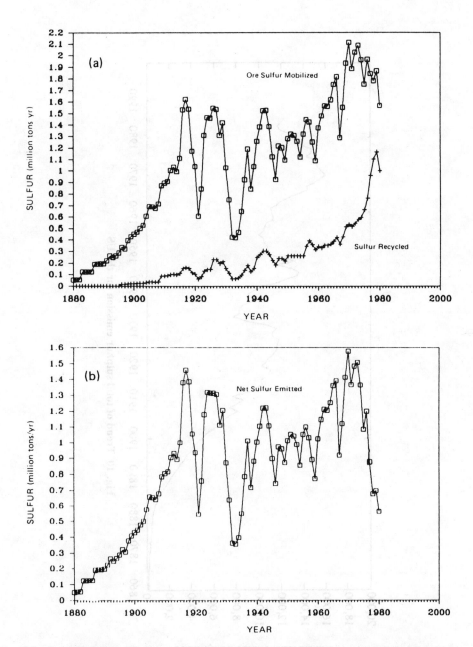

Fig. 9 (a) Trend in sulphur mobilization and recycling from copper and zinc smelting and processing; (b) trend in sulphur emissions from copper and zinc smelting (Source: Husar, 1986)

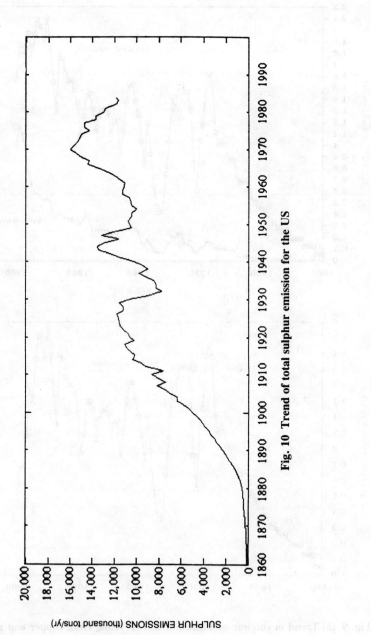

Fig. 10 Trend of total sulphur emission for the US

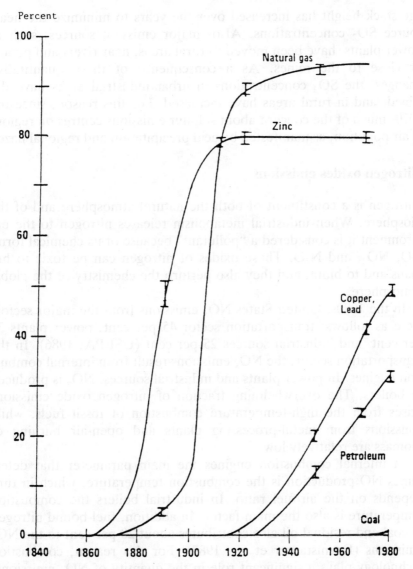

Fig. 11 By-product sulphur recovery rates (Source: Ayres, in Darmstadter et al., 1987)

approaching 50 per cent, with a likely increase in the future. Unfortunately, the S recovery from coal, which is responsible for most of the sulphur mobilization in the United States, is still very low.

There are two other changes in sulphur emissions that are significant from an environmental impact point of view: power-plant stack height and source displacement from urban to rural areas. The average stack height has increased over the years to minimize the near-source SO_2 concentrations. Also, major emission sources, such as power plants, have been moved to rural areas, near rivers and ponds, or close to the mines. As a consequence of these quantitative changes, the SO_2 concentrations in urban/industrial areas have declined, and in rural areas have increased. For this reason, since the 1970s much of the concern about sulphur emissions centres on regional air pollution, as manifested by acid precipitation and regional haze.

Nitrogen oxides emissions

Nitrogen is a constituent of both the natural atmosphere and of the biosphere. When industrial metabolism releases nitrogen to the environment it is considered a "pollutant" because of its chemical form: NO, NO_2, and N_2O. These oxides of nitrogen can be toxic to humans and to biota, and they also perturb the chemistry of the global atmosphere.

In the 1980s, United States NO_x emissions from the major sectors were as follows: transportation sector 45 per cent, power plants 35 per cent, and industrial sources 25 per cent (USEPA, 1986). In the transportation sector, the NO_x emissions result from internal combustion engines. In power plants and industrial sources, NO_x is produced in boilers. The overwhelming fraction of nitrogen oxide emissions arises from the high-temperature combustion of fossil fuels, while emissions from metal-processing plants and open-air burning of biomass are relatively low.

In internal combustion engines the main parameter that determines NO production is the combustion temperature, which in turn depends on the air/fuel ratio. In industrial boilers the combustion temperature is also the main factor. In addition, fuel-bound nitrogen in coal and residual oil also contributes about 20 per cent to the NO_x emissions (Darmstadter et al., 1987). For this reason, combustion technology plays a significant role in the quantity of NO_x emissions. In this sense, NO_x emission estimates, as well as the suitable control strategies, are significantly different from those of sulphur.

Estimating historical emission trends of nitrogen oxides is difficult because most of the nitrogen oxide is formed by the fixation of atmospheric nitrogen at high temperatures of combustion rather than by oxidation of the nitrogen contained in the fuel. Thus, nitrogen oxide emissions depend primarily on the combustion temperature and, to a lesser degree, on the fuel properties. Since combustion processes in internal combustion engines and boilers have undoubtedly changed since the turn of the century, it is likely that nitrogen oxide emission factors have also changed. Because combustion parameters can vary over a wide range, and because information on historical combustion processes is generally lacking, assumptions concerning changes in emission factors over time constitute the major source of uncertainty in developing trends in nitrogen oxide emissions.

NO_x emissions can be obtained from fuel consumption data weighted by an appropriate emission factor. For a given source of combustion, this factor is the quantity of nitrogen oxide emitted per unit of fuel consumed. The emission factors used here were derived from extensive inventories that list nitrogen oxide emission factors according to source type of combustion (USEPA, 1977, 1978). The numerous emission factors listed in these compilations were aggregated into four weighted-average emission factors by fuel type: coal, gasoline, natural gas, and other petroleum products. The emission factors before 1970 were estimated to reflect the fact that the average combustion temperature, and hence the production of nitrogen oxides per unit of fuel consumed, was lower, especially for coal combustion, over the past 100 years (fig. 12). A simple linear trend was assumed for all emission factors. For coal combustion, the emission

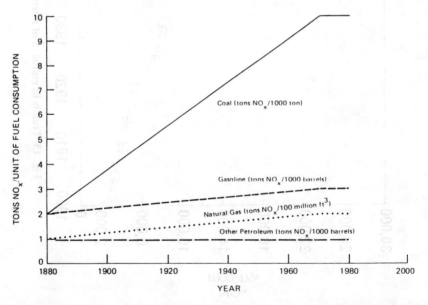

Fig. 12 Trends in emission factors of nitrogen oxide by fuel type (Sources: Emission factors for the period 1970–1980 were derived from data presented by the US Environmental Protection Agency (1977, 1978). For the period 1880–1970, trends of historical emission factors were assumed to be linear, with slopes varying by fuel type)

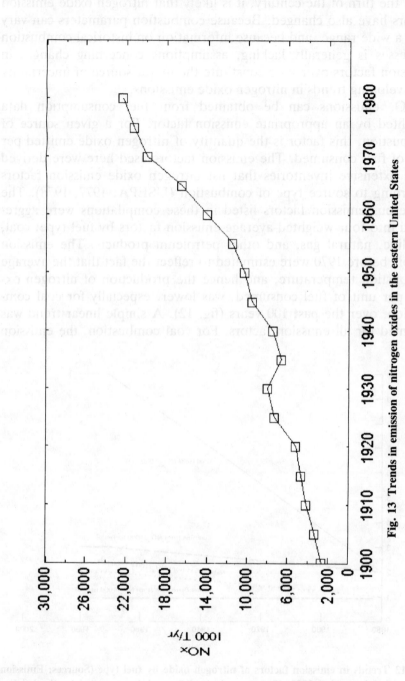

Fig. 13 Trends in emission of nitrogen oxides in the eastern United States

factor was assumed to have increased fivefold from 1880 to 1970. For combustion of gasoline and natural gas, the emission factors were assumed to have increased by 50 and 100 per cent, respectively. The emission factor for other petroleum products was assumed to be constant over time.

On the basis of these estimates of emission factors and data on fuel consumption, national emission trends were calculated as shown in figure 13. It is evident that there was a monotonic increase in NO_x emissions in the United States from the turn of the century to about 1970; since then the emissions have remained roughly constant.

Conclusion

A comparison of the sulphur and nitrogen emissions reveals significant differences:
1. National sulphur emissions have fluctuated between 8 and 16 million tons a year since the turn of the century; nitrogen oxides, on the other hand, monotonically increased until the 1970s.
2. Since the 1970s, the main source of sulphur oxides has been coal combustion in power plants, while nitrogen oxides are contributed primarily by internal combustion engines.
3. Sulphur emissions result from oxidation of the sulphur impurity contained in fossil fuels and metal ores; nitrogen oxides are formed primarily by fixation of atmospheric nitrogen at high temperatures, and to a lesser degree by oxidation of fuel-bound nitrogen.
4. The control of sulphur oxides will have to rely on the removal of sulphur from the fuel or flue gases. Nitrogen oxides controls can be accomplished by technological changes in the combustion itself.

References

Clark, W. C., and R. E. Munn, eds. 1986. *Sustainable Development of the Biosphere*. Cambridge: Cambridge University Press.

Darmstadter, J., L. W. Ayres, R. U. Ayres, W. C. Clark, P. Crosson, T. E. Graedel, R. McGill, J. F. Richards, and J. A. Tarr. 1987. *Impacts of World Development on Selected Characteristics of the Atmosphere: An Integrative Approach*. Vol. 2. Oak Ridge National Laboratory. (ORNL/Sub/86 22033/1V2.)

Energy Information Administration. 1977–1982. US Department of Energy, Quarterly Reports. Washington, D.C.

———. 1981. *Content in Coal Shipments, 1978*. Washington, D.C.: US Department of Energy. (DOE/EIA-0263(78).)

———. 1983. *Coal Distribution, January–December, 1982*. Washington, D.C.: US Department of Energy. (DOE/EIA-0125 (82/4Q).)

Husar, R. B. 1986. "Emissions of Sulfur Dioxide and Nitrogen Oxides and Trends for Eastern North America." In: *Acid Deposition Long-term Trends*. Washington, D.C.: National Academy Press.

Kissock, J. K., and R. B. Husar. 1992. "Population, Economy, and Energy Use's Effect on Sulfur Emission in the United States since 1900." Submitted for publication.

US Bureau of the Census. 1889 and 1919. *Census of Manufacturing*. Washington, D.C.

———. 1975. *Historical Statistics of the United States, Colonial Times to 1970*. Washington, D.C.: US Department of the Interior, pp. 587–588.

US Bureau of Mines. 1933–1980. *Mineral Yearbook*. Washington, D.C.: US Department of the Interior, annual publications.

———. 1957–1977. *Distribution of Bituminous Coal and Lignite Shipments*. Washington, D.C.: US Department of the Interior, quarterly publication.

———. 1971. *Control of Sulfur Oxides, Emissions, in Copper, Lead, and Zinc Smelting*. Information Circular 8527. Washington, D.C.: US Department of the Interior.

US Bureau of Statistics. 1917. *Statistics of Railways in the United States*. Washington, D.C.: Interstate Commerce Commission.

US Environmental Protection Agency (USEPA). 1977. *Compilation of Air Pollutant Emission Factors*. AP-42, 3rd ed., Supplements 1–7 and 8–14. Springfield, Va.: National Technical Information Service. (NTIS PB-275525.)

———. 1978. *Mobile Source Emission Factors*. Washington, D.C. (EPA-400/9–78–005 (NTIS PB295672/A17).)

———. 1986. *National Air Pollution Emission Estimates, 1940–1984*. Research Triangle Park, N.C.: Office of Air Quality Planning and Standards, US Environmental Protection Agency. (EPA-450/4-85-014.)

US Geological Survey. 1880–1932. *Mineral Resources of the United States*. Yearbooks. Washington, D.C.: US Department of the Interior.

11

Consumptive uses and losses of toxic heavy metals in the United States, 1880–1980

Robert U. Ayres and Leslie W. Ayres

Introduction

There has been a disproportionate amount of attention by environmentalists – and regulatory bodies – to controlling pollutant emissions from manufacturing processes.[1] However, manufacturing processes – beyond the extraction (mining) and ore beneficiation stage – are much less important sources of pollutant emissions than post-manufacturing consumption activities. This is true at least for several of the most toxic heavy metals. In six of seven cases for which reasonable historical data can be cited, the consumption contribution to total mobile emissions is growing; in three of seven cases it is close to 100 per cent of total mobile emissions.

In this context, consumption means *dissipative use*. It is not restricted to use by "final consumers" in the usual economic classification. In fact, toxic metal emissions from manufacturing activities are mostly due to intermediate consumptive uses of metallic compounds such as catalysts, fuel or lubricant additives, detergents, pigments, pesticides, preservatives, germicides, fungicides, and so on. The major exception is trace metals in fly ash from coal combustion and fertilizer.

An historical reconstruction of US emissions of toxic heavy metals

259

to the environment, resulting from dissipative consumptive uses, is presented in this chapter. The major implication of this exercise could be to confirm, in quantitative terms, the following assertion: that dissipative (intermediate and final) uses of heavy metals account for more waste residuals than losses from manufacturing processes *per se*. This statement would seem self-evident for "minor" metals such as arsenic, cadmium, and mercury, which have few, if any, uses that would permit recycling. However, it is also true for lead and zinc, at least in the past. Only in the cases of silver, chromium, and copper, whose chemical applications are outweighed by metallic and structural applications, is the matter in doubt.

The eight metals are considered hereafter as a single natural group, not only because of their toxicity, but because of the complex interrelationships in their production and uses. All except chromium are obtained from sulphide ores. Arsenic is a by-product of copper ores (and is also found in iron ores and phosphate rocks); cadmium is a by-product of zinc ore; silver is a by-product of copper, zinc, and lead ores; and copper, zinc, and lead are all contaminants of each other's ores.

On the use side, arsenic, copper, chromium, lead, and mercury have major overlapping and competing pesticidal, fungicidal, and bactericidal uses; lead, cadmium, chromium, and zinc have major overlapping uses as pigments; cadmium, chromium, and zinc have overlapping and competing uses in metal plating; cadmium, mercury, zinc, and silver are all used in electric batteries, and so on.

Production-related heavy metal emissions

Production processes for heavy metals, for our purposes, begin with smelting and refining. We do not include mining *per se*, or associated ore concentration (beneficiation) processes, which are normally carried out near the mine. While these processes generate enormous quantities of waste material, they are normally carried out in fairly remote locations.

In principle, we also include secondary refining in this category. In addition, trace metals are emitted in significant quantities via fly ash from the combustion of coal, oil (especially residual oil), and possibly wood. Though fuels are utilized for residential heating and transportation, as well as for utility and industrial purposes, we class fuel combustion as part of the production of housing and transport services. Thus, all emissions of heavy metals associated with fly ash from fossil-fuel refining are considered to be production-related. On the other hand, we include lead additives to gasoline and zinc additives to lubricating oil as consumption-related.

It must be pointed out that incineration of refuse and sewage sludge also results in heavy metal emissions. But this is an environmental transfer, not a true source of metallic pollutants. All of the metals emitted by incinerators must have been originally embodied in items of consumption discharged as wastes. Incinerator wastes are therefore consumption-related. Data on incinerator emissions are relevant to the extent that they provide evidence of final disposal routes.

Emissions coefficients for production

Emissions coefficients and estimates abound, especially in the "grey literature."[2] Published numbers disagree spectacularly in some instances. Some of the early EPA-sponsored studies (such as NRC, 1977b; GCA, 1973; Davis, 1972, 1980) were admittedly crude, but – being readily available – have been widely quoted, especially in surveys such as those carried out by the National Academy of Sciences/National Research Council in the mid-1970s (NAS, 1980; NRC, 1977a; NRC, 1977c, 1981), and also in the more recent series of symposium volumes edited by Nriagu (Nriagu, 1978, 1980a, 1980b, 1980d). Reasons for disagreement among authors include use of questionable data in some early estimates, aggregation from non-representative samples, failure to distinguish between different process stages (for example in the primary copper industry), failure to distinguish between land-destined and other wastes, and failure to distinguish between gross (uncontrolled) emissions and net emissions after the implementation of controls.[3]

The only truly satisfactory approach for a complex industry is a combination of materials-balance and plant-specific emissions data, as exemplified by *Survey of Cadmium Emission Sources* (GCA, 1981) in the case of cadmium. In the case of copper, the best source we have uncovered is the second edition of *Metallurgy of Copper*, published in 1924 (Hofman and Hayward, 1924). It is regrettable that the few such studies tended to focus on only a single pollutant and neglected to estimate the overall effectiveness of controls in effect at the time of the study. This makes it very difficult to assess the average level of emissions control actually in effect at a given time. We have made our own rough estimates, however, as will be discussed later in more detail.

Tables 1 and 2 summarize our assumed emissions coefficients for

Table 1 Uncontrolled emissions from metallurgical operations (ppm)

Metal (reference)	Steel and foundries	Smelt, convert copper	Smelt, refine lead	Secondary copper	Secondary lead	Secondary zinc
Arsenic (NRC, 1977b; Lowenbach and Schlesinger, 1979)	15.2	8,000 (refinery 800–900)				
Cadmium (GCA, 1981)	3.5–4.0	350–650	1,750–2,100			
Chromium (GCA, 1973)	6.5–7.0					
Copper (Nriagu, 1980a; Davis, 1972; PEDCo, 1980)	17.5–22.5	2,500–5,000		500–1,000		
Mercury (URS, 1975)		26 air 1 water	9 air 0.5 water			
Lead (Nriagu, 1978)	200–300	2,000–5,000 (refinery 25)	20,000–23,000	500–1,000	20,000–23,000	
Zinc (Nriagu, 1980d)	27–370	9,000–11,000	500–1,000	500–1,000	300	9,000–11,000

Table 2 Uncontrolled emissions from fossil-fuel combustion (ppm)

Metal (reference)	Coal	Residual oil	Distillate oil
Arsenic (NRC, 1977b; Lowenbach and Schlesinger, 1979)	0.10 (coal)	0.3	—
Cadmium (GCA, 1981)	0.88 (coal)	2.3	0.150
Chromium (GCA, 1973)	17.00 (coal)	2.9 (oil)	—
	260.00 (ash)	1,300.0 (ash)	
Copper (Nriagu, 1980a; Davis, 1972; PEDCo, 1980)	15.60 (coal)	0.7 (oil)	
	240.00 (ash)		
Mercury (URS, 1975)	0.16	0.13	0.066
Lead (Nriagu, 1978)	4.5		
Zinc (Nriagu, 1980d; Davis, 1980)	4.8–8.5	0.025	

Table 3 Estimated particulate emission control efficiencies over time (percentage of particulates removed, by weight)

	Copper and lead smelters	Other smelters and melting furnaces	Coal-fired utility boilers
1980	99	97	99
1970	95–97	80–90	98
1960	94–96	50–75	97
1950	93–95	0–70	95
1940	92–94	0–65	90
1930	90–93	0–60	85
1920	80–90	0–50	60
1900	30–60	0	0
1880	0	0	0

metallurgical activities and fossil-fuel combustion, respectively. Table 3 shows our assumed particulate emission-control efficiencies since 1880.

Dust- and smoke-control technologies were first applied to some non-ferrous smelters and refineries early in this century, partly because of the inherent value of the flue dust (e.g. to recover arsenic and precious metals). Cottrell precipitators were used, in addition to dust chambers, in the copper industry prior to 1914 (Hofman and Hayward, 1924). In 1915, the Balbach lead refinery in Newark achieved 90 per cent particulate recovery using a Cottrell precipitator (Hofman, 1918); by 1933, virtually all copper smelters included Cottrell treaters obtaining better than 90 per cent dust-collection efficiency. Efficiencies cited in Newton and Wilson (1942, table 5) included Garfield, Utah (90 per cent), Anaconda, Montana (90 per cent),

Table 4 Average annual US metal production (1,000 metric tons)

	Total raw steel production	Total copper smelter output	Primary copper refinery output	Copper recovered from old scrap	Total lead smelter output	Secondary lead, incl. refined from foreign bullion	Slab zinc from scrap
1980	100,250	1,163	1,271	567	539	692	48.4
1970	119,371	1,362	1,526	454	490	538	69.3
1960	86,060	901	1,294	388	366	404	52.1
1950	74,295	793	1,027	408	414	435	52.3
1940	58,133	769	1,075	314	461	284	44.2
1930	37,500	618	868	293	530	278	30.4
1920	35,175	532	715	151	478	160	
1900	11,619	269	242[a]	27[b]	310	225[c]	
1880	1,268	27	25[a]	3[b]	103		

All data are five-year averages centred on year shown, except:

a. 1880, 1900 estimated at 90 per cent smelter output (remainder = old scrap).
b. Assumes secondary production is 10 per cent of smelter output in 1880 and 1900 (probably too high).
c. 1900 estimated from 1899 US Census data (lead refined from imported bullion).

Noranda, Quebec (95 per cent), and Cerro de Pasco, Peru (97 per cent). However, dust recovery efficiency from ferrous melting furnaces was much lower because of the low value of the recovered materials.

It must be pointed out that pollutants (e.g. fly ash) removed from waste streams by "end-of-pipe" control technologies, like Cottrell precipitators, are usually disposed of in landfills. Such disposal is not necessarily permanent. Landfills can (and often do) leak. However, we have not considered the problem of toxic landfill leachates in this paper. To this extent, we have underestimated total emissions.

Table 4 gives the average national production by decade for seven categories of metals: steel, blister copper, primary refined copper, secondary refined copper (from old scrap), lead bullion, secondary refined lead, and secondary slab zinc.

Table 5 gives the average annual national combustion of fossil fuels by decade and by category.

The computation of heavy metal emissions from coal and fuel oil combustion now proceeds in a straightforward fashion by using the gross emissions coefficients (tables 1 and 2), assumed control efficiencies (table 3), national average annual metals production data (table 4), and national average fossil fuel consumption data (table 5). The results are given in tables 6 and 7.

Table 5 Average annual US combustion of fossil fuels (million metric tons)

	Bituminous coal, elec. utility	Bituminous coal, class I railroads	Bituminous coal, industry[a]	Bituminous coal, coke production[b]	Bituminous coal, resid. commerc.[c]	Anthracite coal	Residual fuel oil	Distillate fuel oil	Direct TEL in gas[d]
1980	501.2	0.0	57.8	57.4	5.8	3.4	128.9	160.2	0.12
1970	290.0	0.0	76.8	81.6	11.3	8.0	114.9	137.6	0.19
1960	156.6	1.5	84.1	69.8	27.4	15.6	79.8	99.5	0.11
1950	85.2	57.3	108.3	93.2	72.7	36.5	77.5	57.8	0.08
1940	45.6	81.8	119.2	69.9	75.6	43.9	51.4	23.2	0.03
1930	36.0	85.8	125.3	57.0	83.5	57.8	50.7	30.3	0.00
1920	31.3	110.7	130.7	57.8	87.1	72.5	30.5	25.9	(d)
1900	7.6	57.2	67.2	30.2	28.1	49.3	1.1	2.8	
1880	2.0	14.8	17.4	7.8	7.3	12.8		0.1	
			(a)	(b)	(c)				

a. Includes cement, steel, rolling mills and other.
b. Includes gas manufacture.
c. Residential and commercial establishments (retail distributors).
d. Lead content of tetra-ethyl lead (TEL) in gasoline, not gasoline consumed (see Ayres et al., 1988, vol. II, chap. 8).

Table 6 Average annual US metallic emissions due to metallurgical operations (metric tons)

Year	Arsenic Low	Arsenic High	Cadmium Low	Cadmium High	Chromium Low	Chromium High	Copper Low	Copper High	Mercury Low	Mercury High	Lead Low	Lead High	Zinc Low	Zinc High
1980	169	173	24	31	20	21	90	143	0.4	0.4	1,157	1,556	216	1,285
1970	630	1,182	82	191	78	167	334	969	1.2	2.1	3,866	10,503	799	9,883
1960	874	1,669	114	253	140	301	515	1,432	1.1	1.7	6,742	18,427	1,109	17,079
1950	902	2,498	128	394	145	520	550	2,357	1.3	1.8	7,631	33,565	1,210	29,242
1940	979	2,343	136	350	132	407	526	1,929	1.5	2.0	6,767	25,344	1,202	23,108
1930	852	1,845	133	302	98	263	429	1,446	1.5	2.2	6,118	19,356	1,014	15,318
1920	978	2,028	164	410	114	246	478	1,474	1.9	3.8	6,223	16,911	1,039	14,479
1900	1,230	1,900	295	624	76	81	486	1,229	4.1	7.1	9,536	14,244	1,424	6,680
1880	278	261	194	239	8	9	92	168	1.7	1.7	2,367	2,831	334	877

Table 7 Average annual US metallic emissions – fossil fuel combustion (metric tons)

	Arsenic	Cadmium	Chromium	Copper	Mercury	Lead	Zinc low	Zinc high
1980	39.3	302	504	188	1.3	28	33	56
1970	35.4	273	513	226	2.0	42	48	82
1960	25.0	193	427	222	2.2	48	53	93
1950	25.5	198	619	408	4.3	89	111	195
1940	19.8	156	893	716	7.8	160	211	372
1930	21.9	175	1,287	1,078	12.0	243	322	569
1920	28.7	243	3,425	3,079	33.6	684	942	1,667
1900	24.3	213	4,077	3,738	38.7	821	1,150	2,037
1880	6.2	55	1,054	968	9.9	212	298	527

Consumption-related heavy metal emissions

In the case of the heavy metals Ag, As, Cd, Cr, Cu, Hg, Pb, and Zn, we have found that there are ten categories of consumption that are readily distinguishable in terms of their different degrees of dissipation in use and different modes of release to the environment. These are as follows:

1. Metallic uses, e.g. in alloys. Environmental losses occur mainly in the production stage (discussed previously) and as a result of corrosion in use or discharge to landfills.
2. Plating and surface treatment (excluding paints and pigments) generate some losses in the platings or treatment process and some corrosion losses as above.
3. Paints and pigments generate losses at the point of application and from weathering and wear. Some are ultimately disposed of (e.g. in landfills) along with discarded objects or building materials.
4. Batteries and electronic devices have relatively short useful lives of 1–10 years. Production losses can be significant. Most are discarded to landfills.
5. Other electrical equipment as above, but may be longer-lived.
6. Industrial chemicals and reagents (e.g. catalysts, solvents, etc.) not embodied in products have short useful lives; catalysts and solvents are usually recycled, others are lost directly to air or water.
7. Chemical additives to consumer products include fuel additives,[4] rubber vulcanizing agents and pigments, detergents, plasticizers, photographic film, etc. They are disposed of mainly to landfill or incinerators.
8. Agricultural pesticides, fungicides and herbicides are used dissipatively, on farms, nurseries, etc. Most are immobilized by soil or biologically degraded and volatilized. There is some uptake into the food chain and some amount of loss via run-off.
9. Non-agricultural biocides include the above, as used in homes and gardens, for termite control, etc. These uses are dissipative but most biocides are immobilized by soil, as above.
10. Pharmaceuticals, germicides, etc., are used in the home or in health-service facilities and are largely discharged via sewage or to incinerators.

More detailed discussion of intermediate and final uses of each metal can be found in the Appendix that follows this chapter.

Table 8 Consumption-related emissions factors (ppm)

	Metallic use[a]	Plating and coating[b]	Paint and pigments[c]	Electron tubes and batteries[d]	Other electrical equipment[e]	Chemical uses, not embodied[f]	Chemical uses, embodied[g]	Agricultural uses[h]	Non-agricultural uses[i]	Medical, dental[j]	Misc. NEC
Silver	0.001	0.02	0.5	0.01	0.01	1	0.40	NA	NA	0.5	0.15
Arsenic	0.001	0	0.5	0.01	NA	NA	0.05	0.50	0.8	0.8	0.15
Cadmium	0.001	0.15	0.5	0.02	NA	1	0.15	NA	NA	NA	0.15
Chromium	0.001	0.02	0.5	NA	NA	1	0.05	NA	1	0.8	0.15
Copper	0.005	0	1.0	NA	0.10	1	0.05	0.05	1	NA	0.15
Mercury	0.050	0.05	0.8	0.20	NA	1	NA	0.80	0.9	0.2	0.50
Lead	0.005	0	0.5	0.01	NA	1	0.75	0.05	0.1	NA	0.15
Zinc	0.001	0.02	0.5	0.01	NA	1	0.15	0.05	0.1	0.8	0.15

a. As alloys or analgams (in the case of Hg) not used in plating, electrical equipment, catalysts or dental work. Losses can be assumed to be due primarily to wear and corrosion, except for mercury which volatilizes.

b. Protective surfaces deposited by dip coating (e.g. galvanizing, electroplating vacuum deposition, or chemical bath (e.g. chromic acid). The processes in question generally resulted in significant waterborne wastes until the 1970s. Cadmium-plating processes were particularly inefficient until recently (see discussion in Ayres et al., 1988, vol. II). Losses in use are mainly due to wear and abrasion (e.g. silverplate), or flaking (decorative chrome trim). In the case of mercury-tin "silver" for mirrors, losses were largely due to volatilization.

c. Paints and pigments are lost primarily by weathering (e.g. for metal-protecting paints), by wear, or by disposal of painted dyes or pigmented objects, such as magazines. Copper- and mercury-based paints slowly volatilize over time. A factor of 0.5 is rather arbitrarily assumed for all other paints and pigments.

d. Includes all metals and chemicals (e.g. phosphorus) in tubes and primary and secondary batteries, but excludes copper wire. Losses in manufacturing may be significant. Mercury in mercury vapour lamps can escape to the air when tubes are broken. In all other cases it is assumed that discarded equipment goes mainly to landfills. Minor amounts are volatilized in fires or incinerators or lost by corrosion; lead-acid batteries are recycled.

e. Includes solders, contacts, semiconductors and other special materials (but not copper wire) used in electrical equipment control devices, instruments, etc. Losses to the environment are primarily via discard of obsolete equipment to landfills. Mercury used in instruments is lost via breakage and volatilization or spillage.

f. Chemical uses not embodied in final products include catalysts, solvents, reagents, bleaches, etc. In some cases a chemical is basically embodied but there are some losses in processing. Losses in chemical manufacturing *per se* are included here. Major examples include copper and mercury catalysts (especially in chloride mfg); copper, zinc and chromium as mordants for dyes; mercury losses in felt manufacturing; chromium losses in tanning; lead in desulphurization of gasoline; zinc in rayon spinning, etc. In some cases virtually all of the material is actually dissipated. We include detonators such as mercury fulminate and lead azide (and explosives) in this category.

g. Chemical uses embodied in final products other than paints or batteries include fuel additives (e.g. TEL), anti-corrosion agents (e.g. zinc dithiophosphate), initiators and plasticizers for plastics (e.g. zinc oxide), etc. Also included are wood preservatives and chromium salts embodied in leather. Losses to the environment occur when the embodying productivity is utilized, for example gasoline containing TEL is burned and large-ly (0.75) dispersed into the atmosphere. However, copper, chromium, and arsenic are used as wood preservatives and and dispersed only if the wood is later burned or incinerated. In the case of silver (photographic film), we assume that 60 per cent is later recovered.

h. Agricultural pesticides, herbicides, and fungicides. Uses are dissipative but heavy metals are largely immobilized by soil. Arsenic and mercury are largely immobilized by soil. Arsenic and mercury are exceptions because of their volatility.

i. Non-agricultural biocides are the same compounds, used in industrial, commercial, or residential applications. Loss rates are high in some cases.

j. Medical/dental uses are primarily pharmaceutical (including cosmetics) germicides, also dental filling material. Most are dissipated to the environment via waste water. Silver and mercury dental fillings are likely to be buried with the dead body.

Robert U. Ayres and Leslie W. Ayres

Emissions coefficient for consumption

The term "emission coefficient," as used in this context, means the fraction of the material in question that is released in *mobile* form (to the air or water) within a certain period (a decade, more or less). We exclude wastes that are recycled or disposed of in landfills or in sludge dumped offshore. We exclude toxic metals immobilized in clayey soil. In a few cases we also include production-related losses that were not included in the previous sections (e.g. process wastes in the plating, tanning, and chemical industries). These assumptions are obviously quite conservative, at least in the sense that a case could be made for significantly higher estimates of emissions.

It is unfortunate (and curious) that there are almost no published data on emissions coefficients for consumption activities. Obviously, most analysts so far have not considered such activities to be "sources" of pollutants.[5] In the absence of an existing body of literature (and of time to undertake more intensive research on this topic ourselves) we are led to a rather ad hoc choice of emissions coefficients. These are displayed in table 8. Each coefficient represents the fraction of total consumption in that category that is typically unrecoverable *in principle*.

It should be emphasized that these estimates are rather rough. In some cases, they are little better than "guestimates." The results presented here, therefore, are illustrative rather than authoritative. A task for the future is to improve the approach, and particularly to make it more relevant to major new policy initiatives.

In the case of tetra-ethyl lead (TEL) emissions from gasoline consumption, it is probably not necessary to compute emissions from an emission coefficient. Instead, on the assumption that all lead in gasoline is eventually emitted, input data on lead use as a gasoline additive should suffice. Such data are available from the Bureau of Mines. To compute strictly atmospheric emissions, however, the total lead used as a gasoline additive should be multiplied by a factor of 0.75 to reflect the fact that at least 25 per cent of the lead is trapped in the oil, oil filters, or exhaust system of the cars and not emitted directly to the atmosphere (Hirschler et al., 1957; Hirschler and Gilbert, 1964).

It must be pointed out that, while the numerical estimates in many cases are rather uncertain – sometimes even by a factor of two or three – there are only a few important routes which clearly dominate the rest for each metal.

Historical usage patterns

The next and last step is to allocate total domestic usage of each of the eight metals among the ten categories over the past 100 years. The allocation among uses has been far from unchanging. Many formerly important uses have disappeared, while others have emerged as recently as the last decade. Consumption data by use are available, in general, only since the Second World War. For earlier periods one must rely on a scattering of real data supplemented by a variety of other clues.

Our composite picture of historical heavy metals usage patterns for the United States is summarized in tables A–H in the Appendix. Each table represents one metal, and is arranged as follows:
1. Percentage of metal use by consumptive category.
2. Consumption in metric tons (US).
3. Emissions due to consumptive use (US).

The Appendix also includes a final summary table (table I) of production-related and consumption-related emissions, and the consumption-related fraction, for seven of the eight metals (excluding silver, for which production-related emissions data are not available). The consumption fraction, expressed as a percentage, is plotted for two groups of metals in figure 1.

Conclusions

As noted already, the major results of our analysis are summarized in tabular form in the Appendix (see tables A–H).

The lower part of figure 1 displays, for chromium and copper, the ratio of consumption-related[6] dissipative losses to production-related emissions (not including losses at the mine) in each decade. For these two metals, whose major uses are in metallic form or, in the case of chromite, as bricks for blast-furnace liners, production-related emissions are still dominant, but the consumption share is increasing steadily.

In the upper part of figure 1 the same data are shown for five other toxic heavy metals: arsenic, cadmium, lead, mercury, and zinc.

In two cases, arsenic and mercury, the consumption share has always been high. Arsenic has been used (until very recently) almost exclusively because of its biotoxic properties. Such uses are inherently dissipative. This is also partly true for mercury. For instance, mercury is the basis of a number of commercial fungicides, germicides,

Robert U. Ayres and Leslie W. Ayres

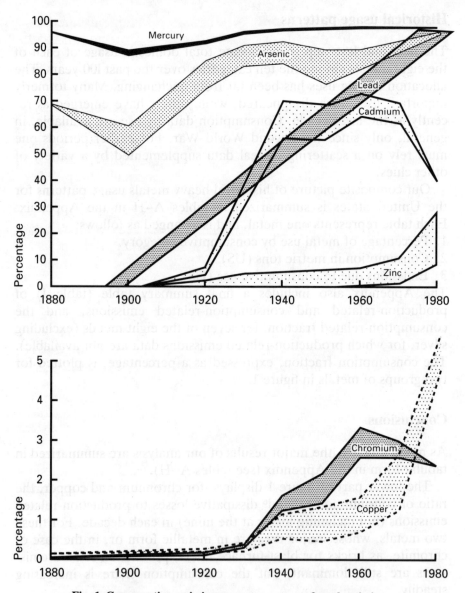

Fig. 1 Consumptive emissions as a percentage of total emissions

and preservatives. The major dissipative uses of cadmium, in the past, were in pigments and as a contaminant of zinc oxide used in tyres. The use of cadmium for red and orange pigments has declined sharply, while metallic usage (mainly in batteries) has increased even more sharply. This accounts for the inverted "U" shape of the cad-

272

mium curve. (As electronic uses of arsenic, in gallium arsenide, may grow in the future, a similar downturn may be expected in the future.)

The increasingly dissipative usage of lead is only partly due to its role as a gasoline additive (largely phased out since 1980, of course). In earlier decades lead was the basis of one of the most widely used agricultural insecticides (lead arsenate). In the nineteenth and early twentieth century, lead was also extensively used as a white pigment for oil-based paints. So-called white lead was later replaced by a zinc-based white pigment (lithopone), which was subsequently replaced by the white pigment now used most widely, titanium dioxide. Red lead was the major metal-protective paint until the last decade or so. The yellow paints currently used on roadways and to protect heavy machinery – such as bulldozers – are largely chromium-based, which accounts in part for the rapid rise in dissipative uses of chromium. Zinc is also used in large quantities in tyres and paper.

As we indicated at the outset, for three of these five metals investigated the dissipative consumption-related emissions far outweigh the production-related emissions; in fact the consumption shares for arsenic, lead, and mercury are close to 100 per cent. In the case of zinc, that share is rising rapidly; for cadmium the consumptive share is still about 50 per cent of the total.

One of the eight metals included in the study was silver. Production-related emissions data are non-existent. However, since silver is a rather valuable metal, and since almost all of it is now obtained as a by-product of lead, zinc, or copper smelting and refining, one could probably argue that production-related emissions are essentially non-existent. On the other hand, one major consumptive use of silver is still in photography. While commercial photographic studios do recycle some silver, a significant fraction is lost. Thus, for silver, too, the consumption-related share of total emissions is probably close to 100 per cent.

The foregoing analysis was entirely historical. But one or two points worth considering for the future emerge clearly. One of them is the fact that several of these toxic heavy metals play a major and increasing role in electronics. These include lead (solder), arsenic (semi-conductors), cadmium (batteries), mercury (switches and batteries), and silver (batteries and connectors). Electronic wastes are accumulating in obsolete equipment at an enormous rate in the United States, and all around the world. Much of this electronic "junk" might be dumped in landfills in future years, and some will be inadvertently incinerated. Many states already classify such wastes as hazardous. Leaching – especially that due to increasingly acid rainfall – and combustion will mobilize some of these toxic materials. There is, therefore, a strong need for more research on ways and means of closing the materials cycle.

Notes

1. This chapter is adapted from a comprehensive three-volume report entitled *An Historical Reconstruction of Major Pollutant Levels in the Hudson-Raritan Basin: 1880–1980* prepared for the US National Oceanic and Atmospheric Administration (NOAA). More details can be found in the original.
2. See, for instance, Nriagu, 1980a, 1980b, 1980c, 1980d; Nriagu and Davidson, 1982; Watson and Brooks, 1979; NRC, 1977b; NRC, 1977c, 1981; GCA, 1973, 1981; URS, 1975; Davis, 1972, 1980; MRI, 1980; PEDCo, 1980; USEPA, 1984; Nriagu, 1978; Little, 1976; Battelle, 1977; Lowenbach and Schlesinger, 1979; Ottinger et al., 1973; APCC, 1956; Hofman and Hayward, 1924.
3. Unfortunately, some of the industry studies sponsored by EPA are almost useless for our purposes because they present a great deal of detailed but disparate and inconsistent data from which it is virtually impossible to generalize. This is particularly true of the EPA's "Industrial Process Profile" series. All things considered, the sources we consider to be authoritative are as follows: arsenic (Lowenbach and Schlesinger, 1979), cadmium (GCA, 1981), mercury (URS, 1975), and lead (USEPA, 1984). In the cases of silver, chromium, copper, and zinc, no single source suffices, and therefore a range of estimates will be used.
4. In our original calculations (Ayres et al., 1988), we included tetraethyl lead (TEL) in the category of fossil-fuel combustion. In this study, it has been shifted to the category of consumption-related (chemical additives).
5. On the other hand, sewage treatment, landfills, and waste incineration have (inconsistently) been treated as if they were sources.
6. For clarity, it should be noted again that the term consumption, as it is used here, includes intermediate consumptive uses of the metal (e.g. as catalysts) as well as so-called "final" uses.

References

Air Pollution Control Committee (APCC). 1956. *Control of Emissions from Metal Melting Operations*. American Foundrymen's Society.

Ayres, Robert U., Leslie W. Ayres, Joel A. Tarr, and Rolande C. Widgery. 1988. *An Historical Reconstruction of Major Pollutant Levels in the Hudson-Raritan Basin: 1880–1980*. Prepared for the US National Oceanic and Atmospheric Administration, Washington, D.C. 3 vols. (NOAA Technical Memorandum NOS-OMA-43.)

Battelle Columbus Laboratories. 1977. *Multimedia Levels Cadmium*. Columbus, Ohio. (EPA-560/6-77-032 (PB 273 198).)

Davis, W. E., and Associates. 1972. *National Inventory of Sources and Emissions: Barium, Boron, Copper, Selenium and Zinc 1969*. "Copper," section III. (APTD-1129 (PB 210 678).)

———. 1980. *National Inventory of Sources and Emissions: Copper, Selenium and Zinc 1969.* "Zinc," section V. Leawood, Kan. (APTD-1139 (PB 210 680).)

GCA Corporation. 1973. *National Inventory of Sources and Emission of Chromium.* Chapel Hill, N.C. (EPA-450/3-74-012 (PB 230 034).)

———. 1981. *Survey of Cadmium Emission Sources.* Chapel Hill, N.C. (EPA-450/3-81-013 (PB 82-142050).)

Hirschler, D. A., and L. F. Gilbert. 1964. *Arch. Environmental Health* 8: 297.

Hirschler, D. A., L. F. Gilbert, F. W. Lamb, and L. M. Niebylski. 1957. *Industrial Engineering and Chemistry* 49: 1131.

Hofman, H. O. 1918. *Metallurgy of Lead.* New York: McGraw-Hill.

Hofman, H. O., and C. R. Hayward. 1924. *Metallurgy of Copper.* 2nd ed. New York: McGraw-Hill.

Little, A. D., Inc. 1976. *Environmental Considerations of Selected Energy Conserving Manufacturing Process Technologies.* Vol. XIV. Primary Copper Industry Report. Cambridge, Mass. (EPA-600/7-76.)

Lowenbach and Schlesinger Assoc. 1979. *Arsenic: A Preliminary Materials Balance.* McLean, Va. (EPA-860/6-79-005 (PB 80-162217).)

Midwest Research Institute (MRI). 1980. *Source Category Survey: Secondary Zinc Smelting and Refining Industry.* (EPA-450/3-80-012 (PB 80-191604).)

National Academy of Sciences/National Academy of Engineering Committee on Lead in the Human Environment. 1980. *Lead in the Human Environment.* Washington, D.C.: National Academy Press.

National Research Council (NRC). 1977a. *Environmental Monitoring.* Vol. IV. Report to US EPA. Washington, D.C.: National Academy Press.

———. 1977b. *Arsenic – Committee on Medical and Biologic Effects of Environment Pollutants.* Washington, D.C.: National Academy Press.

———. 1977c. *Copper – Committee on Medical and Biologic Effects of Environment Pollutants.* Washington, D.C.: National Academy Press.

———. 1981. *Atmosphere-Biosphere Interactions: Toward a Better Understanding of the Ecological Consequences of Fossil Fuel Combustion.* National Academy Press.

Nriagu, J. O. 1978. *The Biochemistry of Lead in the Environment.* New York: Elsevier.

———. 1980a. *Copper in the Environment.* New York: Wiley-Interscience.

———. 1980b. *Cadmium in the Environment.* Part 2. New York: Wiley-Interscience.

———. 1980c. "Global Cadmium Cycle." In: J. O. Nriagu, ed., *Cadmium in the Environment.* Part 1: *Ecological Cycling.* New York: Wiley-Interscience, pp. 1–11.

———. 1980d. *Zinc in the Environment.* Part 1. New York: Wiley-Interscience.

Nriagu, J. O., and C. I. Davidson. 1982. "Zinc in the Atmosphere." In: J. O. Nriagu, ed., *Zinc in the Environment.* Part 1: *Ecological Cycling.* New York: Wiley-Interscience, pp. 113–160.

Ottinger, R. S., et al. 1973. *Recommended Methods of Reduction Neutralization, Recovery or Disposal of Hazardous Waste.* Vol. XIV: *Summary of Waste Origins, Forms And Quantities.* TRW Systems. (PB 224 593/4.)

PEDCo. 1980. *Industrial Process Profiles for Environmental Use: Primary Copper Industry.* Washington, D.C., chap. 29. (EPA-600/2-80-170 (PB 81-164915).)

URS Research Corp. 1975. *Materials Balance and Technology Assessment of Mercury and Its Compounds on National and Regional Bases.* San Mateo, Calif. (EPA-560/3-75-007 (PB 247,000).)

275

Robert U. Ayres and Leslie W. Ayres

US Environmental Protection Agency (USEPA). 1984. *Air Quality Criteria for Lead*. Vols. I-IV (preliminary). Washington, D.C. (EPA-600/8-83-028B.)

Watson, J. W., and K. J. Brooks. 1979. *A Review of Standards of Performance for New Stationary Sources – Secondary Lead Smelters*. McLean, Va.: MITRE. (MTR-7871.)

Appendix

Table A Silver: consumptive uses, United States, by category

Year	Protective cover			Electrical		Chemical		Biocidal poison uses			Miscel-laneous, NEC	Total
	Metallic uses (except coatings and electrical	Plating and coating	Paints and pig-ments	Batteries and equipment	Other electrical uses, in-struments, etc.	Industrial catalysts, reagents, explosives, etc.	Consumer additives, extenders, photo-graphy, etc.	Agricultural pesticides, herbicides, fungicides	Non-agricultural pesticides, except medical	Medical, dental, pharma-ceutical		
Percentage use												
1980	26	0	0	4.8	22	2.5	40	0	0	1	3.0	—
1972	42	0	0	4.0	24	2.2	25	0	0	1	1.6	—
1967	42	0	0	4.0	21	2.0	26	0	0	2	3.0	—
1958	57	0	0	2.0	11	2.0	22	0	0	2	7.0	—
1942	70	0	0	0	7	3.0	15	0	0	2	3.0	—
1929	75	0	0	0	3	3.0	15	0	0	4	0	—
1919	80	0	0	0	0	1.5	12	0	0	6	0	—
1900	85	0	0	0	0	0	5	0	0	5	5.0	—
1880	90	0	0	0	0	0	0	0	0	5	5.0	—
Use in metric tons												
1980	1,096	0	0	202	927.4	105.4	1,686.1	0	0	42	126.5	4,215.3
1972	1,819	0	0	173	1,039.2	95.3	1,082.5	0	0	43	69.3	4,329.9
1967	1,318	0	0	126	658.9	62.8	815.8	0	0	63	94.1	3,137.7
1958	1,790	0	0	63	345.4	62.8	690.8	0	0	63	219.8	3,140.1
1942	1,233	0	0	0	123.3	52.8	264.2	0	0	35	52.8	1,761.2
1929	817	0	0	0	32.7	32.7	163.5	0	0	44	0	1,089.9
1919	906	0	0	0	0	17.0	135.0	0	0	68	0	1,132.1
1900	1,005	0	0	0	0	0	59.1	0	0	59	59.1	1,181.9
1880	420	0	0	0	0	0	0	0	0	23	23.3	466.6

Emissions from consumptive uses

Year											
1980	11.508	0	2.023	9.27	105.4	0	674.4	0	21.08	6.323	830.03
1972	19.095	0	1.732	10.39	95.3	0	433.0	0	21.65	3.464	584.58
1967	13.837	0	1.255	6.59	62.8	0	326.3	0	31.38	4.707	446.84
1958	18.793	0	0.628	3.45	62.8	0	276.3	0	31.40	10.990	404.40
1942	12.945	0	0	1.23	52.8	0	105.7	0	17.61	2.642	192.94
1929	8.583	0	0	0.33	32.7	0	65.4	0	21.80	0.000	128.80
1919	9.510	0	0	0	17.0	0	54.3	0	33.96	0.000	114.79
1900	10.548	0	0	0	0	0	23.6	0	29.55	2.955	66.69
1880	4.409	0	0	0	0	0	0	0	11.67	1.166	17.24

Table B Arsenic: consumptive uses, United States, by category

	Protective cover			Electrical		Chemical		Biocidal poison uses				
Year	Metallic uses (except coatings and electrical	Plating and coating	Paints and pig-ments	Batteries and equipment	Other electrical uses, instruments, etc.	Industrial catalysts, reagents, explosives, etc.	Consumer additives, extenders, photo-graphy, etc.	Agricultural pesticides, herbicides, fungicides	Non-agricultural pesticides, except medical	Medical, dental, pharma-ceutical	Miscel-laneous, NEC	Total
Percentage use												
1980	2	0	0	1	0	5	0	30	60	1	0	—
1970	2	0	0	1	0	4	0	45	45	1	0	—
1960	2	0	0	1	0	5	0	80	10	2	0	—
1950	2	0	0	1	0	5	0	80	10	2	0	—
1940	2	0	0	1	0	5	0	80	10	2	0	—
1930	2	0	0	0	0	5	1	80	10	2	0	—
1920	2	0	2	0	0	5	3	75	10	3	0	—
1900	0	0	5	0	0	10	10	60	10	5	0	—
1880	1	1	10	0	0	10	10	40	20	10	0	—
Use in metric tons												
1980	0.393	0	0	0.197	0	0.983	0	5.901	11.801	0.197	0	19.67
1970	0.513	0	0	0.256	0	1.025	0	11.532	11.532	0.256	0	25.63
1960	0.358	0	0	0.179	0	0.895	0	14.315	1.789	0.358	0	17.89
1950	0.369	0	0	0.185	0	0.923	0	14.762	1.845	0.369	0	18.45
1940	0.592	0	0	0.296	0	1.479	0	23.663	2.958	0.592	0	29.58
1930	0.415	0	0	0	0	1.037	0.207	16.590	2.074	0.415	0	20.74
1920	0.253	0	0.253	0	0	0.633	0.380	9.494	1.266	0.380	0	12.66
1900	0	0	0.190	0	0	0.380	0.380	2.281	0.380	0.190	0	3.80
1880	0.012	0	0.123	0	0	0.123	0.123	0.494	0.247	0.123	0	1.23

Emissions from consumptive uses

Year											
1980	0.039	0	1.97	0	492	0	2,950	5,901	19.7	0	9,364
1970	0.051	0	2.56	0	513	0	5,766	5,766	25.6	0	12,072
1960	0.036	0	1.79	0	447	0	7,158	895	35.8	0	8,537
1950	0.037	0	1.85	0	461	0	7,381	923	36.9	0	8,804
1940	0.059	0	2.96	0	739	0	11,882	1,479	59.2	0	14,112
1930	0.041	0	0	0	518	166	8,295	1,037	41.5	0	10,058
1920	0.025	127	0	0	316	304	4,747	633	38.0	0	6,164
1900	0	95	0	0	190	304	1,140	190	19.0	0	1,939
1880	0.001	62	0	0	62	99	247	123	12.3	0	605

Table C Cadmium: consumptive uses, United States, by category

Year	Protective cover			Electrical		Chemical		Biocidal poison uses			Miscellaneous, NEC	Total
	Metallic uses (except coatings and electrical)	Plating and coating	Paints and pigments	Batteries and equipment	Other electrical uses, instruments, etc.	Industrial catalysts, reagents, explosives, etc.	Consumer additives, extenders, photography, etc.	Agricultural pesticides, herbicides, fungicides	Non-agricultural pesticides, except medical	Medical, dental, pharmaceutical		
Percentage use												
1979	2	50.9	13.0	21.9	0	0	11.0	0	0	0	1.1	—
1970	2	49.9	14.4	3.4	0	0	26.3	0	0	0	4.1	—
1963	2	57.6	15.0	7.4	0	0	17.5	0	0	0	0.1	—
1950	3	68.0	17.0	3.0	0	0	9.0	0	0	0	0	—
1940	4	75.0	20.0	1.0	0	0	0	0	0	0	0	—
1930	4	75.0	20.0	1.0	0	0	0	0	0	0	0	—
1920	0	0	100.0	0	0	0	0	0	0	0	0	—
1900	0	0	0	0	0	0	0	0	0	0	0	—
1880	0	0	0	0	0	0	0	0	0	0	0	—
Use in metric tons												
1979	35.6	907.0	231.7	390.3	0	0	196.0	0	0	0	19.6	1,782.0
1970	89.5	2,332.8	644.3	152.1	0	0	1,176.8	0	0	0	183.5	4,474.6
1963	96.5	2,779.6	732.9	357.1	0	0	844.5	0	0	0	24.1	4,825.7
1950	114.7	2,598.8	649.7	114.7	0	0	344.0	0	0	0	0	3,821.8
1940	134.3	2,517.8	671.4	33.6	0	0	0	0	0	0	0	3,357.0
1930	40.1	752.5	200.7	10.0	0	0	0	0	0	0	0	1,003.3
1920	0	0	67.8	0	0	0	0	0	0	0	0	67.8
1900	0	0	0	0	0	0	0	0	0	0	0	6.4
1880	0	0	0	0	0	0	0	0	0	0	0	0

Losses of toxic heavy metals in the United States

Emissions from consumptive uses

Year											
1979	0.036	136.06	116	7.81	0	0	29	0	0	0.980	290
1970	0.089	334.92	322	3.04	0	0	177	0	0	9.173	846
1963	0.097	416.94	362	7.14	0	0	127	0	0	1.206	914
1950	0.115	389.82	325	2.29	0	0	52	0	0	0	769
1940	0.134	377.66	336	0.67	0	0	0	0	0	0	714
1930	0.040	112.87	100	0.20	0	0	0	0	0	0	213
1920	0	0	34	0	0	0	0	0	0	0	34
1900	0	0	0	0	0	0	0	0	0	0	0
1880	0	0	0	0	0	0	0	0	0	0	0

Table D Chromium: consumptive uses, United States, by category

	Protective cover			Electrical		Chemical		Biocidal poison uses				Total
Year	Metallic uses (except coatings and electrical	Plating and coating	Paints and pigments	Batteries and equipment	Other electrical uses, instruments, etc.	Industrial catalysts, reagents, explosives, etc.	Consumer additives, extenders, photography, etc.	Agricultural pesticides, herbicides, fungicides	Non-agricultural pesticides, except medical	Medical, dental, pharmaceutical	Miscellaneous, NEC	Total
Percentage use												
1980	58.5	3.0	5.0	0	0	0.5	2.7	0	0.4	0	16.5	—
1968	62.5	4.2	5.0	0	0	0.5	3.0	0	0.3	0	25.0	—
1960	54.0	4.0	6.0	0	0	0.5	3.0	0	0.2	0	32.0	—
1950	50.0	4.0	6.5	0	0	0.5	3.0	0	0.2	0	35.0	—
1940	50.0	3.5	14.5	0	0	0.5	4.0	0	0.2	0	27.0	—
1930	60.0	2.5	7.7	0	0	0.5	4.0	0	0.1	0	30.0	—
1920	50.0	0	15.0	0	0	0.5	10.0	0	0	0	25.0	—
1900	0	0	100.0	0	0	0	0	0	0	0	0	—
1880	0	0	100.0	0	0	0	0	0	0	0	0	—
Use in metric tons												
1980	151.8	7.78	12.97	0	0	1.297	7.78	0	1.038	0	42.8	259.46
1968	233.8	15.04	17.91	0	0	1.791	9.67	0	1.074	0	89.5	358.16
1960	176.1	13.04	19.56	0	0	1.630	9.78	0	0.652	0	104.3	326.02
1950	129.9	10.39	16.88	0	0	1.299	7.79	0	0.519	0	90.9	259.73
1940	81.4	5.70	23.61	0	0	0.814	6.51	0	0.326	0	44.0	162.83
1930	41.7	1.74	5.35	0	0	0.347	2.78	0	0.139	0	20.8	69.42
1920	16.9	0	5.08	0	0	0.169	3.38	0	0.034	0	8.5	33.85
1900	0	0	6.49	0	0	0	0	0	0	0	0	6.49
1880	0	0	0.67	0	0	0	0	0	0	0	0	0.67

Emissions from comsumptive uses

Year											
1980	0.1518	0.1557	6.49	0	1.297	0.389	0	1.038	0	2.141	11.659
1968	0.2238	0.3009	8.95	0	1.791	0.484	0	1.074	0	4.477	17.304
1960	0.1761	0.2608	9.78	0	1.630	0.489	0	0.652	0	5.216	18.205
1950	0.1299	0.2078	8.44	0	1.299	0.390	0	0.519	0	4.545	15.532
1940	0.0814	0.1140	11.81	0	0.814	0.326	0	0.326	0	2.198	15.665
1930	0.0417	0.347	2.67	0	0.347	0.139	0	0.139	0	1.041	4.415
1920	0.0169	0	2.54	0	0.169	0.169	0	0.034	0	0.423	3.351
1900	0	0	3.25	0	0	0	0	0	0	0	3.246
1880	0	0	0.34	0	0	0	0	0	0	0	0.337

Table E Copper: consumptive uses, United States, by category

	Protective cover			Electrical		Chemical		Biocidal poison uses			Miscellaneous, NEC	Total
Year	Metallic uses (except coatings and electrical)	Plating and coating	Paints and pigments	Batteries and equipment	Other electrical uses, instruments, etc.	Industrial catalysts, reagents, explosives, etc.	Consumer additives, extenders, photography, etc.	Agricultural pesticides, herbicides, fungicides	Non-agricultural pesticides, except medical	Medical, dental, pharmaceutical		
Percentage use												
1980	99.670	0	0	0	0	0.190	0	0.14	0	0	0	—
1970	99.610	0	0	0	0	0.230	0	0.10	0	0	0	—
1960	99.440	0	0	0	0	0.260	0	0.30	0	0	0	—
1950	99.420	0	0	0	0	0.270	0	0.31	0	0	0	—
1945	99.355	0	0	0	0	0.265	0	0.70	0	0	0	—
1940	99.290	0	0	0	0	0.260	0	0.45	0	0	0	—
1930	99.460	0	0	0	0	0.270	0	0.27	0	0	0	—
1920	99.040	0	0	0	0	0.290	0	0.67	0	0	0	—
1900	99.220	0	0	0	0	0.280	0	1.12	0	0	0	—
1880	93.200	0	0	0	0	0.300	0	3.10	0	0	0	—
Use in metric tons												
1980	2,214.9	0	0	0	0	4.222	0	3.111	0	0	0	2,222.2
1970	1,964.7	0	0	0	0	4.537	0	1.972	0	0	0	1,972.4
1960	1,414.5	0	0	0	0	3.698	0	4.267	0	0	0	1,422.5
1950	1,559.2	0	0	0	0	4.235	0	4.862	0	0	0	1,568.5
1945	1,945.1	0	0	0	0	5.188	0	13.704	0	0	0	1,957.7
1940	1,727.2	0	0	0	0	4.523	0	7.828	0	0	0	1,739.5
1930	723.5	0	0	0	0	1.964	0	1.964	0	0	0	727.4
1920	732.2	0	0	0	0	2.144	0	4.953	0	0	0	739.3
1900	469.8	0	0	0	0	1.326	0	5.303	0	0	0	473.5
1880	151.3	0	0	0	0	0.487	0	5.033	0	0	0	162.4

Emissions from consumptive uses

1980	11.074	0	0	0	4.222	0	0.156	0	0	15.452
1970	9.824	0	0	0	4.537	0	0.099	0	0	14.459
1960	7.072	0	0	0	3.698	0	0.213	0	0	10.984
1950	7.796	0	0	0	4.235	0	0.243	0	0	12.274
1945	9.725	0	0	0	5.188	0	0.685	0	0	15.598
1940	8.636	0	0	0	4.523	0	0.391	0	0	13.550
1930	3.617	0	0	0	1.964	0	0.098	0	0	5.680
1920	3.661	0	0	0	2.144	0	0.248	0	0	6.052
1900	2.349	0	0	0	1.326	0	0.265	0	0	3.940
1880	0.757	0	0	0	0.487	0	0.252	0	0	1.495

Table F Mercury: consumptive uses, United States, by category

Year	Protective cover			Electrical		Chemical		Biocidal poison uses			Miscellaneous NEC	Total
	Metallic uses (except coatings and electrical)	Plating and coating	Paints and pigments	Batteries and equipment	Other electrical uses, instruments, etc.	Industrial catalysts, reagents, explosives, etc.	Consumer additives, extenders, photography, etc.	Agricultural pesticides, herbicides, fungicides	Non-agricultural pesticides, except medical	Medical, dental, pharmaceutical		
Percentage use												
1977	0	0	0	49.2	8.8	20.7	0	1.0	13.2	2.1	0.7	—
1970	0	0	0	25.9	13.5	28.0	0	2.9	19.7	5.2	2.9	—
1960	0	0	0	18.1	12.7	13.5	0	5.9	8.2	7.3	2.5	—
1950	0	0	0	33.8	15.0	12.6	0	12.6	8.7	21.5	1.8	—
1942	0	0	6	9.2	7.1	40.0	0	3.0	5.0	27.7	3.0	—
1928	1.3	0	7	7.3	8.6	43.7	0	1.1	4.7	16.7	9.9	—
1920	5.0	0	7	7.0	8.0	42.0	0	0	8.0	15.0	8.0	—
1900	10.0	0	7	3.0	8.0	42.0	0	0	8.0	15.0	7.0	—
1880	42.0	0	5	0	5.0	30.0	0	0	5.0	10.0	5.0	—
Use in metric tons												
1977	0	0	0	979.54	175.20	412.1	0	19.91	262.8	41.81	13.94	1,990.94
1970	0	0	0	570.46	297.35	616.7	0	63.87	433.9	114.50	63.87	2,202.56
1960	0	0	0	349.10	244.95	260.4	0	111.87	158.15	140.80	48.22	1,928.72
1950	0	0	0	547.01	242.75	203.9	0	203.91	140.80	347.95	29.13	1,618.36
1942	0	0	66.88	102.54	79.14	445.8	0	33.44	55.73	308.75	33.44	1,114.61
1928	11.9	0	64.10	66.84	78.75	400.1	0	10.07	43.04	152.91	90.65	915.65
1920	42.5	0	59.54	59.54	68.04	357.2	0	0	68.04	127.58	68.04	850.52
1900	35.9	0	39.11	16.76	44.70	234.7	0	0	44.70	83.80	39.11	558.70
1880	353.3	0	42.06	0	42.06	252.4	0	0	42.06	84.12	42.06	841.18

Emissions from consumptive uses

Year												
1977	0	0	0	195.91	17.520	412.1	0	15.93	236.52	8.36	6.96	893.3
1970	0	0	0	114.09	29.735	616.7	0	51.10	390.51	22.91	31.93	1,257.0
1960	0	0	0	69.820	24.495	260.4	0	89.49	142.34	28.16	24.10	638.8
1950	0	0	0	109.4	24.275	203.9	0	163.13	126.72	69.59	14.56	711.6
1942	0	53.50	0	20.509	7.914	445.8	0	26.75	50.18	61.75	16.71	683.1
1928	0.595	51.28	0	13.368	7.875	400.1	0	8.06	38.73	30.58	45.52	595.9
1920	2.126	47.63	0	11.907	6.804	357.2	0	0	61.24	25.52	34.02	546.5
1900	2.793	31.29	0	3.352	4.470	234.7	0	0	40.23	16.76	19.55	353.1
1880	17.665	33.65	0	0	4.206	252.4	0	0	37.85	16.82	21.03	383.6

Table G Lead: consumptive uses, United States, by category

Year	Protective cover			Electrical		Chemical		Biocidal poison uses			Miscellaneous, NEC	Total
	Metallic uses (except coatings and electrical	Plating and coating	Paints and pigments	Batteries and equipment	Other electrical uses, instruments, etc.	Industrial catalysts, reagents, explosives, etc.	Consumer additives, extenders, photography, etc.	Agricultural pesticides, herbicides, fungicides	Non-agricultural pesticides, except medical	Medical, dental, pharmaceutical		
Percentage use												
1980	0.16	0	0.06	0.54	0	0	99.2	0.000	0	0	0.017	—
1972	0.12	0	0.03	0.25	0	0	99.6	0.002	0	0	0.019	—
1957	0.25	0	0.06	0.20	0	0	99.5	0.004	0	0	0.019	—
1949	0.42	0	0.11	0.32	0	0	99.1	0.029	0	0	0.016	—
1939	0.76	0	0.37	0.55	0	0	98.3	0.019	0	0	0.009	—
1929	10.18	0	2.70	3.79	0	0	82.6	0.035	0	0	0.669	—
1923	53.73	0	22.99	18.68	0	0	0	0	0	0	4.605	—
1900	60.00	0	30.00	5.00	0	0	0	0	0	0	5.000	—
1880	60.00	0	30.00	5.00	0	0	0	0	0	0	5.000	—
Use in metric tons												
1980	250	0	97	851	0	0	157,400	0	0	0	26.58	158,625
1972	288	0	76	621	0	0	248,300	3.81	0	0	46.96	249,336
1957	374	0	96	301	0	0	147,700	5.70	0	0	28.50	148,505
1949	443	0	115	341	0	0	104,900	30.73	0	0	17.41	105,847
1939	310	0	150	225	0	0	40,000	7.56	0	0	3.78	40,696
1929	419	0	111	156	0	0	3,400	1.45	0	0	27.51	4,115
1923	374	0	160	130	0	0	0	0	0	0	32.05	696
1900	0	0	0	0	0	0	0	0	0	0	0	0
1880	0	0	0	0	0	0	0	0	0	0	0	0

Emissions from consumptive uses

Year												
1980	1.249	0	48.5	8.51	0	0	118,050	0	0	0	1.329	118,110
1972	1.441	0	38.1	6.21	0	0	186,225	0.19	0	0	2.348	186,273
1957	1.871	0	48	3.01	0	0	110,775	0.285	0	0	1.425	110,830
1949	2.217	0	57.4	3.41	0	0	78,675	1.536	0	0	0.871	78,740
1939	1.55	0	74.8	2.25	0	0	30,000	0.378	0	0	0.189	30,079
1929	2.096	0	55.7	1.56	0	0	2,550	0.072	0	0	1.375	2,611
1923	1.871	0	79.8	1.3	0	0	0	0	0	0	1.602	85
1900	0	0	0	0	0	0	0	0	0	0	0	0
1880	0	0	0	0	0	0	0	0	0	0	0	0

Table H Zinc: consumptive uses, United States, by category

Percentage use

Year	Protective cover — Metallic uses (except coatings and electrical)	Protective cover — Plating and coating	Protective cover — Paints and pigments	Electrical — Batteries and equipment	Electrical — Other electrical uses, instruments, etc.	Chemical — Industrial catalysts, reagents, explosives, etc.	Chemical — Consumer additives, extenders, photography, etc.	Biocidal poison uses — Agricultural pesticides, herbicides, fungicides	Biocidal poison uses — Non-agricultural pesticides, except medical	Biocidal poison uses — Medical, dental, pharmaceutical	Miscellaneous NEC	Total
1977	41	35	12.4	0.5	0	0.2	9.9	0.3	0.2	0.1	0	—
1973	45	31	11.7	1.0	0	0.3	8.9	0.2	0.2	0.1	0	—
1968	44	27	12.2	2.2	0	0.5	7.9	0.2	0.2	0.1	0	—
1958	43	33	12.6	3.3	0	0.7	6.8	0.3	0.2	0.1	0	—
1949	25	45	16.8	3.7	0	0.7	7.5	0.2	0.2	0.1	0	—
1940	27	39	19.8	4.1	0	0.5	9.2	0.2	0.2	0.1	0	—
1930	22	39	25.7	2.7	0	0.5	9.9	0.2	0.2	0.1	0	—
1920	26	33	26.0	2.7	0	0.6	5.0	0.2	5.5	0.1	0	—
1900	30	25	25.0	5.0	0	1.0	5.0	0.3	8.0	0.3	0	—
1880	35	30	30.0	0	0	2.5	2.0	0.5	0	0.5	0	—

Use in metric tons

Year	Protective cover — Metallic uses (except coatings and electrical)	Protective cover — Plating and coating	Protective cover — Paints and pigments	Electrical — Batteries and equipment	Electrical — Other electrical uses, instruments, etc.	Chemical — Industrial catalysts, reagents, explosives, etc.	Chemical — Consumer additives, extenders, photography, etc.	Biocidal poison uses — Agricultural pesticides, herbicides, fungicides	Biocidal poison uses — Non-agricultural pesticides, except medical	Biocidal poison uses — Medical, dental, pharmaceutical	Miscellaneous NEC	Total
1977	514.1	438.90	155.50	6.27	0	2.51	124.15	3.76	2.51	1.254	0	1,254.0
1973	643.5	443.29	167.30	14.30	0	4.29	127.27	2.86	2.86	1.430	0	1,430.0
1968	688.6	422.56	190.15	33.65	0	7.83	122.86	3.91	3.13	1.565	0	1,565.0
1958	477.5	366.44	139.91	36.64	0	7.77	75.51	3.33	2.22	1.110	0	1,110.4
1949	217.5	391.50	146.16	32.19	0	6.09	65.25	1.74	1.74	0.870	0	870.0
1940	186.5	269.38	136.76	28.32	0	3.45	63.55	1.38	1.38	0.691	0	690.7
1930	104.8	185.82	122.45	12.86	0	2.38	47.17	0.95	0.95	0.476	0	476.5
1920	102.9	130.59	102.89	10.68	0	2.37	19.79	1.19	21.76	0.396	0	395.7
1900	37.3	31.07	31.07	6.21	0	1.24	6.21	0.62	9.94	0.373	0	124.3
1880	11.9	10.23	10.23	0	0	0.85	0.68	0	0	0.171	0	34.1

Emissions from consumptive uses

Year												
1977	0.514	8.778	77.75	0.063	0	2.508	18.622	0.188	0.251	1.003	0	109.67
1973	0.643	8.866	83.65	0.143	0	4.290	19.090	0.143	0.286	1.144	0	118.26
1968	0.689	8.451	95.08	0.336	0	7.825	18.428	0.196	0.313	1.252	0	132.57
1958	0.477	7.329	69.96	0.366	0	7.773	11.326	0.167	0.222	0.888	0	98.51
1949	0.217	7.830	73.08	0.322	0	6.090	9.787	0.087	0.174	0.696	0	98.28
1940	0.186	5.388	68.38	0.283	0	3.545	9.532	0.069	0.138	0.553	0	87.99
1930	0.105	3.716	61.22	0.129	0	2.382	7.075	0.048	0.095	0.381	0	75.16
1920	0.103	2.612	51.44	0.107	0	2.374	2.968	0.059	2.176	0.317	0	62.16
1900	0.037	0.621	15.54	0.062	0	1.243	0.932	0.031	0.994	0.298	0	19.75
1880	0.012	0.205	5.12	0	0	0.853	0.102	0	0	0.136	0	6.42

Table I Total emissions and consumptive share (quantities in metric tons)

		1980	1970	1960	1950	1940	1930	1920	1900	1880
Arsenic										
Emissions from production	Low	209	666	899	928	999	874	1,007	1,255	265
	High	212	1,218	1,694	2,523	2,363	1,867	2,057	1,924	267
Emissions from consumption		9,364	12,072	8,537	8,804	14,112	10,058	6,164	1,939	605
Total emissions	Low	9,573	12,738	9,436	9,372	15,111	10,932	7,171	3,194	807
	High	9,576	13,290	10,231	11,327	16,475	11,925	8,221	3,863	872
Consumption (% of total)	Low	98	95	90	90	93	92	86	61	70
	High	98	91	83	78	86	84	75	50	69
Cadmium										
Emissions from production	Low	326	354	306	326	292	308	406	508	249
	High	333	464	446	592	506	477	653	837	293
Emissions from consumption		228	846	894	769	714	213	34	0	0
Total emissions	Low	554	1,200	1,200	1,095	1,006	521	440	508	249
	High	561	1,310	1,340	1,361	1,220	690	687	837	293
Consumption (% of total)	Low	41	70	74	70	71	41	8	0	0
	High	41	65	67	56	59	31	5	0	0
Chromium										
Emissions from production	Low	524	590	567	764	1,026	1,385	3,539	4,152	1,063
	High	525	680	729	1,139	1,300	1,550	3,671	4,158	1,063
Emissions from consumption		12	17	18	16	16	4	3	3	0
Total emissions	Low	536	607	586	779	1,041	1,389	3,542	4,155	1,063
	High	537	697	747	1,154	1,316	1,554	3,674	4,161	1,064
Consumption (% of total)	Low	2.18	2.75	3.11	1.99	1.50	0.32	0.09	0.08	0.03
	High	2.17	2.40	2.44	1.35	1.19	0.28	0.09	0.08	0.03
Copper										
Emissions from production	Low	278	560	737	958	1,242	1,507	3,558	4,224	1,060
	High	331	1,195	1,654	2,765	2,645	2,523	4,554	4,968	1,136

		15	14	11	12	14	6	6	4	1
Emissions from consumption										
Total emissions	Low	294	575	748	970	1,256	1,513	3,564	4,228	1,061
	High	346	1,209	1,665	2,777	2,659	2,529	4,560	4,971	1,137
Consumption (% of total)	Low	5.26	2.52	1.47	1.26	1.08	0.38	0.17	0.09	0.14
	High	4.46	1.20	0.66	0.44	0.51	0.22	0.13	0.08	0.13
Mercury										
Emissions from production	Low	2	3	3	6	9	13	36	43	12
	High	2	4	4	6	10	14	37	46	12
Emissions from consumption		844	1,257	639	712	683	596	547	353	384
Total emissions	Low	846	1,260	642	717	692	609	582	396	395
	High	846	1,261	643	718	693	610	584	399	395
Consumption (% of total)	Low	99.81	99.74	99.48	99.22	98.66	97.78	93.90	89.20	97.05
	High	99.81	99.68	99.40	99.15	98.58	97.68	93.59	88.52	97.05
Lead										
Emissions from production	Low	1,185	3,908	6,790	7,720	6,926	6,361	6,907	10,357	2,579
	High	1,585	10,546	18,475	33,654	25,504	19,600	17,595	15,065	3,043
Emissions from consumption		118,110	186,276	110,826	78,739	30,081	2,615	73	0	0
Total emissions	Low	119,295	190,184	117,616	86,460	37,007	8,976	6,980	10,357	2,579
	High	119,694	196,822	129,301	112,393	55,585	22,214	17,668	15,065	3,043
Consumption (% of total)	Low	99	98	94	91	81	29	1	0	0
	High	99	95	86	70	54	12	0	0	0
Zinc										
Emissions from production	Low	250	846	1,162	1,321	1,413	1,336	1,981	2,574	632
	High	1,342	9,965	17,171	29,436	23,480	15,887	16,146	8,717	1,404
Emissions from consumption		103	127	99	98	88	75	62	20	6
Total emissions	Low	353	973	1,260	1,419	1,501	1,411	2,043	2,594	638
	High	1,445	10,092	17,270	29,535	23,568	15,962	16,208	8,736	1,410
Consumption (% of total)	Low	29.3	13.0	7.8	6.9	5.9	5.3	3.0	0.8	1.0
	High	7.1	1.3	0.6	0.3	0.4	0.5	0.4	0.2	0.5

Part 3
Further implications

12

The precaution principle in environmental management

Timothy O'Riordan

Introduction

The principle of precaution in environmental management implies committing human activity to investments where the benefits of action cannot, at the time of expenditure, be justified by conclusive scientific evidence. Other grounds for legitimation need to be present – political, ethical, legal, and moral – in the sense of playing by the same rules as others in protecting the environment. Accordingly, the rationale has to be accounted for in forms that are more overtly judgmental.

Precaution therefore tests science in the realms where it is most vulnerable, namely, where adequate data do not exist or time series cannot yet be modelled, or where the processes being examined operate in such a manner that they are not susceptible to the conventions of prediction and verification.

Precaution also tests political institutions in that they are forced to regulate public and private affairs without recourse to the authority of formal science for their justification. This permits entry into political decision-making by both national and international pressure groups who seek to exploit scientific uncertainty or political indecisiveness.

The global dimension to environmental change places a special burden on the application of the precaution principle, for three reasons. First, there is the fact of pervasiveness across the whole earth; there is no hiding-place, even for the wealthy. Second, there is the potential for irreversibility, at least in terms of the length of time humans would be able to endure before the earth put itself to rights. (The earth itself may recover from the consequences of environmental alteration, but it may not do so in time for humans to survive without much discomfort and possibly economic stress.)

Even if irreversibility is not proven, there is a third point, namely the capacity of human intervention to upset natural processes of dynamic equilibria in particular regions to the point where the disruption to soil, water supply, vegetation, and human health exceeds the capacity of local and national governments, and social and economic adjustment processes, to cope. Combined environmental degradation and socio-economic debilitation is sometimes referred to as environmental criticality.

Global environmental issues therefore involve major ethical implications. They demand a form of sovereignty that is transnational and binding for all states. They raise issues of justice over who should act first and fastest in ensuring equitable compliance. They introduce a new time dimension: we cannot guarantee that our descendants will enjoy the benefits of present economic growth in the same way that previous generations enjoyed the benefits of past progress. And they carry with them important redefinitions of self-interest and sacrifice, and not just for the betterment of the human race: these factors apply to the very ecosystems and geo-biochemical cycles upon which the viability of the earth itself depends.

Precaution therefore becomes more prominent in the lexicon of modern environmental management as science is tested, as problems transcend spatial and temporal boundaries, and as questions of ethics and justice dominate over the more traditional rationales of the natural and social sciences. It is debatable whether there is an appropriate calculus of risk/benefit for precaution. It is also debatable whether there exist appropriate political and legal institutions for the transcendental qualities of managing global environmental change. Wrapped up in the debate over precaution are powerful new ideas, however, that should eventually transform the fundamentals of human knowledge and management.

Precaution and "industrial metabolism"

This book is concerned with directing industrial metabolism towards a closer integration with natural cycles and assimilative capacities. In chapter 1 Robert U. Ayres points out that the state of disruption of these cycles is large and growing, but that the demand on environmental services is falling mainly on common property systems. Ayres also argues that industrial transformations generally promote the cause of efficiency of energy and materials use, but that trends towards more integrated assemblies and blends of natural and artificial substances put limits on substitution and recyclability.

The precautionary principle, as it is discussed in this chapter, will place emphasis on the following:

1. Prevention at source to reduce the discharge of residues that are toxic or environmentally hazardous.
2. Emphasis on a transition from fossil-fuel-based energy sources to energy efficiency, renewable sources (involving cogeneration and much technological inventiveness), and "appropriate-scale" nuclear sources.
3. Promotion of deposit-refund schemes in advance of technological innovation on product development. These schemes would provide cash for conservation where victims cannot otherwise get indemnity from environmental disruption that causes suffering.

All these points are developed below. Suffice it to say here that the precautionary principle is likely to become a significant factor in altering the pattern of industrial activity and pricing. Because the principle is as much political as it is scientific, industry would be wise to anticipate its role and work with non-governmental organizations and governments to define the appropriate response. Such an approach would be novel in its mode of operation, but not in its function. Industry has always tried to anticipate the future and to help shape its influence on the evolution of regulation. Nowadays, however, that will be more of a partnership effort.

Precaution: A case-study

In the southern North Sea algal blooms are common. The water is shallow, currents carry nutrient-rich water over great distances, and in the coastal margins the hydrographical conditions for phytoplanktonic proliferation are very favourable. Along the eastern coastal regions of the Netherlands, Germany, and Denmark nutrient enrichment is particularly noticeable, caused primarily by insufficient removal of phosphorus from municipal sewage-treatment plants, and run-off from agricultural lands, where nitrates are the culprit.

There is controversy over how much of this is anthropogenic. Obviously this is important in the sense that if algal productivity is

caused primarily by humans, regulations or investments aimed at reducing the nutrient burden would be nominally worth while. The economic argument would then be essentially one of identifying the
point where the pay-off of nutrient removal matches the marginal
gains in reduction of algal productivity.

It is not as simple as this, unfortunately. At the heart of this issue
is the relationship between authoritative science and political action
in an international commons.

From a purely scientific viewpoint, there is reasonable evidence
that exceptional algal blooms predate the growth in municipal waste-
water treatment and may be linked to nutrient-rich current inflows
from the north-east Atlantic (see ISQR, 1990). This interpretation,
however, is not conclusive because the necessary time-series data are
simply not available. There is also good scientific monitoring to suggest that nutrient build-up is concentrated in the north-eastern parts
of the southern North Sea, and is confined largely to the coast.

For example, in the German Bight of Heligoland, plankton
biomass has increased fourfold between 1962 and 1985, and an
occurrence of a bloom of *Ceratiumfurca* in September 1981 depleted
oxygen to the point of disrupting a vast area of benthic communities.
Exceptional blooms apply to occurrences of algal productivity that
are sufficiently intense to be noticeable and to have adverse effects on
tourism, fish-farming, and inshore fishing. These may now be more
dramatic owing to more extensive data-collection, greater media
coverage, wider distribution of vulnerable economic activity, and
heightened public sensitivity to environmental change. In addition,
unrelated events, such as the 60 per cent mortality of seals in the
southern North Sea in July 1989, attracted speculation on a link between chemicals generally and environmental catastrophe.

In the public mind, the seal became a symbol like the canary in the
coal mine, the national "barometer of ecological stress" that could
eventually cause environmental catastrophe. To the scientific mind,
the algal bloom is primarily an object for study, not for instant reaction as to cause and effect.

A particularly prominent bloom of *Chrysochromulina polylepis*
occurred in the Skagerrak in May–June 1988. Subsequent investigation suggested that meteorological factors coupled to current movement had advected Atlantic water into the area. This column of
water contained high concentrations of nitrogen, phosphorus, and
silicates, but was stabilized by higher than average rainfall and the
outflow of fresh water from the rivers. This stability led to a high
nutrient density in subsurface levels, which was aggravated by fur-

ther columnar stability due to the presence of a higher than normal outflow of cold fresh water from the Baltic. A spring diatom bloom removed much of the silicate and phosphorus, leaving a high nitrogen to phosphorus ratio in the column.

The rapid bloom of *Chrysochromulina* was probably limited by a lack of phosphorus, a condition which turned the species toxic and affected the shellfish industry across a wide area. A bloom of *Prymnesium parva*, another species of alga with toxic properties, caused $5 million worth of damage to Norwegian fish farms (IQSR, 1990).

At issue here are three interconnected themes. First, the scientific evidence of primarily natural causes is persuasive but not complete. The actual conditions that lead to bloom build-up and to associated toxicity are either unknown or cannot readily be modelled. Second, the damage to commercial interests is serious but not crippling. It is the greater extent of vulnerable economic activity in areas with algal bloom histories that contributes to the demand for action. Third, there is genuine anxiety about the possibility of a catastrophic spread of algal activity across a wide area that may not correlate with meteorological and marine conditions, hence a perceived need to stop the increase of nutrients from waste-water treatment plants and agricultural run-off.

The cost of nutrient removal, of course, will be high. In Germany and the Netherlands, the aim is to remove phosphorus and nitrogen from over three-quarters of municipal treatment plants by 1995 (ICPNS, 1990). This will reduce inputs between 25 and 50 per cent for these nutrients. In addition, Germany intends to tax industry on its nitrogen and phosphorus emissions, and the Netherlands has embarked on a strict ammonia control programme over unprocessed animal manure (Dietz et al., 1992). (Ammonia translates into nitrogen-rich aerosols that are deposited in the open North Sea.)

The British position is that the current level of scientific knowledge does not require the United Kingdom to take such drastic measures. It is said that there is no evidence of significant variation in algal bloom off the UK coast, riverine inputs are estimated as being less than a tenth of total N and P inputs, and though air emissions are considerable they are spread over 525,000 km^2 of ocean surface. Yet the British do concede that the "scientific picture is incomplete and important areas of research are now being addressed, particularly the relationship between gross inputs of nutrients via rivers and the estuarial processes which determine net inputs to the seas" (ICPNS, 1990).

In its declaration on nutrient removal of inputs into the North Sea, the International Conference on the Protection of the North Sea (ICPNS), composed of the Environment Ministers of the eight basin states, agreed in 1990 that each would commit funds for a substantial reduction of nutrients, up to 50 per cent, by 1995. In addition, the European Community, which covers all the eight states except Norway and Sweden, has proposed new directives on both municipal waste water and nitrogen removal in fresh waters that may add further to the costs of environmental protection. The United Kingdom government is, however, resisting the linkage of precaution to these policies.

Nevertheless, as a signatory to the Paris Commission, which deals with pollution from land-based sources, and as a participant in the 1990 ministerial conference, the United Kingdom has committed itself to a $2.5 billion sewage-treatment programme to bring its coastal outfalls up to at least primary levels of treatment. This is in line with the declaration that waste-water treatments plants must be evaluated on a case-by-case basis, and that primary levels of treatment should only be provided where "comprehensive scientific studies demonstrate to the satisfaction of the competent international authorities that this discharge will not adversely affect the North Sea environment at the local or regional level."

The point of this case-study is to show that the kind of argument proffered by the United Kingdom is no longer tolerable where a "commons" resource is perceived to be degraded. A "commons" resource in this case is the assimilative capability of the North Sea to absorb nutrients yet still remain ecologically viable and diverse. Where a group of nations believes that they collectively are responsible for that assimilative capacity, they will tend to support the principle of "equivalence of burden." This is also a part of the precautionary principle. Put simply, it means that each responsible party to a commons regime must share its commitment to the collective well-being of the resource and of its other partners. This means that, to a point, and irrespective of the scientific evidence, the United Kingdom must simply play its part.

In fact this was the outcome of the 1990 North Sea Conference, and the United Kingdom is committed to reducing nitrogen and phosphorus from its waste discharges into the North Sea, even though the government still protests that the benefits of nutrient removal are not justified, on grounds of scientific evidence, given the costs involved.

It is true that the ICPNS has limited the precaution principle to the narrow area of avoiding potentially damaging impacts of substances "that are persistent, toxic and liable to bio-accumulate." In its guidance note, the UK government comments as follows:

The UK government . . . will take action to minimise inputs of such substances wherever there is reasonable evidence to suggest a causal link between emissions and effects even though such a link cannot be proven. The UK government...also considers that account should be taken of the costs of a measure in relation to its benefits. (Department of the Environment, 1990)

What is interesting in the nutrient case is a relaxation of the non-precautionary approach in a case where it would normally be justified, in favour of a shift towards a precautionary investment to meet international obligations and to be seen to be "pulling weight" on the costs of reducing coastal eutrophication. In short, the United Kingdom was forced to modify its purist stance in favour of recognizing that at least an element of precaution can be justified on political and moral grounds.

This shift may not look like much, but it shows that the politics of precaution are powerful, enduring, and progressive. In the 1990 International North Sea Conference, the United Kingdom agreed not to allow the dumping of sewage sludge in the southern North Sea, even though the government and its advisers claimed there was no scientific case to warrant such a move. The argument was that the sludge contains less than 2 per cent of any of the heavy metals that constitute the European Community "Black List." As regards eutrophication, the British view is that the sludge is disposed of in a region that is actually nutrient-poor. Yet the United Kingdom will now embark on a $600 million programme of sludge repatriation in order to play its part in the protection of the North Sea.

To gain leverage on other issues, notably the nutrient issue, the British government, as it saw the matter, "gave way" on the sludge-dumping controversy. This shows that precaution cannot and should not be divorced from politics and the tortuous tactics of international environmental diplomacy; the politics of precaution are in the ascendant in managing a common property environmental resource such as the North Sea.

History of the precaution principle

The notion of foresight, or *Vorsorge*, first appeared in the public debate in the Federal Republic of Germany in the early 1970s. This was a period of social democratic consensus over both a social market

economy and social welfare policy. It was marked by a desire to create corporatist relations between government, industry, and the trade unions (Weale and O'Riordan, 1991). In developing its environmental programme, the Social Democrat–Free Democrat coalition government propounded four basic principles of environmental policy:
- The polluter pays.
- A common burden where it is impossible to identify the cause of damage.
- Cooperation between the main parties concerned.
- International cooperation for transboundary problems.

In establishing these four principles, the then Interior Minister in charge of environmental policy argued that the protection of the environment ought not to react to manifest damage. Rather, it should seek to prevent future damage by means of planning and precaution. In promoting this concept, the government was linking environmental protection to the efficient and prudent management of an economy and a society in which pro-active planning was a key ingredient.

There were three additional aspects to the original German interpretation of precaution. These were the application of the state of the art of technology (*Stand der Technik*) to protect environmental systems as a whole from harmful effects. So the German concept carried with it both a technology-forcing component and a belief that pro-active planning should be geared to the maintenance of ecological health, not just human health. The third characteristic of precaution was the inclined shift of the burden of proof onto the would-be damager, rather than the putative victim. Precaution means in effect, then, that one is guilty until proven innocent when tampering with the environment in manifestly risky ways.

Precaution thus carried both a technical efficiency element and a bioethic, the protection of the intrinsic rights of natural systems to be allowed to operate with the minimum of molestation. Two distinguished German lawyers have expanded further on the meanings of precaution (Rehbinder, 1988; Von Moltke, 1988). Rehbinder cites five main themes within which the precautionary principle may be applied:
1. Prevention of future damage, even when it may arise indirectly from certain sources. Prevention becomes an objective in its own right.
2. Avoidance of conflict that would arise if stressful conditions were

knowingly allowed to continue. Avoidance becomes a strategic management tool.

3. Minimization of risk where causes and consequences are unknown or where valued environmental resources or assets are in potential danger. Risk is a metaphor for unknowable but potential danger.
4. Protection of the assimilative capacity of natural systems for absorption, assimilation, or restoration, thereby ensuring that there is a cost-effective "natural" way of managing environments in the longer term. This is akin to the notion of a buffer, or hedge against uncertainty.
5. Best practice integrated management to create the least-cost environmental outcomes across all sectors of emissions – land, air and water – and by sound management "up the pipe," or just at the point of emission. Precaution thus takes on the role of environmental and social auditor.

Explicit in Rehbinder's interpretation of precaution, therefore, is a fundamentally fresh approach to environmental management. It should be based on holistic views of the functioning of natural processes. It should address integrated approaches to planning and assessment. It should demand comprehensive auditing in industrial management, product design, and waste-recovery practices, so that the least-damage outcome is pursued throughout the complete management envelope. And it should be sensitive to future needs, that is, to the capacity of natural systems and human societies to absorb and cope with unacceptable environmental stress under almost any condition of an economy or social setting.

These points were made clear in the 1986 *Guidelines on Environmental Precaution* published by the German Federal Government. These guidelines emphasize the justification for state (or public) intervention in a social market economy in the cause of environmental safety. The three overruling principles are:

1. Protection from manifest danger.
2. Avoiding risks to the environment even when they cannot be fully demonstrated.
3. Prospective management of both economy and environment in order to retain the integrity of the natural basis of life for the future.

What is evident here is that even best practice is insufficient. There has to be a spur for even greater effort. That comes in the form of strict environmental quality standards for air, water, and land, and ultimately for whole regions. On this basis the complementary principle of critical load has become established. This is a calculation of the tolerance of the most vulnerable ecosystem to any mix of pollutants so as to create a natural limit to the interference with the functioning of ecosystems.

How far the critical load principle can be taken, however, remains a matter of some speculation. It relies on intensive monitoring, scientific prediction and verification, and modelling of tolerance, vulnerability, and sensitivity of systems that in general are still very poorly understood. Taken to its logical limits, critical load would set a punishing limitation on emissions and environmental alteration. In principle, critical load even sets a requirement that damage should be zero.

According to a review of the critical load principle by Ramchandani and Pearce (1991), this is not applied to any economic calculus or willingness-to-pay function: it is assumed as a given. Thus for critical load to have operational meaning it should be related to perceptions about possible damage and precaution. This in turn relates to how far judgements are made about the resilience or vulnerability of natural systems and human coping strategies. Hence the significance of the criticality arguments raised at the outset. Depending on these judgements, any assessment of costs and benefits will vary greatly, and yet quite legitimately. It is this relationship that will give critical load its meaning in both scientific and policy terms and ultimately in economic analysis.

In this sense, therefore, critical load couples three powerful notions in contemporary environmental management into a unity. These are:

1. The environmental audit of policy, programme development, and individual projects, as well as of the sectors of economic activity and of industrial enterprises. The audit is a comprehensive account of the environmental "draw" of a proposed policy on economic activity from onset to completion. It would look at the implications for natural systems, resource availability, emissions reduction, waste recycling, and impact on vulnerable areas and sectors of society. No one has yet undertaken such a complete audit, but interest in the idea is growing.
2. The strict liability principle through which any agent altering environmental conditions in the future would be liable to pay compensation for any affected parties or natural systems, even if best practice and appropriate regulatory rules were being followed. This is a particularly burdensome requirement. It has already

emerged in the field of waste management, and may well extend to other areas of environmental policy before long.

3. The public trust doctrine through which any agent causing minimal, but necessary, damage to environmental integrity or social well-being must compensate the losses by equivalent investments offsetting the damage. This could, for instance, apply to the planting of trees to absorb the carbon dioxide that a new fossil-fired power station would emit into the atmosphere.

So we see that underlying the principle of precaution are profound, and possibly radical, approaches to environmental accounting, auditing, and management that are as yet largely untried.

Having noted this, the application of the precautionary principle will create many difficulties for an industrial society seeking a more harmonious relationship with its natural environment. The critical load approach has been criticized for its scientific naivety in the face of prevailing ignorance over the functioning and adaptability of ecosystems (Ramchandani and Pearce, 1991). As already mentioned, however, such a judgement rests on certain perceptions of resilience and criticality, perceptions which are by no means value-free.

The strategy of "best available techniques not entailing excessive costs" (BATNEEC), now accepted practice in many European Community member states, avoids any coherent and consistent economic and technical rules as to what constitutes "excessive." Similar production functions for emission reductions are almost as unclear as the likely environmental gains from the increase in BAT. It is apparent that the economics of precaution are still at a very nascent stage. This is why more care will be needed, via industrial case-studies, to examine how far data gaps affect managerial decisions on the relative cost-effectiveness of environmental protection measures. This will be a tiresome yet necessary quest. The objective in harmonizing future industrial metabolism with environmental processes must be to ensure that the precaution principle operates through a phase of cost-effectiveness analysis allied to a substantially upgraded metascience of regional environmental functioning. Carefully thought-out examples from good industrial practice should be a higher priority for future research.

The precaution principle in international agreements

The precaution principle is not yet formally enshrined in international environmental law. But it has begun to appear in a number of national and international agreements and looks for further extension in formal law. For example, the US Federal Water Pollution Control Act of 1972 contains a provision for zero discharges of pollutants, based on the best available technology. The Federal Insecticide Fungicide and Rodenticide Act of 1976 places the burden of proof on the manufacturer to show that a proposed formulation is safe. Other national legislation relating to toxic or potentially bio-accumulative substances adopts similar positions (see Cameron and Abouchar, 1991, for a review).

In practice, the precautionary principle is being applied in various stages:

Stage 1: A ban on substances that are known or presumed to be toxic, or persistent, or bio-accumulative in commons arenas (e.g. seas, space, atmosphere).

Stage 2: A strict control, using burden of proof on promoter and application of best available technology, on activities or substances where a causal link to possibly severe environmental damage is deemed likely.

Stage 3: The control of hazardous wastes, via the application of scientific and economic balancing, notably BATNEEC (see below), clean technology, company audits, and regulatory audits where the balance of probabilities favours action sooner rather than later.

Stage 4: The reduction in nutritive elements in common areas where accumulation could prove costly, and where staged action is consistent with a "least regrets" policy.

Stage 5: The coupling of more research and programmed preventative investments in global change issues, notably global warming, sealevel rise, and loss of biodiversity.

The prior statement of the precautionary principle came in the London Declaration of the Second North Sea Conference, 1990: "In order to protect the North Sea from possibly damaging effects of the most dangerous substances, a precautionary approach is necessary which may require action to control inputs of such substances even before a causal link has been established by absolutely clear scientific evidence."

This has been converted into programmes of action by the Oslo and Paris Commissions for controlling the deposition of toxic wastes to air and land respectively. Subsequently the Bergen Ministerial Declaration on Sustainable Development in the ECE region (May 1990) stated: "Where there are threats of serious or irreversible damage, lack of full scientific certainty should not be used as a reason for postponing measures to prevent environmental degradation." Article 130R of the Single European Act of 1985 also refers to the principle of preventative action.

All these positions are not absolute. Coupled to them is a call for more research, so as to be sure that risky strategies of precaution are always advanced with the support of carefully judged scientific and economic appraisal. This is not a cop-out. It is a recognition that, under conditions of uncertainty, there could be serious inefficiencies of resource allocation in acting too expensively, too precipitously. Precaution thus is not an unfettered principle.

Precaution on the European stage

All this is having a profound effect on the character and structure of environmental regulation in Europe. To begin with, the European Commission was content to argue in favour of the "polluter pays" principle, by which it meant that a discharger would have to meet the costs of regulation as imposed, and the "prevention at source" principle, by which the aim was to reduce harm by controlling emissions at the point of occurrence (see Johnson and Corcelle, 1989). The First Environmental Action Programme of the EC Commission already included the statement that "any exploitation of natural resources or of nature which causes significant damage to the ecological balance must be avoided." These two principles, however, were a long way from the concept of precaution as it has evolved in the 1980s.

The first development was to create the notion of air and water quality targets, namely levels of environmental quality that would set yardsticks for individual emissions control. This was superseded by the principle of regional "bubbles" of environmental quality, in which cross-border cooperation would try to establish a common programme of emissions control. Latterly this has involved the application of cross-subsidy payments, allowing the poorer and less efficient plants to be cleaned up by wealthier nations who stand to gain by the improvement in overall environmental quality. (Example: Poland gets payments from West European countries to install desulphurization devices.)

All this is shifting regulation in Europe in three main ways:
1. Towards the concept of a common database and monitoring network that should be the prime purpose of the future European Community's Environmental Protection Agency.
2. Towards a commitment to best available techniques not entailing

311

excessive costs (BATNEEC), which will push the "state of the art of technology" anywhere on the globe to each industrial sector irrespective of its economic vulnerability, with safeguards for subsidies and providing time for adjustment. In this regard, the NEEC component of BATNEEC, which some regard as a watering-down of the "polluter pays" principle, will essentially lose its force. Because precaution is advancing as a concept in contemporary environmental management, so NEEC is weakening.

3. Towards an international environmental regulatory institution, together with "environmental inspectors," who will have powers to investigate any failure to comply at the national level on the basis of a reasonable complaint from an individual or a group of people.

In the European community the BATNEEC principle is now effectively in place, most particularly for toxic and hazardous substances and processes contained in the Black, Grey and Red Lists as defined by member states, but more generally for awkward industrial processes. The cost justification element is steadily being restricted. If the technology is available, or can be developed in a reasonable time, it should be deployed. This gives less room for manoeuvre for the regulatory agencies in negotiating compliance. Thus, precaution is beginning to standardize the regulatory process and provide a basis for uniform and comparative scrutiny. The degree to which interested parties have a right to know with regard to regulatory details, however, still varies from one member state to another. Even in the United Kingdom, where secrecy is officially decreed, there is now much more openness than there once was. Yet progress is slow and far from complete (Birkenshaw, 1992).

The "European Environmental Agency" at the time of writing is still stalled owing to political argument. Ostensibly the problem lies in the lack of agreement amongst member states as to the location of the new agency. But it has to be added that few countries, least of all the United Kingdom, have environmental monitoring and state-of-environment reports of sufficient quality and clarity to meet the needs of this new agency. The agency will, however, be created, and when it begins work it will help to standardize the state of environmental reporting in the member states, and generally upgrade the quality of monitoring and data interpretation. This is very much in line with the steadily evolving international application of the principle of precaution. By contrast, the introduction of some sort of environmental ombudsman in the Community, specifically aimed at upgrading compliance with regulating principles, is still some way off. But as the notion of a "European Social and Environmental Chapter" gains ground, so it is more than likely that developments in citizen environmental rights will follow.

Precaution as a science–politics game

Table 1 illustrates the dilemma facing a decision maker confronted with a demand for action yet unsure of the pay-off. The options for action are:

1. Do nothing but monitor the environmental situation. This is nowadays politically untenable, but where uncertainties are very great or the environmental system is regarded as tolerant it may still be a sensible course.
2. Do nothing but embark on a programme of research. This is the desired British position, at least as expressed by the government in its environmental policy statements of 1990 (HM Government, 1990). Of course, if the UK government were serious about this view it should be supporting research, at least to the point where a reasonable judgement could be made over the degree of advance investment required.

Table 1 Pay-off matrix: science, economics, and politics in precaution

	Strategy			
Outcome	Monitor and do nothing	Research and do nothing	Research and take sequential action	Take action and research
No serious damage	High pay-off	Prudent investment	Political insurance	Economic waste, political embarrassment
Regional damage	Political authority challenged	Avoidable political pressure	Deficit political pressure	Create precedent
Irreversible damage	Catastrophe	Loss of scientific prestige	Undermine scientific and political legitimacy	Establish political and scientific legitimacy

3. Combine research with action to contain pollutants. This is a form of "environmental insurance," and is a tactic adopted by the North Sea states. It is vital that the research mode combines both scientific investigation and economic valuation of removal or status quo, based on sensitivity analysis and public debate.
4. Take action in advance of definitive/final research. This is the pressure for making precaution legitimate, in which science is subservient, or at least secondary. This tactic can result in avoidable economic waste in the minor damage case, but can be vital in the case of irreversible damage.

It can be seen that the optimal strategy requires a combination of innovative science, economics, and politics, working sequentially and progressively. This is why we need to embark on extending science into the realms of economic and political analysis, to weld the concepts of negotiation, adaptation, and learning into political institutions and economic valuations. At the same time we need to find ways of depicting the outcomes of each of these pay-offs so that the interested public can negotiate and participate in the outcome as it weaves its way backwards and forwards through the matrix. Public involvement based on well-founded images of possible futures and their economic consequences provides one way of characterizing the valuation of uncertain environmental situations. It is this "negotiated science" that becomes one of the off-springs of the precaution principle.

Precaution on the global stage

In the Bergen Conference of 1990 that followed up the response by the wealthy northern countries to the Brundtland Report on sustainable development, there was a frightful row over the meaning and role of the precaution principle for global policy and diplomacy. In her opening address, the Norwegian Prime Minister, Mrs Brundtland, called for action in advance of certainty: "If we err in our decisions affecting the future of our children and our planet, let us err on the side of caution," she declared. The scientific community, one of five non-governmental organizations directly involved with the Conference, provided this wording: "After taking into account the possible costs of being wrong, it will be better to find out we have been roughly right in due time than to be precisely right too late" (NAVF, 1990).

It is evident that the furore over the precise wording also applied to the various degrees of commitment by the major greenhouse gas emitting nations to limit their emissions. The Americans are far from convinced of the scientific argument and until now have remained opposed to any specific commitment to reduction. The British will only lower emissions if other countries follow suit, but will not take a lead. The Japanese remain ambivalent, but are now willing to accept the European Community target of stabilization of CO_2 by the year 2000, should all its competitors also follow suit. The trouble, of course, is that greenhouse gas reduction cannot be undertaken on a country-by-country basis if it is to be effective. It requires programmed and comprehensive commitment at least by all major emitters, together with patterns of technology transfer and training provision for the developing world, so that they can develop in a manner that does not create more global warming than is saved by reductions in the North. So far, none of this is forthcoming; hence the political and legal interest in extending the principle of precaution to international environmental conventions.

There are some dangers in getting too carried away with the application of precaution at any cost. In the absence of comparative risk assessment, the consequences of curtailing potentially beneficial activity and creating another set of unforeseeable risks for an unprepared society could be greater than proceeding step by step with prudent caution. This is in part the lesson of the North Sea algal blooms. To reduce greenhouse gases willy-nilly could cripple an economy with no demonstrable evidence of a net advantage at the margin. Prudent science coupled to genuine dialogue with the public, linked in turn to meaningful images of possible outcomes for staged investment in the curtailment of environmental nuisance, is a better synthesis for precaution than precaution as an end in itself. This seems to be the way forward on the international and global stage.

Cameron and Abouchar (1991) have sought to identify four key principles for a legal definition of precaution in international law:
1. A threshold of perceived threat against which advance action would be deemed justifiable. The degree of threat need only be established by common consent, but could be coupled to compensatory exchanges of technology or financial resources to facilitate early action.
2. A burden of proof on the proto-polluter to show that a proposed policy or action will not cause actual harm. Costanza and Perrings (1990) have proposed that nations and/or aid agencies and/or international corporations deposit an environmental performance bond in advance of any investment, the money to be payable for

315

any unforeseeable damage or hardship, or to be returned to the depositor as a sign of best practice. In both arguments the shift of the burden of proof passes from the aggrieved, who are usually the most vulnerable, to the promoter of change, who is usually the most culpable but capable of avoiding downstream and trans-national externalities.

3. A duty of positive obligation that would require decision makers to be fully informed about the possible consequences of environmental change. This duty, which amounts to a comprehensive environmental audit of policies and programmes, would have to be backed by enforceable scrutiny of the justification for action.

4. A liability for omission that would fall upon any party that failed to act on the grounds of insufficient scientific evidence, bearing in mind the threshold principle (above) and the duties of due care and attention.

The objective here is to establish internationally a set of legal principles that would become incorporated into national law, citizens' rights, and full-scale audits of policies, programmes, and projects. This was always the intention of the original provisions of the US National Environmental Protection Act of 1969 which created the practice of "environmental impact assessment." Now that the Euro-

Table 2 The extension of precaution

Constitutional principle

Framework law

Substantive conventions on climate, biodiversity, and international trade

Administrative procedures, both quasi-judicial and inquisitorial, to discover facts and uncertainties and define staged actions

Legal arrangements on liability, burden of proof, fiscal incentives, citizens' action

Precautionary remedies, such as deposit bonds, injunctions, mandamus

Monitoring and enforcement agencies linking national to regional to international obligation and coupled to an expert secretariat

Access to information, and rights to be informed, via state of the environment reports and environmental audits

Policy audits by governments, official agencies, corporations and international regimes that would be examinable and related to an explicit duty of environmental care

---

Source: Based on Cameron and Abouchar, 1991.

316

pean Community has committed itself to a process of taking into account the environmental implications of all policies – agriculture, transport, energy, overseas trade – before action, there is scope for extending the precaution principle across a wider range of international action.

Cameron and Abouchar (1991) have produced a framework for national and international evolution of the principle, which is presented in table 2. The diagram summarizes much of what was discussed in this chapter. For the issue of precaution must not be confined to law, but to social change generally and fundamental principles of justice and welfare. This encompasses rights to know and to be informed, rights to seek redress over legitimate grievances, rights of international agencies to place pressure on non-complying states or agencies through some kind of consensus over environmental security and cooperation, and rights of sharing and exchanging information, understanding, and technology so that the weak and vulnerable are not suffocated in the stampede to save the world.

References

Birkenshaw, P. 1992. "Overcoming Impediments on Access to Information." In: E. Likke and D. Fluharty, eds. *Achieving Environmental Goals: The Concept and Practice of Environmental Performance Review*. Oslo: Fridtjof Nansen Institute.

Cameron, T., and J. Abouchar. 1991. "The Precautionary Principle. A Fundamental Principle of Law and Policy for the Protection of the Global Environment." *Boston College International and Comparative Law Review* 14, no. 1: 1–27.

Conway, G. R., and G. N. Pretty. 1991. *Unwelcome Harvest. Agriculture and Pollution*. London: Earthscan.

Costanza, R., and C. Perrings. 1990. "A Flexible Assurance Bonding System for Improved Environmental Management." *Ecological Economics* 2: 57–75.

Department of the Environment. 1990. *UK Guidance Note on the Ministerial Declaration, Third International Conference on the Protection of the North Sea*. London: Department of the Environment.

Dietz, F. J., U. E. Simonis, and J. van der Straaten. 1992. *Sustainability and Environmental Policy, Restraints and Advances*. Berlin: Edition Sigma.

HM Government. 1990. *This Common Inheritance: Britain's Environmental Strategy*. London: HMSO. (Cm360.)

International Conference on the Protection of the North Sea (ICPNS). 1990. *The Implementation of the Ministerial Declaration of the Second International Conferences on the Pollution of the North Sea*. The Hague/London.

Interim Quality Status Report. 1990. *1990 Interim Report on the Quality Status of the North Sea*. The Hague/London.

317

Johnson, S. P., and G. Corcelle. 1989. *The Environmental Policy of the European Communities*. London: Graham & Trotman.

NAVF. 1990. *Sustainable Development, Science and Policy. The Conference Report*. Oslo: Norwegian Research Council for Science and the Humanities.

Nitze, W. A. 1990. *The Greenhouse Effect. Formulating a Convention*. London: Royal Institute of International Affairs.

O'Riordan, T. 1991. "Towards a Vernacular Science for Environmental Change." In: L. E. Roberts and A. Weale, eds., *Innovation and Environmental Risk*. London: Belhaven Press, pp. 149–162.

Ramchandani, R., and D. W. Pearce. 1991. *Alternative Approaches to Setting Effluent Quality Standards: Precautionary, Critical Load and Cost Benefit Approaches*. Report no. LR93. Medmenham: Water Research Centre.

Rehbinder, E. 1988. "Vorsorgeprinzip im Umweltrecht und präventive Umweltpolitik." In: U. E. Simonis, ed., *Präventive Umweltpolitik*. Frankfurt/New York: Campus Verlag, pp. 129–141.

Von Moltke, K. 1988. "The Vorsorgeprinzip in West German Environmental Policy." In: Royal Commission on Environmental Protection, *Best Practicable Environmental Option*. London, pp. 57–70.

Weale, A., T. O'Riordan, and L. Kramme. 1991. *Controlling Pollution in the Round*. London/Bonn: Anglo-German Foundation.

13

Transfer of clean(er) technologies to developing countries

Sergio C. Trindade

Introduction

Most of the environmental problems of today result from the technological choices of yesterday. Therefore, ecological restructuring of the world economy calls for the choice of cleaner technologies now and in the future. In this connection, "industrial metabolism" may be a powerful analytical concept for the assessment of candidate technologies.

As the world goes through an extraordinary period of reorganization – politically, economically and militarily – the environment has become a concern of decision makers everywhere. In this context an ecological orientation of policies could emerge, based on the global industrial metabolism concept that implies both the delinking of economic growth from energy- and materials-intensive inputs and preventive approaches to economic restructuring.

Countries and organizations are affected differently by these developments. Industrial countries, by and large, have the knowledge and the financial resources necessary to respond to these challenges. But most countries on earth are small developing countries, which have limited capacity to take initiatives and must be helped towards a sustainable development path. Some organizations fear the additional

319

costs of economic restructuring whereas others, who are ready for it, see many opportunities ahead.

Any analysis of the transfer of technologies to developing countries thus requires the use and understanding of several key concepts: sustainable development; clean technology; industrial metabolism; knowledge and technology transfer; and endogenous capacity, i.e. the capacity for managing technological change.

Sustainable development

The World Commission on Environment and Development, in its report (the Brundtland Report), considered sustainable development to be a process of change that meets the needs of the present without compromising the ability of future generations to meet their own needs.

In most industrial countries, environmentally sound development is now a key concept. For most developing countries, the central concern is still development; to them the environment is at best a subsidiary dimension of development.

Ekins (1992) analyses sustainable development by looking at sustainability and development and their interaction. On sustainability he says that

in order for economic activity...to be environmentally sustainable, certain conditions need to be adhered to concerning the use of renewable and non-renewable resources, the emission of wastes and associated environmental impacts. These conditions can be defined. The first principle of sustainable development is that these conditions have absolute priority over GNP growth.

Ekins states further that development and GNP growth are not the same thing: "Development is a qualitative improvement, an achievement of potential. GNP growth is a quantitative increase. There are many examples of GNP growth resulting from, or in, maldevelopment." Therefore, the second principle of sustainable development is that "people and societies must be the subjects of their development, its creators and implementors, based on their knowledge and resources, rather than its objects or even its victims." (Ekins, 1992).

Both poverty and affluence have caused environmental impacts in the past and are likely to do so in the future unless increased awareness of the environment is converted into initiatives that address sustainable development from a global point of view.

320

Environmentally sound technology, clean(er) technology

"Environmentally sound, and clean(er) technology" are relative concepts in time and space. The time dimension relates to the availability of knowledge. For instance, asbestos was implicitly considered environmentally sound until its negative consequences on human health became known.

The space dimension has a societal (economic, political, cultural) connotation. For example, information about the role of CFCs in destroying the stratospheric ozone layer is widely available, but the readiness to take action varies considerably, irrespective of the fact that many countries ratified the Montreal protocol.

This is why, although technology – a form of knowledge – is crucial, it does not constitute a sufficient condition for achieving sustainable development.

"Clean(er) technology" can be understood as equivalent to environmentally sound technology, with special reference to industrial processes in which the management of wastes constitutes a major issue. According to De Larderel (1991), the clean(er) technology concept involves a new global approach to production:

All phases of the life cycle of a product or of a process should be addressed with the objective of prevention or minimization of short and longterm risks to humans and the environment. This includes a "cradle-to-grave" approach, minimizing wastes and emissions into air, water and soil, pollution prevention as well as minimizing energy consumption and the use of raw materials. It means not only developing new technologies but also good operating practices.

Industrial metabolism

The "industrial metabolism" concept may help us to understand better the complex chain of steps from raw materials and energy inputs to final products, and enhances awareness of the concomitant production of wastes and by-products: "Industrial metabolism encompasses both production and consumption, the entire system for the transformation of materials, the energy and value-yielding process essential to economic development" (Ayres, 1989).

Application of the industrial metabolism concept involves detailed accounting of the flows of materials and energy through human activities, and so helps to reveal opportunities to save energy and materials (with little or no investment), thus resulting in decreased resource ex-

Sergio C. Trindade

But it has been justly observed that "the history of the chemical industry is one of finding new uses for what were formerly waste products" (Ayres, 1989), a process that may be enhanced by the right price signals.

Sometimes the disposal of the product itself, after its useful life, constitutes an environmental hazard. The industrial metabolism concept thus calls for a long-term global perspective that will stimulate the cutting down of wastes and increase the recycling of residues.

Knowledge and technology transfer

Knowledge must be holistic or integral to be useful for sustainable development. Knowledge has many facets, such as science, technology, management, organization, etc.

History shows cases where countries – such as France – had a long tradition of scientific excellence without, until recently, technological prowess. The reverse situation – as in the case of Japan – can also be found.

For developing countries, Enos' perception may be relevant:

A technically competent nation has to climb through many rungs of the competence ladder. . . . Its rungs represent accomplishments; the lower, the simpler and more easily attained; the upper, the more complex, attained with more difficulty. . . . The highest rung represents . . . a society which, having achieved it, is then capable of choosing, utilising and advancing any appropriate technique. (Enos, 1991)

Technologies carry with them a set of built-in decisions that reflect markets, level of economic development, attitudes, directions, and policies that emanate from their place of origin. When they are transferred to another country they tend implicitly to transfer the values attached to them. Consequently, when clean(er) technology is to be transferred from one place to another, there are at least two key issues to consider.

The first is the effectiveness of the transfer, i.e. the fitting of the built-in socio-economic options of the source country or organization to the conditions prevailing in the receiving country or organization.

The second is the efficiency of the process, i.e. the extent of absorption by the receiving end of the essential skills and knowledge – a feature of capacity – of the transferred technology.

This is why sustainable development requires from the developing countries the creation of an array of competences that support an

322

ploitation and environmental pollution (and even in lower running costs).

Although wastes constitute an environmental issue, they may not have a sufficiently high market value to warrant further processing. autonomous decision-making capacity for transfer or development of clean(er) technology.

Years ago, at a conference on petrochemicals in Brazil, I was confronted with a statement by a representative of a transnational corporation. He said that technology was not really worth discussing because it was not a major cost element: it made up, at the most, 5 per cent of the sales price of typical petrochemicals. The statement was factually correct but it hid an important dimension – related to the efficiency concept described above – which entirely justified the discussion. The point can be illustrated with the help of a simple equation that defines the perceived value of technology (Trindade, 1980):

$$P^* = \$_o/Q$$

where P^* is the perceived value of knowledge; $\$_o$ is the going (commercial) value of knowledge; and Q is a cumulative measure of competence, skills, and endogenous capacity.

The graphic representation of the argument clearly communicates the idea that the perceived value of technology depends on the cumulative skills of the buyer and the seller of technology (fig. 1). For a given technology the resulting curve is a hyperbola, asymptotic to both axes. The range of interest for the present argument is Q within 0.0 and 1.0.

The above equation is simply a convenient way of arguing the importance of the different value perceptions of the buyer and seller of technology, which depend on their respective cumulative knowledge. For a given clean technology it is possible to move down the slide of the curve. The perceived value of an increment of knowledge or technology declines as an organization learns over a period of time, i.e. increases its level of competence, skills, and endogenous capacity.

The intuitive argument above suggests that if a society or an organization is at a level of competence equivalent to Q close to zero, not even all the money in the world would make a difference in the short term. It would thus be useless to promote the idea of industrial metabolism on a global scale if the majority of countries lacked the capability to implement it.

That is another way of saying that the perceived value of knowl-

323

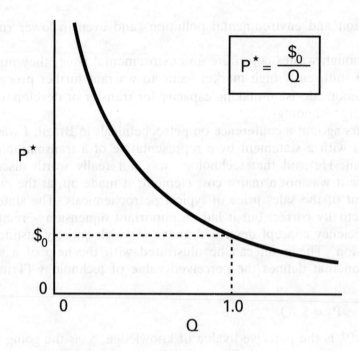

$$P^* = \frac{\$_0}{Q}$$

P^* = Perceived value of knowledge

$\$_0$ = Going (commercial) value of knowledge

Q = Measure of cumulative competence, skills, and endogenous capacity

A seller of knowledge always operates at $Q = 1.0$

A buyer of knowledge operates at $Q \varepsilon (0,1.0)$

Fig. 1 The value of technology depends on the skills of the buyer

edge to a society (or a given stakeholder) can be very large for those who have limited knowledge (as Q approaches zero, P* tends toward infinity). Buyers in this situation, however, are ill equipped to make choices about clean(er) technologies and have limited bargaining power. Consequently, the wide difference in value perception may lead to disagreement between the transferring parties.

By contrast, when the recipient (a particular stakeholder) is at the "state-of-the-art" level, the perceived value of knowledge equals the commercial value (for Q = 1.0, P* = $o). In this case buyers are competent choosers and have strong bargaining power; little disagreement will arise between the transferring parties.

Concretely, for a given technology, it is possible to increase knowledge, that is, to decrease perceived value along the curve (as Q increases, P* decreases). This argument applies particularly to the transfer of clean(er) technologies to developing countries, as they require a higher level of cumulative knowledge.

It is also important to note that knowledge that is not used can be lost to a society. The historical loss of traditional technologies (e.g. iron-making in Africa) illustrates the point. Some of these technologies have been cleaner than the "modern" technologies that replaced them.

Today, even if clean(er) technologies were given away free of charge, the majority of the developing countries could not make use of them because of lack of absorptive and implementation capacities. Clean(er) technologies can only be effectively utilized when the recipient (country or corporation) possesses an endogenous decision-making capability. When such "endogenous capacity" is lacking, progress in handling environmental issues (at country or corporation level) requires the building of competence in relevant fields through experience, training, and education (UN, 1989).

Endogenous capacity

A society that is developing should be a society where productivity and value-added are rising, and, in the future, where clean(er) technologies (and products) are increasingly penetrating the market. This brings in the issue of equity – that is, the sharing of the benefits of development.

In general, development should be equitable to all stakeholders in the development process, that is, all segments of society that are affected by the process of development. Furthermore, to be sustainable development should also be equitable to future generations. Implicit in this conclusion is the importance of knowledge in the development process. Sustainable development can only be achieved with knowledge and by a decision-making capacity – sensible and autonomous – at all levels of society. This capacity to manage technological change can be called endogenous capacity. It seems that a new frame of reference is required, in which the capacity to make autonomous and sensible decisions on the choice of technologies is more important than the development of the technologies themselves. Achieving "technological autarchy" has at least become an obsolete pursuit, since all countries in the world import technology, some more, and others less.

The current universal trend of more participatory decision-making in human affairs is stimulating a novel approach in which more, and eventually all, relevant stakeholders in society partake. Since both poverty and affluence have brought about environmental problems, albeit of a different nature, stakeholders at all levels of income must engage in dialogue to help set new priorities, regarding development in an environmentally sound(er) way.

Technology change will be central to the management of development and the environment in the future. As such, future ventures will be intensive in knowledge, information, measurement, and concept. This is particularly true of radical approaches to design based on the idea of industrial metabolism.

Endogenous capacity can be defined as the set of human and institutional capabilities necessary to address the question of managing clean(er) technology, either indigenously developed or adapted from abroad. Building endogenous capacity is thus a difficult task and will take time, often decades. While every country has some indigenous capabilities in science and technology, such as infrastructure, scientists and technicians, research institutions, etc., these are not sufficient in themselves to respond to the demands of an environmentally sound development process. Endogenous capacity goes beyond indigenous capacity, as it also includes the ability to understand and manage the linkages to the educational system, the productive sectors, the social structure, and the processes of governance and decision-making.

Endogenous capacity is also time-bound in the sense that, though it can be acquired, unless it is maintained it will be lost. In sum, the capacity for environmentally sound development is one of participatory decision-making and implementation in the broadest context.

Crucial elements of endogenous capacity-building

The following, to my mind, are the crucial elements of endogenous capacity-building that facilitate the move from concept to reality:
1. Provision of a favourable policy climate, based on equity concerns

and on participatory decision-making; stakeholders' dialogues will help people focus on opportunities for market stimulation and public intervention regarding clean(er) technologies and products.
2. Generation of portfolios of prioritized initiatives on clean(er) technologies, to guide programmes and projects in focused niches.
3. Domestic and international research partnerships to overcome critical mass limitations.
4. Provision of basic education, including environmental education; this should include emphasis on the education of women.

The implementation of these crucial elements requires domestic resources, reallocated to promote the priorities agreed upon, as well as newly conceived international cooperation schemes in support of clean(er) technology transfer. While this is an ongoing process in most countries, history suggests that linkages are missing between science and technology initiatives and the mainstream of socio-economic activities – that there has not been an adequate consensus among the relevant stakeholders, and that equity has often been neglected.

Thus, technology assessment must be expanded to encompass the industrial metabolism concept in its methodologies. It should constitute a basic approach for the future regarding sourcing, developing, adapting and evaluating technologies (Trindade, 1991). After all, the environment is fast becoming an important source of business opportunities. Gustav Berle's *The Green Entrepreneur* (1991) could be a useful primer, with a wealth of cases that illustrate the fundamental role of private initiative in converting sustainable development into concrete business propositions. Although it concentrates on the United States, it could inspire entrepreneurs in the developing countries as well.

Governments are stakeholders with special responsibilities. Sometimes they are representative of the population, often they are not. The current wave of demands for participatory, transparent, societal decision-making that is sweeping all societies on earth offers an ideal opportunity for governments to play a more constructive role in building up, among all relevant stakeholders, the consensus that is necessary for sustainable development. The resource demands raised by environmental concerns compound, of course, the debt burden of the developing countries, and therefore call for new concepts in international cooperation. It is thus expected that more open and participatory decision-making will enhance equity, both intranational and international, in future development strategies.

327

International cooperation for clean(er) technologies

It has been proposed (UNCED, 1991a) that each country will need to develop policies and programmes to implement Agenda 21 (the action plan adopted at the United Nations Conference on Environment and Development, UNCED). How can international cooperation promote clean(er) technology transfer, particularly to the large number of small developing countries which lack the critical mass of human and other resources to cope with the future?

One response to this challenge is the establishment of a variety of research and technology partnerships, supported by international funds to sponsor a network of centres in various regions of the world. This network of research, training, and technology transfer could focus, for instance, on chlorofluorocarbon substitutes; cleaner production processes and hazardous wastes; energy efficiency; cleaner coal technologies; sustainable biological production systems, etc.

These international partnerships should be conceived in a flexible fashion and operate as facilitators under the overall guidance of competent international bodies. One of their roles should be as demand-oriented clearing-houses for their technologies. They could make use of ongoing initiatives such as: (a) UNEP's International Cleaner Production Information Clearinghouse (ICPIC); the clearing-house on CFC-free technologies under the Montreal Protocol; (b) OZONETT, an international private clearing-house on CFC-free technologies, linked to ICPIC; and (c) CADETT and other clearing-houses on energy-efficient technologies (UNCED, 1991b).

Conclusions

Clean(er) technology transfer is conceptually not so distinct from technology transfer at large. But it requires a higher intensity of cumulative knowledge in society. The ability of countries to respond to this challenge varies widely according to their capacity to manage technological change. Most countries on earth are small developing nations, which so far lack this capacity and are thus deprived of new opportunities for environmentally sound development.

The UNCED forum provides a new opportunity to redress this situation. From the Global Agenda 21 endorsed in Rio de Janeiro in June 1992 there should emerge National Agendas 21 for each and every country, based on a consensus-building stakeholders' dialogue. Consistent policies at the national level and a continuity of relationships in the international arena are at the base of any new framework for clean(er) technology transfer to developing countries.

Two case-studies

The two brief case-studies on cleaner technologies, presented below, follow the concepts laid out on pages 326–327 above regarding the crucial elements of endogenous capacity-building.

Cubatóo: From industrial cesspool to survival

Summary and conclusions of the case (Zulauf, 1991)
Cubatóo lies in a coastal plain near the large conurbation of São Paulo, Brazil. The industries located in Cubatóo can be divided into three complexes, namely petrochemical (one oil refinery for over 150,000 barrels a day and 16 petrochemical plants, plus a paper mill and two concrete plants), steel (one fully integrated steel mill with 4 million tons capacity), and fertilizers (seven plants, plus a cement plant). The latter two complexes are located next to each other.

The installation of this massive industrial agglomeration, from the 1950s to the 1970s, was free from any environmental impact assessment or permit requirements. As a result, at a later stage, there were 320 pollution sources identified, 230 for air, 44 for water, and 46 for soil, all producing intense environmental degradation.

The main air pollutants were particulate matter, fluorides, ammonia, hydrocarbons, nitrogen oxides, sulphur oxides and others (chlorine, carbon dioxide, carbon monoxide, benzene, etc.). The main environmental parameters monitored in water were pH, dissolved oxygen, biochemical oxygen demand, total nitrogen, ammonia nitrogen, total phosphorus, mercury, phenol, and faecal coliform.

The pollution-control programme implemented since 1984 has reduced particulate emissions by 72 per cent, short of the 92 per cent target as a result of the inaction of the steel complex. Fluoride emissions have been cut by 92 per cent, ammonia by 98 per cent, hydrocarbons by 88 per cent, nitrogen oxides by 97 per cent, and sulphur oxides by 37 per cent.

Water pollutants have also been considerably reduced: organic load by 93 per cent, heavy metals by 97 per cent, fluorides by 92 per cent, phenols by 79 per cent, and settleable wastes by 90 per cent.

Solid wastes have been recycled, treated for storage, and disposed of properly on land.

Overall, it appears that the investment made in cleaner technologies paid off handsomely. The steel complex, however, did not invest adequately in cleaner technology owing to depressed prices for steel products and lack of profitability.

Despite all of these impressive relative reductions in pollution, the original level was so high that the current emissions still remain terribly high in absolute terms and further compound the environmental deterioration of four decades. For instance, the current load of particulates is still 32,000 tons per year, hydrocarbons 4,000, sulphur oxides 18,100, nitrogen oxides 1,700, ammonia 75, and fluorides 73. Regarding water pollution, the remaining load is 1,600 tons per year, of which heavy metals make up 44, fluorides 103, phenols 5.5, and settleable wastes 22 tons per year. The steel complex still dumps 860,000 tons per year of solid wastes on land.

This case, however, illustrates the importance of the stakeholders' dialogue in promoting "end-of-pipe" technology transfer. It also points out, in the case of the steel complex, the difficulties involved in bringing state-owned, loss-making enterprises in line with the overall consensus achieved.

Policy climate
Earlier attempts to redress the situation in Cubatóo met with failure. Before 1980 local industries and government launched an advertising campaign called "Valley of Life" to change the image of Cubatóo without seriously addressing the environmental issues. By 1980 the federal government had set up an interministerial committee. This generated technical assessments, but failed to engage the support of the relevant local stakeholders, as its work was opaque to the interested parties. On the basis of these experiences, a new state government decided, in 1983, to operate in a more transparent way, engaging the main stakeholders, including the press, in the decision-making process.

Portfolios of initiatives in cleaner technologies
The State Environmental Agency, CETESB, engaged the local industries in discussions about the choice of technologies and timetables for implementing them, in accordance with priorities agreed upon in advance. For instance, the abatement of emissions of fluorides, particulate matter, and ammonia was the top priority in the

air-pollution field. After rounds of dialogues among the key stakeholders, the programme was agreed upon and implementation began in July 1984, with the endorsement of industry leaders, politicians, and other stakeholders such as environmental, religious, community, and union organizations.

Every three months an open meeting – in the presence of all interested stakeholders – was held to monitor progress in the implementation of the programme; there the participating parties were held accountable for delays and occasionally fined. The press published the results of these meetings, thus stimulating the good performers and pointing out those who did not meet their commitments.

Domestic and international partnerships

The equity in industries in Cubatóo is in the hands of private parties, Brazilian and foreign, and the state (federal and state). Those firms with transnational equity had access to their parent companies in implementing the programme. Brazilian firms, private and state-owned, obtained technologies from local and foreign sources. CETESB conducted studies and surveys in the Cubatóo area and expanded the environmental monitoring infrastructure. In the course of this, CETESB worked in partnership with some 35 other state and private organizations involved with technology, sanitation, water, and power.

The World Bank provided financing for the pollution-control programme (PROCOP), which was refinanced by local banks and managed, from the technical point of view, by CETESB. During 1984–1990 fines amounting to US$1 million penalized the non-performers and provided an additional income to the state.

Educational activities

Two important measures of the programme were a local environmental education project and community participation, engaging the key stakeholders. Information on the environment was shared with the Cubatóo stakeholders to allow them to engage in the dialogue that had been established in order to generate concrete proposals and to achieve consensus on directions to pursue. There were 13 community associations, 5 religious groups, and 10 unions involved in the process. Leaflets in support of environmental education were issued, covering the various facets of the Cubatóo problem. Meetings, seminars, and conferences took place to disseminate further information and to engage the stakeholders. There was, however, no particular effort to engage women in the process.

Sergio C. Trindade

Borregaard/Riocell: Environmentally sound pulping

Summary and conclusions of the case (Slongo, 1991)

Brazil is currently the eighth largest pulp producer in the world. Borregaard, of Norway, conceived, in the late 1960s, a scheme to integrate short-fibre pulping operations in southern Brazil with bleaching and global marketing in Norway. The project, in fact, gave Borregaard access to cheap fibre stock and shifted the pollution caused by pulping from Norway to Brazil. The return freight load of the ship that brought the unbleached pulp to Norway consisted of the chemicals required for the pulping and other processes in Brazil.

Borregaard had total control over the sales of the 190,000 metric tons per year pulp scheme, because unbleached short-fibre pulp has no international market. Nevertheless, as the project was implemented, the Brazilian National Social and Economic Development Bank became the major shareholder, although the operational control remained with Borregaard. Total investment at the time of start-up, in March 1972, reached US$76 million. The plant employed 2,500 people. Sales were planned at US$22 million per year.

The environment was certainly not among the key criteria in the conception and location of the project. In fact, the lack of public concern over the pollution caused by much smaller plants, located near the pulp plant, was used, by the project promoters, as a licence to pollute even further. Straight economic feasibility was the yardstick for the assessment of the project. As plant operations began, its aggressive-smelling atmospheric emissions were regularly brought, by the prevailing winds, to the state capital of Porto Alegre and other nine neighbouring cities, with a total population of over 1.6 million inhabitants. The local newspapers started a press campaign that helped mobilize the population; and the plant was shut down in December 1973 for four months. At that time, the concentration of sulphur oxides in the atmosphere reached 1,800 parts per million (ppm), against the maximum limit set by the World Health Organization of 70 ppm!

In response to this challenge, cleaner technologies were gradually introduced over a period of 10 years. Meanwhile, the equity control changed from the bank to a private pension fund, and finally, in 1975, to a consortium of three Brazilian private companies. The name of the company was then changed to Riocell, to reflect the new ownership. More recently, after the bleaching plant started up, the company also changed its market strategy to move away from the commodity pulp market into the higher value-added customized pulp market, with substantial investment in automation.

In 1989 Riocell's annual sales reached US$223 million, with an average employment of 2,500 people. The output totalled some 310,000 tons per year (up from the design capacity of 190,000) and consisted of 260,000 tons of bleached pulp, 20,000 tons of soluble pulp for viscose making, 15,000 tons for paper and cardboard, and 15,000 tons of unbleached brown pulp.

Policy climate

Public clamour, fuelled by a press campaign, led to a change in the local policy climate that favoured the market penetration of cleaner technologies. This happened at a time when the press in Brazil was strictly censored on political grounds. But apparently the impact of the plant's pollution affected most parties equally. The change in ownership of the firm also brought the local concerns with regard to the environment and marketing closer to the decision-making of the company.

This case illustrates the importance of public opinion in bringing about change, even in a situation of limited freedom of expression. It also demonstrates that concentration of efforts towards endogenous capacity-building is a key to the ability to absorb and develop technologies for both end-of-pipe and process change approaches.

Portfolios of initiatives in cleaner technologies

Successively cleaner production technologies were introduced to respond to the pollution problem. First, air oxidation was applied to the strong black liquor, to reduce sulphur emissions. Next, cheap sodium sulphate was replaced by the more expensive sodium hydroxide pulping. In 1975, a gas and condensate output treatment was introduced, which reduced by 90 per cent the biochemical oxygen demand of the liquid effluent. In 1979, a residual recovery system was implemented to prevent pollution at the source. In 1983, after a US$240 million investment (with 15 per cent for environmental protection alone), a fully-fledged bleaching plant began operation. In further response to external pressure, and in line with its newly found environmental zeal, Riocell invested US$19 million in a complete (all the way to tertiary treatment) effluent-treatment station. Over the years the firm spent some US$42 million for environmental protection activities.

The attitude of the firm towards the main stakeholders affected by its operations changed, over time, from neglect to respect. The additional investment required to redress the environmental impacts caused by its operations led the firm to seek a higher value-added strategy for its output in order to be able to stay competitive as well as environmentally sounder.

Domestic and international partnerships

As the firm evolved, from wholly owned subsidiary of a foreign concern to a Brazilian-owned private company, its attitude changed from one of total dependence on foreign knowledge to one that was enthusiastic about building endogenous capacity. A centrepiece of this strategy was the establishment of a technology centre.

The process started by the end of 1973, when the staff designed a plant for air oxidation of the strong black liquor. This plant converts the sodium sulphide into non-volatile sodium thiosulphide, thus reducing the emissions of sulphur into the atmosphere. The next step took place in March 1974, with the replacement of sodium sulphate by sodium hydroxide in pulping, which drastically reduced the emissions of sulphur.

In 1975, a Swedish company was engaged to design a gas and condensed output treatment unit. This was followed in 1979 by the implementation of a residual recovery system. Competence was being built and a critical mass of human resources and knowledge was accumulating in the firm during this period. Later, this pool of competence became the basis for developing pulp and paper technology throughout Brazil.

The company also learned how to interact with the relevant stakeholders and find consensus on directions for the future. The firm's management gradually developed an environmentally responsible posture, based on the adoption of cleaner technologies and a growing technological decision-making capacity derived from its investment in research and development. Riocell appears to have found that investment in environmental control can lead to greater efficiency and positive economic returns.

Educational activities

In this case, there has been no special effort to provide basic education on the interaction between economy, environment, and technology change. The press, however, played an important role in raising the awareness of the relevant stakeholders on environmental matters, even at a time when there were limitations on freedom of expression in the country.

References

Ayres, R. U. 1989. "Industrial Metabolism." In: J. H. Ausubel and H. E. Sladovich, eds., *Technology and Environment*. Washington, D.C.: National Academy Press, 1989, p. 23.

Berle, G. 1991. *The Green Entrepreneur*. New York: Liberty Hall Press.

De Larderel, J. A. 1991. "Cleaner Production: A Worldwide Goal." Background document to the 11th session of the United Nations Intergovernmental Committee on Science and Technology for Development. New York, p. 77. (Manuscript.)

Ekins, P. 1992. *Sustainable Development North/South – Contradictions and Hard Choices*. Paper presented at the Malente Symposium IX: The Economic Revolution: Challenge and Opportunity for the 21st Century. Lübeck: Draeger Foundation.

Enos, J. L. 1991. *The Creation of Technological Capability in Developing Countries*. London: Pinter.

Slongo, L. 1991. "Environmental Issues and Riocell's Technological Strategy." In: J. Markovitch et al., *Brazilian Experiences on Management of Environmental Issues: Some Findings on the Transfer of Technologies*. Research Paper no. 1. Geneva: UNCED Secretariat, pp. 6–19.

Trindade, S. C. 1980. "Technology Development in Developing Countries: The Case of a Private R&D Institution in Brazil." *R&D Management* 10, no. 2: 77–82.

———. 1991. "Environpeace." *ChemTech* 21, no. 12: 710–711.

UNCED. 1991a. "Capacity Building for Sustainable Development. Preliminary Draft." Geneva: UNCED Secretariat.

UNCED. 1991b. "Transfer of Environmentally Sound Technology, Draft Options for Agenda 21." Geneva: UNCED Secretariat.

United Nations. 1989. *End-of-Decade Review of the Implementation of the Vienna Programme of Action*. Report of the Secretary-General of the United Nations. New York. (A/CN. 11/89.)

Zulauf, W. E. 1991. "Industrial Pollution Control in Cubatóo." In: J. Markovitch et al., *Brazilian Experiences on Management of Environmental Issues: Some Findings on the Transfer of Technologies*. Research Paper no. 1. Geneva: UNCED Secretariat, pp. 46–78.

Bibliography

Heaton, G., R. Repetto, and R. Sobin. *Transforming Technology: An Agenda for Environmentally Sustainable Growth in the 21st Century*. Washington, D.C.: World Resources Institute, 1991.

OECD. *Managing Technological Change in the Less Advanced Developing Countries*. Paris: OECD, 1991.

Sergio C. Trindade

United Nations Advisory Committee on Science and Technology for Development. Report. New York, 1991. (A/CN.11/91.)
United Nations Workshop on Creative Financing for Environmentally Sound Technologies. Workshop report. New York: UN Centre for Science and Technology for Development, 1990.

14

A plethora of paradigms: Outlining an information system on physical exchanges between the economy and nature

Marina Fischer-Kowalski, Helmut Haberl, and Harald Payer

Introduction

The notion of industrial metabolism draws attention to a materialistic view of the economy as a physical system, driven by energy flows.[1] Such a conception is less trivial than it seems, since money functions as a unifying principle of economy to such an extent that it is difficult to raise awareness and understanding of physical (non-monetary) concepts. The physical dimensions of the economy usually are discussed only as tools for the development of monetarization, not as autonomous concepts.[2] Similarly, the social sciences, as well as economics, tend to view social reproduction as a system of communication, and not in physical terms.

If you conceive of the economy as a physical system, drawing physical inputs from its natural environment, processing them internally, and generating physical outputs to this environment, you have to define a boundary between the "system" and its "natural environment": you have to be able to tell what is "inside" and what is "outside." This boundary is both omnipresent and fugitive. It certainly cannot be a "physical" or topographical boundary: The same physical elements will be both part of the economic system and part of its natural environment, depending on the point of view. One can only construct a functional boundary, and this has to be done with care. Two approaches may be chosen.

First, an a priori theoretical approach would discuss the possible functional labels of physical entities and processes that should define them as inside or outside the system. This might be their function as goods and services in markets (a narrow approach that would leave aside the so-called "free goods," and could not easily be applied to elements of subsistence economies); it might be their function for "humans" in terms of a biological species (which would be a very broad approach, difficult to connect to a specific concept of economy). We feel the most promising approach would be the functional link to property: property is specifically human and it constitutes a functional connection between physical entities and economic "subjects." But we will not pursue this question here, though we would like to encourage such a discussion. As long as this question is not resolved satisfactorily on a theoretical level, we prefer to speak of the "socio-economic system" rather than of "industrial economy." Sometimes we also use the term "economy," implying a wider historical range of modes of production.

Another, second, approach is a strictly constructivist one. It presumes that society "constructs" the boundary of its natural environment by the environmental information system it uses. The environmental information system itself defines what is to be considered part of the system and what is to be considered as an element of its (relevant) "natural environment." Practically speaking, this is the approach we chose in this paper; it leads to an implicit definition of the boundary between the socio-economic system and its natural environment.

This leaves us with the need for a mode of selection of physical processes that are relevant within an environmental information system that is supposed to describe socio-economic metabolism. This mode of selection should be self-referential to the socio-economic system, in the sense that it selects, for the possible present or future, harm that feedbacks from the natural environment to the system may cause. In view of our limited knowledge of interdependencies, it should also take into account the self-regulating qualities of natural systems for their own sake.

The second section of this chapter, therefore, attempts to outline what we think are the basic paradigms for conceiving of such interdependencies. The third section is devoted to the overall structure of an information system that might qualify for the standards set. We have proposed this information system to the Austrian government, with some chances of success. In the last two sections we provide empirical illustrations of how the Austrian economy would perform within such an information system.

Distinguishing between "harmful" and "harmless" characteristics of socio-economic metabolism with its natural environment

There exists a variety of conceptions to distinguish between what is good (or at least harmless) and what is bad (harmful) for the environment. These conceptions vary according to scientific discipline and according to political (or ethical) understanding of man–nature relationships.

This variety of conceptions can be ordered into four basic paradigms:
- Poison paradigm.
- Natural balance paradigm.
- Entropy paradigm.
- Conviviality paradigm.

Each of them is guided by a specific reference concept, and each of them is able to catch important aspects of the possible meaning of the "damage" society causes to its natural environment. The paradigms are not mutually exclusive in the sense that one specific aspect of environmental damage might not occur in more than one of them. But they cannot be reduced upon one another, nor can they be merged into one single "grand paradigm."[3] Each has its own specific structure of reasoning, its own scientific and political tradition, and its own audience. But all four paradigms taken together permit a complete scanning of what might be meant when people talk about the socio-economic system "causing environmental damage" (fig. 1).

Let us illustrate the functioning of the four paradigms for a special case: the damage caused by car traffic.
1. In the poison paradigm, the main argument would be: Car traffic causes about 60 per cent of the toxic gaseous emissions to the atmosphere (CO, NO_x, C_xH_y). Thus limiting volumes for the exhaust should be issued. Catalytic converters are a good solution, since they reduce toxic emissions by 80 per cent or more.
2. In the natural balance paradigm, it would be said that car traffic contributes about 15 per cent to the destabilization of the earth's climate, and also severely affects several ecosystems. Catalytic

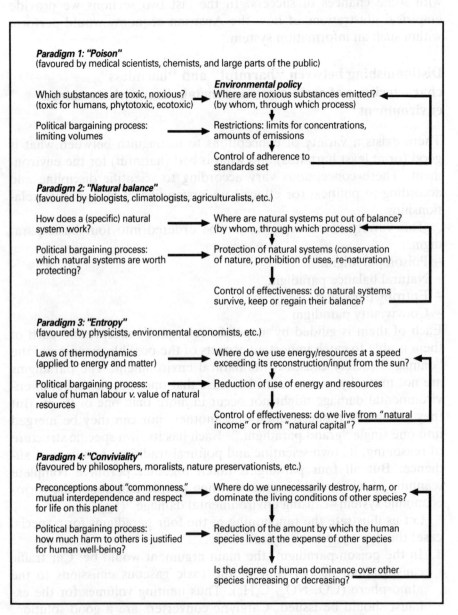

Fig. 1 "Environmental damage" caused by the socio-economic system: four basic paradigms

converters would not do, since they cannot reduce CO_2, but maybe electric or solar cars could.

3. In the entropy paradigm, it would be argued that car traffic requires about 50 per cent of the end-consumption of liquid fossil fuels. Thus we need a technological innovation towards solar cars, for example, while catalytic converters are relatively irrelevant or even counterproductive, since they require platinum, a very rare resource.

4. In the conviviality paradigm, attention would be drawn to car traffic as a major cause of unintentional and useless animal killing (insects, birds, rodents, amphibious animals, etc.). One would also draw attention to the road system reducing the living space of many species to areas too small for a decent life and exposing them to all kinds of disturbances. Solar cars wouldn't help.

We think that an information system on the environmental impacts of the socio-economic system should refer to all these four paradigms and should present evidence concerning the central set of variables in each of them. It should not deprive any one line of reasoning of its possible empirical basis, or favour one over the other. Political discussion and the political decision-making process would then have to weigh arguments and to solve existing contradictions.

This recommendation can also be supported by considering the epistemological qualities of the four paradigms (fig. 2). Regarding the horizontal dimension, the poison paradigm and the entropy para-

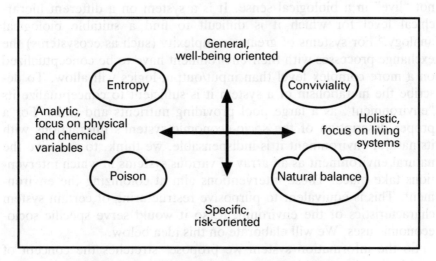

Fig. 2 Epistemological qualities of the four paradigms

digm are more closely related to established ways of analytical thinking in chemical and physical dimensions, whereas the natural balance paradigm and the conviviality paradigm present holistic views referring to living systems. These two are more difficult to relate to analytical systems such as (economic) national accounting – but holistic approaches may be the way of the future. The vertical dimension, specific *v.* general, and at the same time risk-oriented *v.* well-being-oriented, also has implications for the possible acceptability of the paradigms. For the time being it is easier to argue for political measures against specific risks than for ones in favour of long-term well-being. But this (we hope) may change within the next few decades, and an information system that is being created now should be open to such changes.

Outline of an information system for the metabolism of the socio-economic system with its natural environment

Let's come back to the notion of "metabolism." In biology, this term is commonly used to describe the internal biochemical pathways of organic and anorganic inputs and their conversion to organic/anorganic outputs which are necessary for an organism to grow, live, and produce its offspring.[4] Functionally, a specific metabolism is all an organism needs to survive.

Strictly speaking, the socio-economic system is not an organism: it is not as highly integrated internally, nor can it die, because it does not "live" in a biological sense. It is a system on a different hierarchical level for which it is difficult to find a suitable biological analogy.[5] For systems of greater complexity (such as ecosystems) the exchange processes with their environment have to be conceptualized on a more complex level than input/output-logics will allow. To describe the metabolism of a system it is sufficient to conceptualize its "environment" as a large pool providing nutrients and sinks. For a proper description of the socio-economic system's interactions with its natural environment it is indispensable, we think, to conceive the natural environment as an array of various systems in which interventions take place. These interventions aim at colonizing the environment. This is equivalent to purposive restructuring of certain system characteristics of the environment, so it would serve specific socio-economic uses. We will elaborate on this idea below.

So the information system we propose[6] stretches the concept of metabolism by considering not just inputs from and outputs to the

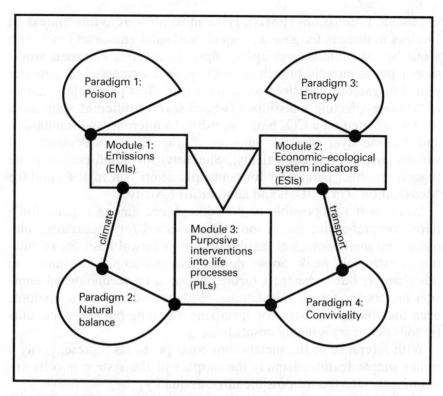

Fig. 3 The relationship between the proposed sets of indicators and reference paradigms of environmental damage caused by the socio-economic system

natural environment, but also interventions in various natural systems.

Figure 3 gives an overview of the information system that we propose in relation to the four paradigms described above. There are three modules of indicators that differ in their theoretical reference, in their (natural sciences) background, and in their databases. Methodologically, though, they have common features: they are all expressed as physical flows over the (systemic) border between the economy and its natural environment per time period (a year); they are all formulated on a level of abstraction that (in principle) allows all economic actors to produce such flows[7]; and they are all attributable to specific economic actors (branches of activities, including private households) on an institutional, not a functional basis.[8]

So, what distinguishes the information modules? What is their content? And how do they relate to the concept of metabolism?

Module 1, emissions (EMIs), is the most obvious in this context. It specifies indicators for gaseous, liquid, and solid emissions (each with a number of subindicators agreed upon in a series of expert workshops) per economic branch of activity, and expressed in tons per year. For gaseous emissions we suggest two effect parameters, namely "climate-affecting emissions" (where several different substances are recalculated on a CO_2 basis according to international standards), and "ozone-layer-affecting emissions" (again a recalculation of various gases in F21-equivalents). Similarly, for liquid emissions we suggest an effect parameter for "eutrophication" (in total P) and for "deoxidation" (in BOD_5), and another for toxicity.

Whereas it was possible to find acceptance among experts for a fairly comprehensive list of indicators selected for importance, ubiquity, and methodological feasibility, the empirical basis for calculation is extremely weak. So we do not give any empirical example in this chapter, but we suggest further research on technological emission factors for future calculations. With regard to solid emissions, even the conceptual basis for specifying anything but sheer amounts (in tons per year) is highly unsatisfying.

With reference to the metabolism concept, EMIs represent only a rather simple feature, namely the outputs of the system into its environment, selected for possible noxious quality.

Module 2, economic-ecological system indicators (ESIs), gives information about the physical dimensions of the economy in terms of matter, energy, and time/space. This rests upon the assumption that, *ceteris paribus*, the economy will have the less impact upon its environment the smaller the physical quantities handled by the system are. Several aspects can be expressed by this module. One aspect is the "size" of the economy relative to its natural environment. Another aspect is the ecological "wastefulness" of the economy: the more energy, matter, and movement (space/time) is processed for a given degree of need-satisfaction, the more ecologically wasteful the system is. Yet another aspect is the relative "closedness" of the system: how much input from the environment does it need and how much output does it produce in relation to the amounts circulated within the system?

The indicators in this module are expressed in physical amounts. (For example, how many tons of materials are handled per year, imported from and exported to the environment? How much energy in terms of joules per year is consumed resp. downgraded? How many tonne-kilometres are being transported per year?) These amounts are

344

very meaningful in absolute terms, be it for comparisons over time or between branches of economic activity. In a second step they can also be related to the monetary side of the economy and expressed as "intensities," e.g. net energy used per unit of gross domestic product. This draws attention to the relative independence of the physical and the monetary size of the economy: an economy may very well shrink in physical terms (which should be environmentally beneficial) and at the same time grow in monetary terms (which would be environmentally rather neutral).

What these indicators have in common is that they are fairly close to standard economic statistics, in the sense that they represent their physical dimensions. They also have in common a number of (sometimes overlapping) environmental implications. (We will come back to this for the case of materials and material intensity below.[9])

ESIs have a close relationship to the concept of metabolism: on a very general level they allow, in combination with economic input-output analysis, the screening of the whole transformation process that this term implies.

Module 3, purposive interventions into life processes (PILs), is the most unconventional of the modules. It is distinguished from emissions in that it seeks to operationalize purposeful actions. Emissions may be regarded as unintended side-effects of economic production and consumption, whereas here we aim at interventions in favour of a particular social use. Roads, for example, purposefully eradicate vegetation and animal life in a particular area in order to remove barriers to human mobility. Agriculture purposively uses pesticides to prevent other species from eating the crops. Pesticides are not an "emission" (or not unless they, as a side-effect, get into rivers), but are applied for a specific economic purpose.

PILs, in common with EMIs, do not portray the metabolism within the economy but the flows over its boundaries to the environment. Other than with EMIs these flows cannot be properly identified as either "intakes" or "outputs," but have to be described (on a different functional level) as interventions in environmental systems. An example is given below.

An empirical example for ESIs: Material balances and intensities for the Austrian economy

We regard the materials intensity of economic processes as one of the basic general criteria for their environmental impact. Most of the cur-

345

rent environmental damage is significantly connected with the extraction, transportation, processing, and use of materials.[10] Therefore the aim is to devise a consistent set of macro-indicators for materials intensity, which should give information on the physical extension (and efficiency) of economic activity.[11]

The suggested indicators for materials intensity trace the material flows from the environment through the economy and back into the environment. The concept of flows, as shown in figure 4, follows the laws of thermodynamics, which state that materials cannot be used up in a physical sense. Nothing gets lost. Macroeconomic material balances always end up with identical sums of material inputs and outputs in terms of mass. The concept of material flows is thus perfectly compatible with the monetary input-output cycles basic to the System of National Accounts (SNA).

The material balances include the total material throughput of the economy in millions of tons (as a measure of mass) per time period. Figure 5 presents a quantitative overview of the material throughput of the Austrian economy in millions of tons per year, calculated by Steurer from all sources available. The economy very much resembles a living system: 88 per cent of the throughput is water (more than half of that for cooling purposes), another 8 per cent is air (combustion only), and only 4 per cent consists of other materials. These other materials are mainly accounted for by construction mat-

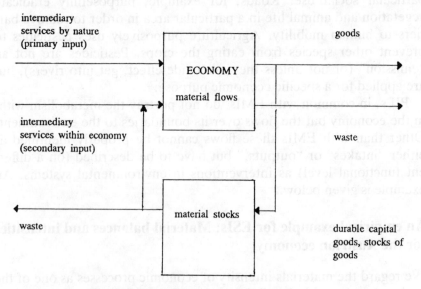

Fig. 4 The concept of material flows and stocks

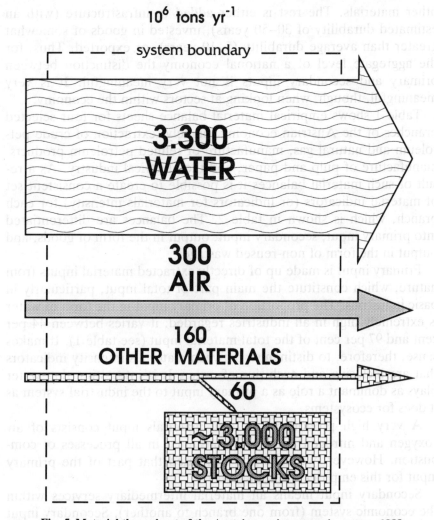

10^6 tons yr^{-1}

system boundary

3.300
WATER

300
AIR

160
OTHER MATERIALS

60

~3.000
STOCKS

Fig. 5 Material throughput of the Austrian socio-economic system, 1988

erials, food, and energy carriers. Just 1.6 per cent of the yearly primary input adds to stock. The whole stock could be estimated to amount to no more than 80 per cent of the yearly throughput; more than 90 per cent of the stock consists of buildings and roads.

On the level of the whole socio-economic system, in effect almost all inputs are directly drawn from nature: even the imports are clearly dominated by primary inputs such as energy carriers, and most outputs are released into nature within the course of a year. This holds true for practically all water and air, and for about half of the other materials. The rest is either added to infrastructure (with an estimated durability of 30–50 years), invested in goods of somewhat greater than average durability (5–10 years), or exported. Thus, for the aggregate level of a national economy the distinction between primary and secondary inputs is not very meaningful. It is very meaningful, though, when looking at sectors within the economy.

Table 1 shows empirical material balance sheets for four selected branches of the Austrian economy, namely, extraction of crude petroleum and natural gas, manufacture of refined petroleum products, manufacture of pulp and paper, and the electrical industry. As a result of such material balances it is possible to create a consistent set of material indicators (or indicators for materials intensity) for each branch, which is shown in table 2. The balances are differentiated into primary input, secondary input, output in the form of goods, and output in the form of non-reused wastage.

Primary input is made up of directly extracted material inputs from nature, which constitute the main part of total input, particularly in basic industries. The proportion of primary input in the form of water is extremely high in all industries regarded: it varies between 44 per cent and 97 per cent of the total material input (see table 1). It makes sense, therefore, to distinguish between materials-intensity indicators that are inclusive and exclusive of water. It is interesting that water plays as dominant a role as a primary input to the industrial system as it does for ecosystems.

A very high proportion of total materials input consists of air (oxygen and nitrogen), which is consumed in all processes of combustion. However, we have not calculated that part of the primary input for this empirical presentation.[12]

Secondary input means all material intermediary services within the economic system (from one branch to another). Secondary input can be divided into re-used waste material, renewable resource input, and direct packaging input. Secondary input in the form of durable capital goods or stocks of goods is not defined as material flow and therefore is not significant in terms of the flow concept, but forms part of the material stock balances.

One strategic gap in material flow balances is the difference between total input and total output in the form of goods. That difference is identical with the total material wastage (in gaseous, liquid, or solid form) of production, which will not undergo any further socio-economic processing and is deposited in the environment in one form or another. The amount of that difference, i.e. the total wastage, has

Table 1 Material balances for four selected branches of the Austrian economy, 1988 (in millions of tons)

		Extraction of crude petroleum and natural gas	Manufacture of refined petroleum products	Manufacture of pulp and paper	Electrical industry
Input					
Primary input (intermediary services of nature)	Directly extracted resources	2.153	—	—	—
	Water	1.761	12.598	220.700	13.811
	Oxygen and nitrogen	?	?	?	?
	Other resources	—	—	—	—
	Energy carrier	0.063	0.664	0.386[a]	0.041
Secondary input (intermediary services of economy)	Other[b] secondary input	0.005	8.247	5.427	0.686
	(Thereof: reused waste materials)	—	—	3.825[c]	0.005
	(Thereof: direct packaging input)	0.000	0.000	0.051	0.035
Total		3.982	21.509	226.513	14.538
Output					
Goods		2.153	8.129	4.105	0.607
Total material wastage		1.829	13.380	222.408	13.931
Total material wastage (excl. water)		0.068	0.782	1.708	0.120
Total		3.982	21.509	226.513	14.538
Employees (annual average)		2.813	3.391	12.474	77.379
Production value in billions of AS		2.916	16.571	36.446	60.415

Source: Own calculations.
a. Excluding combustible waste material.
b. Including deliveries of unprocessed primary inputs by other branches.
c. Including combustible waste material.

Marina Fischer-Kowalski, Helmut Haberl, and Harald Payer

Table 2 Indicators for material-intensity for four selected branches of the Austrian economy, 1988

		Extraction of crude petroleum and natural gas	Manufacture of refined petroleum products	Manufacture of pulp and paper	Electrical industry
Total input per employee (tons/em.)[a]	Incl. water	1.416	6.343	18.159	201
	Excl. water	790	2.628	466	10
Total input related to production value (tons/1.000 AS)[a]	Incl. water	1.37	1.30	6.22	0.24
	Excl. water	0.76	0.54	0.16	0.01
Material wastage per employee (tons/em.)	Incl. water	650	3.946	17.830	192
	Excl. water	24	231	137	2
Material wastage related to production value (tons/1000 AS)	Incl. water	0.63	0.81	6.10	0.23
	Excl. water	0.02	0.05	0.05	0.00
Material efficiency[b]	Incl. water	0.54	0.38	0.02	0.04
	Excl. water	0.97	0.91	0.71	0.83
Packaging intensity[c]		0.00	0.00	0.01	0.06

Source: Own calculations.

a. Excluding oxygen and nitrogen.
b. Percentage of material output in the form of goods to total material input.
c. Percentage of direct packaging input to material output in the form of goods.

a high information value with regard to the checking, controlling, and completion of emission data; the current availability of such data in Austria, however, is very limited. According to table 1 the total material wastage amounts to 46–98 per cent of the total input (if water is included), and from less than 3 to 31 per cent (if water is excluded).

In order to compare different industrial activities, time periods, and countries, we suggest the establishment of indicators such as those shown in table 2.

As can be seen from the table, the variability in material intensity between the branches of the economy is very high: whereas in the electrical industry only 10 kg of material input are needed to achieve a production value of 1,000 Austrian Schillings, in the petroleum extraction industry 790 kg correspond to this production value.

The indicator for material efficiency shows quite a different pattern. Here the manufacture of pulp and paper appears to be the most wasteful of the branches analysed, and the petroleum extraction industry the least wasteful. In these cases, therefore, there exists no positive correlation between the value of the input and the efficiency with which it is handled.

In order to be able to analyse and properly interpret data of this kind, it would be necessary to investigate several more branches of the economy and more points in time than is possible for the purposes of this example. As economic statistics in Austria are currently organized, it would be a tedious task to calculate a complete physical input–output matrix of this kind, let alone to reconstruct material flows within the economy. Nevertheless, we believe that such work is indispensable if one is to give an empirical description of "industrial metabolism."

Purposive interventions into life processes (PILs)

Purposive interventions in natural ecosystems are historically the oldest form of modification of the environment for economic purposes. They characterize the beginnings of agriculture and animal breeding. This exchange with the environment is quite different from simple "input" – for example, the intake of plants or meat as nutrition – and it is specifically human, at least as specifically as the use of tools.

There are many indications that PILs will gain even more importance in the future. As Moscovici (1990) and Oechsle (1988) state, emissions are a typical problem caused by a "mechanical" mode of economic production (and a corresponding mechanical paradigm of nature). The necessity of reducing emissions is now broadly accepted, and in the long run their importance will certainly diminish in relative terms. On the other hand, a new, "cybernetic" mode of economic production (and paradigm of nature) is arising, which is characterized by qualitatively new and enhanced possibilities of human control over nature.

There are many examples of this new tendency. The application of analytical-chemical methods yields new possibilities for directing and utilizing natural processes in order to meet human demands (Korab, 1991); new biological technologies are developing rapidly and are being strongly promoted – not least because it is hoped that they will lead to "clean technologies." This tendency can be described as replacing EMIs with PILs, for example, by using biological instead of chemical techniques (Fischer-Kowalski et al., 1991b).

Module of indicators

We developed the following module of indicators in order to mirror relevant processes by which the socio-economic system intervenes in life processes in favour of particular social uses (Fischer-Kowalski et al., 1991a; Haberl, 1991; Wenzl and Zangerl-Weisz, 1991):

1. Interventions into biotopes. Indicators for socio-economic efforts to change the structure of natural ecosystems. The most important efforts of this kind are interventions in water systems, the appropriation of photosynthetically fixed energy (see below), and the input of technically produced substances (fertilizers, pesticides).
2. Violence towards animals. Indicators for social activities that cause suffering and pain to animals. This subset contains two indicators, one for the circumstances in which animals are kept (long-term aspect), and one for short-term aspects: the killing of animals and animal experiments.
3. Interventions in evolution. Indicators for direct (genetic engineering) and indirect (breeding techniques) influences on the gene pool (see Wenzl and Zangerl-Weisz, 1991).

This systematization is based upon the different biological hierarchical levels on which these interventions take place (fig. 6).

Interventions in biotopes: An empirical example

Energy is the "motor" not only for industrial metabolism, but also for natural systems. Ecosystems can be conceptualized as compartment

352

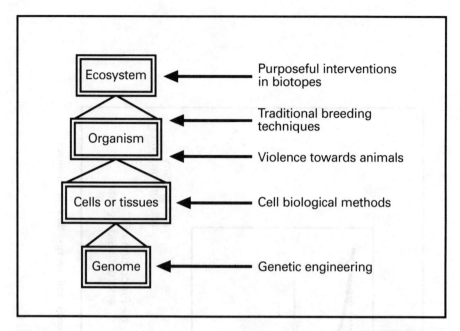

Fig. 6 PILs according to the level of intervention (Source: Fischer-Kowalski et al., 1991b)

models, in which (more or less closed) materials circles between the compartments are driven by a flow of energy. In fact, the development of ecology as a theoretically integrated discipline in the natural sciences began with the investigation of energy flows by Eugene P. and Howard T. Odum (see Odum, 1983, 1991).

Today, the following concept – described in rather simplified terms – is broadly accepted: Green plants convert the radiant energy of the sun into chemical energy by the process of photosynthesis. The accumulated energy – the net primary production (NPP) – is available to all other (heterotrophic) organisms. Consequently, "photosynthetically fixed energy ultimately supports the great diversity of species that inhabit the world's ecosystems" (Wright, 1990).

NPP is the photosynthetically fixed energy accumulated by green plants in a certain period of time (usually one year). It is an important figure for several reasons. First, empirical studies show that "energy flow can be related to numbers of species with species-energy curves" (Wright, 1990). This means that if the amount of energy remaining in the ecosystem is reduced, the number of species living in this ecosystem will diminish (see figure 7). Secondly, there are limits

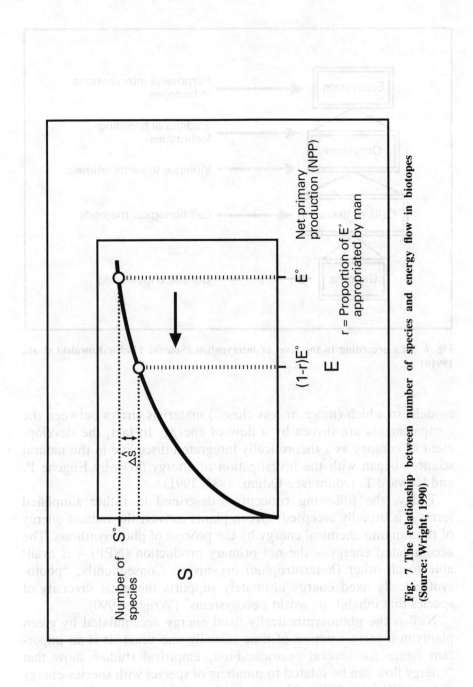

Fig. 7 The relationship between number of species and energy flow in biotopes
(Source: Wright, 1990)

to the fraction of NPP which can be used in a sustainable manner. The human appropriation of NPP is currently estimated at between 20 and 40 per cent of the total terrestrial NPP (Wright, 1990; Max-Neef, 1991). Even if it is not clear at which percentage of human appropriation of NPP the limits of sustainability are reached, the current amount is already considerable, and obviously cannot be increased without further speeding up the extinction of many other species.

We therefore propose to use the appropriation of NPP by the socio-economic system as one of three indicators for purposeful interventions in biotopes (Haberl, 1991). The indicator is formulated as the difference between the hypothetical NPP of the undisturbed ecosystem and the actual NPP.

What does this mean? The hypothetical NPP_h (per space unit and year) depends upon morphological and climatic circumstances. Under Austrian conditions it may vary from about 5 TJ/km^2 in alpine grasslands to 50TJ/km^2 in flood plains.[13] If man did not intervene, this biological energetic basis would be available to all other species. The socio-economic system may intervene in qualitatively different forms, but they boil down to two strategies: (a) the building of structures

Table 3 Appropriation of net primary production in Austria, 1988: first estimation

Socio-economic uses	Area concerned (km^2)	Photosynthetically fixed energy[a]		
		Hypothetical, NPP_h (PJ/a)	Appropriated by man, NPP_a (PJ/a)	Distribution of approp. NPP (%)
Agriculture[b]	15,900	370	250	40.4
Grassland, alpine pastures	21,000	280	180	29.0
Forests (logging)	34,300	580	110	17.7
Gardens	1,700	40	20	3.2
Traffic zones	1,600	40	40	6.5
Buildings	700	20	20	3.2
Other[c]	8,000	40	0	0.0
Total	83,200	1.370	620	100.0

Sources: Bundesamt für Eich- und Vermessungswesen, 1989; BMLF, 1989a; BMLF, 1989b; ÖSTAT, 1990; own calculations.
a. First estimates based on international literature.
b. Including wine.
c. Including waters and wasteland.

(such as highways or buildings) that prevent or drastically reduce the NPP in a certain area (the same road prevents a certain NPP_h each year by its very existence);[14] (b) consumption, in that certain amounts of NPP are harvested (or grazed off by cattle) and serve as inputs to the socio-economic system, thereby being no longer available to the ecosystem. What is shown in table 3 as NPP_a appropriated by the socio-economic system is therefore the sum of "prevented" NPP and "consumed" NPP.

The hypothetical NPP on Austrian territory is estimated to be around 1370 PJ/yr. Thus the socio-economic appropriation of the products of photosynthesis in Austria (620 PJ/yr) amounts to about 45 per cent of the total production.[15]

This means that the socio-economic system produces and reproduces environmental structures that leave more than half of the current photosynthetically fixed energy for all other species apart from human beings. This certainly is highly relevant from the viewpoint of both the natural balances paradigm and the conviviality paradigm.

Conclusions

The concept of metabolism provides a very useful way of directing attention to the physical exchange processes between industrial economy (or, as we prefer to call it, the socio-economic system) and its natural environment. As we have tried to show empirically for Austria, a description of such exchange processes fits in well with standard economic statistics, and in a way mirrors some of the logical structure of the monetary SNA on a physical level.

Deciding which aspects of this metabolism should be described requires a careful selection process. This process may be guided by four basic paradigms for the relationship between the socio-economic system and its natural environment. We have described these as the poison paradigm, the entropy paradigm, the natural balances paradigm, and the conviviality paradigm.

These paradigms draw attention to very different ways in which the socio-economic system causes damage in its natural environment, thereby possibly threatening its own survival. This calls for an information system on "metabolism" that is sophisticated enough to take in a variety of aspects without becoming unwieldy.[16]

One of the examples we demonstrated empirically was the calculation of "material balances" and "material intensities" for selected branches of the economy. The question of how much material input (in terms of weight) the economy needs either as direct extraction from the environment or from other parts of the economy, and how much material output it produces, either as goods for further use or as wastage expelled into the environment, is a crucial element of the description of its metabolism. Empirically it is interesting to note that, in the socio-economic system, water plays as central a role as it does for ecosystems.

Nevertheless, the concept of "metabolism" in its organismic analogy does not take into account a type of interaction between system and environment that is specific for, and typical of, the industrial economy. It does not just consume certain outputs of its environment (resources), and deposit used-up elements as its own output (emissions, wastes), but it purposively intervenes in the structures of the environment – it "colonizes" its environment. This implies a basic asymmetry between the socio-economic system and natural ecosystems. Natural ecosystems may interfere with the socio-economic system (and they do so all the time, sometimes quite forcefully), but they cannot intervene or colonize the socio-economic system in order to make it more useful to them. Under the circumstances of industrial economy, that is as impossible as it is for a monkey to keep a human child as a pet.

So the concept of "metabolism" has to be stretched to come to grips with this asymmetrical process, but without betraying its methodological qualities, which consist in its concentration upon flows (rather than stocks). This is what we are attempting in suggesting (and empirically exemplifying) a measure for the socio-economic intake of photosynthetically fixed energy, which is the basis of most of the life on this planet.

The stunning magnitude of the human interventions in natural systems demonstrate the gigantic size of the industrial metabolism *vis-à-vis* natural biospheric metabolism. Obviously, the socio-economic system is a strong competitor to all natural ecosystems. Yet one doubts that it will be able to drive them completely into extinction without at the same time bringing about its own destruction.

Notes

1. This chapter is based upon a two-year study on "causer-related environmental indicators," partly financed by a programme for "new paths towards measuring the national product,"

run by the Austrian Ministry of the Environment. Its content is, to a large extent, a product of the cooperation of the whole team, which included, besides the authors: Geli Brechelmacher, René Dell'Mour, Peter Fleissner, Anton Steurer, Karl Turetschek, Rudolf Vymazal, Peter Wenzl, and Helga Zangerl-Weisz.

2. Attempts in this direction are becoming somewhat more common now; see, for example, Pearce et al. (1990), and the international examples given there, or Ayres (1991).

3. The notion of sustainability claims to be such a grand paradigm. But in spite of its generality we do not believe it can embrace all aspects of these four paradigms. It excludes the "conviviality" reasoning (paradigm 4) completely, and it would rule out some of the more short-term processes in the poison paradigm. It seems a close relative to the entropy paradigm, also sharing its non-specificity.

4. This term can also be used of lower levels, i.e. the cell, or even parts of cells.

5. One of the main difficulties in finding a biological analogy comes from the fact that it does not have topographical or physical but functional boundaries. For operational purposes a topographical boundary may be defined (such as we do here by analysing the Austrian socio-economic system), but physically it shares its space with all other physical systems.

6. This information system was developed for the Austrian Ministry of Environment for integration into an environmental satellite system for the System of National Accounts (SNA). It is designed to work on the level not only of the national economy, but also of branches of economic activities, in terms of standard economic statistics (particularly input-output statistics).

7. This means, for example, that no indicator such as "growing monocultures" would be included, since this would be on such a low level of abstraction that no other actor but agriculture could be characterized.

8. Using a functional basis is very common in energy statistics, for example "traffic." We differentiate into "transport industry," and, in addition to this, each branch of the economy causes its own traffic. Intermediary services by the transport industry may then be distributed among the other branches by input-output techniques (see Dell'Mour et al., 1991).

9. We have calculated the amount of transport (in tons*kilometres and persons*kilometres per year) and the transport intensities of the Austrian economy on a 10-sector level by means of input-output analysis (see Dell'Mour et al., 1991). The empirical calculation of energy consumption and intensities (separated into renewable/non-renewable and transport/non-transport) by 40 branches of economic activity is available as standard statistics in Austria.

10. However, this does not convey information on specific environmental impacts such as the toxicological risk potential of using matter. That is the explicit function of information on emissions, and indicators for purposeful interventions into life processes.

11. The need for a supplementary system of physical accounting connected to the traditional SNA has gained support in recent years. Ambitious attempts have been started by Norwegian, French, and Canadian statisticians (Corniere, 1986; Friend, 1988; OECD, 1988). The model of material balances and intensities as represented below is a contribution to that discussion in progress.

12. The databases to do so would be sufficient, if confined to processes of combustion (which makes for the major share of the total).

13. $1 \text{ TJ} = 10^{12} \text{ J}$; $1 \text{ PJ} = 10^{15} \text{ J}$.

14. There may also be cases in which the intervention causes an increase in NPP above the "natural" level, for example by growing maize instead of wood. But in practically all such cases this surplus NPP is then extracted from the ecosystem by harvesting.

15. It is interesting to note that the amount of appropriated photosynthetically fixed energy corresponds quantitatively to the end-use of (technical) energy, which for Austria is around 750 PJ/yr.

16. For more detail on this information system as a whole, see Fischer-Kowalski et al.(1991a).

References

Ayres, R. U. 1991. "Materials/Energy Flows and Balances as a Component of Environmental Statistics." Paper presented at the Special IARIW Conference on Environmental Accounting, Baden, 27–29 May 1991.

Bundesamt für Eich- und Vermessungswesen. 1989. "Administrative und statistische Angaben für das Bundesgebiet Österreich: Ausweis der Benützungsarten." *Stand*, 31 December 1988.

BMLF. 1989a. *Bericht über die Lage der österreichischen Landwirtschaftgemäss 3/4 9 des Landwirtschaftsgesetzes 1976 BGBl.* Vienna, p.299.

————. 1989b. *Jahresbericht über die Forstwirtschaft 1988.* Vienna.

Corniere, P. 1986. "Natural Resource Accounts in France. An Example: Inland Waters." In: *Information and Natural Resources.* Paris: OECD.

Dell'Mour, R., P. Fleissner, W. Hofkirchner, and A. Steurer. 1991. *Zur Bestimmung der Transportintensität der österreichischen Wirtschaft und der damit verbundenen Emissionen mittels Input-Output-Modellierung.* Research report. Vienna: IFF/Ökologie-Institut.

Fischer-Kowalski, M., H. Haberl, H. Payer, A. Steurer, and H. Zangerl-Weisz. 1991a. *Verursacherbezogene Umweltindikatoren – Kurzfassung.* Research report. Vienna: IFF/Ökologie-Institut.

Fischer-Kowalski, M., H. Haberl, P. Wenzl, and H. Zangerl-Weisz. 1991b. "Emissions and Purposeful Interventions into Life Processes – Indicators for the Austrian Environmental Accounting System." Paper presented at the Conference on Ecologic Bioprocessing of the Österreichische Gesellschaft für Bioprozeßtechnik (ÖGBPT), Graz, October 1991.

Fischer-Kowalski, M., H. Haberl, H. Payer, A. Steurer, and R. Vymazal. 1991c. "Causer-related Environmental Indicators – A Contribution to the Environmental Satellite System of the Austrian SNA." Paper presented at the Special IARIW Conference on Environmental Accounting, 27–29 May 1991.

Friend, A. 1988. "Natural Resource Accounting: A Canadian Perspective." In: Y. J. Ahmad, S. El Serafy and E. Lutz, eds., *Environmental and Resource Accounting and Their Relevance to the Measurement of Sustainable Development.* Washington, D.C.: World Bank.

Goldsmith, E., and N. Hildyard. 1984. *The Social and Environmental Effects of Large Dams.* Vol. 1: *Overview.* Wadebridge Ecological Centre.

Haberl, H. 1991. *Gezielte Eingriffe in Lebensprozesse.* Research report. Vienna: IFF/Ökologie-Institut.

Immler, Hans. 1989. *Vom Wert der Natur. Zur ökologischen Reform von Wirtschaft und Gesellschaft.* Opladen: Westdeutscher Verlag.

Illich, I. 1973. *Tools for Conviviality.* New York: Harper & Row.

Korab, R. 1991. "Ökologische Orientierungen: Naturwahrnehmung als sozialer Prozeß." In: A. Pellert, ed., *Vernetzung und Widerspruch. Zur Neuorganisation der Wissenschaft.* Munich/Vienna: Profil Verlag, pp. 299–342.

Luhmann, N. 1986. *Ökologische Kommunikation.* Cologne/Opladen: Westdeutscher Verlag.

Max-Neef, M. A. 1991. "Speculations and Reflections on the Future." Official Document no. 1, prepared for the Preparatory Committee of the Santiago Encounter, 13–15 March, Santiago de Chile.

359

Moscovici, S. 1990. *Versuch einer menschlichen Geschichte der Natur*. Frankfurt: Suhrkamp.

Odum, E. P. 1983. *Grundlagen der Ökologie*. Vol. 1: *Grundlagen*. 2nd ed. Stuttgart: Thieme.

———. 1991. *Prinzipien der Ökologie: Lebensräume, Stoffkreisläufe, Wachstumsgrenzen*. Heidelberg: Verlag Spektrum der Wissenschaft.

OECD. 1988. *Natural Resource Accounting: The Norwegian Experience*. Prepared by A. Lone. Paris: Environment Committee, Group on the State of the Environment.

Oechsle, M. 1988. *Der ökologische Naturalismus. Zum Verhältnis von Natur und Gesellschaft im ökologischen Diskurs*. Frankfurt/New York: Campus.

ÖSTAT. 1990. *Ergebnisse der landwirtschaftlichen Statistik im Jahre 1989. Beiträge zur Österreichischen Statistik*. No. 976. Vienna.

Payer, H. 1991. *Indikatoren für die Materialintensität der österreichischen Wirtschaft*. Research report. Vienna: IFF/Ökologie-Institut.

Pearce, D., A. Markandya, and E. B. Barbier. 1990. *Blueprint for a Green Economy*. London.

Wenzl, P., and H. Zangerl-Weisz. 1991. *Gentechnik als gezielter Eingriff in Lebensprozesse. Vorüberlegungen für verursacherbezogene Umweltindikatoren*. Research report. Vienna: IFF/Ökologie-Institut.

Wright, D. H. 1990. "Human Impacts on Energy Flow through Natural Ecosystems, and Implications for Species Endangerment." *Ambio* 19, no. 4: 189–194.

Bibliography

Rüdiger Olbrich and Udo E. Simonis

Aitchison, L. *A History of Metals*. London: Interscience, 1960.

Allen, P. M., and J. M. McGlade. "Modelling Complex Human Systems. A Fisheries Example." *European Journal of Operations Research* 30 (1987): 147–167.

Alloway, B. J., ed. *Heavy Metals in Soils*. London: Blackie, 1990.

Anderberg, S., B. Bergbäck, and U. Lohm. "Flow and Distribution of Chromium in the Swedish Environment. A New Approach to Studying Environmental Pollution." *Ambio* 18 (1989), no. 4: 216–220.

———. *Pattern of Lead Emissions in Sweden 1880–1980*. Swedish National Chemicals Inspectorate Report no. 13/90, 1990.

Andersson, A. "Heavy Metals in Swedish Soils. On their Retention, Distribution and Amounts." *Swedish Journal of Agricultural Research* 7 (1977): 7–20.

Arndt, P., and G. W. Lüttig, eds. *Mineral Resources, Extraction, Environmental Protection and Land Use in the Industrial and the Developing Countries*. Forestburgh, N.Y.: Lubrecht & Cramer, 1987.

Association of the Dutch Chemical Industry (VNCI), ed. *Integrated Substance Chain Management*. Leidschendam: VNCI, 1991.

Ausubel, J. H., and R. Herman, eds. *Cities and Their Vital Systems. Infrastructure: Past, Present, and Future*. Washington, D.C.: National Academy Press, 1988.

Ausubel, J. H., and H. E. Sladovich, eds. *Technology and Environment*. Washington, D.C.: National Academy Press, 1989.

Ayres, R. U. "A Materials-Process-Model." In: A. V. Kneese and B. Bower, eds. *Environmental Quality Analysis. Theoretical and Methodological Studies in the Social Sciences*. Baltimore, Md.: Johns Hopkins University Press, 1972.

———. *Resources, Environment and Economics. Applications of the Materials/ Energy Balance Principle*. New York: John Wiley & Sons, 1978.

361

Rüdiger Olbrich and Udo E. Simonis

——. "Materials and the Environment." In: M. B. Bever, ed., *Encyclopedia of Materials Science and Engineering*. New York: Pergamon Press, 1986.

——. *Self Organization in Biology and Economics*. Laxenburg: IIASA, 1988.

——. "Industrial Metabolism and Global Change." *International Social Science Journal* 41 (1989), no. 3: 363–373.

——. "Industrial Metabolism." In: J. H. Ausubel and H. E. Sladovich, eds., *Technology and Environment*. Washington, D.C.: National Academy Press, 1989.

——. *Eco-restructuring. Managing the Transition to an Ecologically Sustainable Economy*. Laxenburg: IIASA, 1991.

Ayres, R. U., L. W. Ayres, J. McCurley, M. J. Small, J. A. Tarr, and R. C. Widgery. *An Historical Reconstruction of Major Pollutant Levels in the Hudson-Raritan Basin 1880–1980*. Rockville, Md.: National Oceanic and Atmospheric Administration, 1988.

Ayres, R. U., and A. V. Kneese. "Production, Consumption and Externalities." *American Economic Review* 59 (1969), no. 3: 282–297.

——. "Externalities. Economics and Thermodynamics." In: F. Archibugi and P. Nijkamp, eds., *Economy and Ecology. Towards Sustainable Development*. Dordrecht: Kluwer Academic Publishers, 1989.

Ayres, R. U., A. V. Kneese, and R. C. d'Arge. *Aspects of Environmental Economics. A Materials Balance–General Equilibrium Approach*. Baltimore, Md.: Johns Hopkins University Press, 1970.

Ayres, R. U., V. Norberg-Bohn, J. Prince, W. M. Stigliani, and J. Yanowitz. *Industrial Metabolism, the Environment, and Application of Materials-Balance Principles for Selected Materials*. Laxenburg: IIASA, 1989.

Ayres, R. U., and S. R. Rod. "Reconstructing an Environmental History. Patterns of Pollution in the Hudson-Raritan Basin." *Environment* 28 (1986), no. 4: 14–20, 39–43.

Ayres, R. U., and P. K. Rohatgi. "Bhopal. Lessons for Technological Decision-makers." *Technology in Society* 9 (1987): 19–45.

Baccini, P., ed. *The Landfill. Reactor and Final Storage*. Berlin/Heidelberg/New York: Springer, 1989.

Baccini, P., and P. H. Brunner. 1991. *Metabolism of the Anthroposphere*. Berlin/Heidelberg/New York: Springer, 1991.

Bailly, H.-C., and C. Tayart de Borms. Materials Flows in the Post-consumer Waste Stream of the EEC. London: Graham & Trotman, 1977.

Balzer, D., and A. Rauhut. "Verbrauch und Verbleib von Cadmium und seinen Verbindungen in der Bundesrepublik Deutschland (1981–1983)." *LGA-Rundschau*. 87 (1987), no. 3: 73–83.

Beauregard, R. A., ed. *Atop the Urban Hierarchy*. Totowa, N.J.: Rowmann & Littlefield, 1990.

Behrendt, H., and M. Boehme. *Point and Diffuse Loads of Selected Pollutants in the River Rhine and its Main Tributaries*. Research report. Laxenburg: IIASA, 1992.

Benarie, M. "Transport of Pollutants Considered from the Point of View of a Short and Medium-Range Material Balance." *Water, Air and Soil Pollution* 6 (1976), no. 2–4: 329–338.

Bergbäck, B. *Industrial Metabolism. The Emerging Landscape of Heavy Metal Immission in Sweden*. Linköping Studies in Arts and Science, no. 76. Linköping, 1992.

Bergbäck, B., S. Anderberg, and U. Lohm. "A Reconstruction of Emissions, Flow

362

and Accumulation of Chromium in Sweden 1920–1980." *Water, Air and Soil Pollution* 48 (1989): 391–407.

———. "Lead Load. Historical Pattern of Lead Use in Sweden." *Ambio* 21 (1992), no. 2: 159–165.

Block, W., ed. *Economics and the Environment. A Reconciliation.* Vancouver: Fraser Institute, 1990.

Bluestone, B., and B. Harrison. *The Deindustrialization of America.* New York: Basic Books, 1982.

Boeninger, M. *The Carcinogenicity and Metabolism of Azo Dyes.* Technical report. Cincinnati, Ohio: National Institute for Occupational Safety and Health, 1980.

Bomsel, O., et al. *Mining and Metallurgy Investment in the Third World. The End of Large Projects?* Paris: OECD, 1990.

Bookchin, M. *Toward an Ecological Society.* Montreal: Black Rose Books, 1980.

Bosson, R., and B. Varon. *The Mining Industry and the Developing Countries.* New York: Oxford University Press, 1977.

Brading, D. A., and H. E. Cross. "Colonial Silver Mining. Mexico and Peru." *Hispanic American Historical Review* 52 (1972), no. 4: 545–579.

Bradbury, J. H. "Regional and Industrial Restructuring Processes in the New International Division of Labor." *Progress in Human Geography* 9 (1985), no. 1: 38–63.

Braudel, F. *Civilisation matérielle, économie et capitalisme, XVe-XVIIe siècle. Les structures du quotidien: le possible et l'impossible.* Paris: Librairie Armand Colin, 1979.

Brimblecombe, P. *The Big Smoke. A History of Air Pollution in London since Medieval Times.* London/New York: Methuen, 1987.

Brown, L. R., and J. L. Jacobson. *The Future of Urbanization. Facing the Ecological and Economic Constraints.* Worldwatch Paper 77. Washington, D.C., 1987.

Bruce, A. M., F. Collin, and P. J. Newman, eds. *Treatment of Sewage Sludge.* Amsterdam: Elsevier, 1989.

Brunner, P. H., and W. R. Ernst. "Alternative Methods for the Analysis of Municipal Solid Waste." *Waste Management and Research* 4 (1986): 147–160.

Brunner, P. H., and H. Moench. "The Flux of Metals through Municipal Solid Waste Incinerators." *Waste Management and Research* 4 (1986): 105–119.

Bryant, J. "A Thermodynamic Approach to Economics." *Energy Economics* 1 (1982): 36–50.

Cameron, T., and J. Abouchar. "The Precautionary Principle. A Fundamental Principle of Law and Policy for the Protection of the Global Environment." *Boston College International and Comparative Law Review* 14 (1991), no. 1: 1–27.

Catton, W. R., Jr. *Overshoot. The Ecological Basis of Revolutionary Change.* Urbana, Ill.: University of Illinois Press, 1980.

Chandler, W. U. *Materials Recycling.* Worldwatch Paper 56. Washington, D.C., 1987.

Chizhov, N., and M. Styrikovich. "Ecological Advantages of Natural Gas and Other Fuels." In: T. H. Lee, H. Linden, H. Dreyfus, and T. Vasko, eds., *The Methane Age.* Dordrecht: Kluwer Academic Publishers, 1988.

Chynoweth, E., et al. "Catalysts." *Chemical-Week*, 27 June 1990.

Clark, W. C., and R. E. Munn, eds. *Sustainable Development of the Biosphere.* Cambridge: Cambridge University Press, 1987.

Colombo, U. "The Technology Revolution and the Restructuring of the Global Economy." In: J. H. Muroyama and H. G. Stever, eds., *Globalization of Technology. International Perspectives*. Washington, D.C.: National Academy Press, 1988.

Commoner, B. *The Closing Circle. Nature, Man and Technology*. New York: Alfred A. Knopf, 1971.

———. *Making Peace with the Planet*. New York: Pantheon, 1990.

Conell, D. W., and G. J. Miller. *Chemistry and Ecotoxicology of Pollution*. New York: Wiley & Sons, 1984.

Conway, G. R., and G. N. Pretty. *Unwelcome Harvest. Agriculture and Pollution*. London: Earthscan, 1991.

Cook, E. "Limits to Exploitation of Nonrenewable Resources." *Science* 191 (1976): 677–682.

Costanza, R., ed. *Ecological Economics. The Science and Management of Sustainability*. New York: Columbia University Press, 1991.

Dales, J. H. *Pollution, Property and Prices*. Toronto: Toronto University Press, 1968.

Daly, H. E., and A. Umaña. *Energy, Economics and the Environment*. Boulder, Colo.: Westview Press, 1981.

Daly, H. E., and J. B. Cobb. *For the Common Good. Redirecting the Economy toward Community, the Environment, and a Sustainable Future*. Boston: Beacon Press, 1991.

Daniels, G. H., and M. H. Rose, eds. *Energy and Transport. Historical Perspectives on Policy Issues*, Beverly Hills, Calif.: Sage Publications, 1982.

Dasgupta, P., and D. Heal. *Economic Theory and Exhaustible Resources*. Cambridge: Cambridge University Press, 1979.

Davidson, C. F., et al. *Mass Balances for Pollutants in Urban Regions. A Methodology with Applications to Lead, Zinc, Cadmium and Arsenic*. Washington, D.C., 1978. (EPA-600/4–78–046.)

Debus, K. H. "Mining with Microbes." *Technology Review* 93 (1990), no. 6: 50–57.

Dignon, J., and S. Hameed. "Global Emissions of Nitrogen and Sulfur Oxides from 1860 to 1980." *Journal of the Air Pollution Control Association* 39 (1989), no. 2: 183.

D'Itri, P. A. *Mercury Contaminations. A Human Tragedy*. New York: Wiley-Interscience, 1980.

Dixhoorn, J. van, and F. Evans, eds. *Physical Structure in Systems Theory*. New York: Academic Press, 1974.

Douglas, M., and A. Wildavsky. *Risk and Culture. The Selection of Technical and Environmental Dangers*. Berkeley, Calif.: University of California Press, 1982.

Duchin, F. "An Input-Output Approach to Analyzing the Future Economic Implications of Technological Change." In: R. Miller, K. Polenske, and A. Rose, eds., *Frontiers of Input-Output Analysis*. Oxford: Oxford University Press, 1989.

———. "Industrial Input-Output Analysis. Implications for Industrial Ecology." *Proceedings of the National Academy of Science* 89 (1992): 1–5.

Ehrlich, P. R., et al. *Ecoscience. Population, Resources, Environment*. San Francisco: W. H. Freeman, 1977.

Elgersma, F., B. S. Anderberg, and W. M. Stigliani. *Aqueous Emission Factors for the Industrial Discharge of Cadmium in the Rhine River Basin in the Period 1970–1990. An Inventory*. Working paper. Laxenburg: IIASA, 1991.

Enos, J. L. *The Creation of Technological Capability in Developing Countries*. London: Pinter Publishers, 1991.

Epstein, S. S., L. O. Brown, and C. Pope. *Hazardous Waste in America*. San Francisco: Sierra Club Books, 1982.

Faber, M., and J. Proops. "Interdisciplinary Research between Economists and Physical Scientists. Retrospect and Prospect." *Kyklos* 38 (1985): 599–616.

Fainstein, S. S., et al. *Restructuring the City*. New York: Longman, 1986.

Fischoff, B., et al. *Acceptable Risk*. Cambridge: Cambridge University Press, 1981.

Fisher, I. *The Nature of Capital and Income*. New York: Macmillan, 1919.

Foreman, C. T., ed. *Regulating the Future*. Washington, D.C.: Center for National Policy, 1990.

Forman, C. *Industrial Town. Self-Portrait of St. Helens in the 1920's*. Newton Abbot: David & Charles, 1978.

Friberg, L., C. G. Elinder, T. Kjellström, and G. F. Nordberg, eds. *Cadmium and Health. A Toxicological and Epidemiological Appraisal*. Vol. II. Boca Raton: CRC Press, 1986.

Frosch, R. A., and N. E. Gallapoulos. "Strategies for Manufacturing." *Scientific American* 261 (1989), no. 3: 144–152.

Garrels, R. M., F. T. MacKenzie, and C. Hunt. *Chemical Cycles and the Global Environment*. Los Altos: W. Kaufmann, 1975.

Georgescu-Roegen, N. *The Entropy Law and the Economic Process*. Cambridge, Mass.: Harvard University Press, 1971.

———. "The Steady State and Ecological Salvation. A Thermodynamic Analysis." *Bio Science* 27 (1977), no. 4: 266–270.

———. "Myths About Energy and Matter." *Growth and Change* 10 (1979), no. 1: 16–23.

———. "The Entropy Law and the Economic Process in Retrospect." *Eastern Economic Journal* 12 (1986): 3–26.

German Bundestag, ed. *Protecting the Earth's Atmosphere. An International Challenge*. Bonn: German Bundestag.

Goldemberg, J., et al. *Energy for a Sustainable World*. Washington, D.C.: World Resources Institute, 1987.

Goodman, W. L. *The History of Woodworking Tools*. London: G. Bell, 1964.

Goodrich, W. F. *Pulverised Fuel*. London: Charles Griffin & Co, 1924.

Goumans, J. J., H. A. van der Sloot, and T. G. Aalbers, eds. *Waste Materials in Construction*. Amsterdam: Elsevier, 1991.

Government of Japan, Environment Agency. *Quality of the Environment in Japan 1990*. Tokyo, 1991.

Greenpeace USA. *The International Trade in Wastes*. Washington, D.C.: Greenpeace, 1990.

Grübler, A., and N. Nakicenovic. "The Dynamic Evolution of Methane Technologies." In: T. H. Lee, Linden, Dreyfus, and Vasko, eds., *The Methane Age*. Dordrecht: Kluwer Academic Publishers, 1988.

———. *Technological Progress, Structural Change and Efficient Energy Use. Trends Worldwide and in Austria*. Laxenburg: IIASA, 1989.

Gschwandtner, G., K. C. Gschwandtner, and K. Eldridge. *Historic Emissions of Sulfur and Nitrogen Oxides in the USA, 1900–1980*. Report to EPA. Durham, N.C.: Pacific Environmental Services Inc., 1983.

Haber, L. F. *The Chemical Industry during the 19th Century*. Oxford: Oxford University Press, 1969.

———. *The Chemical Industry 1900–1930*. Oxford: Clarendon Press, 1971.

Hahn, E., and U. E. Simonis. "Ecological Urban Restructuring. Method and Action." *Environmental Management and Health* 2 (1991), no. 2: 12–19.

Håkansson, K., B. Bergbäck, S. Karlsson, and B. Allard. "Long-range Spreading of Metals from a Mine Waste Deposit." *Vatten* 45 (1989): 68–74.

Hall, C. A. S., and C. J. Cleveland. "Petroleum Drilling and Production in the United States. Yield per Effort and Net Energy Analysis." *Science* 211 (1981): 576–579.

Harrison, R. M. *Lead Pollution – Causes and Control*. London: Chapman & Hall, 1981.

Hatfield, H. "Earliest Uses of the English Term Capital." *Quarterly Journal of Economics* 26 (1922): 547–548.

Heaton, G., R. Repetto, and R. Sobin. *Transforming Technology. An Agenda for Environmentally Sustainable Growth in the 21st Century*. Washington, D.C.: World Resources Institute.

Heilbroner, R. *An Inquiry into the Human Prospect*. New York: W.W. Norton, 1974.

Herman, R., S. A. Ardekani, and J. H. Ausubel. "Dematerialization." In: J. H. Ausubel and H.E. Sladovich, eds., *Technology and Environment*. Washington, D.C.: National Academy Press, 1989.

Hirschhorn, J. S., and K. U. Oldenberg. *Prosperity Without Pollution*. Washington, D.C.: Van Reinhold, 1991.

Hirshleifer, J. "Economics from a Biological Viewpoint." *Journal of Law and Economics* 20 (1977): 1–52.

Hotelling, H. "The Economics of Exhaustible Resource." *Journal of Political Economy* 39 (1931): 137–175.

Hrehoruk, J., H. Modzelewski, and B. Frydzynska. *Deposition of Zinc, Cadmium and Lead to the Rhine Basin due to Emissions from Local Sources and Corrosion caused by* SO_2. Research report. Laxenburg: IIASA, 1992.

Hubbard, H. M. "Photovoltaics Today and Tomorrow." *Science* 244 (1989): 297–304.

Huisingh, D. Good Environmental Practices – Good Business Practices. Berlin: Science Centre Berlin, 1988.

Husar, R. B., and J. D. Husar. "Sulfur." In: B. L. Turner et al., *The Earth as Transformed by Human Action*. Cambridge: Cambridge University Press, 1990.

Hutchinson, T. C. "Copper Contamination of Ecosystems Caused by Smelter Activities." In: J. O. Nriagu, ed., *Copper in the Environment*. New York: Wiley-Interscience, 1978.

Hutton, M. *Cadmium in the European Community. A Prospective Assessment of Sources, Human Exposure and Environmental Impact*. London: Monitoring and Assessment Research Centre, Chelsea College, 1982.

Hutzinger, O., ed. *The Handbook of Environmental Chemistry*. Berlin/Heidelberg/New York: Springer, 1982.

Jacobs, P., and B. Sadler, eds. *Sustainable Development and Environmental Assessment. Perspectives on Planning for a Common Future*. Ottawa: Canadian Environmental Assessment Research Council, 1990.

Jänicke, M., H. Mönch, T. Ranneberg, and U. E. Simonis. "Structural Change and Environmental Impact. Empirical Evidence on Thirty-one Countries in East and West." *Environmental Monitoring and Assessment* 12 (1989), no. 2: 99–114.

Johansson, T. B., et al., eds. *Electricity. Efficient End-use and New Generation Technologies and Their Planning*. Lund: Lund University Press, 1989.

Jörgensen, S. E., and H. Mejer. "Modelling the Global Cycle of Carbon, Nitrogen and Phosphorus and Their Influence on Global Heat Balance." *Ecological Modelling* 2 (1976), no. 1: 19–32.

Judge, P. C. "Race on for an Electric Car Battery." *New York Times*, 18 July 1990, pp. D1, D7.

Kabata-Pendias, A., and H. Pendias. *Trace Elements in Soils and Plants*. Boca Raton: CRC Press, 1984.

Kerr, C., et al. *Industrialism and Industrial Man*. Cambridge: Harvard University Press, 1960.

Kleiner, A. "What Does It Mean to Be Green?" *Harvard Business Review* 69 (1991), no. 4: 38–47.

Kneese, A. V., R. U. Ayres, and R. C. D'Arge. *Economics and the Environment. A Materials Balance Approach*. Baltimore, Md.: Johns Hopkins University Press, 1972.

Kyrklund, T. "The Use of Experimental Studies to Reveal Suspected Neurotoxic Chemicals as Occupational Hazards." *American Journal of Industrial Medicine* 21 (1992), no. 1: 15–24.

Landes, D. S. *Unbound Prometheus. Technological Change and Industrial Development in Western Europe from 1750 to the Present*. Cambridge: Cambridge University Press, 1969.

Lansdown, R., and W. Jule, eds. *The Lead Debate. The Environment, Toxicology and Child Health*. London: Croom Helm, 1986.

Larson, E. D., M. H. Ross, and R. H. Williams. "Beyond the Era of Materials." *Scientific American* 254 (1986), no. 6: 34–41.

Lee, T. H., H. Linden, H. Dreyfus, and T. Vasko, eds. *The Methane Age*. Dordrecht: Kluwer Academic Publishers, 1988.

Leipert, C., and U. E. Simonis. "Environmental Damage – Environmental Protection. Empirical Evidence on the Federal Republic of Germany." *International Journal of Social Economics* 15 (1988), no. 7: 37–52.

———. "Environmental Damage – Environmental Expenditure. Statistical Evidence on the Federal Republic of Germany." *The Environmentalist* 10 (1990), no. 4: 301– 309; 11 (1991), no. 3: 213–216.

Leontief, W. "Environmental Repercussions and the Economic Structure. An Input-Output Approach." *The Review of Economics and Statistics* 52 (1970), no. 3: 262–271.

Lester, B. L., and A. C. Upton, eds. *Toxic Chemicals, Health and the Environment*. Baltimore, Md.: Johns Hopkins University Press, 1987.

Lieth, H., and R. H. Whittaker, eds. *Primary Productivity of the Biosphere*. Berlin/Heidelberg/New York: Springer, 1973.

Lovelock, J. *Gaia. A New Look at Life on Earth*. Oxford: Oxford University Press, 1979.

———. *The Ages of Gaia. A Biography of Our Living Earth*. New York: W. W. Norton, 1988.

Lovins, A. B. *Openpit Mining*. London: Earth Island, 1973.

Mathews, J. T. "Redefining Security." *Foreign Affairs* 68 (1989), no. 2: 162–177.

McGannon, H. E. *The Making, Shaping and Treating of Steel*. Pittsburgh, Pa.:

United States Steel Corporation, 1964.

McIntyre, A. D., and C. F. Mills, eds. *Ecological Toxicology Research*. New York: Plenum Press, 1975.

McKinsey & Co. *The Corporate Response to the Environmental Challenge*. Amsterdam: McKinsey, 1991.

McLaren, J., and B. J. Skinner, eds. *Resources and World Development*. Dahlem Workshop Report. New York: John Wiley & Sons, 1987.

Meadows, D. H., D. L. Meadows, and J. Randers. *Beyond the Limits*. Post Mills: Chelsea Green Press, 1992.

Meadows, D. H., D. L. Meadows, J. Randers, and W.W. Behrens. *The Limits to Growth*. New York: Universe Books, 1972.

Merian, E. "Introduction on Environmental Chemistry and Global Cycles of Chromium, Nickel, Cobalt, Beryllium, Arsenic, Cadmium and Selenium and Their Derivatives." *Toxicological and Environmental Chemistry* 8 (1984), no. 1: 9–38.

Metallgesellschaft, ed. *Metallstatistik 1977–1987*. 1988.

Ministry of International Trade and Industry. *Direction for Japan's Industrial Structure*. Tokyo, 1974.

Mirowski, P. *More Heat than Light. Economics as Social Physics. Physics as Nature's Economics*. Cambridge: Cambridge University Press, 1990.

Möller, D. "Estimation of the Global Man-made Sulphur Emission." *Atmospheric Environment* 18 (1984), no. 1: 19–27.

Moltke, K. von. "The Vorsorgeprinzip in West German Environmental Policy." In: Royal Commission on Environmental Protection, *Best Practicable Environmental Option*. London, 1988.

Moore, J. W., and E. A. Moore. *Environmental Chemistry*. New York: Academic Press, 1976.

Nakicenovic, N., and A. Grübler. *The Dynamic Evolution of Methane Technologies*. Working paper. Laxenburg: IIASA, 1987.

National Academy of Sciences. *Lead in the Human Environment*. Washington, D.C.: National Academy Press, 1980.

National Research Council. *Arsenic-Committee on Medical and Biologic Effects of Environment Pollutants*. Washington, D.C.: National Academy Press, 1977.

———. *Copper-Committee on Medical and Biologic Effects of Environment Pollutants*. Washington, D.C.: National Academy Press, 1977.

———. *Atmosphere-Biosphere Interactions. Toward a Better Understanding of the Ecological Consequences of Fossil Fuel Combustion*. Washington, D.C.: National Academy Press, 1981.

———. *Acid Deposition. Long-term Trends*. Washington, D.C.: National Academy Press, 1986.

Nelson, R. R., and S. G. Winter. *An Evolutionary Theory of Economic Change*. Cambridge, Mass.: Belknap Press, 1982.

Nielsen, R., and J. P. Meyer. "Evaluation of Metabolism from Heart-rate in Industrial Work." *Ergonomics* 30 (1987), no. 3: 563–572.

Nriagu, J. O., ed. *The Biogeochemistry of Lead in the Environment*. Amsterdam: Elsevier, 1978.

———. *Copper in the Environment*. New York: Wiley-Interscience, 1980.

———. *Zinc in the Environment*. Part 1. New York: Wiley-Interscience, 1980.

———. *Cadmium in the Environment*. Part 2. New York: Wiley-Interscience, 1981.

————. "Global Metal Pollution. Poisoning the Biosphere?" *Environment* 32 (1990), no. 7: 7–11, 28–33.

Nriagu, J. O., and J. M. Pacyna. "Quantitative Assessment of Worldwide Contamination of Air, Water and Soils by Trace Metals." *Nature* 333 (1988): 134–139.

Odum, E. P. *Fundamentals of Ecology*. Philadelphia, Pa.: Saunders, 1971.

————. *Ecosystem Structure and Function*. Eugene, Ore.: Oregon State University Press, 1972.

————. "Input Management of Production Systems." *Science* 243 (1989): 177–182.

OECD. *Technical Change and Economic Policy*. Paris: OECD, 1980.

————. *Environmental Policy and Technical Change*. Paris: OECD, 1985.

————. *The Promotion and Diffusion of Clean Technologies in Industry*. Paris: OECD, 1987.

————. *Environmental Data. Compendium 1991*. Paris: OECD, 1991.

————. *Managing Technological Change in the Less Advanced Developing Countries*. Paris: OECD, 1991.

————. *Technology and Environment. Policy Options to Encourage Environmentally-friendly Technologies in the 1990s*. Paris: OECD, 1991.

————. *The State of the Environment*. Paris: OECD, 1991.

————. Environmental Directorate. *Cadmium and the Environment*. Paris: OECD, 1974.

————. *Mercury and the Environment*. Paris: OECD, 1974.

Ogden, J. M., and R. H. Williams. *Solar Hydrogen. Moving beyond Fossil Fuels*. Washington, D. C.: World Resources Institute, 1989.

O'Riordan, T. "Towards a Vernacular Science for Environmental Change." In: L. E. Roberts and A. Weale, eds., *Innovation and Environmental Risk*. London: Belhaven Press, 1991.

Ophuls, W. *Ecology and the Politics of Scarcity*. San Francisco: W. H. Freeman, 1977.

Pacyna, J. M. *Emission Factors of Atmospheric Cd, Pb, and Zn for Major Source Categories in Europe in 1950 through 1985*. Lillestrom: Norwegian Institute for Air Research.

Pacyna, J. M., and J. Munch. "European Inventory of Trace Metal Emissions to the Atmosphere." In: J. P. Vernet, ed., *Proceedings of the 7th International Conference on Heavy Metals in the Environment, Geneva*. 1989, pp. 144–147.

Pacyna, J. M., J. Munch, J. Alcamo, and S. Anderberg. "Emission Trends for Heavy Metals in Europe." In: J. G. Farmer, ed., *Proceedings of the 8th International Conference on Heavy Metals in the Environment, Edinburgh*. 1991, pp. 314–317.

Pacyna, J. M., A. Semb, and J. Hanssen. "Emission and Long-range Transport of Trace Metals in Europe." *Tellus* 36B (1984): 163–178.

Pearce, D. W., A. Markandya, and E.B. Barbier. *Blueprint for a Green Economy*. London: Earthscan, 1990.

Pearce, D. W., and R. K. Turner. "The Economic Evaluation of Low and Non-waste Technologies." *Resources and Conservation* 11 (1984): 27–43.

Peet, R., ed. *International Capitalism and Industrial Restructuring*. Boston: Allen & Unwin, 1987.

Petersen, G., H. Weber, and H. Grassl. "Modelling the Atmospheric Transport of Trace Metals from Europe to the North Sea and the Baltic Sea." In: J. M. Pacyna and B. Ottar, eds., *Control and Fate of Atmospheric Trace Metals*. Dordrecht: Kluwer Academic Publishers, 1989, pp. 57–83.

Phantumvanit, D., and K. Charnpratheep. *The Greening of Thai Industry. Producing More with Less*. Bangkok: Thailand Development Research Institute, 1991.

Pierrou, U. "The Phosphorus Cycle. Quantitative Aspects and the Role of Man." *Studies in Environmental Science* 3 (1979): 205–210.

Prigogine, I., and I. Stengers. *Order Out of Chaos*. New York: Bantam Books, 1987.

Rauhut, A. *Industrial Emissions of Cadmium in the European Community. Sources, Levels and Control*. Brussels: European Community, 1978.

———. "Cadmium-Bilanz 1978–1980." *Metall* 37 (1983): 271–275.

Rehbinder, E. "Vorsorgeprinzip im Umweltrecht und präventive Umweltpolitik." In: U. E. Simonis, ed., *Präventive Umweltpolitik*. Frankfurt/New York: Campus, 1988.

Reich, R. B. *An Industrial Policy for America*. Washington, D.C., 1983.

Rifkin, J. *Entropy. A New World View*. New York: Bantam Books, 1989.

Roberts, L. E., and A. Weale, eds. *Innovation and Environmental Risk*. London: Belhaven Press, 1991.

Roos, L. L. Jr., ed. *The Politics of Ecosuicide*. New York: Holt, Rinehart & Winston, 1971.

Ross, M. H., and R. H. Socolow. "Fulfilling the Promise of Environmental Technology." *Issues in Science and Technology* 7 (1991), no. 3: 61–66.

Ross, M. H., and R. H. Williams. *Our Energy. Regaining Control*. New York: McGraw-Hill, 1981.

Royston, M. "Responsibility of Industry towards the Environment." *Productivity* 31 (1991), no. 4: 84–93.

Ruhling, Å., and G. Tyler. "Recent Changes in the Deposition of Heavy Metals in Northern Europe." *Water, Air and Soil Pollution* 22 (1984): 173–180.

Sagan, D. "Towards a Global Metabolism – The Sulphur Cycle." *The Ecologist* 16 (1986), no. 1: 14–17.

Sanders, M. E. *The Regulation of Natural Gas. Policy and Politics, 1938–1978*. Philadelphia, Pa.: Temple University Press, 1981.

Sawers, L., and W. K. Tabb, eds. *Sunbelt/Snowbelt. Urban Development and Regional Restructuring*. New York: Oxford University Press, 1984.

Schell, J. *The Fate of the Earth*. New York: Alfred A. Knopf, 1982.

Schmidt-Bleek, F. "Ökologischer Strukturwandel." In: E. U. von Weizsäcker and R. Bleischwitz, eds., *Klima und Strukturwandel*. Bonn: Economica Verlag, 1992, pp. 106–131.

Schmidt-Bleek, F., and W. Haberlan. "The Yardstick Concept for the Hazard-evaluation of Substances." *Ecotoxicology and Environmental Safety* 4 (1980), no. 4: 455–465.

Schmidt-Bleek, F., W. Haberlan, A. W. Klein, and S. Caroli. "Steps towards Environmental-hazard Assessment of New Chemicals (including a Hazard Ranking Scheme, Based upon Directive 79/831/EEC)." *Chemosphere* 11 (1982), no. 4: 383–415.

Schmidt-Bleek, F., L. Peichl, D. Reiml, G. Behling, and K. W. Müller. "A Concept for Detecting Unexpected Changes in the Environment Early." *Regulatory Toxicology and Pharmacology* 8 (1988), no. 3: 308–327.

Schumpeter, J. A. *Business Cycles. A Theoretical, Historical and Statistical Analysis of the Capitalist Process*. Vols. 1 and 2. New York: McGraw-Hill, 1939.

Schurr, S. H., and B. C. Netschert. *Energy in the American Economy, 1850–1975*. Baltimore, Md.: Johns Hopkins University Press, 1960.

Scott, A. J., and M. Storper, eds. *Production, Work, Territory*. Boston: Allen & Unwin, 1986.

Simonis, U. E. "Ecological Modernization of Industrial Society. Three Strategic Elements." *International Social Science Journal* 41 (1989), no. 3: 347–361.

———. "Designing Sustainability of Industrial Society." In: J. Boxall, ed., *Polmet '91. Pollution in the Metropolitan and Urban Environment*. Hong Kong: Hong Kong Institution of Engineers, 1991.

———. "Towards a World Budget. Thoughts on a World Resource Tax." In: A. Vlavianos-Arvanitis, ed., *Biopolitics. The Bio-Environment*. Vol. 3. Athens: Biopolitics International Organization, 1991.

Singer, C., and T. J. Williams, eds. *A History of Technology*. Vols. 1–7. Oxford: Oxford University Press, 1954–1979.

Skinner, B. J. "Resources in the 21st Century. Can Supplies Meet Needs?" *Episodes* 12 (1989), no. 4: 267–275.

Smith, M. P., and J. R. Feagin, eds. *The Capitalist City*. London: Basil Blackwell, 1987.

Socolow, R. H. "The Coming Age of Conservation." *Annual Review of Energy* 2 (1977): 239–289.

———. "The Physicist's Role in Using Energy Efficiently. Reflections on the 1974 American Physical Society Summer Study and on the Task Ahead." In: *AIP Conference Proceedings*. Vol. 135. 1985, pp. 15–32.

———. "Field Studies of Energy Savings in Buildings. A Tour of a 15-year Research Program at Princeton University." *Energy* 12 (1987), no. 10: 1029–1043.

Socolow, R. H., and M. H. Ross. "Energy Conservation. Proceedings of the Soviet-American Symposium, Moscow, June 1985." *Energy* 12 (1987), no. 10: R5–R7.

Söderlund, R., and B. H. Svensson. "The Global Nitrogen Cycle." In: B. H. Svensson and R. Söderlund, eds., *Nitrogen, Phosphorus and Sulphur – Global Cycles*. SCOPE Report, 7. *Ecol. Bull.* (Stockholm) 22: 23–74.

Solow, R. M. "The Economics of Resources, or the Resources of Economics." *American Economic Review* 64 (1974), no. 2: 1–14.

South Commission. *The Challenge to the South*. Oxford: Oxford University Press, 1990.

Speth, J. G. "The Greening of Technology." *Washington Post*, 20 November 1988, p. D3.

———. "Can the World be Saved?" *Ecological Economics* 1 (1989): 289–302.

Spitz, P. H. *Petrochemicals. The Rise of an Industry*. New York: Wiley-Interscience, 1988.

Stigliani, W. M. "Chemical Time Bombs." In: *IIASA Options*, September 1991, p. 9.

Stigliani, W. M., F. M. Brouwer, R. E. Munn, R. W. Shaw, and M. Antonovsky. "Future Environments for Europe. Some Implications of Alternative Development Paths." *The Science of the Total Environment* 80 (1989), no. 1: 1–102.

Stigliani, W. M., and P. F. Jaffe. *Industrial Metabolism. A New Approach for Analysis of Chemical Pollution and Its Potential Applications*. Research report. Laxenburg: IIASA, 1992.

Stone, C. *Should Trees Have Standing? Toward Legal Rights for Natural Objects*. New York: Avon Press, 1975.

371

Tarr, J. A., and B. C. Lamperes. "Changing Fuel Use Behavior and Energy Transitions. The Pittsburgh Smoke Control Movement, 1940–1950." *Journal of Social History* 14 (1981), no. 4: 561–588.

Taube, M. *Evolution of Matter and Energy*. Berlin/Heidelberg/New York: Springer, 1985.

Tchobanoglous, G., H. Theisen, and R. Eliassen. *Solid Wastes*. New York: McGraw-Hill, 1977.

Thoenen, E. D. *History of the Oil and Gas Industry in West Virginia*. Charleston, W.Va.: Education Foundation, 1964.

Tilton, J. E., ed. *World Metal Demand*. Washington, D.C.: Resources for the Future, 1990.

Trabalka, J. R., and D. E. Reichle, eds. *The Changing Carbon Cycle. A Global Analysis*. Berlin/Heidelberg/New York: Springer, 1986.

Trindade, S. C. "Technology Development in Developing Countries. The Case of a Private R&D Institution in Brazil." *R&D Management* 10 (1980), no. 2: 77–82.

Tschinkel, V. J. "The Rise and Fall of Environmental Expertise." In: J. H. Ausubel and H. E. Sladovich, eds., *Technology and Environment*. Washington, D.C.: National Academy Press, 1989.

Turner, B. L., et al., eds. *The Earth as Transformed by Human Action. Proceedings of an International Symposium 1987*. Cambridge: Cambridge University Press, 1990.

Tyler, G. "Leaching Rates of Heavy Metals Ions in Forest Soils." *Water, Air and Soil Pollution* 9 (1978): 137–148.

Udo de Haes, H. A., G. Huppes, and G. Vonkeman. *Cadmium Policy. From Prohibition to Control*. CML/FEEP Report for Commission for Long-term Environmental Policy. The Hague, 1990.

Ullmann's Encyclopedia of Industrial Chemistry. 5th ed. New York: VCH Publishers, 1986.

Ukita, M., N. Nakanishi, and M. Sekine. "Study on Transport and Material Balance of Nutrients in Yamaguchi Estuary (Japan)." *Water, Science and Technology* 20 (1988), nos. 6/7: 199–210.

Ulrich, B. "Stability of Forest Ecosystems." *Forstarchiv* 52 (1981), no. 5: 165–170.

Umweltbundesamt. *Daten zur Umwelt 1990/91*. Berlin: Erich Schmidt, 1991.

UNCED. Transfer of Environmentally Sound Technology. Draft Options for Agenda 21. Geneva: UNCED Secretariat, 1991.

UNIDO. *Industry and Development. Global Report 1990*. Vienna: UNIDO, 1990.

United States Bureau of Mines. *Mineral Facts and Problems*. Washington, D.C.: US Government Printing Office, 1985.

———. *Mineral Commodity Summaries 1991*. Washington, D.C.: US Government Printing Office, 1991.

United States Council on Environmental Quality. *Environmental Quality*. 20th Annual Report. Washington, D.C.: CEQ, 1990.

United States Congressional Office of Technology Assessment. *Serious Reduction of Hazardous Waste for Pollution, Prevention and Industrial Efficiency*. Washington, D.C.: OTA, 1986.

———. *Facing America's Trash. What Next for Municipal Solid Waste?* Washington, D.C.: OTA, 1989.

———. *Materials Technology. Integrating Environmental Goals with Product Design*. Washington, D.C.: OTA, 1990.

Vanderharst, J., F. B. Schmidt-Bleek, K. O. Günther, and J. T. de Krauk. "Conclusions and Recommendations Resulting from the Secotox Workshop Feasibility of Integrated Approaches to Testing of Chemicals, Kyoto 1980." *Ecotoxicology and Environmental Safety* 5 (1981), no. 3: 377–381.

Vitousek, P. M., et al. "Human Appropriation of the Products of Photosynthesis." *BioScience* 36 (1986), no. 6: 386–373.

Voet, E. van der, G. Huppes, and W. G. H. van der Naald. "Guidelines for Pollutants Policy as a Result of Substance Flow Analysis." In: L. J. Brasser, and W. C. Mulder, eds., *Man and his Ecosystem. Proceedings of the 8th World Clean Air Congress 1989*. Vol. 5. Amsterdam: Elsevier, 1989.

Vogg, H., H. Braun, M. Metzger, and J. Schneider. "The Specific Role of Cadmium and Mercury in Municipal Solid Waste Incineration." *Waste Management Research* 4 (1986): 65–74.

Weale, A., T. O'Riordan, and L. Kramme. *Controlling Pollution in the Round*. London/Bonn: Anglo-German Foundation, 1991.

Weizsäcker, E. U. von. "Sustainability. A Task for the North." *Journal of International Affairs* 45 (1991), no. 2: 421–432.

White, R. R. "Urban Metabolism and Sustainable Development. A Fusion of Old and New Concepts for Planners." Toronto: University of Toronto, 1990. (Manuscript.)

Whorton, J. *Before Silent Spring*. Princeton, N.J.: Princeton University Press, 1974.

Williams, R. H., E. D. Larson, and M. H. Ross. "Materials, Affluence, and Industrial Energy Use." *Annual Review of Energy* 12 (1987): 99–144.

Willums, J. O., ed. *The Greening of Enterprise*. Paris: ICC, 1990.

Winner, L. *The Whale and the Reactor. A Search for Limits in an Age of High Technology*. Chicago/London: University of Chicago Press, 1986.

Wolfe, J. A. *Mineral Resources. A World Review*. New York: Chapman & Hall, 1984.

World Commission on Environment and Development. *Our Common Future*. New York: Oxford University Press, 1987.

World Resources Institute. *World Resources 1990–91*. New York: Oxford University Press, 1990.

———. *World Resources 1992–93*. New York: Oxford University Press, 1992.

Wright, D. H. "Human Impacts on Energy Flow through Natural Ecosystems and Implications for Species Endangerment." Ambio 19 (1990), no. 4: 189–194.

Wronskanofer, T., J. Stetkiewicz, and J. Wisniewskaknypl. "Biological Consequences of Metabolic Interaction of Industrial Chemicals and Ethanol." *Alcohol and Alcoholism* 21 (1986), no. 2: A 63.

Zulauf, W. E. "Industrial Pollution Control in Cubatao." In: J. Markovitch et al., eds., *Brazilian Experiences on Management of Environmental Issues. Some Findings on the Transfer of Technologies*. Research paper. Geneva: UNCED Secretariat, 1991.

Vanderhurst, L. F. R., Schmidt-Bleek, K. O. Günther, and T. d. Krause. "Conclusions and Recommendations: Resulting from the Second Workshop Feasibility of Integrated Approaches to Testing of Chemicals. Kyoto 1986." *Ecotoxicology and Environmental Safety* 5 (1981), no. 4: 371–381.

Vitousek, P. M., et al. "Human Appropriation of the Products of Photosynthesis," *BioScience* 36 (1986), no. 6: 368–373.

Voet, E. van der, G. Huppes, and W. G. H. van der Naald. "Guidelines for Pollutants as a Result of Substance Flow Analysis," in L. J. Brasser and W. C. Mulder, eds., *Man and his Ecosystem: Proceedings of the 8th World Clean Air Congress 1989* Vol. 5. Amsterdam: Elsevier, 1988.

Voet, E., H. Braun, M. Metzger, and J. Schneider. "The Specific Role of Cadmium and Mercury in Municipal Solid Waste Incineration," *Waste Management Research* 4 (1986): 65–74.

Weizsäcker, E. A., J. O'Riordan, and I. Kramer. *Consuming Ecology in the Rccess.* London/Bonn: AngAb German Foundation, 1991.

Weizsäcker, E. U. von. "Sustainability: A Task for the North," *Journal of International Affairs* 44 (1991), no. 2: 421–432.

White, R. R. "From Metabolism and Sustainable Development: A Fusion of Old and New Concepts for Planners." Toronto: University of Toronto, 1990. (Manuscript.)

Whorton, J. *Before Silent Spring.* Princeton, N.J.: Princeton University Press, 1974.

Williams, R. H., E. D. Larson, and M. H. Ross. "Materials, Affluence and Industrial Energy Use," *Annual Review of Energy* 12 (1987): 99–144.

Williams, L. O., ed. *The Greening of Enterprise.* Paris: ICC, 1991.

Winner, L. *The Whale and the Reactor: A Search for Limits in an Age of High Technology.* Chicago/London: University of Chicago Press, 1986.

Wells, L. A. *Mineral Resources: A World Review.* New York: Chapman & Hall, 1984.

World Commission on Environment and Development. *Our Common Future.* New York: Oxford University Press, 1987.

World Resources Institute. *World Resources 1990–91.* New York: Oxford University Press, 1990.

———. *World Resources 1992–93.* New York: Oxford University Press, 1992.

Wright, D. H. "Human Impacts on Energy Flow through Natural Ecosystems and Implications for Species Endangerment," *Ambio* 19 (1990), no. 4: 189–194.

Wrona-Stuzel, T. J., Stukszewicz, and J. Wiśniewskaknapp. "Biological Consequences of Metabolic Interaction of Industrial Chemicals and Ethanol," *Archives of Toxicology* 21 (1986), no. 2: 1–63.

Zuzel, W. P. "Industrial Pollution Control in Indhatsza," in J. Markovitch et al. eds., *Brazilian Experience on Management of Environmental Issues. Some Findings on the Transfer of Technologies.* Research paper. Geneva: UNCED Secretariat, 1991.

Contributors

Peter M. Allen, B.Sc., Ph.D. in Theoretical Physics. Director of the International Ecotechnology Research Centre, Cranfield Institute of Technology, Bedford, United Kingdom.

Stefan Anderberg, B.Sc. in Human Geography. Research Scholar, Project on Sources of Chemical Pollution in the Rhine Basin, IIASA, Laxenburg, Austria.

Leslie W. Ayres, B.A., Bennington College. Computer Consultant, Fontainebleau, France.

Robert U. Ayres, B.Sc., B.A., M.A., Ph.D. in Theoretical Physics. Sandoz Professor of Environmental Management, INSEAD, Fontainebleau, France.

Peter Baccini, Dr. sc. nat., Professor and Head of the Department of Waste Management and Metabolism at the Eidgenössische Technische Hochschule, Dübendorf, Switzerland.

Bo Bergbäck, Ph.D. in Environmental Studies. Researcher and Lecturer, University College of Kalmar, Kalmar, Sweden.

Paul H. Brunner, Dr. sc. nat., Chemistry, Environmental Engineering and Waste Management/Materials Management. Professor of Waste Management, Technical University, Vienna, Austria.

Mala Damodaran, M.A. in Business Economics. Research Associate at the Tata Energy Research Institute, New Delhi, India.

Himraj Dang, M.E. in Engineering Management. At present doing consultancy work as an environmental scientist, New Delhi, India.

Hans Daxbeck, Mag. soc. oec. publ. Fellow of the Department of Waste Management and Metabolism at the Eidgenössische Technische Hochschule, Dübendorf, Switzerland.

Contributors

Marina Fischer-Kowalski, Ph.D. in Sociology. Assistant Professor, Institute for Interdisciplinary Research and Continuing Education, Vienna, Austria.
Helmut Haberl, M.Sc. in Biology and Mathematics. Head of the Department of Energy at the Ecology Institute, Vienna, Austria.
Rudolf B. Husar, Ph.D. in Mechanical Engineering. Professor of Mechanical Engineering and Director of the Center for Air Pollution Impact and Trend Analysis, Washington University, St. Louis, United States.
Ulrik Lohm, M.A., Ph.D. in Entomology. Head of the Department of Water and Environmental Studies, Linköping University, Linköping, Sweden.
Rüdiger Olbrich. Student of Environmental Engineering at the Technical University of Berlin, Assistant at the Science Center Berlin, Germany.
Timothy O'Riordan. Professor of Environmental Sciences at the University of East Anglia; Associate Director, Centre for Social and Economic Research into Global Environment, University of East Anglia and University College, London, United Kingdom.
Rajendra K. Pachauri, Ph.D. in Economics and Industrial Engineering. Director of the Tata Energy Research Institute, New Delhi, India.
Harald Payer, M.A. in Economics. Institute for Interdisciplinary Research and Continuing Education, and Department of Social Ecology at the Ecology Institute, Vienna, Austria.
Udo E. Simonis, M.A., Ph.D. in Economics. Professor of Environmental Policy at the Science Center Berlin, and Member of the German Council on Global Environmental Change, Berlin, Germany.
William M. Stigliani, B.A., M.A., Ph.D. in Chemistry. Senior Research Fellow, Leader of the Project on Sources of Chemical Pollution in the Rhine Basin, IIASA, Laxenburg, Austria.
Joel A. Tarr, B.Sc., M.A., Ph.D. in History. Professor of Urban Studies at Carnegie Mellon University, Pittsburg, United States.
Sergio C. Trindade, M.Sc., Ph.D. in Chemical Engineering. President of SE2T International Ltd., an energy, environmental, and technology consultancy, Scarsdale, United States.